Tuning
the
Green Machine

AN INTEGRATED VIEW OF ENVIRONMENTAL SYSTEMS

by

The Institute for Environmental Education

and

The Association of New Jersey Environmental Commissions

1978 • OCEANA PUBLICATIONS, INC. • DOBBS FERRY, NEW YORK

EPA REVIEW NOTICE

This text was prepared under a contract financed by the U.S. Environmental Protection Agency and is approved by the Agency for publication as an important contribution toward implementation of federal programs at the local level. Publication approval does not necessarily signify that the contents reflect the views and policies of the Agency. The mention of trade names or commercial products does not constitute endorsement or recommendation for use.

Library of Congress Cataloging in Publication Data

Institute for Environmental Education.
    Tuning the green machine.

    Includes index.
    1. Environmental protection. 2. Pollution.
3. Conservation of natural resources. I. Association
of New Jersey Environmental Commissions. II. Title.
TD170.I55   1977   363.6   77-17902
ISBN 0-379-00811-4

Manufactured in the United States of America

TABLE OF CONTENTS

CHAPTER 12 • ENERGY, CONSERVATION, AND RESOURCE ALTERNATIVES

PREFACE

TUNING THE GREEN MACHINE was written to aid citizens in making responsible decisions that affect their environment. It was originally conceived as a limited-edition handbook for appointed and elected public officials directly charged with environmental decision-making. This group saw the book as a unique work which satisfied a range of needs for life on planet Earth. Encouragement from educators, planners, and regulatory agency officials has led to its commercial publication. The book first appeared in draft form accompanied by manuals on federal and state tools and rules that apply to environmental protection. The Association of New Jersey Environmental Commissions (ANJEC), under the directorship of Candace M. Ashmun, received a grant from the U.S. Environmental Protection Agency to develop materials and to conduct a pilot training program for local public officials. ANJEC commissioned the Institute for Environmental Education to prepare the text of what was to become TUNING THE GREEN MACHINE.

Earth is "the green machine" whose individual but interdependent systems of water, air, soil, and life must maintain a proper balance if the machine is to run naturally and healthily. When pollution disrupts the systems, the green machine is "out of tune." Environmental degradation and its possible cures, whether natural or manmade, are explored here in relation to those interdependent ecosystems whose elements constitute the life we know today.

The aim of TUNING THE GREEN MACHINE is to provide those who make decisions about the environment — in effect, *all* of us — with an introduction to the principles of practical ecology, so that we see decisions in light of their long range environmental impact. Not only do we need to know about and to appreciate the interconnectedness of natural systems, but also we must know and appreciate man's role as a product and part of those systems.

The environmental principles explored in the following chapters bear on the economic, social, and environmental realities under which we all live. However, since the principles governing Earth's life zones are so logical and intrinsically simple, often we may search for simple solutions. It would be gratifying to come up with a sublime solution to cleaning out any Augean Stable in our community. It was so easy for Hercules. He had only to divert a river to run through the ignored and accumulated wastes of that mythic stable, flushing them downstream and out of sight. Hercules did not have to deal with BOD levels or environmental impact statements. Nor does the account mention how the Herculean effort threatened the health of the hapless Greeks downstream who drew their drinking water from the river.

There are more of us today and our lives are more interconnected; we tolerate pollution less today. The outcry against it, once shrill and emotional, focused on aesthetic values. It has since taken on an undersound that is "not loud but deep." Our many small mistakes, made wittingly and unwittingly, have accrued to an awesome tyranny. That tyranny forces us to live under conditions we do not prefer. Certainly we can try to make fewer mistakes: knowledge about and a greater employment of our natural systems will aid us in doing so. The resilience of those systems will help us to live in a way we do prefer. We must think of pollution as "resources out of place." To put them back into place is to use them to the benefit of Earth's creatures.

Developing new technologies and the necessary areawide planning to effect cures for environmental degradation often is either too expensive or too regionally oriented to serve specific local needs. Successful implementation of local plans, however, occurs only if public officials involve as many citizens as possible in researching, evaluating, and carrying out the plan. Numerous federal and state programs depend on local ordinances to meet standards of regional performance. Public motivation to solve environmental problems is rooted most firmly at the local level.

An aware public will understand that technology does not free us from the responsibility of practical conservation. Reducing our home use of resources — water, energy — can lessen our need to develop expensive new sources of them. In some cases, home septic systems may be more cost-effective and less environmentally degrading than sewer lines to a central facility. The natural assimilative capacity of air, land, and water is the least costly means of treatment we have, the ideal treatment.

Each of the following chapters begins with a perspective, a brief account or a viewpoint that concerns a major issue in the chapter. We urge you as reader, world citizen, decision-maker, and human with many responsibilities to read this book from the overall perspective of an age-old comment: "No one man sees everything."

"We" are a team of some twenty-five citizens brought together to lend our experience to this work. Among us are a businessman, a biologist, a botanist, a chemist, a citizen-activist, educators, an environmental health specialist, an environmental planner, a meteorologist, an oceanographer, public officials, a regulatory water specialist, and a watershed planner.

The primary team for the project, augmented by ANJEC personnel, was the staff of the Institute for Environmental Education. Together they reworked the individual contributors' efforts into a single presentation as informal as possible. In the revising, editing, writing, and adding to, no single contributor's chapter was left in a state to be solely attributed to him or her. We hope the weaving does justice to their work, and serves well the reader's purposes.

The draft text was reviewed, used, and evaluated in workshops in seven states, and then revised to its present form. Throughout these processes innumerable people lent their encouragement and professional expertise. Sincere thanks go to those who aided in reviewing and revising: George Watkins, respected planner and former mayor and present Director of the Three Rivers Watershed District; Maria R. Eigerman of Planning and Environmental Systems, Dalton-Dalton-Little-Newport; and John James, author, botanist, creative humanist, and friend. Others who helped to prepare one or both manuscripts include our illustrator, Mike Aaron, a talented audio-visual artist whose drawings help to elucidate the text; Thorold E. Roberts, who aided in manuscript preparation, proofreading, and indexing; Alison Kerester and Adolph Faller checking factual details; and Janice Pengal and Rusty Anderson who expertly typed the final manuscript under unrelenting time constraints. We also thank the architecture/engineering/planning firm, Dalton-Dalton-Little-Newport for its help and enthusiastic support.

Lastly, we are grateful to the administrative and production staff at Oceana Publications, Inc., for continued interest in the project from its early days. Their encouragement, congeniality, and professionalism have made preparing the manuscript for publication both a pleasure and an adventure.

Joseph H. Chadbourne
Sally F. Gardner
Thomas W. Offutt
Mary M. Roberts

The Institute for Environmental Education

Tuning
the
Green Machine

CHAPTER ONE

THE NATURE OF PLANET EARTH

A PERSPECTIVE

When the first word comes in from outer space, finally,
we will probably be used to the idea. We can already
provide a quite good explanation for the origin of life,
here or elsewhere. Given a moist planet with methane,
formaldehyde, ammonia, and some usable minerals, all of
which abound, exposed to lightning or ultraviolet irra-
diation at the right temperature, life might start almost
anywhere. The tricky, unsolved thing is how to get the
polymers to arrange in membranes and invent replication.
The rest is clear going. If they follow our protocol,
it will be anaerobic life at first, then photosynthesis
and the first exhalation of oxygen, then respiring life
and the great burst of variation, then speciation, and,
finally, some kind of consciousness. It is easy, in
the telling.

Lewis Thomas, The Lives of A Cell

Earth's Constant Change

The writing of one word is like the taking of a snapshot--both fix
time and space and relationships. The writing of many words in book form
is like putting together an album of snapshots: the album presents different perspectives of different events, but every event is fixed--forever.

There is a reluctance, then, to put down any words about the Earth and
our lives upon it, for the first statements, as in the clicking of a shut-
ter, prohibit any further communication of movement. And yet movement of
the Earth, the wind, the seas, our bodies, and our thoughts is precisely
what we want to communicate. We would better serve you if instead of 14
written chapters this book were 14 channels of live action television!
Then, every reader always would have a more accurate picture of the world.

Nonetheless, it is such a current view of the world that we seek in
this book, a perspective of the whole. We want to integrate the words,
the snapshots, in such a way that all of the objects perceived are inte-
grated with each other. We want to do that, because, very simply, that's
the way nature is.

1

That is what this book is all about--the interrelationships of our natural systems. Nature is _our_ connection to _you_. If each chapter's television sequence could reveal exactly and simultaneously all of the relationships between and among the objects projected, then it would be startlingly clear how connected we are. Every move you have made, every move you will make connects to us--and so we have a stake in helping you to understand those connections. If you see and believe in those ties, you will forever after act with a high regard for their continuity. It is true that all of our lives are in your hands, and yours in ours.

The movements among all objects commenced a direction a long time ago. It is these established movements and their direction that require us to deal with the Earth the way it is. As a favorite aunt's Swiss housekeeper put it, "we are stuck mit."

The <u>Physical</u>, <u>Chemical</u>, <u>and</u> <u>Biological</u> <u>Properties</u> <u>of</u> <u>Earth</u>

This book describes the Earth and the subsystems that we are "stuck mit." The first chapter introduces the natural systems and the human adjustments made to them that we discuss throughout the book. The last chapter synthesizes all of the instruction that seems appropriate to extract, and directs it toward the building of a healthy land-use management program. By reading Chapter 1, the summaries at the end of the others, and then Chapter 14, you can view quickly the overall scope of the book.

In this chapter our concern is Earth and its characteristics. Among them we have chosen to focus on those most critical to wise use of our lands:

- the Earth's position in the Universe
- the shape of the Earth
- pathways through space
- mass
- heat contained within the Earth
- magnetism
- atmosphere
- hydrologic cycle
- the surface of the Earth
- weather and erosion
- soils
- energy
- life

The main idea is that Chapter 1 is a photograph of the past; Chapter 14 is a projection of the future. Chapters 2 through 13 are pictures of the present.

The Universe, Galaxies, Stars, and Planets

The Universe is space of unknown limits. Within measurable regions there are clusters of galaxies, one of them the Milky Way, which contains our solar system. This galaxy is 100,000 light years wide, the distance that light would travel at 186,234 miles per second in 100,000 years, or about 600,000,000,000,000,000 miles.* The Milky Way, perhaps one among billions of other galaxies, sprays its countless stars as if a giant pinwheel scattering its myriad sparkles. Overhead, those far flung stars blend in a haze of light. In this profusion of brightness, our own star, the Sun, is still 24 trillion miles from the next nearest star.

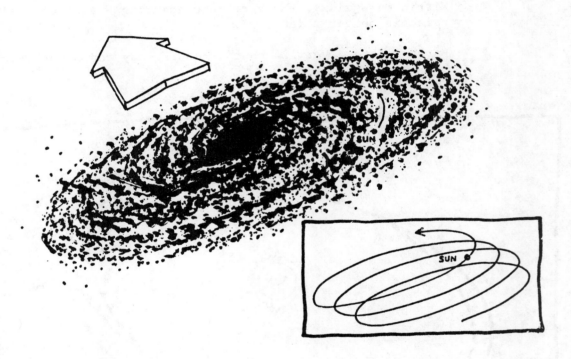

Figure 1: *The Milky Way diverges from the other galaxies, its stars spiralling outward.*

Nine planets orbit about the Sun. The third most distant is Earth. In turn, Earth has one planet, the Moon. It is 1/80th of the Earth's mass and some 250,000 miles away from it. The Moon always faces the Earth and moves about it every 27 1/3 days. Closer to the Earth are invisible magnetic lines

---

* Many statistics, descriptive images, and phrases in Chapter 1 come from the Life Nature Library series volumes on the Earth, mountains, and weather. We commend these excellent books to your reading, along with other sources listed at chapter's end.

of force that arc from one end of the axis of the Earth out 40,000 miles into space and back to the other end. The Sun, the Earth, and the Moon are attracted to one another, but they do not collide because of their circulatory orbiting. Our planet, like others in the solar system, attracts meteoroids, but unlike the others it also holds close to the surface a precious 600-mile thick stuff we call the atmosphere.

Earth in Motion

Earth has 8 major, identifiable spatial relationships:

* The entire Milky Way galaxy is diverging from other galaxies (Figure 1).

* Within our galaxy, the stars are spinning away from their galactic center (Figure 1).

* Earth rotates every 24 hours—causing day and night (Figure 2).

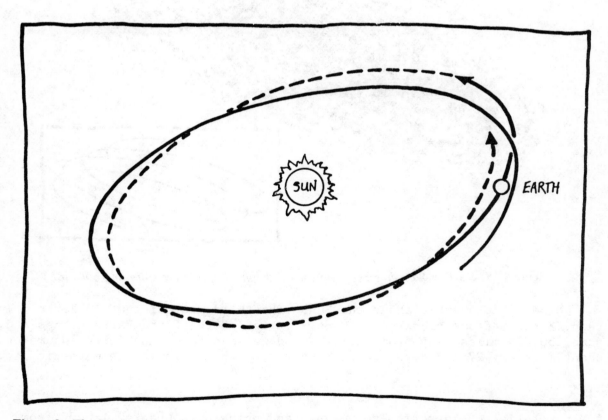

Figure 2: *The Earth rotates each 24 hours. The ratio of "day" and "night" shifts slowly as it also revolves on angled axis about the Sun.*

- The fourth movement is Earth's revolution around the Sun in 365-1/4 days--setting the sequence of our seasons: fall, winter, spring, and summer (Figure 3).

- The Earth's axis of rotation is tipped; the tilt accounts for the greater and lesser amounts of sunlight that make the difference among seasons (Figure 3).

- The Earth and Moon together make a bowling pin-shaped mass as they revolve together about the Sun, but rotating as if on an axis on which each planet is an opposing weight. Because Earth is 80 times larger than the Moon, Earth's path about the Sun is really a wavy one, not a smooth, concentric orbit (Figure 4).

- A distortion in Earth's revolution is caused by two other phenomena. First, the Moon pulls on the Earth, the Sun pulls on the Earth, and vice versa. The combined gravitational forces cause the tides. The ebb and flow of the tides in turn create an unbalanced condition, always shifting the precise center of the Earth's mass from its true center. Second, the Earth is like a top in profile, for it bulges slightly:

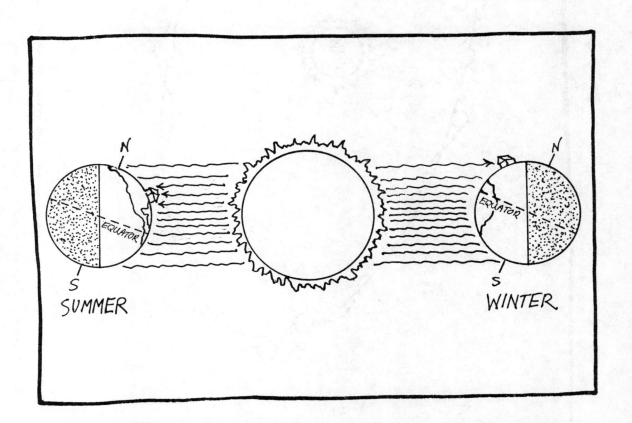

Figure 3: *During its 365-day revolution of the Sun, Earth tilts on its north-south polar axis, so that at any given point on Earth's surface there is more or less light energy — hence the change of seasons.*

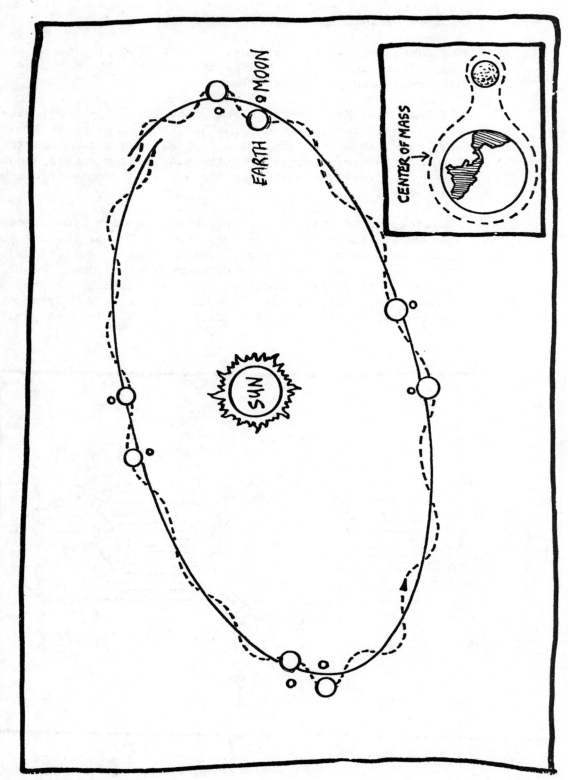

Figure 4: *Earth and Moon — massed together like a bowling pin — eccentrically orbit on a corkscrew-like path.*

26.7 miles thicker around the equator than around the poles. The attraction between Moon and Earth increases when the Moon orbits across the equator, because then that planet is closer to the Earth than at any other time. The combination of the Moon's greater attraction at the equator than near the poles and the unbalanced state of the Earth produce the top-like wobble depicted in Figure 5.

- It takes 25,800 years for an imaginary line through the axis of the Earth to trace a complete cone in the sky. This motion results from the coincident attraction of Sun and Moon on the Earth. The rare alignment of both masses urges a nodding on top of the wobble (Figure 5). The nod takes place once in 18.6 years and for 1/400th of a degree!

These protracted meanders and swirls and wobbles and nods are the physical dispositions that contribute to the more readily perceived, more common phenomena we know as wind, dawn, warmth, humidity, snow, and growth.

Earth's Mass

The planets and their satellites formed, it is believed, when condensing gases gravitated toward one another and, spiralling inward, collapsed inward into very dense bodies. The compression of molecules became greater and greater--until today on the Earth's surface air weighs 14.7 pounds per square inch (psi); the pressure of the water at 5 miles below the surface is 12,000 psi; at 1,800 miles toward the Earth's center, 16,950,000 psi; and at the Earth's center, 40,000,000 psi. At the center this great pressure forces molecules together in mutual bombardments that create radioactive materials and enormous heat.

The Heat Within the Earth

The temperature increases approximately $1/2^\circ$ C for every 60 feet from the crust of the Earth toward the mantle (see Figure 6). At its center the temperature may be 2,000 to 4,000° C, compared to the Sun's surface temperature of 6,000° C. Partly because of the mantle's heat, deep ponds and lakes do not freeze in winter, the shafts of great mines are hot, in shallow crustal areas of the Earth steam breaks through the ground in geysers, the great tectonic plates of the Earth's surface drift against and over one another, and volcanoes burst with molten rocks that ooze over land or explode into the air. New land forms thrust upward, erode, and tumble to form new land below.

The Earth may be expanding from material heat or contracting and creating more heat. It is not totally accurate then to say, over the short period anyhow, that the Earth is cooling down. The heat is a source of

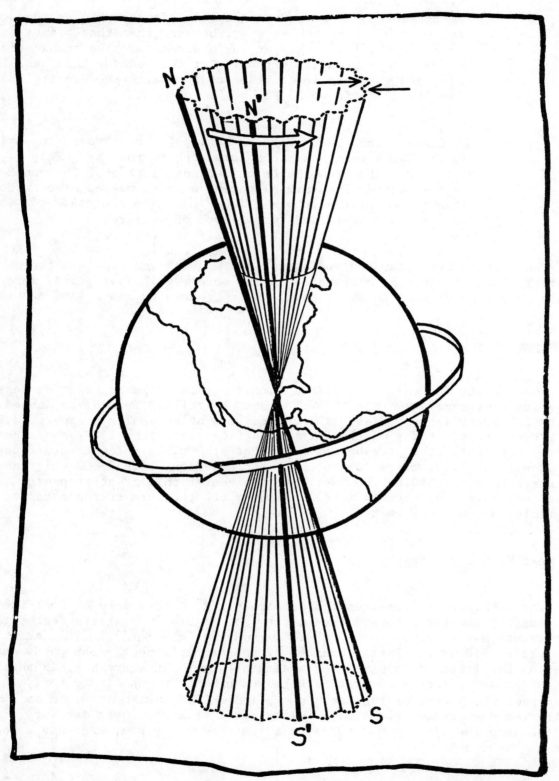

Figure 5: *The north-south axis nods every 18.6 years and pivots in a complete circle every 25,800 years!*

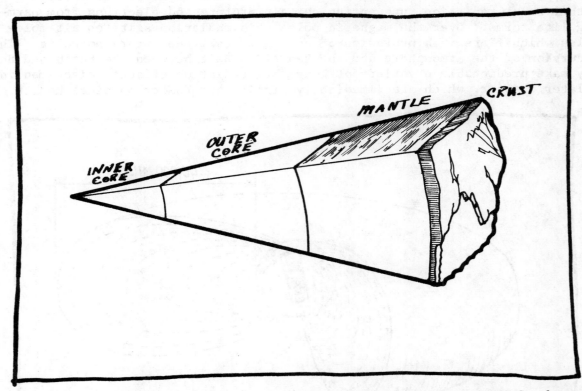

Figure 6: *A section of Earth, from surface to center, with temperatures of 2,000 to 4,000° C at the core.*

energy that we scarcely can tap. The partial venting of this geothermal energy to the atmosphere takes place quite naturally, and in its translation to the free system can be rerouted temporarily to perform work. The mechanisms that cause the Earth to be hot and molten also cause it to be magnetic.

The Earth's Magnetism

The Earth, often likened to a great magnet, behaves as if a gigantic ferromagnetic bar were buried deep within it some 200 miles from its center and some 11-1/2° from Earth's axis of rotation. The probable reason for the magnetic field about the planet may be found in the swirling current of the inner core.

The magnetic lines of force are from one axis out into space and back into the other axis (Figure 7). The fluidity of the Earth's mass may account for the irregularity in the force field. The areas of apparent entry and exit of those lines of magnetic force shift in location: in 1948, the North Magnetic Pole was 70 miles southeast of its present location; in 1904, 270 miles southeast of it. In addition, the strength of the magnetic attraction has also changed, declining about 5% in the last 100 years.

The magnetic field reaches far into space, 600 to 40,000 miles out. Known as the Van Allen Radiation Belt, the Earth's magnetic field traps lethal solar radiation, preventing certain protons and electrons from harming life forms. Over the magnetic poles this radiation agitates air molecules which flare in a profusion of colors we call the aurora borealis. This incursion of the atmosphere and the Van Allen Belt between the Earth and Sun may make predictable a variety of long-term radiation effects, discussed in a later chapter, which are immediately significant to our physical health.

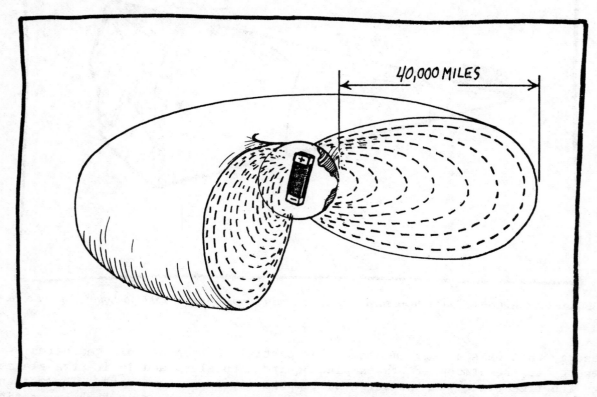

Figure 7: *The Earth, behaving as if a giant bar magnet were buried deep within, ionizes particles in the magnetosphere — the Van Allen Radiation Belt.*

The Atmosphere

Within the magnetosphere and within 19 miles of the Earth's surface lies 99% of our atmosphere. The fluid mixture of gases, mostly nitrogen (78%), oxygen (21%), carbon dioxide (.03%), inert gases (.93%), methane, and hydrogen, as well as traces of others, stratifies to varied thickness and density about the globe. Water equivalent to 1 inch over the entire surface of the Earth is present as a gaseous vapor, liquid drops, and solid ice crystals (rain, hail, sleet, and snow). Coming mostly from the oceans, this water evaporates into and condenses out of the atmosphere in a rhythmic periodicity, the hydrologic cycle.

The Earth rotates beneath this gaseous suspension, dragging some of the lower, denser volumes of air with it. Relative to the atmosphere, the land velocity is 1,050 miles per hour at the equator (25,000 miles around the Earth in 24 hours), and zero at the poles. Partly, the friction or gradient between the poles and the equator sets in motion the laminar flow of great air waves over the Earth's surface.

Simultaneously, the Sun bombards the Earth with light energy. Burning hydrogen at the rate of 4,000,000 tons per second, the Sun has been consuming itself at this rate for 5 billion years, but has some 30 billion years to go. The burning releases energy as "photons," or light energy. This energy headed for Earth each minute is equivalent to 23,000,000,000,000 horsepower (the force required to raise 33,000 lbs. one foot in one minute)--more energy every minute than all of mankind uses in all forms in one year!

The atmosphere reflects back into space about one-half of this solar energy. Carbon dioxide and ozone absorb an additional 15%. The remaining 35% strikes the Earth where several different types of wave lengths boost other molecules into higher energy levels and new directions.

The greater the energy motion of an object, the hotter it feels. The heat from excited molecules is greatest near the equator and during midday: that is where and when the most photons can strike a given area. The newly heated air and water molecules escape energetically up into the sky, pushing the lower gases high into the upper atmosphere ahead of them. There, the gases cool, draw closer together and, becoming heavier, sink toward the poles.

The Hydrologic Cycle

The hydrologic cycle, the polar-equatorial air-land frictional gradient, and the energetics of solar rays are the principal ingredients of weather. However, weather on a global scale is highly modified locally by surface characteristics. The oceans, lakes, ponds, mountains, valleys, and soils as well as the color, texture, and height of vegetation that grows change the relationships among water vapor, wind velocity, and heat energy. Weather wears, wets, dries, and blows the land, altogether transforming it, continuously changing Earth's features.

Surface Features

The Earth's inner and outer core are under constant stress. It may result from the Earth's cooling or heating and its contraction or expansion. But stress--the force exerted by change in temperature, the flow of molten metals, the eccentricities of orbital motions--in sufficient amounts acting on different surface formations creates strains, or shifts, in the position of the crust. We see these surface strains as folds, faults, volcanoes, and domes (see Figure 8).

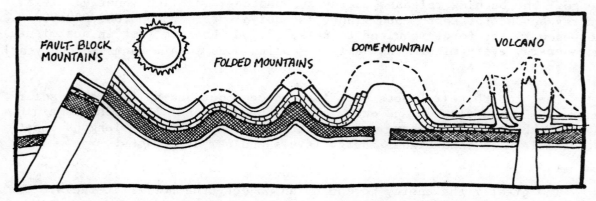

Figure 8: *The four basic geologic structures found on Earth's surface.*

These four land forms are familiar. A <u>fold</u> is a wave of connected earthen crust. Examples are some mountain ranges quite familiar to us: the Appalachians, the Urals. <u>Faults</u> are straight breaks between blocks of land mass, such as the horizontal San Andreas fault in California or the vertical fault of the Grand Tetons in Montana. <u>Volcanoes</u>, such as Vesuvius in Italy or Kilimanjaro in Tanganyika are outpourings of magma, molten rock from within the Earth. <u>Domes</u> push upward when molten rock pulses toward but does not break through the surface (and become volcanic). It presses the crustal rock upward into a blister on the Earth. Dome mountains, such as Utah's Henry Mountain, are basically unerupted volcanoes. Slowly all of these forms blow or erode, eventually to settle, fragment, and wear down to become soil.

<u>Weather and Erosion</u>

Weather beats and blows against the folded, faulted, volcanic, domed protrusions of the Earth's surface. Wedged by alternate freezing and thawing, pressures or stresses, rocks crack and then tumble down streams and rivers, grinding into smaller parts or dissolving into separate molecules and atoms. Slowly, flowing glaciers and rainwater transport the diminished particles downhill toward the ocean. When the river's flow is too slow to carry the particles, they settle in mixture with vegetative matter as sediment.

The atmosphere contains an immense quantity of matter--air molecules, dirt, and water. The weight of the atmosphere is approximately 5,600,000,000,000,000,000 tons, some of it moving at 200 to 400 miles an hour. A single midwestern storm has been estimated to transport some 500,000,000 tons of topsoil. A small cloud may hold from 100 to 1,000 tons of water. In the Gulf of Mexico, water evaporates on a hot afternoon at the rate of 5,500,000,000 gallons an hour, travels north, and may fall in a few days as rain in New York and southern New England. The deserts and deltas, foothills and floods are what we see today as evidence of the atmosphere's sandpapering of the Earth's crust--the reduction of mountain into molehill.

The Formation of Soils

When the mountains become molehills, their particles move in location and change in composition. The general motion of erosion is downhill due to the force of gravity, although some soils which were formed long ago in river basins have been uplifted to higher elevations than nearby mountains. Eroding particles are carried by wind and blown downwind in airsheds, and by water washed downstream in watersheds.

The composition of soils originates with the parent rock. The three major types of rock are igneous, sedimentary, and metamorphic. Initially, the molten interior of the Earth spewed to the surface and cooled as igneous structures. As igneous rock fractured and tumbled downhill, it settled in small, mixed bits and pieces as sediment. Thrown together with other rock sources and plants and animal forms, it compressed into sandstone and limestone, sedimentary rocks. Sedimentary rocks, with pressure and heat and chemicals, fused into harder forms--metamorphic rock--such as marble. The process continues. If not, the metamorphic rock is pressed and heated by the mass of the Earth, and blends once more into the more uniform composition of igneous rock. This simplified cycle is not strictly linear, i.e., from igneous to sedimentary to metamorphic structures. Each major type can be the parent of either of the other two because of the crustal movements mentioned. Each rock type may lie next to another in folds, twists, overlaps, and ruptures and then erode or become layered, pressed, and heated together. Such physical mixtures are often seen in outcroppings along highways and construction sites. These exposed rocks are slowly wearing down and becoming soil.

The basic chemical composition of most of our soil is quite simple. Of over 100 known natural elements, 8 predominate in some 98% of the Earth's crust. Oxygen is in about 50% of the soil. The majority of the remaining constituents are silicon, in 25%; aluminum, in 8%; iron, in 5%; and sodium, magnesium, potassium, and calcium, some 4%. These separate elements combine chemically with one another and a few other rarer ones to form about 2,000 compounds called minerals. In time, these minerals and other less predominant elements and their compounds became the essential ingredients for soils, then plants, then animals--life.

Energy

By now some of the energetics of natural systems are becoming apparent:

- Peregrinations of the Earth in the Universe cause seasons, daylight, temperature.

- The attraction between masses, gravity, purses the oceans into tides, tumbles rocks to valleys, and pulls water to the seas.

- Radioactive minerals heat the Earth and modify other chemicals. Their energy can be harnessed to drive steam turbines.

- Magnetic lines of force repel solar radiation, attract iron-bearing compounds, and induce electrons to flow through wires.

- Atmospheric mixtures dragged over the Earth's surface drive soils and water around the world. Lightning, hurricanes, and fronts churn local weather systems endlessly.

- Great floating crustal plates grind together; the Earth quakes, and uplifts new land forms. In some places subsurface waters turn to steam.

What we have not spoken of yet, however, are the movements--and therefore the energy--in even the smallest parts of this Earth. We are talking about the energy in molecules, atoms, nuclei--and _their_ parts. Atoms have neutrons and protons at their centers and electrons in the distant space around these centers. There are over 100 atoms, or chemical elements, that differ from one another in the numbers of these three particles (see Figure 9). All of the particles move and each has a neutral or a positive or a negative charge. These motions and charges allow them to interact with other moving, charged atoms and combinations of atoms, molecules. All of the Earth's matter is made up of these atoms and molecules.

Life--Its Beginnings

The interaction of these particles and their response to certain conditions in their environment started some remarkable events a long time ago. At some warm, wet, distant time in history, photons--the wave-like particles

I	II											III	IV	V	VI	VII	O
H 1																	He 2
Li 3	Be 4											B 5	C 6	N 7	O 8	F 9	Ne 10
Na 11	Mg 12											Al 13	Si 14	P 15	S 16	Cl 17	Ar 18
K 19	Ca 20	Sc 21	Ti 22	V 23	Cr 24	Mn 25	Fe 26	Co 27	Ni 28	Cu 29	Zn 30	Ga 31	Ge 32	As 33	Se 34	Br 35	Kr 36
Rb 37	Sr 38	Y 39	Zr 40	Nb 41	Mo 42	Tc 43	Ru 44	Rh 45	Pd 46	Ag 47	Cd 48	In 49	Sn 50	Sb 51	Te 52	I 53	Xe 54
Cs 55	Ba 56	See below 57-71	Hf 72	Ta 73	W 74	Re 75	Os 76	Ir 77	Pt 78	Au 79	Hg 80	Tl 81	Pb 82	Bi 83	Po 84	At 85	Rn 86
Fr 87	Ra 88	See below 89-															
		La 57	Ce 58	Pr 59	Nd 60	Pm 61	Sm 62	Eu 63	Gd 64	Tb 65	Dy 66	Ho 67	Er 68	Tm 69	Yb 70	Lu 71	
		Ac 89	Th 90	Pa 91	U 92	Np 93	Pu 94	Am 95	Cm 96	Bk 97	Cf 98	Es 99	Fm 100	Md 101	No 102	Lw 103	

Figure 9: *The Periodic Table of the Elements.*

of energy from the Sun--penetrated to the interior of certain atoms, such
as those of carbon, oxygen, nitrogen, and hydrogen, as well as to compounds
of those atoms. The photons gave these atoms enough energy to combine as a
molecule called an <u>amino acid</u>. After that, amino acids reacted to form
<u>proteins</u>. Still later, more atoms united into <u>fats</u> and <u>carbohydrates</u>. Col-
lectively, with the help of heat and other catalysts, these chemicals
became <u>nucleic acids</u>. Ultimately nucleic acids could do wondrous things:
form twins of themselves, and each twin another twin. In short, they could
replicate their own structures. This capability is what is meant by "life."

The various nucleic acids of plants and animals continued to copy their
chemicals (see Figure 10); in doing so, some of the copies varied slightly by
an atom here and a molecule there. When any parent set of chemicals--
genes--copied inexactly, there were chances that one of the "offspring"
would vary slightly in different ways. The resulting <u>variety</u> of offspring,
Darwin observed, helped ensure there would be "survival of the species."
The probability, however, for survival of diverse mutant offspring is small
because there must be a correspondingly diverse environment.

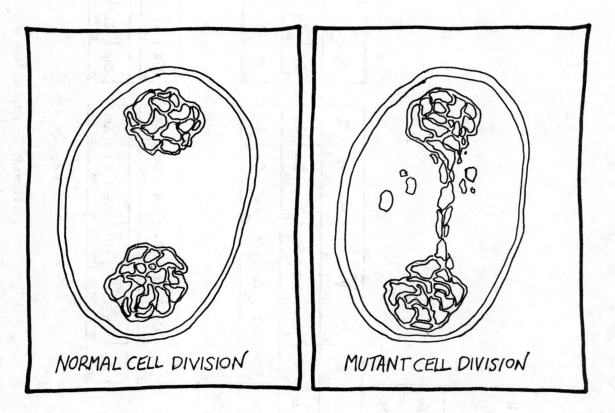

NORMAL CELL DIVISION   MUTANT CELL DIVISION

Figure 10: *Normally, genetic material separates equally during cell reproduction. Quite frequently, it
divides unequally, yielding a new, or mutant, cell type.*

Indeed, at some point certain of the nucleic acids produced a slightly different cell molecule. This molecule could receive photons of sunlight within the ultraviolet frequency range and convert the molecule into a new, excited, energized level of activity. This meant that the cell which had this new molecule did not have to hunt for and gorge itself on fats, carbohydrates, and proteins as energy sources, but instead could get all the energy it needed right from exposure to the Sun. Some of these early, light-sensitive pigments were very much like those which we have in our eyes today, the rhodopsin, for example. The particular chemical that is energized by photons from the Sun rather than electrons from another chemical is chlorophyll.

The activated chlorophyll molecule helps other chemicals to capture CO_2 and H_2O molecules and successively hitch them together into a more complex six-carbon molecule, glucose, $C_6H_{12}O_6$. Plants produce quantities of this sugar and store them in various forms as fixed packets of food. Plants store sugar, the squirrels store nuts, or we store "fat." Sugars (carbohydrates), nuts (fats, carbohydrates, and proteins), and stored fat (carbohydrates and fats) are foods. When chlorophyll-bearing plant cells make food, they use CO_2 and H_2O, and give off oxygen, O_2. Animals cannot make food as plants do; instead they find it in the environment. Both need O_2 to use food and produce as by-products CO_2 and H_2O. (If plants did not produce oxygen, the existing animals and their offspring would use up the oxygen in the atmosphere within about 1,000 years.) There is a reason, then, to talk about the necessity for maintaining a balance of plant and animal life. Each supplies a need and uses the waste products of the other.

We have just discussed that both plants and animals store food. Over a long period of time, some of those stores have become caches of energy which we now use: wood, peat, coal, petroleum, and natural gas.

At one time, swampy areas dense with plant forests covered great sections of the Earth, including about 1/10th of the United States. Following changes in the Earth's crust, the marshes were inundated shallow seas. Sediments from erosion and living organisms settled on top of the dead plants until the level was sufficiently shallow to start another open marsh. This process may have occurred many times. The layers slowly built up, the pressure increased, chemical changes took place, and the decaying vegetation compressed over time into seams of practically pure carbon--coal.

In similar fashion, ancient plants and animals settled to ocean bottoms, compressed, and chemically changed into petroleum. Apparently the organic materials break down, gradually releasing carbon and hydrogen which then chemically recombine as natural gas and oil. Gas and oil migrate upward through penetrable soils, such as sandstone. If trapped by an impervious soil, perhaps sediments compressed into shale, then both fuels are retained until released to the surface by crustal movements or by drilling (see Figure 11).

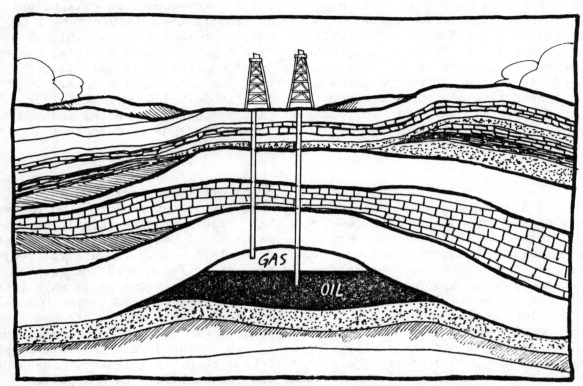

Figure 11: *Gas and oil reserves are trapped beneath impervious rock.*

Gas and oil have been drilled since 1859. Most of the reservoirs have been found, and most of the supplies have been taken from those reservoirs. They took 350,000,000 years to form--how long to use?

These physical, chemical, and biological forms of matter <u>in motion</u> are energy. They have the capacity to perform work. By work we can extract iron ore, construct highways, erect buildings, assemble cars, disperse insecticides, inject antibiotics, preserve parks, jog uphill, write master plans, regulate consumption--and conserve energy.

<u>Species</u> <u>Diversity</u> <u>and</u> <u>Environmental</u> <u>Health</u>

We, then, are the current expression of a long history of variant chemicals falling into a variant environment. Since we take so long to grow into biologically competent individuals, we must be certain that the environment will be able to receive us nurturingly when we do. Once conceived, the systems of our bodies are fixed forever. The environment had better be too.

It is logical to argue, then, that where there are many different types of grasses, shrubs, insects, birds, mice, fish, worms, barnacles, bacteria, and algae, there are concomitant diverse habitable homes or "niches." The presence of diverse species indicates that the physical, chemical, and biological factors mixed in quantity and quality permit energy to be converted in a variety of ways. If that could not happen, we would be talking about an environment with fewer and fewer energy conversions and sources. That would be an unhealthy environment.

We need to have abundant nutrients, moisture, and stable temperatures. Our offspring need them, too; they will not have had the time to adapt to anything less. To ensure a healthy environment takes care and forethought.

"Forethought" is a thinking or a planning out in advance, a consideration of the future. Our past decisions and actions shaped our present conditions. In that continuity, our present extrapolates pretty solidly to our future. In that future, the natural systems that went before will continue, but how healthily depends on our present forethought and subsequent action.

We humans are at present forms of what went before, having evolved and been refined over millions of years. We are not at home in the water or in the air, but on the land: lungs and legs. We are "stuck mit." Land-lovers we will no doubt always be, and as creatures of the land we build on the ground. What we structure on land will make the critical difference in whether our ecosystem survives healthily or perishes slowly. Lack of forethought is already killing some of us--with crowded living conditions that pollute the waters we drink or with manufacturing that emits toxic gases and particulates into the air we breathe.

The chapters that follow discuss how we can best assure a healthy Earth and healthy life to inhabit it.

CHAPTER SUMMARY

1. Earth's characteristics determine the means and degrees to which we can influence life in our biosphere to our benefit or to our detriment.

2. The Earth's position and motion with respect to the Sun and Moon in the Milky Way Galaxy cause day and night, seasons, tidal ebb and flow, and numerous less perceptible motions.

3. Our planet's mass and density cause such pressure at its center that radioactive materials and tremendous heat result, the latter providing geothermal energy we can use as an alternative energy source.

4. Both the magnetic field and the atmosphere of Earth prevent harmful solar rays from penetrating and damaging the life forms vulnerable to them. The atmosphere, solar heat, and the hydrologic cycle make our dynamic weather

systems. Weather and the energetic activity within the Earth continuously transform the surface of our land. The dynamics account for the ongoing formation of soils from developed and then eroded parent materials.

5. The massive scale--in sheer mass, energy, and motion--of Earth in relation to Sun, Moon, the planets, the Galaxy, and all of Universal space is mirrored in infinitesimal scale in the atom and its particles, energy, and motions. Just as eons ago photons of sunlight penetrated the atmosphere of Earth, so at some point photons of sunlight penetrated certain atoms so that amino acids formed, then proteins, then fats and carbohydrates. With these and heat and other right conditions, nucleic acids formed. With their coming, life came to Earth.

6. We are the current expression of a long history of variant chemicals in a variant environment. As a species, humans adjust extremely slowly. To keep our Earth a nurturing environment takes care and forethought about how we will use our land and our planet's other resources.

SOURCES

Beiser, Arthur., et. al. The Earth. New York: Time, Inc., 1962.

Farb, Peter, et. al. Ecology. New York: Time, Inc., 1970.

Leary, Richard L. "Where Has All the Oil Gone?" The Explorer, 19 (Summer 1977), 14-17.

Milne, Lorus J., et. al. The Mountains. New York: Time, Inc., 1962.

Moore, Ruth, et. al. Evolution. New York: Time, Inc., 1962.

Shelton, John S. Geology Illustrated. San Fransisco: W. H. Freeman and Co., 1966.

Spar, Jerome. Earth, Sea, and Air: A Survey of the Geophysical Sciences. Reading, Mass.: Addison-Wesley Publishing Co., Inc., 1965.

Thompson, Philip D., et. al. Weather. New York: Time, Inc., 1965.

SUGGESTED READING

Chemical Bond Approach Project. Chemical Systems. New York: McGraw-Hill, 1964.

Evelyn, G. "The Biosphere." One Biosphere: A Scientific American Book. San Francisco: W. H. Freeman and Co., 1970.

Gore, Rick, et. al. "The Awesome Worlds within a Cell." The National Geographic, 150, No. 3 (September 1976), 354-399.

Sienko, Mitchell J. and Robert A. Plane. <u>Chemistry.</u> New York: McGraw-Hill, 1961.

Thomas, Lewis. <u>The Lives of a Cell.</u> New York: Bantam Books, Inc., 1974.

CHAPTER TWO

THE NATURE OF WATER

A PERSPECTIVE

The Qu'Appelle River flows through 250 miles of the fertile, treeless plain of south-central Saskatchewan in Canada. It is a scenic land, a series of shallow glacial lakes dot the Qu'Appelle (or Calling) River, the largest, Echo Lake. When the first white men came to the area they found Echo Lake full of blue-green algae and smelling from the accumulated carcasses of buffalo that had been stampeded by Indians over the Lake banks for centuries.

The buffalo had long since disappeared by 1941. The river and its lakes ran clear and 200,000 people thrived in the watershed. Over 80% of the people were farmers, the vast majority of these, wheat farmers. Land and water use was in balance with the carrying capacity of the watershed.

By 1971 dramatic shifts had occurred. There were half as many farmers, but nearly a million more acres were devoted to intensive cultivation. Cattle-raising had mushroomed with 60 feed-lots springing up near the river. The population of Regina and Moose Jaw had increased by 111,000 and wastewater treatment had become inadequate. Vacation cottages with no waste treatment provisions sprang up along the lakes. By 1972 Echo Lake smelled foul and was once again covered with algae.

Echo Lake and the Qu'Appelle River are excellent examples of "eutrophication." The nutrient loading rate (nutrients per unit of surface and depth) for Echo Lake in the spring of 1971 was 5 lbs. per square foot of surface (20 times that of Lake Erie). Phosphate in milligrams per litre was 1.09, total nitrogen was 1.75, and total organic carbon was 21.

The Saskatchewan Department of the Environment and Environment Canada have taken tough, realistic steps to address the problems. Consequently, striking improvement has been noted in recent years.

Report of the Qu'Appelle Basin Study Board

All of the water that has ever existed on the Earth is still here. Most of it is on the surface as liquid, some is frozen, a small quantity is in the atmosphere as a gas, and the rest is locked into chemicals in plants and animals.

The oceans hold over 97% of the Earth's total water supply. More than 2% lies frozen in glaciers and the polar ice caps. Less than 1% lies in the lakes, streams, rivers, and underground reservoirs. A fraction of 1% is found in the atmosphere as water vapor, snow, sleet, hail, or rain. However, this last very tiny percentage of all the water of the Earth is a large amount to us, for it is critically important in relation to the forces that change the surface of the Earth and continually bring fresh water to living organisms.

The "hydrologic cycle" that takes place all over the Earth is the continuous evaporation and condensation and precipitation of water. Yearly 80,000 cubic miles of water evaporate from the ocean, and 15,000 cubic miles evaporate from water residing on the land and from plant transpiration. But, because of the condensation which occurs when the cool ocean air passes over land, of the total of 95,000 cubic miles evaporated, only 24,000 cubic miles fall on land. Much of this—some 15,000 cubic miles—soaks into the groundwater supply. The last 9,000 runs over the soil, into the streams and rivers, and in a few weeks (on the average) returns to the oceans.

The airborne portion of the hydrologic cycle is extremely rapid. In the United States 80-90% of each day's precipitation has evaporated from the ocean only 2-3 days before. The quantities and velocities of water moving through the cycle, then, are immense. Weather is the force that moves the water, but it is the chemistry of the H_2O molecule that accounts for water's astonishing behavior. The molecule is a compound of three atoms, two hydrogen atoms and one oxygen atom.* The positively charged hydrogen atoms and the negatively charged oxygen atoms attract one another. However, the positive charge of the single proton cloud of one hydrogen atom repels the like positive charge of the other hydrogen atom. The "resolution" of this tension is that each water molecule assumes a unique shape, with the hydrogen atoms standing apart from each other on the average of 105°. The familiar image to which you might liken the molecule's shape is that of a "V": the two top ends are the hydrogen atoms with small positive charges; the bottom (apex) is the single oxygen atom with a large negative charge.

The water molecule is said to be "dipolar" because of these two oppositely charged ends. The physical structure of the water molecule, a

*The appendix contains a brief review of the properties and structures of atoms and molecules.

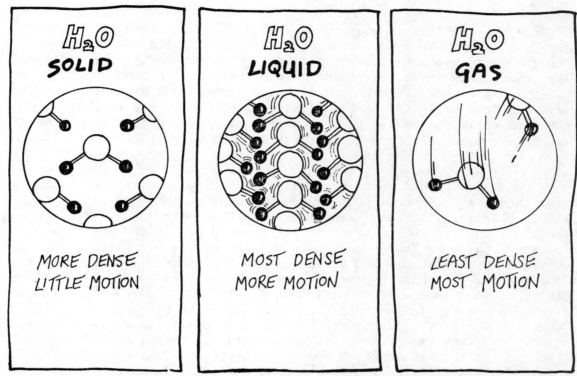

Figure 12: *The three physical states of water: solid, liquid, and gas. Each state is a function of the energy level of the water molecules.*

dipolar V-shaped unit, gives water highly unusual <u>chemical</u> properties. One of its most unusual ones is water's stability at different energy levels or temperatures. Water remains uniformly a liquid throughout the energy level ranging from 0° C to 100° C. Below that range, water is a solid; above that, a vapor. These three physical states are consequences of the molecule's dipolar, V-shape. Figure 12 represents the three states in which H_2O may be found.

<u>The Three States of Water</u>

When the molecules are at a low level of energy due to their sub-zero centigrade temperature, they move little in comparison to the other two states. At this low level of motion water is in the solid state. The intermolecular charges between the tips of the molecules cause the molecules to align themselves equidistantly from one another into a pyramid. The resulting structure is familiar to us--ice. Compared to the liquid state, the molecules are a greater distance apart. Therefore, there are fewer of them in any given volume of ice, such as a milliliter, than in an equal volume in liquid form. Since the molecules as ice are not as dense

as in the liquid state, a milliliter of liquid water weighs more than a
milliliter of solid water (ice).

With the addition of energy, such as heat, the molecules have more
energy and consequently they move faster--causing solid water to melt. As
melting occurs, the molecules move closer together, making the water more
dense; then, less dense ice floats on the surface of a pond or at the top
of a glass of water. It takes 80 calories of heat per gram of water to
change H_2O from the solid to the liquid state. Yet, it takes only 1
calorie to raise the temperature of water one degree per gram. In short,
it takes a lot of heat to melt ice, for it is a very stable form of water.

With the continued heating of water from 0° C, the molecules draw
closer together until at 4° C they are the closest they ordinarily ever
will be; therefore, at this temperature water is most dense. This characteristic of density causes water in lakes and ponds in the northern part of
the United States to "turn over" each spring and fall, a highly important
phenomenon in the biology and weather of such regions. (The details are
discussed later in this chapter.) Water remains totally "liquid" with the
addition of more heat energy until 100° C (212° F). At that temperature
the level of energy in the molecules causes them to overcome the pressure
of air on the surface of the water and to overcome their attraction between
one another: they escape into the air as gas, or vapor; they "evaporate."
The Sun in fact provides enough energy to evaporate in the hydrologic cycle
the 95,000 cubic miles of water mentioned earlier. It takes 540 calories
of heat per gram of water to energize it enough to leave the liquid state
and to become a gas. In effect, a gram of water vapor has the energy equivalent of 540 calories. This heat energy is a major source of fuel for
the global weather system which we will discuss in a later chapter.

Because of water's amazing stability, it is used as a standard of measurement. At 20° C and at 760 mm of mercury (sea level), the specific
gravity of water is called 1. At that temperature and pressure 1 cubic centimeter of water is equal to 1 milliliter and weighs one gram. All other
substances are compared to this reference (see Figure 13).

Water as a Solvent

The dipolar structure and the V-shape of a water molecule partially
explain its ability to dissolve many substances. Although water is by no
means a "universal solvent," it is the most common dissolver in nature.
For example, water seeping through the minerals of America's midwestern
salt flats dissolves the salts. Water molecules bombard the salt crystal
and pull apart the sodium atom and the chloride atom that are held together
by opposite charges. Then the water molecule moves in, orienting its positive hydrogen end to the negative chloride atom, and its negative oxygen end
to the positive sodium atom. Thereafter, successive water molecules break
up the salt crystal entirely by separating all the parts into individual

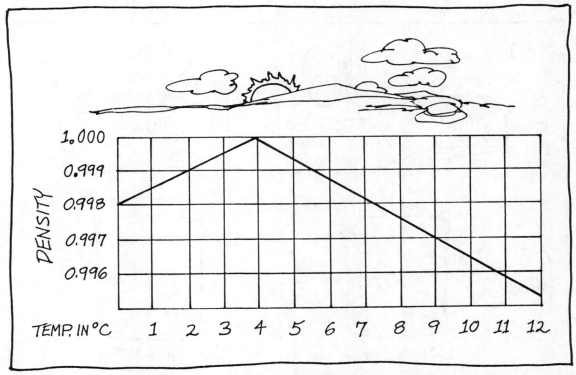

Figure 13: *At 0° C ice floats; at 4° C water is most dense, causing it to sink.*

charged atoms (ions) and by holding them in solution with small attractive forces (see Figure 14). The success of the water dissolving salt is as much to the credit of the polarity of the sodium ion, Na^+, and the chloride ion, Cl^-, as it is to the water molecule's polarities. Water is a less successful solvent when the surrounded substance has many bonds holding its molecules together. Gasoline, for example, does not break into separate ions in water, but remains undissolved, floating on top of it.

Molecules which exist primarily in the gaseous state at the normal temperature ranges, such as carbon dioxide, oxygen, and nitrogen, generally do not dissolve well in water either. However, some are more soluble than others. Oxygen, for example, comprises about 21% of the atmosphere, but only about .001% of water. The oxygen in the air is many times more concentrated than it is in water, and organisms with lungs or with gills have evolved characteristics appropriate to their respective sources of oxygen.

The gas oxygen is a molecule of two oxygen atoms, O_2. The two oxygen nuclei share their orbiting electrons and, by doing so, settle on an energy

Figure 14: *The charged ends of the water molecules attract the oppositely charged sodium and chloride ions, thus suspending them in solution.*

level that is so low that it actually takes a great deal of energy to separate the two atoms. Therefore, they are not attracted to the dipolar, V-shaped water molecule: they do not have the polarity of the positive and negative charges found in salt, NaCl. The fact that oxygen dissolves poorly in water is a tremendously significant factor in the workings of environmental systems.

Because of the higher partial pressure of oxygen in the atmosphere than in water, numerous oxygen molecules will be forced into the water when it is broken up and exposed to the air, as is the case in turbulent, cascading waterfalls. If the water is also very cold, the water molecules move slowly and more oxygen will be able to stay in solution. At low temperature <u>both</u> water and oxygen molecules have less energy; they both move more slowly. Therefore, the oxygen is less likely to escape back into the atmosphere. High oxygen levels are survival requirements for some organisms, such as trout. That is why such fish are found in the rough, cold waters of mountainous northern streams.

Surface Tension

The shape and charge of the H_2O molecule give water a high surface tension. A carefully filled glass of water brims beyond the top but does not overflow. A needle eight times the specific gravity of water will float on water. In nature, water striders and other insects stride on a stream's surface, while others walk on its undersurface. Raindrops fall in tear shapes, upon impact bouncing and reforming into tiny spheres. The surface tension is actually due to the alignment of mutually attracted water molecules at the interface of water and air.

The surface tension can be broken, however. Detergents can do it chemically, while fast-running rapids can do it physically. In later chapters we will examine how the breakdown of the water's surface helps to explain how certain matter is transported as well as how certain pollutants can upset or destroy an insect's niche in the water. Thus, the surface tension of water is of great ecological significance--for life today has evolved to a state where its health depends highly on water and its amazing characteristics.

Dissociation

Water molecules also do something else of great interest and importance: they can dissociate into positively and negatively charged units called ions. In fact, every now and then a molecule--perhaps one in ten million--does so. One hydrogen atom leaves the molecule, creating a loose, positively charged hydrogen ion (H^+) and a loose, negatively charged oxygen-hydrogen ion (OH^-). If the loose hydrogen ion moves toward a regular water molecule, it joins it to make an H_3O^+ ion. These two species (H_3O^+ and OH^-) together are now free to interact as new agents. No longer are they bound as the other molecules of H_2O; rather, they have their own personalities. The H_3O^+ ion might be attracted to the Cl^- from dissolved NaCl, creating HCl, hydrochloric acid. The OH^- might approach the Na^+ ion, joining it to form NaOH, sodium hydroxide. Both of these resultant compounds are potent corrosive agents, themselves able to interact with yet other groups of compounds. In biochemical reactions, especially, the H_3O^+ and OH^- ions have an intermediate balancing role (see Figure 15).

There is a way to express the relative numbers of the H_3O^+ and the OH^- ions. It is called the "pH scale" and it relates the concentration of H^+ present to the normal number expected (1×10^{-7}). In the pH range of 0 to 14, the normal pH of water is pH 7. When the OH^- ions are numerous, the pH number will tend toward 14 and the conditions are said to be basic or alkaline. When the H_3O^+ ions are numerous, the pH number will tend toward 0 and conditions are said to be acidic.

What significance is pH in evaluating the environmental quality of streamwater, for example? The acidity of a stream or other body of water can increase or decrease with the addition of biologically active organic compounds.

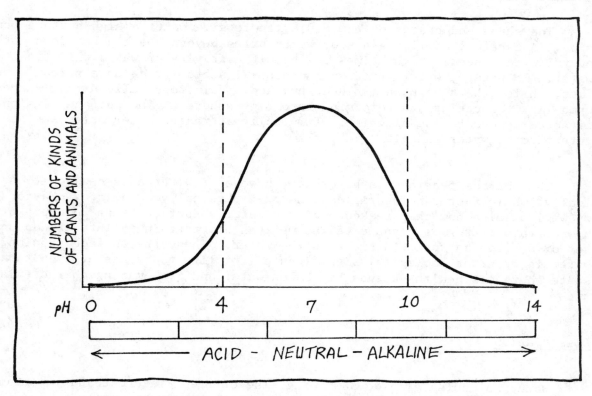

Figure 15: *Most plants and animals survive within a pH rang of 4-10.*

These can come from soil, rocks, rotting leaves, and other sources. Concentrations of ions from inorganic elements such as aluminum, sodium, and calcium increase or decrease acidity, and so do atmospheric gases such as sulfur dioxide, carbon dioxide, and hydrogen sulfide. The basicity of water can increase with biological decomposition products that form chlorides, bicarbonates, and nitrates; or with soil and rock ions of sulfates, carbonate, fluoride, chloride, and phosphates; as well as from the ions of atmospheric gases, such as sulfate and bicarbonate. A pH reading can be put into practical use in water purification: the proper reaction between algae and chemical additives to remove these plants takes place only within a narrow pH range. In farming, soil pH is critical to the uptake of nutrients by plants. Industrial water must not be too acidic or it will corrode certain metals. Fish culture, alcoholic beverage fermentation, and manufacturing of bakery products all require a certain pH level to be successful.*

---

* We can measure conveniently pH levels in two ways. At certain pH conditions, the H_3O^+ ions react with certain chemicals, causing them to change color. A series of chemically treated paper strips can indicate by color the pH of a solution. Ions in solution also cause electricity to flow through a wire; that flow causes a meter needle to deflect. Therefore, we can read pH level directly in terms of electrical conductivity.

Water Is Transparent

We mentioned earlier that water molecules evaporate when they have 540 calories per gram of water. Water molecules intercept photons of light energy from the Sun, but they do not intercept all of them. Enough solar radiation continues downward so that the photosynthesizing plants can capture the photons in their chlorophyll, generally to a depth of 30 feet. The depth of penetration depends upon the particles present in the water--soils, decayed leaves, and others. In highly polluted swamps, the light may penetrate only an inch; in the Caribbean, to some 200 feet; and in Crater Lake, as far down as 400 feet!

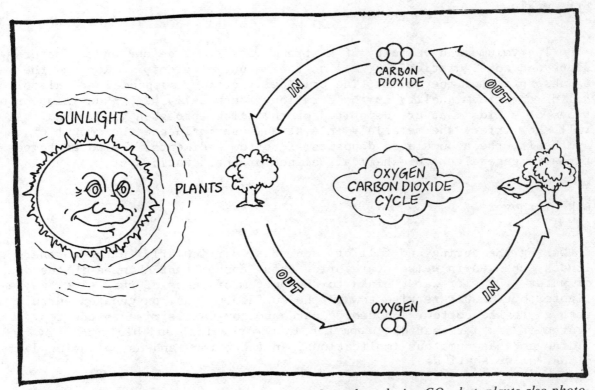

Figure 16: *Plants and animals respire, consuming O_2 and producing CO_2; but, plants also photosynthesize, producing O_2 and consuming CO_2.*

With the addition of soil particles, however, the water becomes opaque or at least so turbid as to prevent light from passing to the lower regions. As plants die, carbon dioxide accumulates and oxygen production decreases. The amount of available light, of course, depends upon the time of day, the season of the year, and the latitude (the angle of incidence of the Sun's rays). But the relative angle to the Sun concerns us less than the particulate matter that diminishes the clarity of water. We want to maintain a balance in the oxygen/carbon dioxide cycle (see Figure 16).

Water turbidity indicates the amount of suspended material transported. In ponds and lakes a visual test using a Secchi dish is used to determine turbidity. For flowing water, a sample is passed through a fiber glass filter. Solids, such as salts that dissolve in water, pass through the filter. Other solids are suspended and non-filtrable and remain on the filter. Non-filtrable solids, commonly called silt, are determined per liter and multiplied by the volume and flow of the stream in cubic feet per second to determine the stream's total sediment load. Filtrable solids in the water have no effect on turbidity and do not block radiation. They usually result from water passing through sedimentary geologic formations and reflect the composition of the minerals in them.

Stream Flow

The volume and velocity of a stream, its flow, depend on the watershed's slope and configuration, as well as the amount of precipitation and the rate of absorption of the soils. The critical factor of suspended and dissolved solids to stream quality is the duration of unusually high quantities or new types of solids that are deposited or that flow through a given area. As we will show later, the materials in a stream can influence the amount of photosynthesis, the accumulated deposits of bottom sediments, the water temperature--in general the biochemical balance of the aquatic system.

Lake Turnover

During the spring and fall of each year, particularly in the northern latitudes, changes in temperature bring about concomitant changes in the density of water. Heavier water sinks to the bottom of lakes at this time, while the lighter bottom waters rise toward the surface. Thus, oxygenated surface waters go to the bottom, and deoxygenated bottom waters rise to the top. This "turnover" is a repeated phenomenon in the physical and biological system. "Turnover" has numerous implications, in fact, for land-use planning decisions, as we shall see.

---

* Impurities are classified by size for their ability to be trapped upon or to pass through a specified filter. Thus, all impurities are either filtrable or non-filtrable solids. A filter is weighed before and after a sample of water has been filtered through it. The gain in weight is the amount of non-filtrable solids. The filtered water is then evaporated from a container that is weighed before and after evaporation. The increase in weight of the container is the amount of filtrable solids in the original water sample. The separate and combined weights are reported, the latter called the total solids. Total solids information is important because filters used may vary in their filtrability, depending on the mix of chemicals in the water. Therefore, official reports require the full information about non-filtrable and filtrable solids. The temperature at which evaporation takes place may help to distinguish between filtrable organic and inorganic matter.

Biannual turnover results from the change in state of the water molecules that comes with the change in atmospheric temperature. We recall that at 4° C the water molecules are most dense. Just before water freezes in the late fall, the surface waters cool down toward 4° C, becoming more and more dense. Gradually they sink toward the bottom, forcing the summer's water beneath to give way to the mass above and to displace to the surface. Again in the spring, as the ice melts and the water warms from 0° C to 4° C, the top water becomes heavier than the warmer, lighter water beneath, and displaces the winter's water to the surface. From this account, a number of facts are now probably clear to you.

First, the heaviest water is at the bottom, at 4° C. Therefore, the bottom waters of ponds and lakes normally do not freeze because the ice and water above blanket them from the cold air. Possibly the Earth's molten center slightly warms the basin of at least the very deep lakes. Second, the lake water stratifies by temperature between turnovers (see Figure 17); thus, there is an opportunity for bottom waters to lose their dissolved oxygen to bacteria that use it as they feed on bottom nutrients. When there are a great many nutrients, say from non-point pollution or from decayed algae, then the bacteria will not be limited by the amount of food, but rather by the amount of oxygen available. When the bacteria also die, the nutrients are no longer decomposed. Instead, they accumulate. Third, this bottom accumulation of nutrients creates problems. As soon as the semi-annual turn-

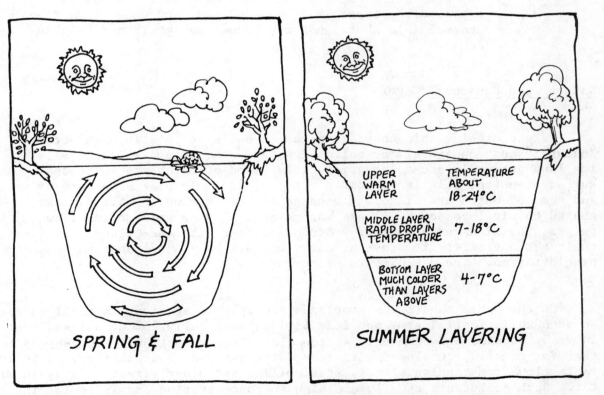

Figure 17: *Lake turnover occurs when 4° C, heavy water sinks, displacing the warm, lighter water to the surface. In periods of constant temperature, water stratifies into layers.*

over occurs, the oxygenless water containing those nutrients carries them to the surface. If it is springtime, the warming ultraviolet light activates the chlorophyll in algae growing at the surface. With the surfeit of nutrients recently brought to these plants by turnover, there is potential for an enormous growth of the algae population--a bloom--for these plants double their numbers with every ten degrees centigrade increase in temperature. The additional organic nutrients, such as phosphorous from detergents, pollute the water because they bring a concentration of nutrients that exceeds the lake's capacity to decompose. Therefore, added nutrients in such a stressed environment sink to the bottom and continue to accumulate. This process over a period of time causes a more rapid aging of the lake than normal. The resulting problems of such algal blooms and nutrient build-ups are many:

- If there are increasingly large areas of deoxygenated water in the lake, then organisms that require substantial amounts of oxygen--such as gamefish--eventually die off altogether, or at least die in great numbers in "fishkills."

- Upon turnover, nutrients will continue to surface and algal blooms will be maintained. The algae interferes with drinking water purification and recreational use of water.

- The water may taste bad; the algae and putrefying fish may wash onto shore; land values may fall; the tax base may erode; property may be abandoned; and once attractive and valuable shorelands may become unsightly and be abandoned.

Natural and Unnatural Water

Before closing this chapter it may be useful to distinguish between "natural" and "unnatural" or polluted water. The rainwater that falls on the land gradually accumulates materials, some of which are suspended by the surface tension, relative specific gravity, and molecular structure of water, and some of which are dissolved because of the charges on this dipolar, V-shaped chemical compound. These waters naturally contain soils, leaves, twigs. The kind and amount of sediments differ with the upland soil types, their susceptibility to erosion, the slope of the ground, and the amount of precipitation. These sediments are natural.

On the other hand, when croplands are open to erosion, rainfall carries so much soil, fertilizers, and insecticides that fully 25% of all sediments in U. S. streams are from this source alone. Other pollutants wash from land that is forested, developed, or cleared for one reason or another, or pollutants flow from canning plants, steel mills, and urban street salting in winter. Such pollutants usually are high in concentration and irregular in source; they constitute qualitative and/or quantative surprises to the natural system. These sediments are unnatural: they are pollutants.

All of the water pollution problems seem to be more manageable if they are viewed in the context of the hydrologic cycle, a flowing system with continuous, alternative pathways, motion, and durability. The properties of water, including its variety of physical states at different energy levels, its strange V-shaped molecular structure, and its ability to ionize and suspend or dissolve materials, give the system a tremendous dynamism and strength. A systemic perspective shows us that with proper management the water can be cleaned a bit more each time through the hydrologic cycle. There are advantages to closing down certain pollution sources. Water is not going to disappear, but the amount of healthful water can be greatly diminished by stressing the natural purifying system to its limits.

CHAPTER SUMMARY

1. The Sun's energy heats the Earth's surface. The heat increases the energy of the Earth's water. Some 95,000 cubic miles of water annually evaporate into the atmosphere, cool, condense, and fall back on Earth through the process called the hydrologic cycle.

2. The smallest integral unit of matter which can be called water is the molecule H_2O, which has one negatively charged oxygen atom and two positively charged hydrogen atoms. The hydrogen atoms oscillate in spaces which on the average are 105° apart. The appropriate picture of a water molecule is a V-shaped wedge that is negatively charged at the bottom and positively charged at the two top legs.

3. The molecules are always in motion. With little motion, water is ice; with greater motion it is liquid; and at high energy levels and greatest movement, it is a gas.

4. The negative (oxygen) end of one water molecule is attracted toward the positive (hydrogen) end of another. Similarly, the positive end of one pulls toward the negative end of another; thus, the molecule is said to be two-poled, dipolar. In water molecules, the V-shape and electrical charges of oxygen and hydrogen account for water's physical and chemical properties.

5. Water molecules hold together over wider temperature ranges than most chemicals--i.e., from 0° C to 100° C; they dissolve other dipolar chemicals and suspend non-dipolar chemicals. Water therefore is a very predictable, dependable chemical that is an excellent carrier and dissolver of others.

6. A small number of water molecules dissociate and form separate positively and negatively charged units called ions--H^+ and OH^-. These chemical species enter into different types of chemical reactions and give water additional characteristics.

7. Water cycles from Earth to air and to Earth again, interacting with and transporting other chemicals during that cycle. Water's stability, availability, and properties are primary concerns of the land-use planner, in particular, and to all of us, in general.

SOURCES

Chemical Bond Approach Project. <u>Chemical Systems</u>. New York: McGraw-Hill, 1964.

Harper, Harold A. <u>Review of Physiological</u> Chemistry, Los Altos, California: Lange Medical Publications, 1963.

SUGGESTED READING

<u>River of Life</u>: U. S. Department of Interior Conservation Yearbook. U.S. Department of Interior, Vol. No. 6 (1970).

CHAPTER THREE

THE NATURE OF AIR AND WEATHER

A PERSPECTIVE

The earth breathes, in a certain sense. . . . There may
have been cycles of oxygen production and carbon dioxide consumption, depending on relative abundances of
plant and animal life, with the ice ages representing a
period of apnea. An overwhelming richness of vegetation may have caused the level of oxygen to rise above
today's concentration, with a corresponding depletion
of carbon dioxide. Such a drop in carbon dioxide may
have impaired the "greenhouse" property of the atmosphere, which holds in the solar heat otherwise lost
by radiation from the earth's surface. The fall in
temperature would in turn have shut off much of living,
and, in a long sigh, the level of oxygen may have
dropped by 90 percent. Berkner speculates that this
is what happened to the great reptiles; their size may
have been all right for a richly oxygenated atmosphere,
but they had the bad luck to run out of air.

Now we are protected against lethal ultraviolet rays
by a narrow rim of ozone, thirty miles out. We are
safe, well ventilated, and incubated, provided we can
avoid technologies that might fiddle with that ozone,
or shift the levels of carbon dioxide. Oxygen is not
a major worry for us, unless we let fly with enough
nuclear explosives to kill off the green cells in the
sea; if we do that, of course, we are in for strangling.

It is hard to feel affection for something as totally
impersonal as the atmosphere, and yet there it is, as
much a part and product of life as wine or bread. Taken
all in all, the sky is a miraculous achievement. It
works, and for what it is designed to accomplish it is
as infallible as anything in nature. I doubt whether
any of us could think of a way to improve it, beyond
maybe shifting a local cloud from here to there on
occasion. The word "chance" does not serve to account
well for structures of such magnificence. There may
have been elements of luck in the emergence of chloroplasts, but once these things were on the scene, the
evolution of the sky became absolutely ordained.
Chance suggests alternatives, other possibilities,
different solutions. This may be true for gills and
swim-bladders and forebrains, matters of detail, but
not for the sky. There was simply no other way to go.

37

We should credit it for what it is: for sheer size and
perfection of function, it is far and away the grandest
product of collaboration in all of nature.

It breathes for us, and it does another thing for our
pleasure. Each day, millions of meteorites fall
against the outer limits of the membrane and are burned
to nothing by the friction. Without this shelter, our
surface would long since have become the pounded powder
of the moon. Even though our receptors are not sensitive
enough to hear it, there is comfort in knowing that the
sound is there overhead, like the random noise of rain
on the roof at night.

Lewis Thomas, The Lives of a Cell

The Sun and Weather

The hydrologic cycle, evaporating, condensing, and precipitating water
through the horizontal and vertical tumult of the atmosphere, is a prime element of the weather. Except for the heat within the Earth, the Sun is
the source of the energy in the weather system. The characteristics of
that energy, then, are helpful to know in thinking about how the weather
relates to the quality of our natural environment, the distribution of
pollutants, and the considerations we must undertake in planning how to
manage the way we use our land.

Max Planck postulated in 1900 that light energy was emitted discontinu-
ously in quanta or packets of light energy called photons and that photons
had different amounts of energy depending on their frequency. Now, when
photons of high frequency strike an atom, its electrons have higher kinetic
energy than before. Low frequency photons do not give the atomic electrons
more energy. The photon disappears when an electron is aroused to a higher
energy level, and it reappears when the electron drops back to a lower
energy level. It appears that a photon behaves like a wave and a particle,
that it can lose mass and become pure energy.

Sunlight contains a large range of photons with different frequencies.
Some of the photons strike us directly, some are absorbed in the upper
atmosphere and readmitted at still other frequencies, and the rest are
reflected out into space. In addition, radiation other than solar penetrates the atmosphere: some of it is high energy rays from outer space,
which are called cosmic rays. These high energy radiations may have their
origins in the normal decay of stars. In addition to visible light, emissions from distant galaxies also include low frequency radio waves which
can be detected by radio telescopes.

The frequencies of solar waves range from about 60 Hz* to 10^{20} Hz. Some comparisons of familiar frequencies help to show the range of those solar waves:

- Household alternating current   60 Hz (60 cycles/second)

- Radio waves 10^5 to 10^9 Hz

- Microwaves 10^9 Hz

- Infrared rays 10^{11} to 10^{14} Hz

- Visible (that light we know) 4×10^{14} to 7.5×10^{14}

- Ultraviolet 7.5×10^{14} to 10^{17} Hz

- X-rays 10^{16} to 10^{20} Hz

- Gamma rays (lasers) 10^{19} to 10^{23} Hz

To give usefulness to these numbers, consider these familiar sources of frequencies. If you sit before a hot stove, you receive low-frequency infrared radiation. You become hot. However, none of your body's electrons become excited, as they do if you sit in the Sun--even in mid-winter-- where you will be struck by high frequency ultraviolet solar light which excites certain pigments of the skin, if you have them, causing a sunburn. Heavier doses of ultraviolet light, of course, can increase the chances of skin cancer or even genetic mutations which could be precursors to birth defects. These physiological changes in human health we discuss later on.

Fortunately, not all of the Sun's radiation penetrates to Earth; the atmosphere prevents it. Like the glass and polyethylene in greenhouses, the atmosphere absorbs most of the frequencies in the ultraviolet range that cause burns. About 50% of the Sun's wide-ranging frequencies of photons reach the surface of the Earth, some absorbed, some radiated, depending on the angle of the Sun to the Earth and the time of exposure of objects receiving radiation. Most plants can absorb energy from wave lengths that are lower in frequency than those that cause burns in many humans. Consequently, they can flourish in the warm greenhouse. Plant leaves absorb about 83% of all of the light striking them, reflecting about 12%, and passing through some 5%. Of the 83% absorbed, only 4% travels to the light-responsive chemical with energy-transferring properties, chlorophyll. The remainder is converted into heat and radiated or otherwise lost to the atmosphere. Ice and water, on the other hand reradiate practically

---

*The Hertz is the international unit for frequency. One Hertz is equal to one cycle per second; 60 Hz equals 60 cycles per second. The higher frequency waves are 600,000,000,000 cycles per second!

all of the Sun's radiation. Therefore, the surface features of the Earth affect the amount of energy reflected, or reradiated, from the Earth's surface back into the atmosphere. This energy becomes the driving force of our weather system.

Composition of the Atmosphere

The Earth's atmosphere is a mixture of various gases, mostly oxygen (21%) and nitrogen (78%). Because of our planet's shape, its rotation, and the effects of gravity, atmospheric gases tend to layer out in three main strata:

- Low (troposphere)--from 5 miles at the north and south poles to a bulge of 10 miles at the equator. This is the stratum encompassing the biosphere.

- Middle (stratosphere)--from 10 to 15 miles from the surface of the Earth.

- High (ionosphere)--from 15 to 600 miles, the gases layer out differentially.

Within the troposphere the predominant weather movements take place-- the hydrologic cycle, cloud formations, and other phenomena. Between this lowest layer and the stratosphere are the jet streams, an exceptionally high velocity ribbon of wind that travels around the world between the two major layers. They often stir and drive the pressure systems and temperature fronts.

The Winds

The Sun does not heat the Earth uniformly, as it would if the Earth were a flat plate with no atmosphere. Because of the equatorial bulge at Earth's middle, the Sun's energy radiates more intensely there in the daytime than at any other place or time. The result of this high energy impact at the equator we have already foretold in Chapter 1--a great amount of equatorial air rising into the sky, carrying with it tons of water evaporated from the sea.

As this hot, light, moisture-laden air rises above the equator, it cools, becomes more dense, and the moisture becomes precipitation. Pushed by more hot air rising beneath it and pulled to Earth by gravity, it has nowhere to go except in the direction of the north and south poles. The air currents created by moving vertically upward from the equator, then horizontally to the poles, and then vertically downward are called "Hadley's Cells." (See Figure 18.)

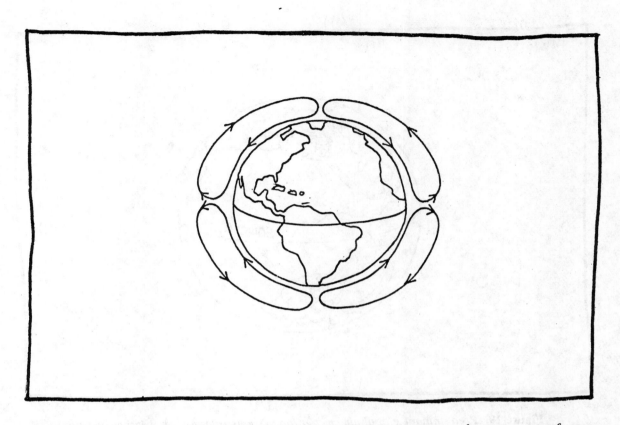

Figure 18: *The equatorial movement of cold, polar air and the continuing polar movement of warm equatorial air is a Hadley cell.*

As you examine the drawing, recall that the Earth is rotating from west to east (left to right in the drawing). The velocity of the globe's surface at the equator is 1,100 miles per hour, so that it rotates through 25,000 miles in 24 hours. At New York City, the velocity is about 770 miles per hour. One foot from the axial pole, the distance covered in 24 hours, would be a circle six feet in circumference, a fraction of a mile an hour. Therefore, the Earth's surface at the equator is moving very rapidly below the rising, hot, moist air, and decreasingly toward the poles. As a result, the air mass in the Hadley Cell moves clockwise in the northern hemisphere; counterclockwise in the southern hemisphere.

To illustrate the direction of the two major weather motions, let's imagine a free-floating balloon released at the north pole. It would drift in the cool air of the Hadley Cell close to the surface of the Earth. Looking down from the balloon, watching the Earth move faster and faster from west to east as we approach the equator, upon arrival we would not be due south of the release point, but substantially west of it. In the northern hemisphere, observers of the balloon would report that it was travelling south and west, southwest. There is not enough friction between air and Earth to hold the atmosphere directly overhead, so the air slides over the Earth. The composite direction is suggested in Figure 19.

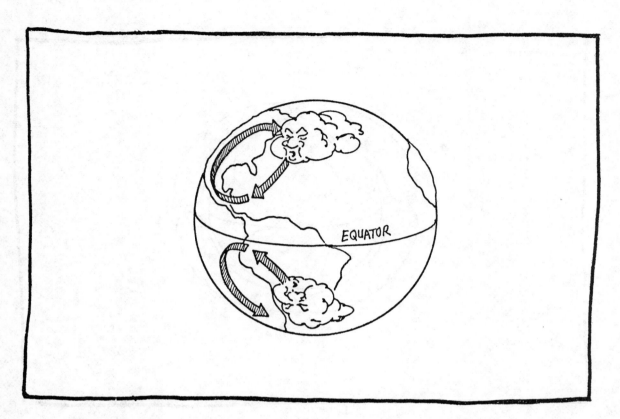

Figure 19: *Predominant global air circulation systems that govern weather conditions.*

The wind blown from the polar region southward and eastward leaves a vacuum which pulls in air to fill it. The arrow tracing the movement from south and west toward north and east shows the path of the predominant westerly winds that blow across the United States.

The differences in energy associated with the differences in season direct the two general wind patterns. Earth's axis of rotation tilts 23-1/2° from the plane formed by the Earth orbiting around the Sun at 16,000 miles per hour. Therefore, during the winter, the northern hemisphere is tilted away from the Sun. In the summer, it is tilted toward the Sun. Consequently, in the northern hemisphere we have longer nights and colder weather in winter, and longer days and warmer weather in the summer. These temperature differences create yet other air patterns. In the southern hemisphere, this same difference in energy and of the tilt of Earth's axis of rotation produce opposite patterns.

Certain wind patterns fairly consistent throughout the year are associated with certain kinds of weather. Looking at Figure 20 we see that in the region of the equator shown in the cross section at the far right, most of the movement is vertical rather than horizontal. In this pattern of air movement the rising air will create vertical energy movements, so that

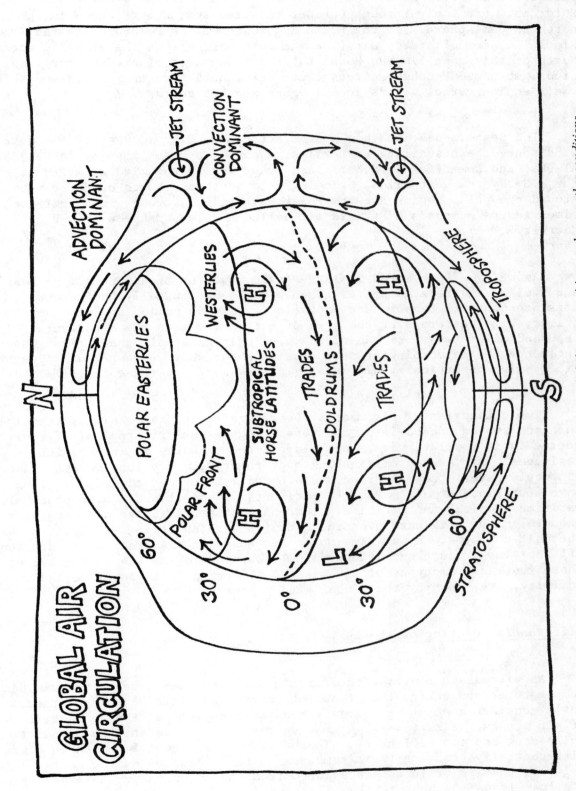

Figure 20: *Temperature, moisture, rotation, gravity, and planetary position produce weather conditions.*

thunderstorms occur almost daily, hence the name of the wind pattern, the Doldrums. From July through October the area spawns hurricanes in the northern hemisphere. To the north and south of the Doldrums are the Trade Winds, an area of steady air from the northeast across the Atlantic Ocean. North of this zone lie the Horse Latitudes, an area of predominantly calm winds, so named because sailors often jettisoned from their becalmed ships their equine cargo. Winds in this zone are hot and dry.

The west-to-east weather system across the U.S. is part of the next wind zone--the prevailing Westerlies. Weather systems forming in Canada, Alaska, and sometimes in Siberia are swept across the middle latitudes of the U.S. by the Westerlies, bringing cold weather. North of these winds around the polar region are the Polar Easterlies, strong winds that some-times generate mounds of frigid air called a Polar Outbreak or a Blue Norther.

As we have seen, wind is large-scale movement of air caused by heating and cooling in the atmosphere. When wind is horizontally homogeneous in moisture content, temperature and velocity, it is called an "air mass." The primary wind pattern over the area of origin may move the air several thousand miles away from the ocean. The origins of all these air masses influence the meteorologist's conclusion about what weather conditions are likely with a particular air mass.

Two categories of air masses are recognized on the basis of tempera-ture and two on the basis of moisture. Sea masses are <u>tropical</u> if their source is in low latitudes, and <u>polar</u> if their source is in the high latitudes. Air masses originating over relatively dry land masses are <u>con-tinental</u> masses; those over oceans are the moister <u>maritime</u> ones. Thus, we have four kinds of air masses: continental tropical and continental polar; maritime tropical and maritime polar. A continental polar air mass, for example, might originate over the Canadian Rockies, bringing winter snows to the United States. A maritime polar air mass, on the other hand, develops off the Alaska coast and brings rain, snow, and fog to the west coast states. These four general types of air masses, differing in temperature and humidity, are blown by the global wind patterns.

<u>Differential</u> <u>Heating</u> <u>of</u> <u>the</u> <u>Earth</u>

As air masses traverse the Earth's surface, they take on the humidity, temperature, and energy that translate moving air into "local" weather. Let's consider some of the variables as well as some of the characteristics of air masses. First, we know that vegetation absorbs the Sun's radiation, while snow and ice reflect it. Therefore, the surface of the Earth heats differentially, causing the air masses to be influenced by the energy and moisture that is or is not reradiated from these surfaces. A large north-ern lake loses its heat to the winter winds much more slowly than forests do. Therefore, in the spring the temperature of warm southerly air blowing toward the lake will be fairly constant until it moves across the lake. Because the waters still hold the lower winter temperatures, they will cool the prevailing warm winds, making them colder as they arrive at the opposite shore. In the winter, the same lake has a warming influence on the cold northerly winds, for well into the winter the water retains its heat from the previous summer's warm temperatures. Thus, the temperature above and below the lake can be markedly different, even though the opposite sides of the lake are only a few miles apart and are exposed to the same basic weather conditions.

Secondly, changes in the elevation of the air mass and changes in the ground features create varying degrees of humidity. Typically, maritime masses contain a great deal of water. The westerly Pacific masses that blow across the California coast immediately flow against mountainsides and rise into the cooler atmosphere. There the evaporated water condenses and precipitates into the valleys below. The air mass that continues onward is dry. When it descends into the plains region, the Sun heats it, removing any remaining moisture and thereby creating desert conditions.

Thirdly, the air masses themselves compress against one another, forming crests and valleys in accordian-like fashion. The crests are high pressure fronts, while the valleys are low pressure ones. Clear air low in humidity is associated with the highs; dark, rainy weather typifies the lows. We make such designations of "high" or "low" pressure on the basis of the amount of air amassed over the point measured. Normal atmospheric pressure is the mass (amount) of one square inch of air pressing upon the Earth at sea level. The weight is 14.7 pounds on that square inch. This amount of air pressure (on anything) will exert enough force on a pool of mercury to push some of the liquid metal up a calibrated tube 30 inches high (a barometer). An average barometric pressure is 30 inches of mercury. A reading of 29 inches means there is less mass above the barometer; therefore, the pressure is less on the pool of mercury. Over 30 inches is a high pressure air mass.

Fronts and Weather

There is a certain wave-like periodicity to the weather fronts. In the northeastern United States a new front passes about every 8th day in the summer, about every 6th day in the winter. The sharp changes in weather occur at the interface of masses differing considerably in moisture content. In Figure 21 we see that warm, moist air--probably a low pressure mass--is covering the region. Soon a cold, dry high pressure mass moves in from the west. Since cold air is more dense than warm, it is closer to the ground. In moving from west to east, the cold front acts like a wedge, forcing the warm air upward. The rising, moist air gradually cools, approximately 6° C for every 1,000 feet. The water vapor loses its 540 calories per gram, and recondenses as water--the rain falls.

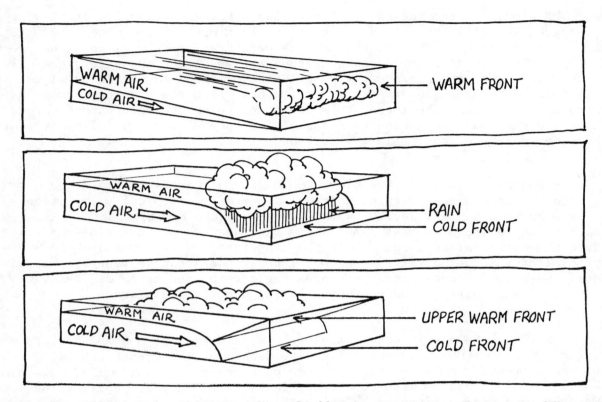

Figure 21: *Weather fronts result from warm and cold air mass movements. Temperature differences cause condensation and then precipitation.*

When such action takes place slowly, the rain falls gradually; it drizzles. If the action occurs rapidly, thunderstorms, possibly tornadoes, follow. The condensation in these latter conditions may take several forms, but it occurs in the first place because of ample available moisture, a lowering of temperature, and the presence of condensation nuclei, such as dust particles.

The first drops of rain or the first formed ice crystals of snow are tiny, but they increase in size with collision and motion, falling finally when they are too heavy to be supported as rain or as ice particles. Rain falling from high, warm air through colder air will freeze and land as sleet. A raindrop travelling up and down through a thunderstorm cloud, often passing above and below the freezing level, eventually may fall to the ground as a hailstone. The enormous exchanges of energy caused by freezing, evaporating, and condensation may cause lightning. The energy exchange rate and friction between moving moisture droplets is so strong that the normal balance of electricity is upset. An excess of positive ion charges above the freezing level accumulates, and an excess of negative ion charges forms below the freezing level. With the friction created by the falling droplets, a violent reaction will take place--flashes of lightning. Such flashes usually occur inside clouds, but often will strike the ground. The effect then is a bolt of lightning attracted to Earth by the ground's surplus of negative charges. The energy released by the bolt is great enough to produce shock waves that we hear as claps of thunder.

Lightning has killed people, shorted massive power nets, and ignited dry forests. However, routinely and more benignly it makes available atmospheric nitrogen to plants and therefore to animals. Along with nitrogen-fixing bacteria that live in algae and leguminous plants, lightning energizes the nitrogen molecule, N_2, so that N_2 combines with oxygen to form a compound readily usable by plants. Nitrogen is one of the elements in the amino acids, nucleic acids, and other compounds needed for life. Therefore, even though lightning is an unusually short-lived, powerful manifestation of weather, it is as normal and necessary a part of the natural system as the rotation of the Earth about the Sun, the hydrologic cycle, or the relentless shift of high and low pressure fronts.

Air Inversions

Air inversions are unusual weather conditions which may result in unusual pollution conditions. When warm air blankets over a cold, dense mass, pollutants concentrate in the lower mass because air is trapped and cannot carry away the gases and particulates.

Normally, the Sun heats the land, the land reradiates some of the energy as heat, and the heat agitates the air molecules, causing them to move faster. The only direction they can move is upward, and so the warm air mass rises into the sky, losing energy (cooling) as it goes. Eventually it becomes colder, more dense, and settles back to Earth again—there to be rewarmed and driven skyward.

Upon rising, the air mass creates a pull or vacuum behind itself. That vacuum draws in new air that may not be contaminated, and so pollutants are continuously carried from an area by the Earth's heating of the overlying air.

But, an inversion may take place if the ground cannot reradiate enough energy to make the molecules rise. That can happen when (1) a cold air mass settles over the ground and (2) cuts off the reradiation to the static, warm air above, so that (3) the warm air does not rise, thereby preventing the Sun's heat from reaching the ground. Thus, the cold air sits directly above the ground; the warm air hovers above the cold mass, and the Sun's rays do not reach Earth to warm it. At such times air pollutants can concentrate very rapidly and cause us great physical distress because there is literally no air movement to disperse the gas and particulates. Since the Sun's radiation cannot penetrate, only a very strong outside break in the weather can change the conditions. Inversions have lasted for days over major urban areas before a strong wind, heavy rain, or a combination of those forces could move the warm air from its blocking position.

The Perspective to the following chapter illustrates exactly what happens when inverted air concentrates pollutants over a major city. Now emergency industrial shutdowns and automobile restrictions are standard procedures where urban air inversions are likely threats to human health. Local officials and citizens responsible for the master plan for land-use in the area must know the prevailing weather--its overall effects as well as its site-specific extremes--if they are to make decisions with social and economic benefit, as well as to plan land-use that is environmentally sound over time. For example, an area's weather largely determines the nature of its airshed. Therefore, zoning for residential and industrial sites might consider alternatives, such as the following weather-related ones. An industry will be dispersing airborne pollutants. If the prevailing winds and concomitant weather are known:

- Zoning might place all residential areas upwind of the plant.

- That particular industrial plant might be banned in areas especially susceptible to air inversions.

- Restrictions might be placed on the industry regarding times during which it may be permitted to emit airborne pollutants, that decision based on knowledge about when winds will be such as to disperse the pollutants quickly.

Prevailing weather patterns determine where residential sites can be placed most energy-efficiently--preferably in those areas where there is warmth in winter and coolness in summer due to natural protection and to other protection from the extremes of the local weather system. It is economically and environmentally wise to allow industry proximity to natural waterways for efficient transportation. Therefore, a certain section of land along a river might be zoned industrial. However, if that area floods regularly with spring rains, neither industrial or residential needs would be met, and far more energy would be expended "living with" a poor land-use decision than would be spent if weather conditions had been considered.

These variables and many others are all part of the information bank we can draw on in using land to achieve the highest possible environmental quality, while serving the myriad individual needs of the community.

CHAPTER SUMMARY

1. When the Sun's hydrogen atoms fuse, they let some of their energy escape. The form of that energy in waves is called photons. The waves of particles are reflected from the Earth's surface to our ocular cells where chemicals re-

act to that energy and transmit messages to our brain--as a result, we see light.

2. More photons strike the Earth at noon than in the morning or the afternoon. More photons strike near the equator than at either of the poles.

3. Photons entering the systems of atoms and molecules give them more energy. Energized matter moves faster, reacts with other chemicals more frequently, and often can be sensed as heat.

4. Heated water evaporates and rises into the atmosphere, the most water rising at the equator. The action sucks cold, heavy air toward the equator from both poles. These two movements are fundamental determinants of "weather."

5. Standing at the equator, a person travels 25,000 miles in 24 hours, about 1,000 miles an hour. Moving toward the poles, the velocity slackens to zero. The earthbound person rotating through the atmosphere reports the effect as "wind."

6. Air masses move constantly from solar heating, Earth's rotation, and the evaporation and condensation of water. The movements cause high and low pressure subsidiary cells. Extreme movements are hurricanes, or Doldrums; their conversion into other energy forms are thunderstorms, lightning, and heat.

7. Pollutants transported by air are subjected to the energetics of photons, Earth's movements, the hydrologic cycle, and local weather systems.

SOURCES

Calder, Nigel. _The Weather Machine._ New York: Champion International Corp., 1975.

Greulach, Victor and J. Edison Adams. _Plants: An Introduction to Modern Botany_. New York: John Wiley & Sons, Inc., 1967.

Hidore, John J. _A Geography of the Atmosphere._ Dubuque, Iowa: William C. Brown Co., 1970.

Miller, ALbert and Jack C. Thompson. _Elements of Meteorology._ Columbus, Ohio: Charles E. Merrill Publishing Co., 1975.

Weather for Air Crews. AFM 105-5. Washington, D. C.: U. S. Air Force, 1967.

CHAPTER FOUR

AIRSHEDS AND AIR POLLUTION

A PERSPECTIVE

The weather was sunny and warm that November in 1966.
There would be no rain to spoil Thanksgiving plans.
Only those in Long Island who were interested in sail-
ing were disappointed--no wind was forecast. The cool
air near the Earth was held there by the warm air above.
With no morning breeze, the cool air was not mixed and
a definite layer of heavy warm air formed about 700
feet above the city.

New York City was about to experience a classic thermal
inversion, and all of us would once again be reminded
that in spite of our technological progress--and in
this case because of it--we were at the mercy of the
weather.

Light morning fog was mixed with the exhaust of commuter traffic on Riverside Highway. The Consolidated
Edison Company continued to generate electricity for
the demands of the city, in the process emitting sulfur dioxide to be trapped beneath the layer of warm
air. Across the river and up in the Bronx, life went
on as usual, which meant tons of hydrocarbons, nitrous
oxides, and particulates were added to the smog that
was beginning to settle over the city. Even well
adapted natives began to rub their eyes. Some
scurried into air conditioned office buildings, while
others turned on their apartment units. Those that
worked outside and were not so fortunate breathed
in the mixture. . . .

The tiny water droplets of the morning fogs transformed the sulfur dioxide into sulfurous acid mist
and carried it deep into the lungs of millions. The
sulfur dioxide level held at .4 ppm, and the "excess
death" level began to rise. People with heart and
respiratory trouble--especially the old and the
frail--suffered the most. The inversion lasted
seven days, and one hundred sixty-eight people
died--from air pollution combined with weather conditions that could indeed recur, not only in New
York but also in a number of other cities.

Virginia Brodine, "Episode 104"
Environment, Volume 13, No. 1,
January/February 1971

Airsheds

The weather is the system that transports everything that goes into the atmosphere--oxygen from photosynthesis, carbon dioxide from plant and animal respiration, water from the hydrologic cycle, dust from the winds and thermal currents, and all the rest. The "rest" is what we're really worried about. And we're worried about it at the global, international, national, regional, and local levels.

In the summer of 1976 China exploded an atomic device that produced radioactive wastes which the world's air currents still carry. Radioactive fallout occurred in the U.S. two months later, and was reported in the milk of cattle in Massachusetts. Volcanic eruptions as long ago as 1883 spewed non-radioactive dust into the atmosphere that persists there today. Indeed, it is possible for both man and nature to suspend sufficient material in the atmosphere to block solar radiation, our number one energy source. Let's consider a classic example from the 19th century.

Krakatoa in the Sunda Strait between Java and Sumatra had once been a single island consisting of a volcanic mountain built up from the ocean bottom. On August 26, 1883, part of the island stood 2,400 feet above the surface of the ocean. On August 27th it was gone, and the base of the island was 600 feet under water. A gigantic volcanic explosion had blown the cone to bits with a blast heard on islands off the African Coast 2,200 miles away. A pressure wave in the air was recorded by barographs around the world.

Columns of extremely fine ash and pumice soared miles into the air. Astonishing as it may seem, most of the debris actually was suspended for five years before it began to fall out. Visible material was swept along by the upper air currents and studied by meteorologists throughout the world who, for the first time, could measure the speeds and directions of such currents high above the ground. During the five year period, sunsets throughout the world were of abnormal hues. A reddish-brown circle known as "Bishop's Ring," which was seen around the sun under favorable weather conditions, gave evidence not only of the continued presence of dust in the air, but also of the approximate size of the pieces, just under .002 millimeters--very small. The global temperature during the first five years fell an average of 5.5° C. This gains full import if we consider that an extended drop in temperature of about 10°C will begin a new advance of continental glaciers. Further, the early 1890's were characterized by severe winters and cool summers across the northern hemisphere: it even snowed in Boston in July of 1892.

Let's return now to the 20th century. Suspended particulates and carbon dioxide have been increasing in the atmosphere for the last several decades, but not in amounts out of keeping with the geological cycle we are in. Theoretically, the particulates may shield solar radiation from reaching the Earth--producing a cooling effect, while the carbon dioxide may retain the radiation which does reach the earth, reflecting it back up into the atmosphere and producing a heating effect. This speculation is currently subject to much controversy.

The Ozone Layer

One of the contemporary worries is the ozone/fluorocarbon issue (see Figure 22). Ozone (O_3) absorbs a dangerous solar radiation frequency range type B ultraviolet light, which is used to decontaminate food, medicines, and surgical instruments because its particular light-frequency kills any living tissues. No living system has evolved protection against this form of radiation. The ozone layer absorbs 99.9% of all type B ultraviolet light from the Sun. Fluorocarbon (CF_4) compounds of fluorine and carbon bonds are used as an inert gas propellant in spray cans for dispensing deodorants, paints, cleaners, food, and similar substances. But fluorocarbon attacks ozone.

Figure 22: *The Earth's ozone layer absorbs harmful solar radiation. The carbon dioxide layer reflects heat back onto Earth.*

As the contents leave the can, the fluorocarbon propellant begins a slow ascent through the atmosphere. When the CF_4 molecules are bombarded by the sun's ultraviolet light, they are energized and then break apart, releasing the fluorine, F_2. The free fluorine reacts with ozone, converting it from O_3 to O_2. The fluorine molecule then reacts with a second ozone molecule (it is estimated that fluorocarbon gas can exist in the atmosphere for 200 years). If atmospheric ozone is diminished, then the penetration of ultraviolet type B rays will increase. As a result, skin cancer, crop damage, and unusual turns in the global weather system may also increase. There are alternatives to the use of CF_4 as a propellant. Many consumers choose products without fluorocarbon gas now that the probable effects of the compound have been so widely publicized. Time is on our side at the moment. Global temperature patterns change slowly, and experiments can be made in the reduction of carbon dioxide, particulates, fluorocarbons, and other atmospheric contaminants. But we are institutionalized in a technology that burns fossil fuels which, in turn, produce sulfur dioxide (SO_2) and other pollutants, and manufacturing processes that generate particulates.

Air Pollution

Reduction of excess contaminants must be a collaborative effort of all nations; as yet there is no international machinery for this purpose. The only such organizations that might help are the United Nations and its affiliates, the World Meteorological Organization and the World Health Organization. Continental-scale air pollution means basically the transport of pollution across international borders. The industries of Great Britain and Germany caused acidified rain which fell into the Netherlands, Belgium, and Scandinavia, resulting in decreased pH (see Chapter 2) of their waters and soils. A great number of pine forests and food crops were severely damaged. In another case, photographs from satellites show sulfur oxides emanating from sources in Germany and contaminating and destroying crops as far away as Pakistan. The Canadian Trail smelter discharged sulfur oxides which caused crop damage in the U.S. A lawsuit settled with the Canadian firm paid Idaho farmers for damages. In these cases, pollution originated in one country and traveled to another via the prevailing Westerlies and the Northwest Trade Winds. Therefore, regulation must occur by negotiations among countries, but the political process of reaching settlements calls on the work of many people, often for a period of years. Pollution is apolitical and observes no boundaries.

Urban Air Pollution

Next to solving the urban health problems caused by air pollution, the United States' greatest concern is the protection of air in areas now unpolluted. Air pollution is generally considered an urban problem that one can avoid by going to the country, but increasingly much of that air is polluted. Supposedly country-clean rural air masses that move into cities may well be dirty air from another city, or even recirculating air from the same city. Cleveland, Steubenville, Los Angeles, New York, and the

Chicago-Gary area once led as contaminators of the air. But in 1976 the mile-high pride of the Rocky Mountains, Denver, Colorado, led even those offenders. Denver's problems originated both in California and right at home with its own automobiles. Smog that forms over California is transported by Westerlies to Denver. NASA satellites track the movement of smog and ozone to determine the extent of just such interstate problems. In another location, photographs from satellites of the Dallas-Fort Worth smog reveal that it is carried up the Mississippi River Valley and across Lake Michigan. It may even damage crops in Wisconsin and Minnesota.

Interstate contamination of air also has sources in non-urban regions. Phenomena such as the dust bowls and forest fires are persistent concerns. Crop sprays, plant and animal processing wastes, and airborne topsoils all add to air loadings. These sources must be controlled by state management. Passing the legislation to control them and educating the public to see that the laws are enforced, however, is often the work of many years.

In the United States' cities, severe gaseous and particulate concentrations accumulate when horizontal and vertical wind motions fail to move the mass at a sufficient rate and volume to pull in cleaner air. A horizontal calm and a vertical inversion can do the job. Donora, Pennsylvania in 1948 and New York City in 1966 (see Perspective to this chapter) were locations where air pollution caused many deaths during short-term air pollution episodes.

Tall structures of the city barricade air motion, and their surfaces absorb a great deal of solar energy in the daytime. That energy warms the air, which rises and then spreads out like a mushroom. As it does so, it also cools, becomes heavier, settles to the ground, and recycles again, starting at the mushroom's base. A self-contained circulatory system drives the pollutants around and around. Only a strong wind can break up the system, as Figure 23 suggests.

Scaling ourselves down to microscopic size for a closer look at such a system, we see that the circulating air contains great amounts of very small solids and liquids, less than 1/1,000,000 of a meter in size, or 1 micron. Their mass is so slight that they behave very much like the nearby gases, floating in the air and drifting with the winds. These are aerosols; they rise, sink, and recirculate. Their numbers are so great that they form a visible "dust dome" or "haze hood."

The aerosols cover the city as the atmosphere covers the Earth. They reflect the Sun's radiation and so prevent the Sun from heating a large enough mass of ground air to lift the pollution "mushroom" away from the city. Meanwhile, underneath this darkening umbrella, the air collects more and more aerosols, gases, and debris.

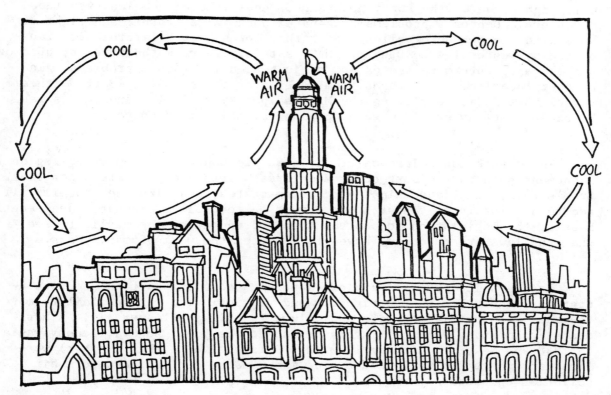

Figure 23: *Daytime radiation warms the atmosphere. More radiation is absorbed by urban surfaces than rural fields and waters. The heat rises, cools, and recycles, accumulating and returning the city's pollution. At the worst, an air inversion occurs.*

If the city is located near a large body of water--as a case in point, consider Boston, which has all of these conditions--the cool air over the water will move right into the "mushroom system." The offshore air is clean as it starts through the cycle, but the next time around it carries a load of aerosols. It can make as many as three round trips in an 8-hour period and become more polluted with each trip.

While the predominant local weather conditions disperse pollutants in a predictable direction and over a predictable distance, solar radiation changes the air's temperature and hence its motion. Basically, wind transports pollutants, whereas turbulence disperses them. The higher the wind speed and turbulence, the lower the concentration of pollutants. Mechanical turbulence caused by land forms, buildings, aircraft, and thermal turbulence induced by reflected solar heat and industrial and business operations help disperse air and its contaminants. Prevailing Westerlies or Northeast Polar and Trade Winds are locally modified by valleys, slopes, sea and land breezes, as well as by the solar and mechanical effects within the airshed. Relationships between dominant weather factors and development siting are predictable, but most important is that the concentration of pollutants in a small airshed can absorb up to 60% of the incoming solar energy, thus diminishing the potential for thermal turbulence and in turn reducing the airshed's capability to move and disperse airborne contaminants.

Air Pollution Index

A national air pollution index for use by local governments and the news media has been developed by a federal task force. The new system standardizes the many different indices now being used. With this index the maximum measured daily air pollution level converts to a simple 0-500 scale. Intervals on the scale are related to the potential health effects of the daily measured levels of carbon monoxide, oxidants (or ozone), particulates, sulfur dioxide, and nitrogen dioxide. The air pollution index and the associated health effects are:

0-50 good

50-100 moderate

100-200 unhealthful

200-300 very unhealthful

300-500 hazardous

Local communities can and do initiate pollution reduction actions at certain index levels. A 200-level in Cleveland, for example, triggers an "alert stage" which prohibits open burning and requires cutbacks in some industrial production. At 300, a "warning situation," authorities call for further industrial cutbacks and prohibit the use of incinerators. And at 400, the city is under an "air pollution emergency": industries and businesses must shut down, and motor vehicle use is prohibited except for emergencies.

What must be remembered in taking corrective action, however, is that urban pollution problems reach into many political jurisdictions. Many small cities can do no more than regulate their city-located polluters. Clusters of large cities often face a more complex situation; pollutants cross state lines, making questions of jurisdiction difficult.

But there are local problems which officials can identify and do something about. Choking bus exhaust roiling through the air we breathe at a traffic intersection is a good case in point. Pedestrians and occupants of nearby buildings suffer from such exhaust pollution, too. Fumes, eye irritations, lung congestion, and a high measure of carbon monoxide all indicate an immediate, identifiable pollution source. The problem may be helped by a lull in the morning's traffic, a stiff wind, or by an overall shift in the air mass movement--these are all happy circumstances but not controllable ones. Planned actions, such as rerouting, staggered work hours, and more mass transit could help alleviate the immediate, short-lived problem before it grows so large as to warrant prohibition of all vehicular traffic, as an index of 400 requires in Cleveland, Ohio.

As in the hydrologic cycle, there really is no discontinuity among global, continental, national, regional, and local air pollution problems. Air problems are global, but the solutions are local. If we all do our part, none of us will have to worry about the quality of the air in our own localities. Control of local air pollution is our modest but indispensable contribution toward clean air in the biosphere.

CHAPTER SUMMARY

1. The composition of the Earth's atmosphere and the global and local weather patterns are fixed, natural conditions which characterize the airsheds in which we live.

2. When certain matter in certain concentrations is freed from the Earth's surface into the atmosphere, we have pollution. Volcanic ash, radioactive fallout, fluorocarbons, eroded soil, automobile exhausts, and industrial air emissions are examples. Such pollutants may have both short- and long-term effects.

3. The volcano Krakatoa exploded in 1883. Most of the fallout remained suspended in the atmosphere as long as five years. The temperature of the Earth's atmosphere during that period fell over 5° C. Dust from the explosion is <u>still</u> in the atmosphere.

4. Atmospheric ozone screens out 99.9% of the Sun's Type B ultraviolet light. Carbon tetrafluoride, CF_4, converts O_3 to O_2, thus removing the screening agent. Skin cancer, crop damage, and weather changes may be associated with increases in ultraviolet light.

5. The entire world is influenced by dust bowls, forest fires, crop sprays, auto emissions, and other sources of air-borne particulates and gases because of predominant weather systems. Cities are especially burdened by automobile and industrial air emissions because of the mushrooming effect of heated urban air that rises, cools, and then returns with its load of contaminants.

6. The federal air pollution index is based on daily levels of carbon monoxide, oxidants, particulates, sulfur dioxide, and nitrogen dioxide: 0-50=good; 50-100=moderate: 100-200=unhealthful; 200-300=very unhealthful; 300-500=hazardous.

7. <u>Total</u> air pollution control begins with <u>local</u> air pollution control because everything we contribute as a pollutant inevitably pollutes the airshed of the entire biosphere.

SOURCES

American Lung Association. <u>Air Pollution Primer</u>. New York: National Air Conservation Commission, 1971.

American Lung Association. <u>Controlling Air Pollution</u>. New York: National Air Conservation Commission, 1974.

Bach, Wilfrid. Atmospheric Pollution. New York: McGraw-Hill, 1972.

Division of Air Pollution Control. 1973 Annual Report. Cleveland, Ohio:
    Cleveland Division of Air Pollution Control, 1973.

Division of Air Pollution Control, Cleveland, Ohio. Window, 3, No. 1,
    1976.

Leet, Don L. and Sheldon Johnson. Physical Geology. Englewood Cliffs, New
    Jersey: Prentice-Hall, Inc., 1971.

Stern, Arthur, et. al. Fundamentals of Air Pollution. New York: Academic
    Press, 1973.

SUGGESTED READING

American Lung Association. Air Pollution Primer. New York: Air Conservation
    Commission, 1971.

CHAPTER FIVE

AIR POLLUTION SOURCES AND CONTROLS

A PERSPECTIVE

What does air pollution mean to people? Region V of
the U.S. EPA answered this question in a personal
interview with one of the growing numbers of middle-
aged persons suffering from pulmonary diseases. This
is the story of Thomas Watson, a businessman in
Chicago. He has emphysema.

Mr. Watson listens carefully to the early morning pollution readings. He knows that any type of air pollution means he might not be able to breathe. Pollutants
often cause an infection in his lungs which then fill
with phlegm. He coughs and struggles for oxygen.

"Once," he said, "I was going home on the commuter
train when it broke down not too far from my station.
I was in the 'no smoking' car but after awhile of just
sitting there the commuters got impatient. They
started lighting cigarettes.

"Soon, the smoke made it difficult for me to breathe.
Then the conductor came by and asked if we could get
out and walk the last mile or so to the station. I
couldn't. I looked healthy but I wasn't getting
enough air to make the walk."

At home, and in the office, Watson must have air
cleaners running constantly. He has to hire someone to mow his lawn because he can't take the
mower's exhaust fumes. Family trips and social
engagements have been cut. Business trips are
very difficult. Watson can't carry a suitcase for
any distance. Smokers and atmospheric changes in
an airplane cause him to struggle for breath.

The emphysema has affected his emotions as well.
When breathing is a struggle, he grows anxious;
the more distressed he becomes, the more air he
needs.

U.S. EPA, Region V, Environment Midwest
(July 1976)

Air Pollution: Where It Comes From, What It Is

We have some sense, now, of the interrelatedness of solar energy, the atmosphere, air, and water. Altogether they support life on Earth, and an imbalance in any one of them threatens life itself. Now let's examine further the condition of our air, especially with attention to (1) present sources and forms of pollutants, (2) means for controlling and abating those pollutants, and (3) the regulatory programs that are now effectively achieving those goals.

The "major sources" of pollution are quite well known:

- fuel-consuming modes of transportation

- fuel combustion from stationary sources

- industrial processes

- solid waste disposal

- innumerable others--controlled agricultural and forest burning; solvent and gasoline evaporation; accidental burning of coal, refuse, and forests.

Less familiar to us are the variety of pollutants these sources generate. According to the EPA they include:

- sulfur dioxide (SO_2)

- suspended particulates

- nitrogen oxides (NO, NO_2, N_2O_4)

- hydrocarbons (C-H compounds--1000 known variations)

- carbon monoxide (CO)

- photochemical oxidants and miscellaneous "others."

Amounts of emissions for gases are measured as the numbers of parts of pollutant in 1,000,000 parts of ordinary air (parts per million, ppm); or, for particulates, as the weight of pollutants in a cubic meter, usually as millionths (micro-) of a gram, ug/m^3.

Just for comparison:

- a micron (u) is 1/1,000 of a millimeter, or 1/1,000,000 of a meter

- viruses are between .01-.1 micron

- bacteria are between 1-25 microns

- fog droplets, 5-60 microns

- raindrops, 200-5,000 microns.

A comment about each major category of emission follows. Much of the information comes from the American Lung Association's <u>Air Pollution Primer</u>, a handy pocket guide.

Sulfur Dioxide

Sulfur-containing compounds, such as coal and oil, upon combustion with oxygen produce sulfur dioxide. SO_2 is a heavy, colorless gas of "rotten egg" odor that combines readily with water vapor to form sulfurous acid (H_2SO_3). This acid, colorless and mildly corrosive, is used as a bleaching agent in industry, can form yellow spots on your car, and--most unfortunately--reacts with free oxygen to yield the extremely corrosive sulfuric acid (H_2SO_4). Or, sulfur dioxide pouring from a stack, diffusing rapidly, may first oxidize to sulfur trioxide (SO_3) and then react with water to form sulfuric acid.

The national ambient air quality standard for sulfur dioxide is 80 ug/m^3 (0.03 ppm) as an annual arithmetic mean,* and no more than 365 ug/m^3 (0.14 ppm) for a single 24 hour period per year. These oxides can interfere with the growth of vegetation, destroy the paper in books, corrode iron and steel, deteriorate leather, weaken natural and synthetic fibers, and dissolve marble. In humans they can aggravate respiration, constrict air passages, and trigger asthma attacks.

Particulates

Particulates are small-sized liquids and solids that include smoke, fumes, dust, and mist. If we were unfortunate enough to have a close-up view of smokestacks belching out these wastes, we could identify several types as they passed. Smoke, a byproduct of combustion, is comprised of solid and liquid particles under 1 micron. Smoke may contain fumes, dust, and mist. Fumes are caused by the solid particles under 1 micron

---

*Arithmetic mean: the quotient obtained by dividing the sum of the highest and lowest number by 2; e.g., AM of 2, 4, 15 is $\frac{2+15}{2} = \frac{17}{2} = 8.5$.

that smelting, refining, and similar processes produce. Dust generally refers to soil particles and fly ash from coal-burning, both types are from 1-10 microns in size. Mist is liquid droplets of 100 microns or more in size, dispersed by industrial processes, agricultural spraying, condensation of water, or even photochemical action on automobile exhaust.

In the most severely fouled sections of our most polluted cities, particulates fall in quantities of 50-100 tons per square mile each month. New York City unleashes 335 tons of particulates on a good winter day. Los Angeles coughs up 40 tons of aerosols (solids or liquids under 1 micron in size) a day just from gas-powered vehicles. Kansas City, not to pass unnoticed, records dustfall in the winter of 67 tons a square mile each month. This is weighty data.

Atmospheric particulates, such as the very small aerosols (.001 - .1 microns), provide nuclei on which vapor condenses easily, so that fogs, ground mists, and rain may increase in aerosol-laden air. Suspended particles of 2-3 microns can be carried into the alveoli of the lungs, along with any accompanying solution of chemicals. And, as we have already mentioned, it is extremely dangerous that aerosols can absorb radiant energy. If high altitude jet planes such as the SSTs release enough aerosols, a thin veil between Sun and Earth will form blocking radiation to the surface of the earth, jeopardizing biospheric life.

The following are the National Ambient Air Quality Standards for particulates ("Primary" health standards relate to effects of pollutants on human health and are more permissive than the "secondary" or welfare standards which relate to indirect effects on health, such as poor visibility, harm to crops, and the like):

Primary (health standard)

    75 ug/m^3 as an annual geometric mean*

    260 ug/m^3 maximum concentration for a 24 hour period,
    not to be exceeded more than once per year

Secondary (welfare standard)

    60 ug/m^3 as an annual geometric mean

    150 ug/m^3 maximum concentration for a 24 hour period,
    not to be exceeded more than once per year

-----

*Geometric mean: the nth root of the product of n numbers; e.g., the GM of 2, 4, 15 is $\sqrt[3]{2 \times 4 \times 15} = \sqrt[3]{120}$ = approximately 5.

Nitrogen Oxides

Nitric oxide (NO) is a colorless, somewhat toxic gas formed at high temperatures from nitrogen and oxygen in the air. Temperatures this high are reached in the combustion engines of automobiles. The high and low concentrations especially when hydrocarbons and sunlight are present, nitric oxide and air form nitrogen dioxide (NO_2).

Nitrogen dioxide absorbs much of the ultraviolet light from the Sun and is the trigger for the photochemical reactions that produce smog in polluted air. The smog can decrease the yield of crops as well as inhibit growth of leaves or injure those already mature. It also can alter paints, bleach out dyed fabrics, and combine with water vapor to form the strongly corrosive nitric acid (HNO_3). Apparently, nitrogen oxide compounds also aggravate symptoms of acute respiratory diseases; they tend to constrict the lung's air passages. Increasingly, such compounds are linked to the incidence of emphysema.

The National Ambient Air Quality Standards for nitrogen dioxide are:

100 ug/m^3 (0.05 ppm)

Hydrocarbons

Hydrocarbons contain carbon and hydrogen only, but in varying numbers of carbon and hydrogen atoms. Some are gases: methane (CH_4), ethane (C_2H_6), and propane (C_3H_8); some are liquids, some solids. They are found in fossilized plants and animals, and are released to the atmosphere by combustion and evaporation of substances such as coal and oil, which are the product of plant and animal remains compressed for millions of years underground. Most hydrocarbons are harmful only in high concentrations; a few may cause cancer. Many take part in light-catalyzed chemical reactions that contribute to the generalized pollutant, smog.

The National Ambient Air Quality Standards for hydrocarbons are:

160 ug/m^3 (0.08 ppm) (this is the maximum 3 hour concentration (6:00-9:00 AM), not to be exceeded more than once per year)

Carbon Monoxide

Carbon monoxide (CO) is the all-too-prevalent colorless, odorless gas that displaces oxygen on the red blood cell's hemoglobin molecule in the human body. At critical concentrations it causes death. Fatigue, headache, confusion, and dizziness commonly experienced by people in or near high traffic congestion are typical symptoms of carbon monoxide poisoning.

The gas forms through the incomplete combustion of carbon in air; complete combustion produces carbon dioxide. Automobiles are the largest source, making drivers its more frequent targets.

Laboratory studies show that an 8-hour exposure to 10-15 ppm of CO impairs one's ability to judge time intervals. At 30 ppm, vision and physical responses are abnormal. Under actual driving conditions, the necessary concentration to impair varies somewhat, but those with heart disease are in danger because the heart has to pump harder to circulate a greater amount of oxygen-deficient blood. In a recent study in 15 cities, surveyors found that people in moving vehicles in heavy traffic are at times subject to sustained levels of 50 ppm of carbon monoxide.

The National Ambient Air Quality Standards for Carbon Monoxide are as follows:

10,000 ug/m^3 (9.0 ppm)--maximum 8-hour concentration, not to be exceeded more than once per year.

40,000 ug/m^3 (35 ppm)--maximum 1-hour concentration, not to be exceeded more than once per year.

Photochemical Oxidants

A variety of chemicals interact in the atmosphere upon exposure to solar radiation. The products are collectively called smog, the Los Angeles variety familiar to many of us.

The typical photochemical reactions are these. Nitrogen dioxide in the presence of hydrocarbons and ultraviolet light separates into nitric oxide and atomic oxygen ($O^=$). The single atom oxygen reacts with auto exhaust constituents and molecular oxygen (O_2), forming several products, including ozone (O_3). Ozone then takes part in numerous reactions, many of which are continuous. Some of the hundreds of products are peroxyacetyl nitrate (PAN), formaldehyde, and--once again--nitrogen dioxide. Nitrogen dioxide then continues the process of separating more hydrocarbons into more nitric acid and atomic oxygen.

Ozone's sharp, pungent odor often can be noticed around electric motors. Unlike oxygen, this gas can cause coughing, eye irritation, choking, headache, and severe fatigue. It can harm vegetation and can damage fabrics and rubber. But in addition to all of this harm, ozone also helps to protect us from type B ultraviolet radiation by forming ozone layers in the atmosphere.

The National Ambient Air Quality Standards for photochemical oxidants are:

160 ug/m^3 (0.08 ppm)—maximum 1 hour concentration not to be exceeded more than once per year.

Miscellaneous Air Pollutants

There are other pollutants in the miscellaneous category, such as carbon soot, fluorides, lead and other heavy metals, asbestos, tobacco smoke, pesticides, and radiation. Plain carbon pours from every home and industry that burns coal; soot is still one of the most prevalent of solid pollutants. Carbon soot has a high surface-to-weight ratio and adsorbs many other chemicals, among them some hydrocarbons known to produce cancer in animals. Many soot particles are small enough to be carried into the lungs, taking their adsorbed material with them. In 1775 soot was singled out as a causative agent in the high incidence of cancer of the scrotum among chimneysweeps.

Fluorides occur naturally in some groundwaters and artificially in many drinking water sources where law requires them for their benefit to bones and teeth. However, airborne fluorides can accumulate to dangerous levels at which they cause a range of illnesses. These compounds are the waste by-products of aluminum and iron ore smelting, fertilizer production, and ceramics processing. The airborne particles can be taken in by plants which, when eaten by livestock, can cause the animals severe illness. Continuous exposure of humans to industrial sources of fluoride pollutions has caused eye and skin irritation, respiratory tract inflammation, and overall breathing difficulty.

Leaded gasoline cutbacks will help to reduce vehicular combustion sources of fine lead particles which may or may not be harmful to humans. Accumulations of lead are dangerous, however, particularly for young children who ingest leaded paint by mouthing or peeling off and eating chips from painted areas in old and badly maintained dwellings. Blood tests are easily administered to detect serum lead levels.

Beryllium, along with asbestos and mercury, is designated as a hazardous pollutant by the EPA. Beryllium has been a fatal poison to workers in and to residents near processing plants that use it, such as in the manufacture of rocket fuels and alloys for space probe equipment. Similarly, arsenic from copper smelting, pesticide compounding, and agricultural spraying operations is an accumulating poison suspected of causing cancer.

Asbestos, a mineral comprised of long fibers, is used for roofing, automobile brake shoes, household tile, and insulation. In addition to its appearance in drinking water supplies in most major American cities, asbestos is also released into the air as a result of using and consuming the products of which it is a component. Researchers still have not established, for legal purposes, that asbestos is a carcinogen, but it does cluster in and destroy lung tissues. Lung cancer appears to be a synergistic effect among cigarette smokers who work in asbestos-producing industries. Much has been written about the problem, and litigation continues over the Reserve Mining Company's discharge of 67,000 tons per day of "asbestos-laden tailings" into the waters of Silver Bay, Minnesota. "Asbestos-like fibers from the tailings have appeared in the drinking water of Duluth and adjoining cities," according to Environmental Quality: 7th Annual Report of the Council on Environmental Quality.

Agricultural sprays, dusts, pesticides, fungicides, and herbicides also cause illness in humans. When chemically long-lasting, such as DDT, they are washed into the water system via the hydrologic cycle to be taken up by phytoplankton, zooplankton, fish, birds, and, of course, man. The cycles go on, the story is endless, and the threats to the health of all life are very real ones.

Now, let's consider radiation. Here, as above, we are relying heavily upon the American Lung Association's indispensable book, Air Pollution Primer. Let's imagine ourselves once again as microscopic in size so we can look closely at the nuclei of atoms, which contain neutrons* and protons. In relation to the nucleus the electrons are very far away, orbiting about it. For illustration's sake, if we were at the nucleus we would be the size of the period at the end of this sentence. The electrons, however, would be flying about in a space the size of a house. The forces holding a nucleus together are far greater than those holding the electrons to atoms or holding atoms within their molecules. For some reason, radium nuclei spontaneously fly apart. When they do, they produce alpha rays, which can be stopped by paper; beta rays, which can be stopped by aluminum foil; and gamma rays, which can penetrate living tissue.

Much radiation is dangerous to us because it is so energetic that it tears electrons from otherwise stable atoms and molecules. Naturally occurring cosmic radiation and radioactive materials in the ground give each of us a dose of about 0.1 rems** per year. Federal regulations limit exposure of workers to 5 rems per year. Since radiation causes damage to the body that is not apparent, a person could be exposed to a lethal dose without even knowing it.

---

*A neutron is a proton coupled with an electron.
**A rem is the unit measure of radiation absorbed by man.

There are normal, natural background sources of radiation, such as in the spontaneous breakdown or decay of uranium. Radiation also originates from amassing uranium, causing a high intensity of cross bombardment. Because great heat results, this energy source is used to heat water to steam that drives turbines to produce electricity. Radioisotopes are slight variations of uranium that are used in industry, agriculture, medicine, and research. All of these applications are possible sources of radiation to humans. In addition, though, the reactants slowly lose strength and therefore efficiency, becoming wastes to be removed and replaced. But, the wastes are still radioactive--what do you do with them? The safe disposal of such "spent" energy sources poses an ongoing problem to land-use management, public health officials--to all of us. The United States Atomic Energy Commission set standards that permit a yearly exposure limit of 170 millirems for the general population. This limit refers to man-made radiation, excluding medical sources. The standard indicates how much radiation an average person is thought to be able to tolerate without risk of harm.

Natural background radiation gives a dose of 70-200 millirems annually. On a coast-to-coast jet flight, one may be exposed to 5 millirems from cosmic radiation; with one chest X-ray, 50 millirems; near nuclear power operations, 1 millirem. Theft of radioactive materials or accidents involving radioactive matter can, of course, expose many people to quite harmful amounts of radiation.

Iodine-131, Cesium-137, Strontium-90, and X-rays are radioactive substances used in medicine and research; they are also found in the ambient air. We can't do too much about halting natural production of them, but it's clearly in our best interest to avoid any unnecessary exposure to them.

Abatement and Control

Air pollution can be controlled at its source in a number of different ways. The two most popular means of pollution control are (1) preventing the pollutants from forming and (2) collecting the pollutants after they have formed but before they reach the outdoor atmosphere.

The first may be accomplished by replacing or changing the fuel or raw material used, altering the production process, redesigning the equipment, improving operation and maintenance practices, enclosing the operation, controlling land use, and developing transportation strategies. While these are effective means of control, more than preventive measures may be needed to limit atmospheric pollution.

Therefore, a second way to control pollution is to collect the pollutant for cleansing and/or disposal, instead of emitting it directly into the atmosphere.   In this approach a pollutant may be trapped, changed, or destroyed before it reaches the ambient air.   The methods for this are often called "tail-end techniques," since they apply after the pollutant forms in the industrial process or the combustion equipment.   There are four major types of controls, with numerous variations of each.   The crucial point to remember about control equipment is that every smoke stack and every control unit is unique, and therefore each unit has to be custom designed and ordered for each manufacturing situation.   The four basic types of collectors are (1) cyclones, (2) baghouses, (3) precipitators (electrostatic and wet), and (4) scrubbers.   Some equipment is designed to trap particulates, while others are designed for gas (and odor) elimination.   Some types can even be used for both gaseous and particulate matter.

     Cyclone collectors rely on inertial force as well as gravity for their operation.   The gas stream is rushed into a cylindrical chamber

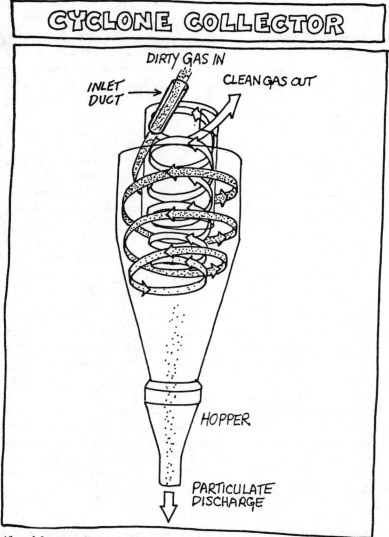

Figure 24: *Centrifugal force pulls heavy particulates to the outside wall of the cyclone container. Through friction and gravity, the particulates fall to the hopper, while the lighter cleansed air returns to the atmosphere.*

through a tangential inlet duct (one set at an angle to the chamber wall) at the top of the cylinder. This combination of shapes sets the stream whirling downward with increasing rapidity toward a cone-shaped base. Centrifugal force throws the entrained particles out of the spinning gas stream onto the wall of the chamber. From there they fall into a collecting hopper where an air stream then swirls them upward through a tube in the center, as illustrated in Figure 24. Depending on design, cyclone collectors remove particles as small as 3 microns, although high-efficiency collection cannot be expected for particles under 15 microns. We rate the efficiency of a collector according to the percentage of pollutants removed. A high-efficiency particulate collector can remove over 95%, by weight, of the particles. Multiple cyclones--that is, several low-capacity units instead of a single, large one, are popular because they can increase collection efficiency without using more power.

Baghouses work on the same principle as a vacuum cleaner bag. The bags for industrial collectors, though, may be 20 feet or more in length. In operation, the gas stream that carries a burden of particles passes through a woven fabric in which the particles themselves are caught. These widely used, very versatile collectors come in many materials, including cotton, wool, asbestos, glass fiber, and any of a number of synthetics. The choice of fabric is based on the temperature and chemical composition of the gas and the physical and chemical characteristics of the particulate matter.

Cloth filter collectors are used for fine particles; some can remove close to 100% of particles as fine as 0.4 micron. These baghouses are used to trap particulate emissions from cement kilns, iron foundry cupolas, primary steel production furnaces, and many other sources. The most common type of arrangement is in the mounting of multiple units. Custom-designed installations can be as large as a good-sized building (see Figure 25).

Electrostatic precipitators capture particles electrically through the use of electrodes that conduct an electric current to the non-metallic part of a circuit. These precipitators use a small-diameter negative electrode--usually a wire--and a grounded positive electrode plate, so that in operation, a strong electric charge from the negative electrode sets up a one-directional electric field. The particles passing through the field pick up the charge and are then drawn to the positive collecting surface where they are neutralized, either falling or being shaken into a collection hopper.

Electrostatic precipitators can remove many different kinds of particles as small as 0.1 micron with as much as 99.9% efficiency. In spite of the drawbacks--among them, a sensitivity to the composition and electrical properties of the substances passing through them--they are used in a great many plants, including those producing power, sulfuric acid, paint, plastics, chemicals, and automobile tires. A wet precipitator uses the same principle as the electrostatic precipitator, but removes the particles by <u>washing</u> them off the electrode plate (see Figure 26).

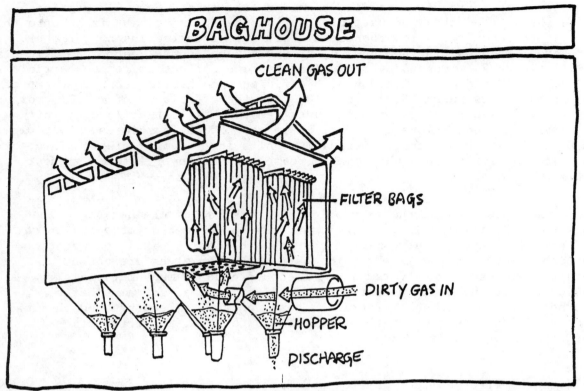

Figure 25: *Baghouses are gigantic vacuum cleaners. Dirty air flows through bag filters, straining out large particles which are then collected in hoppers.*

Scrubbers using either water or some other liquid may be combined with a number of other techniques to pick up and dissolve or wash out solid or liquid pollutants. Such scrubbers are used mainly in the removal of gaseous and odorous pollutants. Of the variety of scrubbers on the market today, one of them is the centrifugal spray scrubber. Here the gas stream is sent spinning through the scrubbing chamber, while a liquid is sprayed against the gas particles, wetting them and the chamber wall. The centrifugal force of the swirling gas throws the wetted particles against the wall; from there they are washed down. Efficiency as high as 96% is possible for particles of two and three microns (see Figure 27).

Another popular type is the Venturi scrubber in which the gas stream passes through a Venturi tube, a short tube with flaring ends and a constricted middle which forces an increase in a gas stream's speed and a decrease in its pressure. A coarse spray of water injected at the throat of the tube through radial jets becomes atomized by the speed of the gas to drops of about 50 microns in size. These collide with and trap the dust particles. Venturi scrubbers can collect from 97% to 99% of particles as small as 0.5 microns.

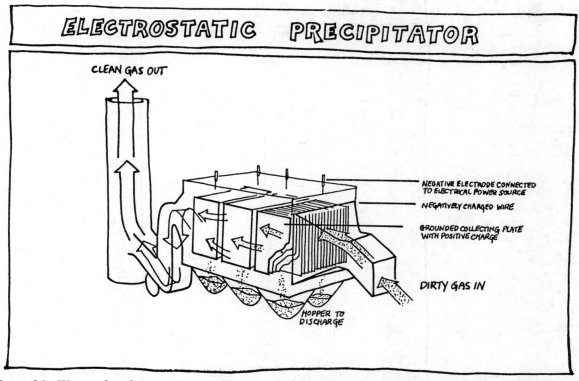

Figure 26: *Wet or dry electrostatic precipitators clean air with positively and negatively charged fields. Incoming particles receive a negative charge, and then are drawn to a large positive surface for neutralization, after which they fall into a collection hopper.*

Scrubbers, though they answer many needs and are widely used, have serious drawbacks. Like all wet collectors, they solve an air pollution problem, but create a water pollution problem in that the wash water becomes laden with particulates and must be treated as polluted effluent. In addition, scrubbers require high power to cool the gas stream so that it cannot easily disperse into the atmosphere. They are noisy and generally less effective than baghouses or electrostatic precipitators in removing very fine particles.

Clearly what was said about the "Million Dollar Man" could also be said about pollution control: "We've got the technology." To use that technology wisely, however, we must choose the most appropriate and cost-effective equipment. In the meantime, we must at least maintain, and not permit deterioration of, air quality.

Maintenance

The Clean Air Act of 1970 requires in new production facilities the "best available control technology." Not all types of technology for all types of industries are yet specified, but this standard which demands the best technology is a means for designing a viable maintenance plan.

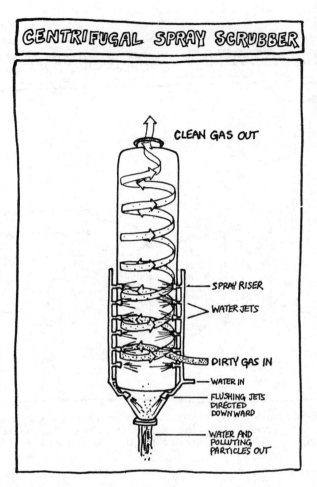

CENTRIFUGAL SPRAY SCRUBBER

CLEAN GAS OUT

SPRAY RISER

WATER JETS

DIRTY GAS IN

WATER IN

FLUSHING JETS
DIRECTED
DOWNWARD

WATER AND
POLLUTING
PARTICLES OUT

Figure 27: *Scrubbers may be used to pick up, dissolve, or wash out solid or liquid particles. Centrifugally spinning gas loses its particles to the wet wall surface where particles are washed downward for collection.*

The Act also authorizes EPA to designate Air Quality Maintenance Areas for regions anticipating pollutants in excess of the ambient (surrounding) standards. The Act requires those Areas to manage growth and prevent violation of the standards. Community planners and leaders will be intimately involved with such planning, bringing to bear knowledge about meteorology, topography, present pollutant levels, and projected growth factors. The Act requires EPA to set standards for new and modified stationary sources of pollution. These standards constitute direct emission limits for all major pollutants from specified types of sources.

While Congress intended that clean air areas be maintained and protected from deterioration, legislators noted that such restrictions can hamper "growth." The legal framework leaves to the state and local governments the decision on how much degradation will be allowed in a given area. Clearly, the challenge to officials is to balance land use with the adequate protection of the local, state, national, continental, and global ambient air quality. That approach now taken to protect the environment in the face of growth is discussed in Chapter 14.

CHAPTER SUMMARY

1. Major air pollution sources include fuel-consuming modes of transportation; fuel combustion from stationary sources; industrial processing; solid waste disposal; and miscellaneous but nonetheless broadly contributory controlled burning, solvent and gas evaporation, accidental burning of coal, refuse, and forests, and similar events.

2. Such sources generate SO_2; suspended particulates; NO, NO_2, N_2O_4; hydrocarbons of some 1,000 variations; CO; photochemical oxidants, and others.

3. Emissions are measured in the number of parts of pollutants in 1,000,000 parts of ordinary air--parts per million (ppm).

4. Natural radiation, destruction of the ozone layer by fluorocarbons, and other phenomena that alter the chemical make-up of the ambient air expose plants and animals to varying kinds and degrees of harm.

5. Abatement and control of air pollution from stationary industrial sources typically follows one or both of the following methods: 1) preventing the pollutants from forming in the process or operation; 2) collecting the pollutants after they have formed but before they have reached the outdoor air. Four types of collectors include 1) cyclones; 2) baghouses; 3) precipitators; 4) scrubbers.

SOURCES

Background Information on National Emissions Standards for Hazardous Air Pollutants. Washington, D. C.: U. S. EPA, October 1974.

Brucato, Cynthia. "The Reserve Mining Decision: 60,000 Tons of Health Menace vs. 3,000 Jobs." *Environment Midwest* (May 1974).

Controlling Air Pollution. New York: American Lung Association, 1974.

Corman, Rene. *Air Pollution Primer*. New York: American Lung Association, 1974.

Council on Environmental Quality. *Environmental Quality, 1975: The Sixth Annual Report of the Council on Environmental Quality*. Washington, D. C.: GPO, 1975

Racki, Matt. "How the Environment Affects Our Health." *Environment Midwest*, Special Issue (1976).

SUGGESTED READING

Governmental Approaches to Air Pollution Control. Washington, D. C.:

Institute of Public Administration, July 1971.

Scientists' Institute for Public Information. <u>Air</u> <u>Pollution</u> <u>Workbook</u>. St. Louis, Mo.: SIPI, 1970.

The <u>Air</u> <u>Pollution</u> <u>Primer</u> is a concise summary of air pollution causes and types, testing procedures to determine type and quantity, and current information on the effects of certain types at given levels. The book's approach is a straightforward, non-technical one. Many of its major points have been summarized in this chapter.

Seven annual reports of the Council on Environmental Quality highlight the following subjects:

   I. Carcinogens
  II. Pollution: water, air, noise, solid wastes, and hazardous pollu-
       tants. In addition, use of resources: land, water--in con-
       junction with public land, outdoor recreation, wildlife areas,
       foresting, mining, and others.

  III. Environmental Conditions and Trends

   IV. Environmental Economics

    V. Global Environment

   VI. National Environmental Policy Act

  VII. CEQ Studies--fluorocarbons and the environment

Altogether, they may well be considered one of the local official's most indispensible resources.

CHAPTER SIX

WATERSHEDS, SOILS, AND WATER

A PERSPECTIVE

The famous Scottish missionary, David Livingstone, explored southern and central Africa for over three decades, from 1841 until his death in 1873. He reached the Botletle River, in what is now the country of Botswana, in 1849. He wrote, "It is a glorious river. . . . The banks are extremely beautiful, lined with gigantic trees." Early explorers who followed him all described the Botletle as having swampy beds of reeds as well as forest along its margins, with populations of buffalo, elephant, and species of marsh-dwelling antelope. Immediately away from the river were open grasslands supporting giraffe, zebra, and various plains antelopes.

In 1851, exploring some 150 miles to the north of the Botletle, Livingstone crossed an open grassland of about 15 miles diameter. (Recently, an old man who first entered the area around 1900 confirmed that it had been a grassland then, with a few palm trees on the minor elevations protruding above the plain.)

Midway between this area and the Botletle is the Mababe River. Old people along the Mababe remember when wagons had to be floated across, while the oxen were unhitched and swam. That was back around the turn of the century.

Our first written descriptions of the Molopo and Nosob rivers, some four hundred miles to the south of the Botletle, also come to us from European explorers of the nineteenth century. Like the Botletle, they were lined with forest and swamps; the grassland away from the rivers contained springs favored by the wild animal populations. Even away from the springs, the people could suck water from the soil with a reed. The name of the village of Letlhakeng means 'place of reeds,' indicating a considerable amount of moisture in the area.

Today, Livingstone might find it difficult to recognize the places he visited. The forests and reed beds along the Botletle are gone, and the grassy plains back from the river have given way to bare

ground, scattered bushes, and small thorn trees. The
same is true of the grassy plain north of the Botletle.
The Mababe, where wagons floated while oxen swam, is
now perennially dry. The story is repeated along the
Nosob and Molopo in the south. The rivers still contain
some water, but the forests, swamps, and grasses have
yielded to scrub bush. The springs are gone, and the
people can no longer suck water from the soil with a
reed. The large wild animals have either disappeared
altogether or have been replaced by species that can
browse on thorn trees and get by on little water.

And there are no more reeds at Letlhakeng.

Such changes have been carefully documented over all
of what is today the nation of Botswana. In just a
little over a century, there has apparently been
a marked deterioration toward desert conditions. Rainfall records have been kept for eighty years and indicate no downward trend, yet the area's water table has
obviously made a significant drop, accompanied by
pronounced changes in flora and fauna. What has
caused the change?

Large numbers of people and their cattle migrated into
the area in the 1800s, fleeing from tribal warfare
elsewhere. In the last quarter of the century the warfare both within and outside the area was suppressed
by the British, and the people were able to adopt a
more settled way of life. As modern medicines were
made available, a population explosion occurred among
both people and cattle. Settled areas were overgrazed
and a vicious cycle set in. Reduction of grass cover
by grazing cattle exposed the soil, allowing more
evaporation and faster runoff of water under the sear-
ing subtropical sun. This lowered the water table,
thus making a less favorable habitat for grass, thus
leading to more evaporation and runoff, and to the
replacement of grass by scrub bush. In a large area
along the Botletle, it appears that the process was
caused by the setting up of a cattle-holding station
by the Colonial Development Corporation in 1949. Up
to ten thousand head were grazed in an area too
fragile to accommodate them. In the grassy area which
Livingstone found to the north of the Botletle, the
cattle experienced a catastrophic die-off in the early
1950s, reducing a well-to-do village to poverty in
three years. The entire country experienced severe
drought in the mid-1960s. With soil no longer able to
retain moisture, crops failed. Food had to be
imported, and the people dug deep into dry river beds
to obtain their water by the cupful. The cattle,

which were the basis of the country's main industry, had to be disposed of; the single meat-processing plant was closed and has not reopened.

And there are no more reeds at Letlhakeng.

> Thomas R.Tanner, Ecology, Environment, and Education

The Earth's biosphere is the physical space with the identified chemicals, transmissible energy, and spectrum of conditions in which the present, known life forms have evolved, including us. Within that space, the sequence of actions and reactions led to various phenomena--caused by the rotation of the Earth, the periodicity of the elements, and the evaporation and condensation of water, as well as the change from high-energy states to low-energy states. In concert these comprise the total system which maintains the biosphere's integrity.

Watersheds

Subsystems of the biosphere, or ecosystems, are communities of life forms and the physical and chemical environment in which they interact. The most definitive components of an ecosystem are its watersheds. Just as the smallest, completely functional unit of a chemical compound is an atom, so the smallest, completely functional unit of an ecosystem is the watershed. Because of its natural history, we will argue here that a stable watershed offers the greatest hope for a stable ecosystem and a habitable community.

Stability, not size, may be the watershed's most fundamental property. Any watershed's character is the consequence of the relationship among the Earth, Sun, and Moon; the Earth's geologic history; and the present available energy. The smaller the watershed, the more dependent its character is upon the precise substance of the local weather patterns and the composite of activities of all plant and animal behavior (including human). It is at present the end product of the collections of chemicals in bacteria, worms, mosses, shrubs, frogs, birds, and humans that have already competed and survived or else died off. It is also the starting point for every evolutionary event that takes place from now on. The inextricability of all observed movements, organisms, and reactions in the watershed are what is so impressive. They are not really subdivided, categorized, classified, or ordered by taxonomy; those are inventions of man for his purposes. Contrarily, those movements, organisms, and reactions are the "snapshots" we mentioned in Chapter 1. The fluidity of energy, the holding of a chemical, the transforming of life is what we cannot see. At any one time, every drop of water, each bit of soil, an insect pupa, a flowering plant, a molecule of oxygen, a rise in temperature, a photon of sunlight are related--"knotted," if you will--to every other member in a special way. The connections are "lifelines"; the knots tie them together in a network.

The network's integrity is related directly to environmental quality. Environmental quality is stability.

This interconnectedness becomes more meaningful if we understand the nature of watersheds themselves. A watershed is defined at its outer and upper limit by the mountains, ridges, and hilltops that divide and shed precipitation to one collecting land gradient or another, and at its lower terminus by its intersection with the ocean. Just as the peak of a house top, the rim of a bathtub, the lip of a bowl determine the future pathway of falling water, so does the gradient of the watershed, as precipitation gathers and is retained on or below the surface of land, until the water either evaporates or flows into the seas. In nature, companion raindrops falling separately into different watersheds do not meet again until they mix in the ocean or the atmosphere.

Continuous availability of water is required by all plants and animals; they, in turn, are required for stability of the watershed. The watershed's stability is essential to the ecosystems, and maintenance of the ecosystems is imperative for sustenance of the biosphere.

Figure 28 represents this sequence. At the left, rain falls over the surface of many watersheds. That surface water then flows over rocks to lakes and ponds, or soaks into the top few inches of soil. Later, water may seep down into sand and porous rock substrate. This water-bearing (aquiferous) rock provides a reservoir from which water may gush when drilled (an artesian well) or may be pumped.

Eventually the elevation of freshwater reaches that of sea water--zero. The right-hand side of Figure 28 attempts to reveal what happens. Freshwater is moving from left to right. At sea level, the underground freshwater has a great deal of pressure, or "head," because it is pushed from new reserves that are above it in elevation. In addition to its pressure, freshwater weighs less than sea water, and therefore, it floats over sea water. The result is that freshwater acts as a barrier to salt water. Representation of this standoff is indicated graphically in the white and stippled areas at angles to one another.

The salty sea water presses against the freshwater, and vice versa. If a well point is in that interface, it may from time to time pump fresh and saline water. The consequences of depleting the freshwater so that it cannot hold out the sea water are serious. Discussion of this form of pollution continues later in this chapter.

Within a watershed, no matter if it is thousands of miles in area or a few feet square, water gathers. The gathering is actually a simple relationship between soil and the water's tendency to run to the sea. The

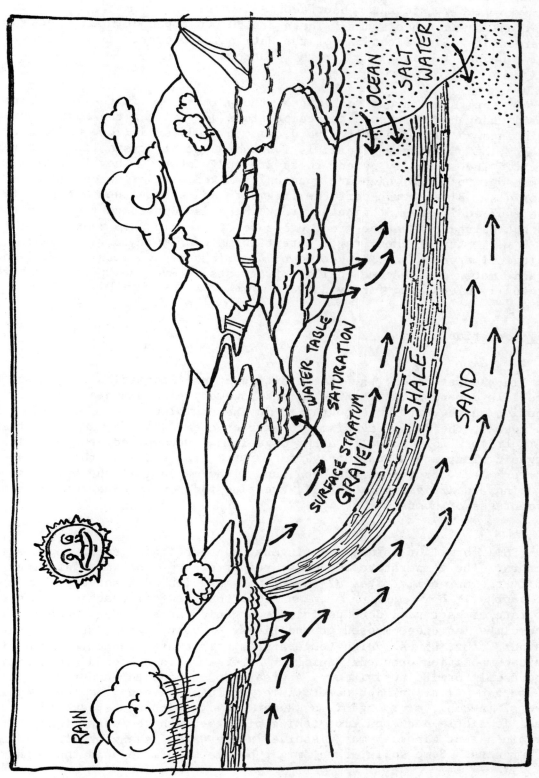

Figure 28: *Watershed, water tables, and aquifers.*

soil is the important factor. In Chapter 1 we presented a cursory review of soil formation, indicating that soils derive from parent rock structures. Whether water pours over the surface of the land, as it does in parking lots, or soaks deeply into the subsurface as it does in a desert, is a matter relating to watershed soils. There are 80,000 types of soil. These are intermediate classifications of the National Cooperative Soil Survey. Each soil type has implications for the planner.

Of the three parent rock types, the primary one is the igneous rock formed under high pressure and temperature deep within the Earth during its beginnings as a molten ball. Hard, smooth obsidian is igneous rock cooled quickly; New England's granite is igneous material crystallized out very slowly. The secondary parent rocks are sedimentary. They form from broken outcroppings which are eventually mixed with organics and other materials. Rivers transport the fragments and settle them out into familiar layers of sediment. Sedimentary rock which is compressed and recrystallized, but not melted by heat or great pressure, is metamorphic rock, the third rock type. Any of these three parent forms can, by physical, chemical, and biological processes, be broken down, distributed, and with the addition of organic materials, become enriched fragments or even new parent rock that eventually blend into finely divided soil that is high in nutrients.

Soil Formation

In the watershed, the rate and type of soil formation from these parent materials depend greatly on which and how many plants and animals can flourish on the nutrients contained in the crumbled parent material. Lichens and mosses, the first organisms to extract chemicals from the rock fragments, are nutrients for growth of other organisms. Decomposed, they provide humus (organic plant and animal decay) for ferns, grasses, and other herbaceous plants. Next, bacteria, protozoa, and algae metabolize the dying plants, aerating and irrigating the soil, creating finer particles and greater percentages of humus.

Soil formation is also contingent upon certain physical and chemical factors. The temperature and moisture patterns of the immediate locale modify the metabolic rates of the organisms which successively live upon one another. Low temperatures mean slower biochemical reactions, hence a low rate of bacterial decomposition. Organic matter under these conditions accumulates as undecomposed ground litter--leaves, twigs, stems, cadavers, feathers, fur, bones. High temperatures accelerate biochemical reactions, and decomposition proceeds rapidly. Water amounts and conditions similarly alter soil forming activities. A great amount of water underground and near the surface, i.e., a high water table, occludes oxygen from the deeper soil layers. Aerobic microorganisms cannot survive without oxygen; therefore, there is little decomposition taking place beneath the water line. Or, certain parent minerals may dissolve in the water, changing its acidity or hardness. Some soils, then, might become much more acid than others.

In such soils, which earthworms and snails disdain, the physical mixing between surface litter and subsurface mineral matter will not take place as rapidly as in neutral or slightly alkaline soils.

As the layers accumulate above the original parent soil particles, rain-water percolates downward, leaching soluble materials from the upper levels and carrying them to lower ones. The size of the soil particles, the number of interstices in the soil, as well as the temperature, frequency, and volume of the "watering" modify the impact of leaching. Deeper water, saturating the soil above the parent rock, may rise so close to the top-soil that capillary action will pull some of the water in a reverse direction--up through the original parent soil particles, again modifying the composition of the various soil layers. The distance of the water table from the surface, its total depth to bedrock, and its variations in level constantly change the condition of the soil. Figure 29 illustrates this process.

The net effect of these movements is a variety of material deposits discernible as layers. These are seen in roadside cuts, freshly dug pits, or other cross-sectional exposures. Many of the physical and chemical transfers shown in Figure 28 cause the differences in thickness, color, amount of moisture, and pH in these layers. Knowledge of soil history is essential for comprehending the workings of a watershed. With such understanding we can plan ways to improve contaminated areas and to maintain naturally health ones. Our success in both can be measured in the quality of many environments, especially the human one.

Lifelines--The Biological Network

The biological network within the surface layers of soil will have a different organization from point to point because of the variation in soil types and other ecological factors. Again, a knowledge of the network, its "knots" and "lifelines," is critical to making wise decisions about land-use. A few of the connections are described here. The conclusion by many scientific investigators who have examined thousands of biotic inter-relationships is that there are two and three or more ties between organisms, so that the loss of one organism or one "knot" in the mesh may not be crucial. On the other hand, the loss of one knot could start a "run," in biological terms. The loss of not one individual, usually, but perhaps a population or an entire species could presage a natural condition that might lead to the loss of other, closely related organisms. Just as one cut thread in a fabric can be the undoing of a hundred other threads, so it is possible that the death of one species might lead to the extinction of a community.

But it is not a sense of fragility of the natural world that we wish to convey. On the contrary, some sense of the intricacy, toughness, and beauty of the fabric is hoped for as we now begin our closer examination of the life we find in the soils themselves.

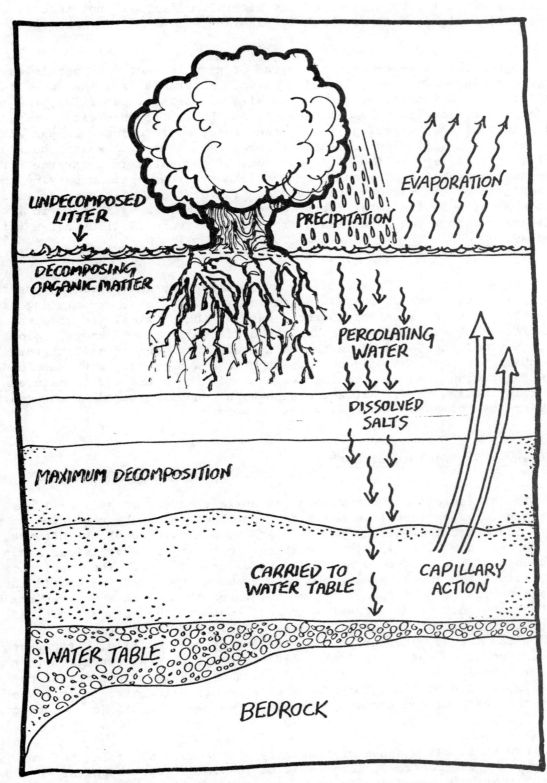

Figure 29: *Weather, precipitation, surface litter, soil type, compaction, depth to water tables and bedrock — all modify the capacity of the soil to assimilate water.*

Viruses

Viruses are clusters of proteins and genetic materials visible only by electron microscopy and "alive" only after invading and acting upon the nuclear material of a host cell. Although much studied, soil viruses are still little understood. We do know that they may specifically attack bacteria, plants, or animals and that they are related to airborne viruses that cause polio, swine flu, measles, and colds. However, the connection between their presence in soil and the potential they hold for benefit or harm is not certain. One such virus, nucleopolyhedrosis, is a proven pesticide to the Tussock moth which kills northwestern Douglas firs; in lieu of DDT, this virus has just been approved for control use against the moth.

Bacteria

Bacteria, on the other hand, are perceived as the only organism group upon which we depend for decomposition of dying plants and animals which otherwise would quickly pile up around us. Bacteria are small (250,000 could fit into the dot of this "i") and prolific (in 24 hours, with the right conditions, one bacterium alone could produce a 30-centimeters-thick colony large enough to cover a football field). Some soil bacteria require free oxygen and therefore porous soil; others do not. This group is able to function with or without free oxygen. These are the anaerobic decomposers. Each type plays a certain role in the reduction of a large molecule into smaller molecules which can be absorbed by plants or released into the atmosphere. For example, it is well known that legumes such as peas, soybeans, and clover have root nodules which host bacteria. Together, the plant and the Rhizobium bacterium can take free nitrogen from the circulating soil atmosphere and "fix" the nitrogen into nitrites and nitrates. In these forms nitrogenous compounds are assimilable into the biochemical cycles of plants and animals. Some bacteria can also disassemble certain of the man-made insecticides and pesticides. In doing so, they can interfere with the intended use of the poison by preventing its entry into the life cycles of the target organism.

Actinomycetes

Like bacteria, actinomycetes are decomposers of complex molecules. They, too, are small (100,000 to 100,000,000 single organisms estimated in a gram of soil). They resemble a blend between bacteria and fungi: they are single-celled with long branching tubes. They play a role in decomposition, since their work begins where that of viruses and bacteria stops. One form, Streptomyces, is used to produce the antibiotic streptomycin.

Fungi

Fungi are larger and more specialized than bacteria. They exist as spores for long periods. Then, with proper moisture, nutrients, and temperatures, they beome long, multi-filamentous structures that decompose the more complex plant molecules--cellulose, lignin, and starch--that bacteria cannot. Symbiotically, some mycorrhizal fungi serve as roots to some plants, transporting to them water and dissolved nutrients from otherwise infertile soil. The spreading of molds on bread, potatoes, fruit, and earth demonstrates how rapidly fungi can reduce a large mass to tiny, assimilable chemical forms.

Protozoa

Protozoa, too, are single-celled soil organisms. Many devour bacteria, a single protozoan consuming as many as 40,000 bacteria in 12 hours. Amoeba, euglena, flagellates, and ciliates reproduce exponentially from field grass placed in water. In such high-moisture conditions they are found in great numbers, but aside from a few interdependent (symbiotic) or parasitic relationships, little seems to be known about the functions of protozoa in the vitality of the soil network.

Nematodes

Of 10,000 known species of nematodes, about 2,000 inhabit the soil. As many as 30,000,000 individuals live in a cubic meter of soil. They thrive in the water that clings to soil particles. Free-living forms feed on bacteria, small algae, and actinomycetes. Others penetrate plant roots, ingesting the circulating juices and often damaging or killing the plants. Before their own death, the nematodes leave eggs which drop into the soil, hatch, and repeat the process. Farmers must control the growth of nematodes because they can harm cash crops. Reciprocally, there is some control by nematodes of protozoa as well as other nematodes. As with the protozoa, we know little about how nematodes influence the overall healthiness of the soil.

Earthworms

Earthworms are found in moist soils high in humus content and deep in surface litter. They tunnel for food, feeding mostly at night, descending to depths of 9 to 12 feet when the soil becomes dry. As they tunnel more deeply, earthworms push mineral-rich soil up to higher layers. Simultaneously they leave tunnels which retain water for dryer periods. At the surface they take in remains such as leaf bits, mixing them with inorganic materials and leaving remains which bacteria, actinomycetes, and other decomposers reduce to food for rooted vegetation. The earthworms alone physically transform the soil more than all other soil organisms combined.

Other Life in the Soil

Other life contributes to the charcter of soils. Terrestrial snails and shelless slugs digest decaying wood and other organic matter, including algae, lichens, and fungi. Others feed on earthworms. Snails and slugs may range in numbers from 7,500 to 600,000 per acre; they decompose woody litter, but they require a loose, uncompacted soil.

Also decomposing the matter that forms soils are large numbers and varieties of insects--some 750,000 species. Millipedes, centipedes, wood lice, and mites are found under decaying leaves and wood. Ants and termites range everywhere, but the termites contribute more significantly to decomposition as they chew through fallen trees at incredible rates. Beetles quickly devour dead birds and rodents. Flies lay eggs in rotting flesh, while their larval forms--maggots--aid in the rapid breaking down and removal of the carcasses of animals large and small. Vertebrates such as moles, woodchucks, gophers, chipmunks, and rabbits feed on the various plant and animal forms we've already surveyed. They subsequently defecate organic wastes of their own. As burrowers, they also leave air and water spaces in the earth, providing still another means of continuous recycling of the soil's components.

All of these processes are part of the continual flow of events. First, these organisms assist in the physical breakdown of rock and in the chemical breakdown of its minerals. Next, they churn and stir the soils, mixing in air and water, incessantly preparing and repairing the land for others. Lastly, each organism is part of the energy pathway--from Sun to us. A description of the pathway appears in every science book from Malthus to the present day, a story that is told and retold but probably cannot be told enough.

We considered earlier that the Sun and the heat contained within the Earth are our original and continued sources of energy. The Sun radiates energy (photons of light) which is captured by the photochemicals in the chloroplasts of green plants and chlorophyll-bearing animals. The light energy allows the plants to synthesize small chemical particles into larger molecules which in effect are new forms of the original solar energy. Thus, a leaf is a large packet of energy. When that leaf falls to the ground as litter, it is methodically taken apart into its separate, smaller energy components--first by the bacterial decomposers, then by the actinomycetes, and so on. These organisms distribute the energy which is taken up next by consuming nematodes, earthworms, insects, and others. Multi-celled animals are bundles of transformed solar energy. At each transition, some of the energy is lost as heat in the activity of taking apart and putting together, so that the amount of energy stored is less than the previous amount available. Plants--sometimes assisted by bacteria and nematodes-- also consume the small energy molecules, and eventually produce another chlorophyll-containing system which can trap additional solar energy.

All this is basic but essential: at any given time, energy is packaged as a nematode, an earthworm, an insect, a mushroom, a clover plant, wheat, corn, a chicken, a pheasant, a sheep, a cow . . . and we are able to convert any of these forms into energy that we can use. Obviously, the "forms" include wood, coal, oil, and gas which can be converted again into yet other forms--steam, gasoline, electricity, and chemicals. It follows that if there are few organisms in the soil, there is little energy in it; if there is little energy in the soil, it cannot provide energy for us. With all this in mind, let's now reconsider the general importance of soil in the watershed.

Soils, Rainwater, and Subsurface Waters

The breakdown of parent rock to soil and the subsequent mixing by organisms greatly affects the watershed's water retention. We know that an unpacked, coarse surface allows precipitation to penetrate to the subsurface. Underlying, loosened soil also permits the water table's moisture to be absorbed upward. Both downward gravitational and upward capillary movements deliver water to microorganisms and rooted plants, in stable amounts which are independent of the weather conditions. The greater the soil's water-holding capacity, the longer and more uniform is the potential growing (energy-producing) season. But there are other reasons for our wanting to restore or to maintain a water table's capacity for water retention.

Clearly, rainwater which soaks into the soil does not carry off soil, fertilizers, or pesticides, nor does it run into urban storm sewers to add to the volume of water needing treatment. It does not add to the flow of streams beyond their banks. Thus, retained water is not flood water. Absorbed water offers greater potential for use and less potential for damage than water that runs off the surface. Subsurface waters, aquifers, are underground reservoirs. As seen in Figure 28, the water just below the surface may move to nearby streams, constantly maintaining the stream flow regardless of surface run off. Such movement contributes to a steady supply of streamwater for drinking, industry, commerce, recreation, and especially hydroelectric power generation--the largest single use of surface waters.

The 1970 figures indicate that we use 2,600,000,000,000 gallons of water per day (2,600 bgd*). Seven-eighths of it (2,285 bgd) is needed for hydroelectric power, although this represents use and not consumption of water. Of the 315 bgd remaining, 177 bgd is used for industry, 120 for

---

* billion gallons per day.

irrigation, 16 bgd for public utility supplies, and 2 in rural and urban consumption. Excluding water used for hydroelectric requirements, future demands through the year 2020 are estimated as follows:

1970:	315 bgd
1980:	383 bgd
2000:	786 bgd
2020:	1,148 bgd.

On the average, each American uses 40-100 gallons each day. Some typical volumes include the following:

Washing dishes:	10 gallons
Flushing a toilet:	3 gallons
Taking a shower:	20-30 gallons
Taking a tub bath:	30-40 gallons
Washing clothes:	20-30 gallons.

All of this water originates daily from within some watershed.

Salinity

Other rainwater which soaks deep into the ground through the sandstone rock--the small spaces between gravel and sand--is available for drinking water and industrial purposes by drilling and pumping. Its slow permeation through the substrates helps to dissolve minerals; thus, these deep reserves become increasingly salty as aquifers are recharged by waters passing through different geologic formations. Composition of the salts varies, and the change in salinity level is gradual. Rainwater contains less than 10 ppm of dissolved solids; most rivers and lake waters have less than 500 ppm. But groundwaters are generally much more saline--having even 10,000 ppm of salt. At the extreme, sea water (which can intrude into the aquifer) has approximately 35,000 ppm of salt.

Certain types and quantities of dissolved solids, like salts, gain importance with certain uses. Calcium and magnesium in household water, for example, make it "hard." The ions of these salts react chemically with soap to form a gummy clot in fabrics. Sodium chloride gives water the familiar salty taste, sulfur the pungent odor. Limestone releases calcium, carbonates, or sulfates; feldspar contains oxygen, silicon, aluminum, and sodium.

When limestone and feldspar salts are dissolved, the water deposits them as solids in pans, kettles, and industrial tanks or boilers. The deposit builds into a thick scale that decreases heating efficiency. A coating 1/8 inch thick in domestic waterpipes, for example, requires 10% more heat than uncoated pipes to reach the same temperature as the uncoated ones. Sodium in irrigation water forms hardpan in soils, a deposit which blocks water migration to the plants. Heavy concentrations of other salts in soils actually can kill vegetation. Once in the soil, salts can again be dissolved by rainwater to soak into the aquifer or to run off into nearby streams. In either location, the salts may affect the stream quality and may require, for subsequent use, that the ground or stream waters be additionally treated.

Underground saline waters pose ongoing threats to drinking water supplies. In the Chicago area and southern Illinois, for example, potable water exists in various geologic strata down to certain levels, but at 1,800 feet in Chicago and 300 feet in lower Illinois, underlying water becomes extremely salty. Ocean water also can pollute underground freshwater supplies, for the same rock stratum that contains freshwater extends under the ocean. Pressures there force seawater landward. Such saltwater has seriously contaminated freshwater supplies in Long Island, New York and in California, Florida, New Jersey, and southern Texas.

In shoreline areas, at least, the removal of freshwater from groundwater aquifers at rates exceeding replenishment has caused the freshwater/saltwater interface to move progressively closer to the pumping stations. Previously, the saltwater was held back by the freshwater, as in Chicago and other areas in Illinois. As we saw above, freshwater is lighter in weight than saltwater, and so blockades the saltier water. But once pumping starts to withdraw the freshwater, saltwater creeps inland against the retreating freshwater/saltwater interface. In some cases, so much freshwater has been pumped out that the interface becomes close to or directly under the well points. Then, the only reasonable choices left to those regions are (1) reduction of pumping, (2) acceleration of freshwater recharge, (3) a combination of both, or (4) abandonment. Some attempts have been made to re-inject freshwater--a fifth possibility for inhibiting the movement of saltwater intrusion.

The major concern is that as greater proportions of saltier underground water are used, the surface waters will become saltier. The more saline underground waters passing through industrial and commercial systems eventually are discharged into the lakes, streams, and rivers. Maintaining the quality of both ground and surface waters requires regular, careful analysis and appropriate treatment. The U. S. EPA established maximum containment levels for dissolved solids (among the types of contaminants) in drinking water. Atomic absorption is used to measure the types and amounts. Maximum contaminant levels proposed as of May 17, 1976 for 10 elemental species are in numbers of milligrams in a liter of sample water: Arsenic, .05; Barium, 1.0; Cadmium, .01; Lead, .05; Mercury, .002; Silver, .01; Fluoride, 2.4-1.4 ranges; and Nitrate, 10.0. Greater amounts than these are believed hazardous to public health.

It is clear now that protecting soils is a means of pollution prevention. If soils retain water, the water feeds slowly into reservoirs, lakes,
and ponds and thereby furnishes us with quantities of useable, low-salt water. Obviously, then, we would use less of the underground water which is
high in potentially harmful dissolved salts and heavy metals.

Soil Quality and Environmental Planning

A vigorous, healthy, high-energy soil is crucial to environmental quality. If we must have sound judgement about how to preserve soils as we use
them, we also must have sound data about present conditions of soils. Then
we can carefully plan for safe uses of land: which land should be left open
to receive and absorb precipitation? What kind of lime, potash, and fertilizers can be used to make soil agriculturally productive? Where is bedrock
poor for soils but sound for buildings? How can we ascertain a balance between aquifer input and output? Where are soil layers and slopes unsuited
to dwellings? What changes will ensue following highway construction? What
criteria for use and soil type do we apply in resolving land-use conflicts?
The information necessary to make such judgements begins with a land capability analysis. A key resource is the soil survey prepared by the Soil
Conservation Service. It includes soil data and engineering interpretations
based on specifications in "Soil Memorandum SCS-45 (Rev. 2)." The relationship among SCS, the engineer, and the local officials is based on the Soil
Conservation Service's years-old function of aiding the farmer. The Service's vast data bank provides engineers with essential information about
the natural condition of the soil. The engineers use it to make recommendations for construction of facilities. With SCS data and engineers' in-
terpretation, local officials can make policies, decisions, laws, and enforcement procedures that are best for the watershed and its communities.

The need for such practical planning is dramatically illustrated in
the following account. The City Public Service Board of San Antonio, Texas
ran into unsuspected sandstone float-rocks while laying a 30-inch gas supply line. Every test hole drilled failed to locate the float-rocks, but
the continuous trenching machinery encountered many of them, each requiring
laborious and costly work with air hammers to remove them. Yet, soil scientists knew that in certain parent materials there would be float-rocks.
Their presence would have been predicted by soil maps, but the soil survey
was completed just after the pipeline installation was finished! The city
planners then did use a soil survey to lay out a greenbelt plan. The kinds
of soils suitable for special uses helped them to decide where to place
parks, nature areas, agricultural fields, drainageways, and rights-of-way
for utilities and streets. The boundaries of each were adjusted to reflect
sources of construction materials, stream beds, flood plains, and areas
that were more suitable for horticultural purposes than for structural
foundations.

In fact, soil surveys have been used to establish preferential tax as-
sessments--taxing more for highly productive land and less for soils that
can generate little income. This use of soil information helps to keep

assessments uniform, readily explainable, and administratively economical. Naturally, there are difficulties--the lack of modern soil surveys for some areas under consideration or insufficiently trained personnel to interpret the surveys. The Soil Conservation Service, however, can help offset such limitations with its range of available information.

As we cautioned, information on soils is not infallible. In another actual case, soil maps in Broome County, New York--located in the Allegheny Plateau region--were useful but did not show the very different capacities of the soils to handle septic tank effluents. Such variations in soil capacities can occur within short distances. The surveyor reported that Chenango soils are very permeable and that seepage fields with tile lines in gravel can be used in them according to standard design curves. Nearby Volusia soils, however, are practically impermeable below the topsoil because of a dense fragipan and compact till. Volusia soils, therefore, need artificial sand filters that do not use the natural soil for absorption. Other soils, like Lordstown and Tioga, are rated shallow and diminish to bedrock or are even flooded. For subsurface sewage disposal, seepage fields are needed in specified loamy fill. Fragile soil, bedrock, or swamps pose leaching problems. The County funded Cornell University to consider the universal mix of clearly located soil types in a detailed report on the Broome County soils--ultimately saving many thousands of private dollars and great costs to public health.

Another case shows how soil permeability can produce potentially toxic conditions in drinking water. Long Island is heavily dependent on wells for its public water supply. The Grumman aircraft assembly plant, with 20,000 employees, in Bethpage, Long Island closed five wells when polyvinyl chloride, a suspected cause of a rare form of liver cancer, was discovered in them. The source of contamination (reported in the Washington Post on December 10, 1976) was believed to be neighboring Hooker Chemical Company, which was disposing of its PVC waste underground. Presumably, adequate information about the soils, water movement, and PVC might have meant a far different means of disposing of the polyvinyl chloride.

Probably the oldest and most familiar impact of improper soil management on man is flooding brought about partly by erosion. The quantity of eroding soils varies dramatically with soil conditions. For example, streams drawing from the Adirondack watersheds in New York State are surrounded by unpopulated slopes; porous, rocky soils; and heavy vegetation. The sedimentation after each rainfall averages fewer than 100 tons per square mile of watershed. But in western Iowa, as much as 2,000 tons per square mile of watershed will be carried downstream with each rain due to erodible soil and lack of vegetation.

The Mississippi River transports 330,000,000 tons per year of suspended solids and 130,000,000 tons per year of dissolved solids. The soils along the Mississippi sequentially change from gravel to sand to silt and to clays, the extent of open land exposed for erosion by the river shifting according to the land use: forestry, construction, mining, grazing, and farming.

The soils are lost to farming, and any extensive accumulation of sediments increases the probability of flooding.

Flooding and Flood Control

When streams and rivers crest their banks, they inundate the areas adjacent to the channel at depths and widths that vary with the rainfall, floodplain soils, and the uses made of the land. Farmers, developers, industrial managers, and water treatment engineers base their tilling or designs for basements or storage facilities on how much and when flooding will take place. Local officials attempting to control flooding in their regions also need to know how far they should go in proposing flood protection to communities that are subject to flooding; naturally, those in the floodplains must plan accordingly.

All rivers flood. Ordinarily, with sufficient rain and snowmelt, there is enough water to reach bank level about twice each year. They overflow their banks about every two years. Less frequently, perhaps once in 25 years or less, a massive downpour will cause violent flooding. The Ohio River in January, 1937; the Kansas River in July, 1951; and the Connecticut River in 1955 are examples. On the last occasion, 14 inches of rain fell in one day, the Connecticut River rose 19 1/2 feet; it was estimated that the floodwaters damaged property valued at over two billion dollars and killed 186 people. The flood could not have been predicted or stopped, yet flood damage can be minimized with management of upstream water retention facilities and with maintenance of floodplains to absorb spreading flood waters. This last practice necessitates restricted development in the floodplains, but in most urbanized communities today it is already too late to effect such restrictions. In more rural, outlying areas the opportunity exists to protect floodplains so that they can continue to serve their natural functions of storage and absorption.

As a first step in flood control, analysts chart the height of the water surface above a given reference marker. These charts show the peaks associated with significant flood damage. Upon comparing peaks occurring in one year, ten, fifty, or one hundred years, governments can decide whether to protect the community from every flood that might occur in one year or from a flood that might occur in ten, fifty, or perhaps one hundred years. The decision is based upon the relationship between costs to protect and costs to compensate for flood damage.

Control actions might include channel dredging, diking, damming, or building ponds, flood-proofing, and controlling land use. Thereafter, the system must be maintained. Sediments accumulating behind dams must be removed and floodplain absorption capacity must not be significantly reduced --when possible, it should be increased. Building in floodplains increases flood heights by displacing floodwaters. Flood prevention might further require leaving cover on cropland soils to reduce erosion; enforcing regulations governing construction, forestry, mining, and soil protection; planting cover along stream banks; and generally restoring the watershed's soils so that they can receive and retain precipitation.

Rivers with broad, undeveloped floodplains reduce potential future flood damage. Broad, flat rivers, such as the lower Mississippi with its wide adjacent floodplains, quickly dissipate their crests by overflowing onto assimilating soils. The porous riverbank soils reduce the volume of floodwater.

Clearly, any workable flood prevention plan must consider how the natural assimilative capacity of the watershed can be used. Permitted uses of a floodplain might include agriculture--ideally with low erosion potential and low fertilizer application rates, recreation, parking lots, navigation facilities, equipment storage yards, and other open-space uses. One local government required that

> . . .no vacant regulatory floodplain land shall be occupied or used and no building hereafter erected, altered, moved, or occupied until the applicant submits to the appropriate local official a certification by a registered professional engineer designated by the local governing body that the finished fill and building flood elevations or other flood protection measures are in compliance with appropriate floodplain zoning provisions and other floodplain regulations.

Local governments are now empowered to make needed policies, ordinances, and enforcement commitments consistent with the best available information about watershed history, soil types, weather conditions, and population needs.

The watershed is the logical planning unit. As we said in the Preface, the system is essentially simple, but it is not highly respected. The penalty for not making an effort to understand the watershed system as a whole will inevitably grow more severe, for the biosphere suffers when its parts break down. By planning intelligently, we can sustain those water and soil resources that now serve us, and perhaps restore many of those that once did.

CHAPTER SUMMARY

1. Ecosystems are communities of life forms and the chemical and physical environment in which they interact. The "life-net" of interrelatedness among all life forms is sustained by the interconnectedness of watersheds in the hydrologic cycle. The stability of a given watershed in a healthy ecosystem is perhaps the watershed's and ecosystem's most essential characteristic for ongoing life support.

2. The underlying material in a watershed determines by its kind, amount, and quality, the nature of the water it absorbs, transports via aquifers,

and stores in water tables.

3. Three parent rock types--igneous, sedimentary, and metamorphic, in their distribution and contiguity to one another--produce soils, determine the depth of water table, and overall lend to an area's watershed a given set of characteristics.

4. The organic material decayed and accumulated, the relative compactness of the soil, the size of soil particles, and the number of interstices influence percolation of water and therefore its leaching capacity.

5. Layerings occur in the process of water percolation, typically in this order: precipitation; undecomposed litter; decomposing organic matter; percolating water; dissolved salts; maximum decomposition; transport zone to water table; and bedrock.

6. A biological network spreads throughout the layers of soil and underlying matter: soil viruses, bacteria (aerobic and anaerobic), actinomycetes, fungi, protozoa, nematodes, earthworms, snails and shelless slugs, insects, millipedes, centipedes, wood lice, ants, termites, etc., are supported by the soil at various depths for various periods during their life cycles. These life forms, their part in breaking down parent rock to form soils, and the subsequent capacity of the soils to absorb water all play a part in determining the amount of available water for human and other use in a watershed.

7. Certain dissolved salts (calcium and magnesium) picked up through percolation cause hardness of water; at certain loads such material causes inefficient heating and damage to plant and animal life. Salt water intrusion threatens the water supply at fresh/salt water interfaces. Therefore soil stability, type, and other factors determine the quality and quantity of drinking water available.

8. Environmental quality depends upon a healthy, high-energy soil. Land-use management must consider water table and soil characteristics when deciding about extensive covering of an area, as by asphalt or concrete; when determing relative productivity of land for taxing purposes; and appropriateness of soils for certain construction purposes.

9. The watershed is the logical planning unit. It is geologically and biologically the presentation of a long evolutionary history. Watershed systems are therefore time-tested ones. As a consequence, planning that considers the holding capacities of both the biology and the geology of the watershed has a high probability of being solidly founded and successful.

SOURCES

American Public Health Association. Standard Methods for the Examination of Water and Wastewater. Washington, D.C.: American Public Health Association, 1971.

Andrews, William A. A Guide to the Study of Soil Ecology. Englewood
    Cliffs, New Jersey: Prentice-Hall, 1973.

Bartelli, L. J., et al. Soil Surveys and Land Use Planning. Madison,
    Wisconsin: Soil Science Society of America and American Society
    of Agronomy, 1966.

Biological Sciences Curriculum Study. Solid Waste. Menlo Park,
    California: Addison-Wesley Publishing Company, 1975.

Clairborne, William. "N.Y. to Probe PVC in Water at Grumman's Aircraft
    Plant." The Washington Post, December 10, 1976.

Committee On Geological Sciences. The Earth and Human Affairs. San
    Francisco, California: Canfield Press, 1972.

Davis, S. N. and R. J. DeWeist. Hydrogeology. New York, John Wiley and
    Sons, Inc., 1966.

"Injection Wells to Be Regulated." Chemecology. Washington, D.C.:
    Manufacturing Chemists Association, October 1976.

Leet, L. D. and S. Judson. Physical Geology. Englewood Cliffs, New
    Jersey: Prentice-Hall, 1959

Leopold, Luna B. and Kenneth S. Davis. Water. New York: Time, Inc.,
    1966.

Linslev, R. K., et al. Hydrology for Engineers. New York: McGraw-Hill,
    1958.

Meinzer, O. E., ed. Hydrology. New York: McGraw-Hill, 1942.

Ohio Department of Natural Resources. Land Capability Analysis--the
    Wolf Creek Project. Columbus, Ohio: ODNR, Planning Services
    Section, Division of Planning, February 1974.

Ohio Department of Natural Resources. Minimum Criteria for the Regulation
    of Ohio Flood Plains. Columbus, Ohio: ODNR, Flood Plain Manage-
    ment Section, March 1973.

Omohundro, William. "Interceptors and Suburban Sprawl." Environment
    Midwest. September-October 1976.

Penman, H. L. "The Water Cycle." The Biosphere. San Francisco: W. H.
    Freeman, 1970.

Reid, Frank. "Drinking Water Quality Regulations: Measuring, Monitoring,
    and Managing." Water and Sewage Works, 123, No. 6 (June 1976).

"Scientists Drilling in Floor of Atlantic for Fresh Water." Environment
    News, October 1976.

CHAPTER SEVEN

WATER POLLUTION SOURCES

A PERSPECTIVE

The Merrimack River rises in the White Mountains of
New Hampshire and drains 5,000 square miles of New
England until it flows into the Atlantic at Newbury-
port, Massachusetts. In 1965 it was thoroughly polluted. That it has recovered somewhat is a tribute to
the resiliency of natural systems, the effectiveness
of the EPA's enforcement and regulations, and the
concern and hard work of local and state officials.

The river once supported a fishing industry, but in
1965 the average dissolved oxygen level was below
the level required by most species for propagation.
The coarse fish that survived were tainted with oils,
phenols, and dyes. Waste solids covered the river
bottom destroying plant and macroinvertebrate animal life.

Recreation was hazardous. In 1964 not one town on
the main stream of the Merrimack treated its wastes.
Downriver of several of these, total coliform levels
exceeded 1,000,000 colonies per 100 ml. of water.
The river carried high concentrations of topical
pesticides and exotic wastes such as cyanide. In
summer the river ran black or black tainted with the
particular variety of industrial waste currently
predominant. An article reported, "Oil slicks, grease
balls, black oozing sludge, fecal debris, and condoms
float by on top of the stream."

The Merrimack still served as the drinking water source
for the towns which fed their raw wastes into her
waters. Sudsy water ran from faucets--the ammonia
level was so high as to reduce the effectiveness of
chlorine treatment. At times the taste and color of
the water made it undrinkable. As early as 1887 the
Massachusetts Department of Public Health had recommended
against using the river for drinking water.

By tremendous margins the communities consistently
defeated bond issues for sewerage plant construction
(37,166 to 5,087 in Lowell in 1947). Federal involvement was initiated by Governor Endicott Peabody, but
vehemently contested by municipalities and industry.

A city solicitor attested: "I have been delegated by the
city manager of the City of Lowell, by a vote of the City
Council, to oppose any action . . . which would require
the expenditure of money by the City of Lowell" (for sewerage plant construction).

Even the chairman of the Nashua River Committee claimed
that" . . . it cannot be said that the use of the River
by Massachusetts paper mills endangers the health of
persons living in either Massachusetts or New Hampshire."

A newspaper editorial argued, "Purification is in the
class of . . . an ermine coat, something nice to have
but something we don't need."

This was 1965.

Leonard Wolf, "Cleaning up the
Merrimack," Bulletin of the
Scientists (April, 1965)

Report on Pollution of the Merrimack
River and Certain Tributaries (US
Department of the Interior, Federal
Water Pollution Administration,
August 1966)

Water Pollution--What Is It?

As we saw in Chapter 6, the distribution of water on land is a function
of watershed geology, form, and location. And the nature of that water
is the momentary consequence of its time and history within the watershed.

Surface waters include a wide range of types and concentrations of
non-aqueous matter. This matter's constituents may be living or dead,
harmful or beneficial, simple or complex, filtrable or non-filtrable, hot
or cold, many or few, constant or changing--in short, endlessly varied.
Water is polluted if plant and animal life in the ecosystem is harmed by
the substances in the water. What is pollution for one body of water, however, is not necessarily pollution for another. Salt from icy roads may
pollute a narrow, shallow stream, but not a wide, deep one--when the amount
of salt flowing to both of them is the same. The difference is a relative
one that asks us to consider: How healthy is the life already in the
streams? How fast do the waters flow? What other factors do they share or
differ in? Our natural waters contain soil, leaves, and animal wastes.
These are natural to the water, but if there is too much of any, pollution
results. Natural waters can take in some fertilizers, some city sewage, but
if the concentration of any of these is too much or the chemistry too
foreign for life in the ecosystem, then we have pollution.

Therefore, the concept of pollution applies to a system that is above or below its natural character or state. A statement about pollution is made independently for each body of water because each is unique.

For 3,000,000,000 years now watersheds have received water, and water has received foreign substances. The winds and rains over millions of years brought it dust, grasses, twigs, leaves, salts, hair, and bones. The plant and animal populations (biotic setting), multiplying in enormous numbers but with minute generational genetic changes, faced the unique environment in each stream. The caddisfly larvae cemented pebbles, sticks, or other material into a little house in which they survived the hail of sediment passing downstream. The protozoa that haplessly fell victim to an invasion of photosynthesizing bacteria collectively produced enough oxygen to survive in the unaerated waters. The tiny worm that bored into the dorsal aorta of a polychaete worm remained untouched by predators. Each survivor in his own way struggled against these forbidding environments and came to terms with them. The outcome is what we call the intricate "web of nature."

Over time and distance, the stream's adjoining lands became more heavily used, first as forests, then as farmlands, next as homesites, and finally for cities and industries. Correspondingly, the quantities of natural matter increased. The ratio of their mix shifted. The introduction of substances with new, synthetic compositions began. These changes, which took place very rapidly from an evolutionary perspective, greatly affected the surface waters. The impact caused changes in the stream that were substantially unlike those of its multi-million year prehistory. The factors of change are different <u>quantities</u> of the natural materials and different <u>qualities</u> of unnatural materials. Altogether, the natural and unnatural materials are pollutants.

Pollutants that enter the waterways from many and various sources, such as cropland sedimentation and urban stormwater, are designated by the EPA as "non-point source pollutants." Those discharged by pipe or other means from identified sources of known function, such as pickling acid from a steel plant or hot water from an atomic power plant, are designated as "point source pollutants." These classifications arose from the need to distinguish among kinds of pollutants and to arrive at means to control each. The EPA reports that 60% of <u>all</u> pollution is non-point; 40% is point source pollution.

A later chapter presents the history which led to a legislative permit program for point sources (the National Pollutant Discharge Elimination System, or the NPDES Permit System), but no such system exists for non-point sources. Point sources were believed to be more easily regulated by practical controls, whereas non-point sources would be less so. In fact, that conclusion is one reason why this manual was written and is the principal reason for its emphasis on non-point water pollution--that local officials will plan implementable procedures to reduce non-point pollution.

Non-Point Pollution

We have already established that the watershed is the underlying system that governs non-point pollution. Further, we know that the watershed has a predictable capacity for processing known pollutants--such as sediments, nutrients, acid rains--and that it is a very <u>inexpensive</u> "treatment plant" to run.

An appropriate non-point pollution control plan must seek to prevent excessive loadings on any one component of the system. It is helpful, then, to look first at the system as a whole--a lifeline--in order to recognize the limits of stress which can be applied to its "knots."

The types of pollutants which enter streams and lakes from non-point sources include, but are not limited to, these categories and examples: sediments (bits of rock, dirt, minerals); organic nutrients (farmlot manure, artificial fertilizers, plant and animal remains); oils and greases (street washings, marine wastes, spills); dissolved solids and gases (highway salts, acids and bases, carbon dioxide, sulfur dioxide); organics (PCBs, PBBs, DDT, Endrin, Lindane); inorganics (nitrates, phosphates, arsenic, lead, mercury); and biota (algae, bacteria, viruses); radioactivity (fallout from atomic testing), and others. The list could be very long, particularly if unnaturally occurring chemicals were included. One chemical company alone sells 50,000 different chemical compounds; their release and resulting random recompounding in the natural environment--as with photochemical smog--could increase the list substantially.

Sources of Non-point Pollution

To identify different types and quantities of non-point pollution, the Federal Water Pollution Act (Public Law 92-500) in Section 208 requires the U.S. EPA Administrator (1) to provide guidelines for identifying and evaluating the nature and extent of non-point sources of pollutants, and (2) to provide processes, procedures, and methods to control pollution resulting from:

1. agricultural and silvicultural activities, including runoff from fields and crop and forest lands:

2. mining activities, including runoff and siltation from new, currently operating, and abandoned surface and underground mines;

3. all construction activity, including runoff from the facilities resulting from such construction;

4. the disposal of pollutants in wells or in subsurface excavations;

5. salt water intrusion resulting from reductions of freshwater
    flow from any cause, including extraction of ground water,
    irrigation, obstruction, and diversion; and

6. changes in the movement, flow, or circulation of any navigable
    waters or groundwaters, including changes caused by the construc-
    tion of dams, levees, channels, causeways, or flow diversion
    facilities.

Of all the pollution resulting from these 6 sources, 50% is sediment--
fragmented rocks, soil, and litter. Chemical, physical, and biological
mechanisms originate and transport the sediment, but in each geographic
location, variety of sedimentation is a function of the watershed.

The sources of streamwater sediment identified in an EPA research
project were ranked as follows, from highest to lowest volume of contribution:

1. cropland

2. gullies

3. residential and commercial construction

4. highway construction

5. poorly managed range, and idle and wooded areas

6. unstable streambanks

7. surface mining areas

8. unstabilized roadbanks

9. bare areas of non-cropland

The first-ranked use--cropland--accounts for one half of all stream
sediment, or 25% of the nation's total stream pollution. Since this is
the largest identifiable non-point source pollutant, and since the
principles revealed over years of control application are essentially
useful for most of the other categories, we have chosen to concentrate
on that one source.

Actual cropland conditions differ on each farm, and less significantly
with each crop. The amounts of soil lost as sediments always have
concerned farmers, for the crop yield and economic gain or loss is
linked directly to soil depth and quality. Therefore, the motivations

have been simple and the actions direct in the farmers' efforts to reduce soil loss. Their success should be an example to others whose activities cause sedimentation problems.

Erosion by rain can be controlled best by leaving or growing cover on fields. In fact, one new farming theory advocates no tilling at all. No-till farming means no plowing or harrowing, and sowing by injection. This leaves the prior crop's post-harvest debris as cover for the soil, protecting it from erosion by wind and rain. One study of no-till farming in Coshocton, Ohio, reports reduction of sediment loads by 25%. However, at another Ohio location, no-tilling on very flat fields in some cases reduced seed germination frequency. There are many experimental projects to investigate the advantages and disadvantages of no-till methods.

Velocity of cropland runoff has been steadily reduced through the tried, proven, and now common principles of contouring, terracing, and strip planting of grass plots or other close cover. These formations interrupt the overland flow of water, permitting sediment to settle and water to be retained to infiltrate the soils to underground waters.

The total volume of sediment is, of course, reduced through use of soil cover and reduction of velocity of runoff, but even that which is washed loose can be restrained. Where it is obvious that heavy rains will flow over the terraces and strips, grass waterways--rather than gouged out channels or gullies--are used, and grass filter strips will strain out some of the soil. These waterways and strips are not as easily eroded as exposed channels and gullies are. Finally, since most farms have ponds for one purpose or another, they can be located to allow the ponds to serve also as sediment retention basins. Such a basin is a costly abatement practice, but variations of dammed depressions and excavations can be employed to slow the eroding waters, settle out their loads, and prevent both from running onward to the nearby stream.

Since pollutants are associated with the sediments, there is a multiple benefit in halting soil erosion. Since fertilizers, pesticides, and herbicides may adhere to soil particles, soil-retention will simultaneously keep the desired chemicals where they can do the most good--on the crops. Application of chemicals on frozen ground or before predictably high rainfall portends their probable loss to the cropland and their subsequent transport to surface waters.

Pastureland, by contrast, does not produce as much sedimentation as cropland. This is particularly true in the northeastern states, less so in the western ones. Much pasturage, in particular that under federal ownership, is severely overgrazed. Once stripped of vegetation, it is incapable of retaining water, is exposed to the wind, and then quickly erodes. The federal government controls 31% of the nation's rangeland, some

373,000,000 acres. The Bureau of Land Management in 1975 described 28%
of this total as follows: "Range in poor condition has lost so much
vegetative cover and topsoil that it produces only a fraction of the
forage grown on similar sites in fair, good, or excellent condition.
Few of the more valuable perennial plants remain. Only 2% of BLM's
total rangeland is in 'excellent condition.'" Since rangeland, unlike
cropland, is not regularly worked, there is little alternative to erosion
control, except to reduce the numbers of livestock per acre of land,
especially land in borderline condition. This is easy to recommend, but
difficult to finance and regulate.

Feedlot operations, where large numbers of stock are herded for
pre-market fattening, concentrate the harmful effects of overgrazing,
soil disruption, and nutrient production. If nutrients enter surface
waters or penetrate to underground waters, contamination of both resources
is inevitable. The U.S. EPA has now designated all feedlots for 1,000
cattle or more as point sources of pollution, requiring NPDES controls.
All smaller lots are considered non-point sources. Feedlot waste can be
drained, treated, and stored in lagoons where bacteria can digest it.

Several of the 9 major sources of non-point sedimentation involve
the removal or destruction of rooted vegetation, which exposes the soil
to erosion. In highly developed construction sites, some of the soils
are highly unstable, due to their slope and composition. The Los Angeles
hillside housing developments are well-known case histories:

In 1950, Metropolitan Los Angeles had no flat, open
land left. With little understanding of the geology,
drainage, or soil conditions, housing developers
turned to the hillsides. They followed standard flat-
land building practices, and moved millions of cubic
yards of earth in the standard cut-and-fill fashion.

The rains came, and houses that had perched picturesquely
in June, tilted precariously in January. Broken pipes,
cracks, and tumbled chimneys became commonplace for
these home owners. With each rainy season more and
more houses slid downhill on the shifting, sliding soil
on which they had been built.

By 1963, regulations were implemented which governed
grading, density restrictions, and consultation with
engineering-geologists before building. In February 1969
Los Angeles County received the heaviest rainfall in 85
years. Of the 11,000 sites developed since 1963, damage
was limited to a total of $182,000. Sites developed
before the regulations suffered damages of more than
$6,300,000.

Precautions can be taken to abate sedimentation after construction has started. For example, runoff entering the site can be diverted around the exposed area. Vegetative wind and rain buffers and plateaus can be left before clearing ground or established afterward. In both cases, grass cover rather than earth-exposed gullies will slow runoff velocity and will filter particulates. Erosion checks--hay bales, sand bags, small dams, etc., as in farmland retention--are simple, inexpensive, and in some applications reusable. Final grading and revegetation can include covering the seeded areas with sawdust or wood chip mulch, jute and fiberglass netting, or seeding an area by hydrospraying with a mixture of seed, water, and fine mulch. Two guidelines for construction site rehabilitation are 1) to minimize the exposure time of uncovered soil and 2) to restore the water retention capability of the soil to no less than what it was before construction began.

In-stream Sources of Non-point Pollution

Let's consider now several sources of in-stream, non-point pollution: dams and impoundments, channelization, and dredging. The nature of their influence on surface water quality is abstracted from EPA's Impact of Hydrology Modifications on Water Quality.

Construction of dams and impoundments generally is done under dry conditions after diverting the stream to a temporary bed. This type of construction affects water quality in ways similar to those of highway construction: high sediment loss from exposed subsoil, washings from concrete mixing and finishing operations, etc. Of greater and longer-term impact, however, is the post-construction effect. Dams and impoundments modify downstream waters by several mechanisms:

1. Trapping and retaining sediment behind the dam--this alters the established downstream sedimentary equilibrium (e. g., a sharp reduction in organic nutrients for normal stream nutrients); if later the sediment is dredged out (see dredging, below), then the shock-loading again adversely affects aquatic life downstream.

2. Thermal stratification--layering by temperature, density, and chemical and biological makeup introduces a different orientation of stream conditions, again modifying the established ecosystem.

3. Decomposition of trapped organic material--accumulated products of decomposition take dissolved oxygen from the water.

4. Nitrogen saturation--violent mixing of air and water released from turboelectric generators or in high velocity tailwash causes the water to become supersaturated with atmospheric nitrogen; this condition kills fish downstream.

5. Surface evaporation--the large, relatively warm surface area of impounded water permits rapid evaporation, thus increasing the concentration of salts and other dissolved and suspended constituents in the impounded water.

Channelization and stabilization of channels for drainage, irrigation, and stream realignment cause severe erosion, mostly around the Great Lakes and in coastal areas where 77% of the 20,000 miles of existing channel modifications are concentrated in ten states. The coastal states suffer the greatest known damage by sedimentation of estuarine areas. This adversely alters the survival rates of young fish and other aquatic life in these rich breeding areas.

Dredging activities (removal, lifting, or disposal) resuspend or redissolve some of the polluting materials accumulated on the waterbody bottom. If disposal is on land, then the pollutants have an opportunity to enter the groundwater. Annual dredging volume is about 400,000,000 cubic yards and is increasing. Most of this takes place near densely populated areas; therefore, high-impact potential is concomitant. The types of pollutants released are primarily sediments, but this can vary with every situation. (For case histories see the EPA reports.)

Other Sources

Lumbering and mining practices initiate many of the same sequences of problems that lead to high stream-loadings. The general correctives which help farmers and contractors to reduce sedimentation apply here as well. One controversial practice of miners and lumberers--clear-cutting, as opposed to selective-cutting of trees--can also be planned and conducted so that erosion is slight. Using cropland control principles, a deliberately placed tangle of small brush, branches, and horizontal trees on a cleared slope act as thousands of tiny check dams, holding moisture and soil until primary vegetation succeeds. In fact, much helpful vegetation flourishes in these sunny areas.

Haulways are also a major cause of erosion. Arranging them in contours at low elevation helps to abate it. Surface mining exposes bare soils to weathering conditions, and it places extracted overburden-- the material lying between the surface and the resource deposit--where precipitation can dissolve its minerals and transport them to the surface and subsurface water systems. Although the principles of drainage and land restoration are appropriate, they are difficult to enforce. Many states, particularly those where drainage from surface mining is blatant (Ohio, Illinois, Iowa, Tennessee, and Kentucky) have passed mined land reclamation laws which require that the land be returned to the original contour or better and be revegetated.

However, a serious problem lies in the nature of the laws governing mining--the Mining Law of 1872 and the Mineral Leasing Act of 1920. They limit the federal government's control over mineral development on its own land. The first law allows virtually anyone staking a claim to gold, silver, iron, copper, lead, bauxite, zinc, tungsten, and uranium to take possession of the land upon mining it. The 1920 Act applies to coal, onshore oil and gas, oil shale, phosphates, potassium, sodium, and asphalt. It provides for a sharing of returns with the federal and state government for public benefit. But, there are no environmental provisions in either law. Subsequent regulations, especially in coal mining, have been prepared, but in 1974 and 1975 laws with provisions for the environmental standards were vetoed by the President. He believed they would restrict coal production and employment; hence, mining operations persist as non-point pollution sources.

Underground mining operations which discharge polluted water from water-extraction processes are considered point sources. Unregulated, the overburdened soils, like those from surface mining, are dumped in piles of mine-tailing from which minerals are leached. These large-grained materials are not conducive to growing vegetation and so are placed behind a dam, covered with soil, and then seeded.

Domestic septic tanks, leach fields, cess pools, and similar household treatment facilities should not be a problem. However, when located in permeable soils, below or near the water table, or in groundwater recharge areas, they can contaminate surface and subsurface resources. Clearly, the number of tanks which can safely be placed in a given area depends on the geology--soil type, slope assimilative capacity of the soil--as well as the efficiency of the septic tanks.

Before tank installation, soil permeability can be tested by placing water into a hole and measuring the time required for it to percolate from the hole into the soil. Permeability then can be predicted by examining Soil Conservation Service maps as well as by having the SCS investigate and assess the site. Soil borings and percolation tests are generally required before issuing a building permit, particularly in high density, lowland areas. These tests should be conducted at the time of year when the water table is at its highest. High water tables can cause septic tank overflow. Flooded soils cannot "treat" the wastes; instead they permit nutrients and potentially hazardous microorganisms to enter subsurface water which may be used for drinking.

Solid Waste Leachates

Sanitary landfill leachates are a severe and vexing source of pollution. Sanitary landfills are planned excavations, filled with solid waste, compacted, and covered with soil. By definition, all these steps must be taken within 24 hours of each fill. The covering soil should be impervious clay and silt. The overall site is graded both to divert external flow from the site and to minimize internal flow. Theoretically, landfills are excavated above impermeable soils at least ten feet above the water table. Since each 24-hour cell is sealed, ideally no leaching into surface or groundwaters should occur. It does. Wastes, including "hazardous materials" (such as PCBs, Kepone, pesticides, mercury compounds and lead paints, fluorocarbons, vinyl chlorides, asbestos, etc.) are contained in the cells. Many of these chemicals are long-lived and must be prohibited from entering the atmosphere or ground-waters for a long and unknown period of time. Rigid controls and monitoring are <u>sine</u> <u>qua</u> <u>non</u> companions of effective solid waste management. The key to control is sound planning and constant enforcement of regulations.

The best hope, however, is that solid waste landfills can become obsolete. Waste source reduction, recycling, and conversion to other useful forms, usually by pyrolysis, are the present means of prevention, control, and treatment.

Source reduction, by legislative banning or taxing of nonreturnable beverage containers has been introduced in 50 state legislatures and numerous county and city councils since 1971. As of mid-1975, Oregon, Vermont, and South Dakota have laws restricting beer and soft drink containers, and Minnesota has a law affecting all major types of packaging wastes. Oregon reported these results after its 4-year ban on nonreturnable beverage containers:

- Beverage container litter has been decreased by an estimated 66%.

- Beer and soft drink sales are unchanged.

- Beer and soft drink prices are lower on the average than previously.

- Job losses have occurred in the container manufacturing and canning industries.

- Jobs have been created in the brewing, soft drink, and retail sectors of the economy.

Recycling has not proved effective in the last few years because there are many disincentives to the recycling of scrap, including lower taxes, tariffs, and freight rates for virgin over scrap materials. However, environmental quality and energy conservation are two powerful incentives encouraging use of recycled matter. The National Commission on Materials Policy in its interim report of April 1972 states, "Secondary processing-- i.e., recycling of materials after end-use and reclamation of waste prior to end-use--plays a major role in attaining both goals of enhancing environmental quality and conserving materials for more effective utilization of our natural resources." In a report adapted from an article in

Environmental Science and Technology, author Howard Ness reported that at a hearing of the Economic Committee of Congress to identify the restraints and impediments to expanded recycling, the Committee was told that inequitable federal tax policies are the chief barrier. Present tax policies provide economic encouragement for continued and expanded use of primary or virgin products to the direct economic disadvantage of recycled material. Tax policies should be changed, the Committee said, to:

- provide manufacturers a realistic incentive factor for utilizing more recycled materials through a recycling tax deduction or credit;

- encourage new and expanded plant investment in recycling facilities and equipment through rapid write-off and amortization of such investments;

- provide a basis for expanding research and development activities by industrial firms capable of recovering recycled materials.

Discriminatory freight rates on recycled materials discourage the use of them, since rates are as much as 50% higher than those for comparable primary or virgin materials. Changes in these rates could encourage the use of recyclable waste products. Revised government procurement policies, too, could specify either (1) the use of scrap in manufactured products, or (2) revising certain state product performance standards, which might compel the use of scrap, rather than compel the use of virgin materials. Such practices will stimulate the demand for products containing recycled paper, metals, and plastics. Demand for recyclable wastes is now essential to open the economic door to the supply of them.

Many towns, cities, and even the federal government have licensing, zoning, and tariff ordinances that also diminish the potential flow-through of scrap. Municipalities, for example, may zone and license scrap dealers and processors out of business. The federal government places an export tax on overseas scrap shipment; such tax is but another hurdle in the supply/demand system. However, in some situations local, state, and federal governments have cooperated in planning and establishing waste recovery systems. Some of these recovery systems are discussed in Chapter 12.

Nationwide, there are numerous municipal waste recovery systems in operation. Other systems are underway, and 20 communities are actively preparing to install more recovery systems. Currently, nationwide, about 6% of these wastes are being recovered. Most systems concentrate on energy recovery, either by producing steam for off-site use, or oil and gas from pyrolitic waste conversion or by feeding the waste directly to utility boilers—a practice in Connecticut.

The Connecticut Resources Recovery Authority plans ten facilities that will process 84% of the state's waste by 1985. These are energy recovery facilities that principally will prepare municipal wastes for use as fuel in utility boilers, while separating the unburnable residue for possible recycling. A later chapter discusses waste as a source of supplementary energy.

Some of the most severe non-point problems are associated with those toxic and hazardous pollutants produced as by-products of unusual industrial processes, or from mine tailings, and from agricultural residues such as pesticides, herbicides, fungicides, heavy metals, and other toxic and hazardous substances. The U.S. Government's efforts to abate or totally eliminate toxic and hazardous pollution can be traced historically in legislation: in 1910 a pesticide control law; in 1954, the Atomic Energy Act; in 1970, the Clean Air Act; in 1972, the Pesticide Control Act, the Ocean Dumping Act, and the Federal Water Pollution Control Act; in 1974, the Safe Drinking Water Act and, effective January 1, 1977, the Toxic Substances Control Act.

Under the 1972 Federal pesticides law, application of some 81 pesticide ingredients--out of the 1,400 now in thousands of farm and non-farm pesticides--will be limited to certified farmers and commercial applicators. Certification requires an EPA-approved, state-administered program on the safe handling, use, and storage of potentially hazardous pesticides. The new Toxic Substances Control Law (in which pesticides are not considered toxic substances for regulatory purposes) concentrates on preventing dangers that can result from producing a new toxic substance. Before production can commence, manufacturers will have to furnish information for review by the EPA regarding the composition, production, use, disposal, and effects of a new substance, according to the February 1977 Environment Midwest, Region V, magazine of the U.S. EPA. Together, these Acts move toward control of existing and anticipated future non-point source pollutants.

However, it is the disposal of wastes containing these materials that is the non-point problem. How can we prevent those chemicals, which are already buried in and leaching through sanitary landfills, from entering the nation's waterways and estuaries, and eventually the world's biosphere?

CHAPTER SUMMARY

1. The distribution of water on land is a function of watershed geology, form, and location; the nature of that water is the momentary consequence of its time and history within the watershed.

2. Judgements about pollution are made on the basis of the prior and present health of organisms in the water and of those that use it less directly. Varied factors--whether waters are moving or still, eutrophying or not, recovering from previous natural or man-made pollutants--determine water's carrying capacity to withstand and to recover from pollution.

3. Non-point pollution is the broad spectrum of contaminants from many diffused sources: the sediments, fertilizers, rural and urban stormwater runoff. Non-point sources comprise 60% of the nation's water pollution.

4. The Federal Water Pollution Control Act requires the U. S. EPA to provide guidelines to identify and evaluate the nature and extent of non-point pollution sources and to provide processes, procedures, and methods for controlling pollution from 1) agriculture and silviculture; 2) mining and related activities; 3) all construction activity; 4) disposal of pollutants in wells; 5) salt water intrusion; 6) changes in water movements caused by dams, levees, and other construction.

5. Cropland erosion causes 50% of all stream sedimentation. Sedimentation is 25% of all U. S. stream pollution. Fertilizers, pesticides, and other matter accompanying cropland sedimentation further pollute the water.

6. Major sources of in-stream non-point pollution are dams, impoundments, channelization, and dredging. The first two pollute via trapping and retaining sediments, by causing thermal stratification, by decomposition of trapped organic material, by nitrogen saturation, and by surface evaporation. Channelization and stabilization contribute pollution especially to estuarine waters; dredging resuspends or redissolves much bottom-polluting matter.

7. Other serious non-point pollution sources include lumbering, mining, clear-cutting, and other planned and unplanned erosion-conducive processes. Haulways also contribute to severe erosion of soil. Domestic septic tanks, leach fields, cess pools, and similar uses of impermeable soils often cause water table pollution. Sanitary landfill leachates due to broken covering soils or permeable underlying ones also contribute to soil and water pollution.

8. Legislative efforts to control solid waste pollution are exemplified by Oregon's prohibition on non-returnable containers. Oregon's findings after its 4-year ban are: beverage container litter decreased by 66%; beer and soft drink sales went unchanged; beer and soft drink prices are lower on the average than previously; job losses have occurred in the container manufacture and canning industries; jobs have been created in brewing, soft drink, and retail sectors of the economy.

9. To encourage recycling, to preserve resources, and to abate pollution, the Economic Committee of Congress recommended the following tax policies: give manufacturers a realistic incentive for using recycled material by introducing a tax deduction or credit for recycling; encourage new and expanded plant investment in recycling facilities and equipment via rapid write-off or amortization of such investments; provide a basis for expanding research and development activities by industry capable of recovering recycled materials.

SOURCES

Council on Environmental Quality. Environmental Quality—1975: The Sixth Annual Report of the Council on Environmental Quality. Washington, D. C.: GPO, 1975.

National Academy of Sciences. The Earth and Human Affairs. New York, N.Y.: Canfield Press, 1972.

Ness, Howard. "Recycling as an Industry." Solid Waste. Menlo Park, Calif.: Addison-Wesley Publishing Co., 1975.

Penman, H.L. "The Water Cycle," The Biosphere. San Francisco, Calif.: W.H. Freeman, 1970.

U.S. Environmental Protection Agency. Impact of Hydrologic Modifications on Water Quality. Washington, D.C.: Office of Research and Development, April 1975.

Loading Functions for Assessment of Water Pollution From Non-Point Sources. Washington, D.C.: GPO, 1976.

_____. Management of Nutrients on Agricultural Land for Improved Water Quality. Washington, D.C.: GPO, 1971.

_____. Methods for Identifying and Evaluating the Nature of Non-Point Sources of Pollutants. Washington, D.C.: GPO, 1973.

_____. Pollution of Subsurface Water by Sanitary Landfills. Washington, D.C.: GPO, 1971.

_____. Processes, Procedures, and Methods to Control Pollution Resulting From All Construction Activity. Washington, D.C.: GPO, 1973.

_____. Processes, Procedures, and Methods to Control Pollution From Mining Activities. Washington, D.C.: GPO, 1973.

_____. Public Law 92-500, 92nd Congress, S. 2770, Federal Water Pollution Control Act Amendments of 1972. Washington, D.C.: GPO, October 18, 1972.

_____. Toward Cleaner Water: The New Permit Program to Control Water Pollution. Washington, D.C.: GPO, 1974.

CHAPTER EIGHT

WATER, STREAM BIOLOGY, AND POLLUTION

A <u>PERSPECTIVE</u>

The degree to which we are all involved in the control
of the earth's life is just beginning to dawn on most
of us, and it means another revolution for human
thought.

This will not come easily. We've just made our way
through inconclusive revolutions on the same topic,
trying to make up our minds how we feel about nature.
As soon as we arrive at one kind of consensus, like an
enormous committee, we found it was time to think it
through all over, and now here we are, at it again.

The oldest, easiest-to-swallow idea was that the earth
was man's personal property, a combination of garden,
zoo, bank vault, and energy source, placed at our
disposal to be consumed, ornamented, or pulled apart
as we wished. The betterment of mankind was, as we
understood it, the whole point of the thing. Mastery
over nature, mystery and all, was a moral duty and
social obligation.

In the last few years we were wrenched away from this
way of looking at it, and arrived at something like
general agreement that we had it wrong. We still
argue the details, but it is conceded almost everywhere that we are not the masters of nature that we
thought ourselves; we are as dependent on the rest
of life as are the leaves or midges or fish. We
are part of the system. One way to put it is that
the earth is a loosely formed, spherical organism,
with all its working parts linked in symbiosis.
We are, in this view, neither owners nor operators;
at best, we might see ourselves as motile tissue
specialized for receiving information--perhaps, in
the best of all possible worlds, functioning as a
nervous system for the whole being.

Lewis Thomas, <u>The Lives of A Cell</u>

We are going to follow the course of a brook which begins in the mountains and eventually wends its way to the ocean. Our main concern is the life that first makes its modest start in that brook and what life is added to it or taken away as it joins other brooks that later form a stream. We will consider why certain life forms carry on through a range of water conditions; why the essential chemical processes in the stream require certain basic ingredients if they are going to take place, let alone succeed in balancing the life of the stream. Along the way we will wander a bit more than that stream does, recalling some information we may have forgotten and anticipating a good deal more we'll have to learn if we are to understand why certain life, simple or complex in form, is in good or frail health. Since all life systems touch, the health of one may be a measure of the health or future health of the others. Let's begin once again with earth, water, and air.

Water Temperature, Flow, and Dissolved Oxygen

In a mountain brook, white water foams over rocks in miniature waterfalls, each bubble exchanging oxygen between air and water. Through these rapids the water acquires more oxygen than it can hold. In this supersaturated state its dissolved oxygen count is 11 ppm. The temperature of the water 12° C.   This physical interaction between air and water is one of the most meaningful phenomena in nature, for the dissolved oxygen (DO) level directly affects water quality. The amount of oxygen available to aquatic plants and animals alone can determine the kind and variety of life in a stream. DO level influences water quality, and water temperature influences the dissolved oxygen level. As temperatures rise, oxygen is driven off. At 1°C, water can hold 14 ppm; at 30°C it can hold only 7.6 ppm.

Because dissolved oxygen plays a crucial role in determining water quality, let's consider briefly how one can test the DO level. Having done so, we'll return to the brook to follow its path with a better sense of what knowledge we need to assess water quality:

The test for dissolved oxygen is called a Winkler titration. Three chemicals are added to a known volume of water carefully collected to preserve the in-stream oxygen content. The chemicals cause release of iodine equivalent to the amount of oxygen.

The iodine then can be titrated with a known concentration of sodium thiosulfate. The amount of titrant used is equivalent to the iodine released, which is equivalent to the oxygen concentration. The amount of oxygen is expressed in milligrams of oxygen per liter of water, mg/1 or parts per million, ppm.

Returning to the headwaters of the mountain brook, we find the temperature is cold and the dissolved oxygen content high, but the brook is moving too fast for animal life to survive unless it clings to the under surface of the rocks. Here the velocity of the water is 4 feet per second--as fast as the water will flow in its long trip to the ocean. Occasionally a rock slips and rolls downstream, breaking loose in the current dozens of macroinvertebrates. Mayfly and stonefly nymphs, riffle beetle larvae, flatworms, and caddisfly larvae with their distinctive food-catching nets float downstream to quieter waters.

Life in the Stream

Behind larger rocks the first fish appear, darters. Unlike other fish, they are heavier than water and are able to survive the torrent. The brook deepens. The descent becomes less steep and the water slows slightly. Here in the riffle areas we find the most productive part of the brook. The water is clear, allowing photosynthesis to occur, and the large rocks allow a stable environment of numerous niches where insects can strain their food from the water. There are many different kinds of plants and animals, each an evolutionary adaptation to a special environment. There are other kinds of caddisfly larvae here which build cases of tiny pebbles. Thousands of black fly larvae hug the undersides of rocks, and microscopic browsers feed on the algae and mosses. Pools in the brook provide habitat for dragon fly nymphs and brook trout. These pools also offer additional shelter for other fish and support a rich assortment of benthic organisms. As the brook flattens toward the valley it links with other brooks and spreads out. Now water striders and frogs join the animal and plant life, most of which had existed upstream.

Now let's consider a different situation. Another brook, smaller than this started in a watershed that had been forested the year before. Heavy logging has left the hillside along the brook exposed, so that the waters run turbid with silt and clay. Light penetrated the water, but the suspended particles there concentrated the sun's energy, raising the water temperature and lowering the dissolved oxygen level. Since the sunlight couldn't reach the submerged photosynthesizing green plants, oxygen levels fell even further below that needed by most organisms to live. Even some of the complex life was affected: heavy suspended particles abraded the sensitive gills of fish, killing them. And then, as the stream slowed, these particles settled over an entire benthic community, smothering it. The dead plants and animals then washed downstream with the lighter particles of silt and clay.

When this tributary joined with our larger stream, its sediment and decomposing organic load mixed with the clear water. The combined streams flowed, broadening the valley where a glacial-aged river had left wide floodplains for farmland on either side of the stream. The land has been cultivated: non-point nutrients, pesticides, and soils washed from the farmlands into the waters.

As the combined flow of the two streams descends through the valley channel to the coastal plain, the Sun warms the sediments, heating the waters to 25°C. The volume of flow is greater even though the velocity is low, only 1 ft./sec. Some rapids provide niches for insect larvae, crayfish, nematodes, freshwater sponges, water mites, and rotifers. The deeper, slower waters house water spiders, hydras, bryozoans, tardigrades, and many other mostly unfamiliar bottom-dwelling organisms. Farmers channel water to their lands for irrigation, and an occasional dam provides quiet stretches where people living nearby come to fish and swim.

Downstream, a pipe draws off water for treatment before serving a city of 40,000 people. Alum flocculates the suspended solids; sandbeds filter finer particles; chlorine kills bacteria; then the water is pumped to a high storage tank. Each person uses about 80 gallons a day for drinking, washing dishes and clothes, showering and flushing, sprinkling lawns and washing cars, manufacturing, cooling, swimming, extinguishing fires--and then the water is returned to the stream.

This town is building a sewage treatment plant, but it will be another year until it is on-line. For the time being, raw sewage flows from a second pipe below the town directly into the stream. Figure 30 shows how sewage depresses the dissolved oxygen level, with a corresponding impact on plant and animal life in particular and water quality in general.

Nutrients from the sewage provide food for bacteria. And bacteria use oxygen, removing it from the water for their own biochemical activities: to make enzymes, with the enzymes to digest sewage, to synthesize new cell membranes and nucleic chemicals--in short to reproduce more cells of their own kind.

Directly below the sewage outfall there is an accumulation of sewage molds and sludge. This matter is made up of solids and usually a distinctive gray-white filamentous bacterium known as Sphaerotilus. It is an easily-identified bacterium whose presence indicates raw sewage.

The stream's nutrient load is digested slowly, and waste products settle out with the silt. The dissolved oxygen level slowly returns. The great hordes of leeches and bloodworms and other low-oxygen "sewage" life diminish; a greater diversity of life successively appears. As shown in Figure 31, the oxygen level was lowest 24 miles downstream, but is back to normal 70-100 miles beyond the discharge point. The recovery point can never precisely be known, particularly during the different seasons, since biochemical activity doubles with every 10°C rise in temperature. Decomposition is much faster in the summer months--consequently, the dissolved oxygen level rises much sooner.

Figure 30: *Sewage discharge depresses dissolved oxygen levels, increases turbidity, and affects health of invertebrates, plankton, and fish. Normal assimilative capacities reduce the pollutant loading, modifying harmful effects and restoring stream quality.*

Variations in activity occur during the day and night and on cloudy days. Sunlight is needed for photosynthesis; without it little oxygen is produced, so the bacteria use much of that available. Since the suspended solids and algae prevent light from reaching bottom chlorophyll-containing organisms, sunlight can only act on those close to the surface. Consequently, bottom organisms die and surface organisms "bloom." An algal bloom further depletes the dissolved oxygen; eventually the algae die as well.

There are over 20,000 individual kinds of algae. Of these, 260 are listed as "important to water supplies." The more common groups include diatoms, desmids, euglenoids, and green and blue algae. They are extremely efficient in converting the nutrients of sewage--i.e., phosphates and nitrates and some industrial wastes--into more algae. Certain algae link into strings and ropes--slime. They block drains and cooling systems, clog sand filters, corrode concrete and metal, and release noxious gases.

Biochemical Oxygen Demand

But algae also produce a lot of oxygen, releasing tiny, visible bubbles of it into the atmosphere during the daytime. Eventually the plants die and drift to the bottom where their bacterial decomposition requires great amounts of oxygen. The algae, like the sewage wastes, create a secondary demand on the oxygen load of the stream.

The uptake of oxygen is called "biochemical oxygen demand" (BOD). A 5-day test for it quantifies the oxygen removed from a sample of water by the biological and chemical "demands" made upon it. When oxygen is reduced to a level insufficient to support life, the BOD load is too great; the result is a septic or toxic stream condition. That level is different with each body of water; BOD has to be related to each stream's known assimilative capacity. Therefore, the sluggish stream with a BOD of 5 mg/l may be in danger of imbalance, while a larger, faster moving one with a BOD of 50 mg/l may not.

BOD is measured by comparing the difference in dissolved oxygen between a water sample on day 1 with a water sample which has been incubated at $20^{\circ}C$ on day 5. The oxygen depletion per volume of water sampled is the reported amount of BOD in that stream at that time, expressed in milligrams per liter.

(summarized from Standard Methods for Examination of Water and Wastewater)

The oxygen demand in our stream is approximately the same at night as during the daytime, but with little oxygen input at night, the dissolved oxygen level falls and is lowest before dawn. Samples taken on a sunny afternoon are, therefore, not a good indication of the stream health.

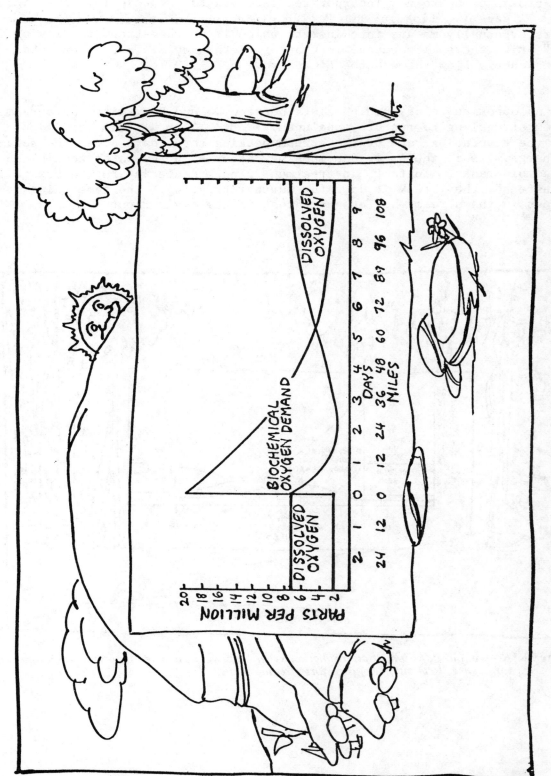

Figure 31: *Sewage inflow decreases the amount of dissolved oxygen in water, while increasing the amount of biochemical oxygen demand. About 60-72 miles downstream, recovering waters assimilate the pollution and return to nearly normal conditions.*

BOD can change from biochemical to biological form and become incorporated into potential BOD. This means that the organic wastes which were just broken down are now incorporated into plants and animals, "crawling BOD." Algae are "floating BOD." The sludge worms, mosquito larvae, and others eventually mature into insects which leave the stream as "flying BOD." Like the soil sequence in Chapter 6, the aquatic BOD is one phase of the energy flow through the biosphere.

An opposite relationship exists between DO and BOD, with the stream system struggling to restore a balance. Figure 32 shows both conditions, with the reaeration rate of the stream peaking three days after the sewage discharge. As in the soil, decomposing bacteria in the water accomplish incredible tasks. In fact, in treatment plants bacteria are the sewage "digesters"; they break it down for further treating. The same thing happens in the stream, but at great cost to the environment.

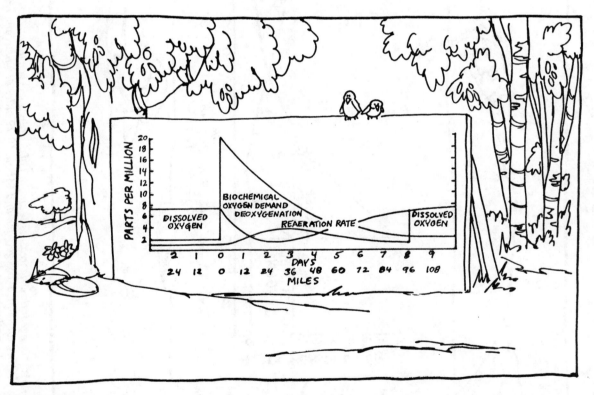

Figure 32: *Reaeration, diffusion of atmospheric oxygen into water, is aided by low temperatures and turbulence. Reaeration helps restore stream balance.*

Waterborne Bacteria: The Coliforms

   Bacteria are smaller by far than the cells of plants and animals. Reproducing exponentially, they are infinitely adaptable. And, there are about 1,500 different species: certain kinds exist in the soil, air, and water, while other kinds exist inside of us and all other animals. A few cause serious illness, but most are beneficial in their role of decomposers and recyclers of waste.

   One genus of bacteria, the coliforms, are found in large numbers in the intestines of warm-blooded animals. They pass with feces into stream-water, surviving briefly but not reproducing. Their presence suggests that potentially pathogenic gastroenteric organisms causing dysentery, typhoid, cholera, and other diseases also may be present.

   The numbers present of two kinds of coliforms give us one piece of information in determining the overall quality of the water. Although total coliforms are found in the water and serve as an official criterion of sanitary water quality, they are also found naturally in soil. In contrast, fecal coliforms occur only in the intestines of warm-blooded animals and do not survive for long outside of this environment. Thus, they are also an excellent indicator of recent fecal contamination of the water and are being used more as such by regulatory agencies.

   It is also possible to identify positively the "warm-blooded" animal that caused the contamination by testing for fecal streptococcus. The following chart shows that there exists a consistent ratio between fecal coliforms and fecal streptococci. Domestic animals and birds have more streptococci bacteria than fecal coliforms, but the opposite is true for man. By using this ratio it is possible to identify positively the source of the pollutant:

Average Indicator Density Per Gram of Feces

Animal	Fecal Coliform (Million)	Fecal Streptococci (Million)	Ratio FC/FS
Man	13.0	3.0	4.4
Sheep	16.0	38.0	0.4
Cow	0.23	1.3	0.2
Turkey	0.29	2.8	0.1
Pig	3.3	84.0	0.04

Data from Bureau of Water Hygiene, Environmental Protection Agency, Cincinnati, Ohio.

Total and fecal coliform and fecal streptococci concentration are determined in one of two ways:

A water sample is collected in a sterile bottle at a designated stream site. Later at the lab small quantities of the water are placed in test tubes containing nutrients for growth in a dilution series in which each successive tube has a fraction of the water sample in the one before it. The tubes are incubated at constant temperature for a fixed time. If bacteria are present in the water sample, they grow in numbers and, in decomposing the nutrient, produce gas. This gas is collected in small inverted tubes over the water sample. Eventually one tube will have no gas. That is the least fraction of water tested. The tube before is a count or number, such as 1/100th of the original sample. This figure expresses the numbers of bacteria present in the original stream water, in this case, if 10 ml were used, there was 1 bacterium in 1 /100th of 10 ml, or 10/100 ml.

Another procedure is to filter the water sample through a special membrane: The water passes through, leaving the bacteria trapped on the filter. The membrane is then placed on a pad soaked in nutrient. Incubated for a period of time, the bacteria reproduce, each one yielding a round colony, the totals of which can be counted by eye. The number of colonies represents the numbers of bacteria originally present in the sampled water. Bacteria are reported in both cases as the number per 100 milliliters of water.

Another bacterium found in water for drinking and recreation, <u>Pseudomonas</u> <u>aeruginosa</u>, can cause infections of the upper respiratory tract. It causes 50% of the eye, ear, nose, and throat infections related to water sports. Like the coliform and streptococcus, this organism is also used as a water quality indicator.

The <u>Diversity</u> Index

Figure 33 shows how bacteria grow in the presence of the hypothetical sewage discharge and also how they break the organic wastes into chemical nutrients.

Before such wastes were discharged into the clean waters above the city, aquatic life consisted of a great number of <u>different</u> species and not so many of any <u>one</u> species. This diversity is an indication of a healthy stream. At the point of sewage discharge, the number of different species is replaced by a different association of aquatic life. It is marked by significantly <u>fewer</u> species but a great number of <u>individuals</u> of each species, demonstrating a drastic change in the environment. The animals now present are adapted particularly to an environment with low oxygen and great accumulations of sludge and sediment. Figure 34 demonstrates this species diversity graphically. By examining organisms at various points along the

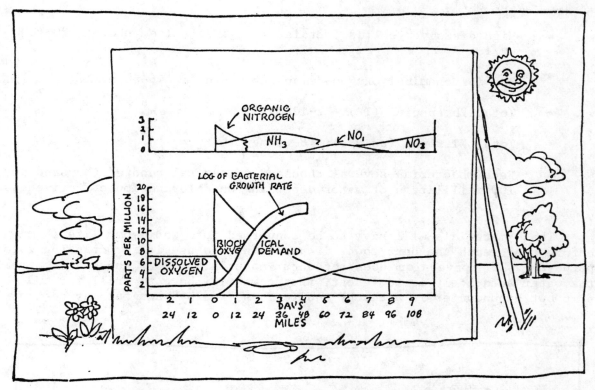

Figure 33: *At zero-point, sewage discharge provides nutrients for massive bacterial reproduction. DO level falls and BOD soars — nutrients are decomposed. Nearing 100 miles downstream, pre-pollution stability is restored.*

stream, it is possible to obtain a measure of diversity and present it as a number, a diversity index.

Since the animals in a stream spend much of their entire lives there, they are perhaps the best indication of the stream's health. A "slug" of chemicals can be discharged into a stream, killing certain sensitive life, and then flow downstream. A chemical test the day following would indicate that the water quality was good. A biological test such as the diversity index would give a much more accurate measure of the stream's health.

Pollutant Loads in a Stream

Even after the treatment plant for the city is completed, pollutants will still be discharged into the stream. The effectiveness of the treatment system will determine the load, but the levels probably would range from:

- High suspended solids (silt, dirt, organic particles, etc.): 20-600 mg/l;

- High dissolved solids (metals, inorganic salts, etc.): 20-1000 mg/l;

- BOD (biochemical oxygen-demanding wastes): 16-50 mg/l;

- Total Phosphorus (TP): 2-12 mg/l;

- Total Nitrogen (as NH_3): 8-20 mg/l;

- Fecal bacteria--several thousand to several hundred thousand per 100 milliliters of water depending on chlorination effectiveness.

These materials will have to be converted into wholesome life forms before they reach the next town, if people are to use it for drinking water purposes. If conversion does not occur naturally, or if the cost to treat the water adequately is too great, that town will have to drill for and pump out groundwater in a nearby aquifer. A "nearby" aquifer may be too

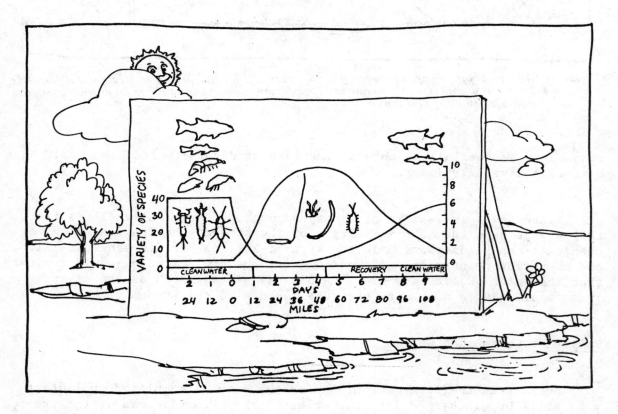

Figure 34: *Clean water is characterized by a relatively large number of widely differing species. Polluted water has fewer types of species, but often very large populations of those species.*

far away. Ocean City, Maryland, has a freshwater aquifer some 7 miles out to sea; Nantucket Island has a 10-12,000-year old water supply 1,500 feet beneath the surface. But surface waters are still the most economical to tap. Connecticut prohibits any sewage discharge into certain streams, thereby preserving potable water supplies--a geologically and economically sound water-use resolution.

One can imagine how that second town, many times larger than the first, might repollute our slowly recovering stream. If time, weather conditions, and other factors conspire against it, the water may become sluggish and noxious again. Under most conditions, however, some biota would have reestablished themselves--crayfish, dragon fly larvae, and the like in slowly moving stretches; and bluegill, clams, and stone fly larvae in riffles and fast-moving areas.

A large city with a typical industrial and commercial profile would further degrade the water by adding its various wastes, such as acids, bases, hot water, metals, salts, adhesives, dyes, paints, oils, greases, paper, animal renderings, and other life-threatening matter. What was once a stream now takes on the character of an open sewer. The natural interrelationships among water, plants, and animals is seriously stressed, if not altogether destroyed.

The essential impact of one, more, or all of such foreign pollutants is that of upsetting the relative "balance" of any established stream community. The interlacing energy and chemical bonding activities, the physical dynamics, the prey-predator food sequences--all of these can be disrupted. As we mentioned in an earlier chapter, each disruption can have wave-like consequences. The extinction of one organism or a population of that species may forebode the extinction of those that feed upon the population. Consequently, when we talk about "how much" pollution can harm a stream, we're talking about effects unique to each stream. But the common quality they all share is some degree of imbalance in their system whenever pollutants are introduced.

Industrial Pollutants

Since it is impossible to discuss each of the industrial wastes that enter our nation's waters, we have selected the effects of one industrial pollutant to examine in detail.

Polychlorinated biphenyls (PCBs) generically describe several manmade organic compounds in use since the 1930s in coolers and electrical insulators, and more recently in use as pesticide extenders. PCBs also find their way into the environment in the ink, dyes, and adhesives used in paper manufacturing. When cardboard is recycled, for example, the ink print dissolves and PCBs leave the plant in its wastewater. The PCBs are more resistent to degradation than DDT and equally capable of bioaccumulation.

Testing in the early 1970s revealed fish with low levels (below 1 ppm) of PCBs, but by the end of the food chain, these had concentrated thousands of times over. Water containing PCBs at .1 ppm is fatal to juvenile shrimp, but freshwater mussels and fish can survive far greater concentrations. When seals eat many mussels and fish with such levels of PCBs, they themselves accumulate levels of 5-21 ppm (a 50-200 multiplication). Eagles that feed on such fish accumulate up to 240 ppm (a 2400 multiplication). At these concentrations PCBs kill game birds; reduce reproductive capacity of fish-eating mammals, such as mink and seals; reduce viral resistance in laboratory mammals; and in a recent series of tests have proven to be carcinogenic to laboratory animals as well.

Recent testing has found eels in the Hudson River with residue values as high as 403.4 ppm, and concentrations in bottom sediments at Glenn Falls in the Hudson have exceeded 18,000 ppm. The reports on PCB levels in ocean fish are even more disturbing. The CEQ report states that:

> The total input of PCBs into the oceans of North America has been calculated at about 3.3 million pounds and for DDT at about 110 million pounds. Yet samplings in the North Atlantic indicate that PCB residue levels in the water are at least as high as those of DDT, despite the much greater load of DDT discharges. The implication is that PCBs are even more persistent in ocean water than long-lasting DDT.

There is only one U.S. producer of PCB, the Monsanto Chemical Company. Its sales of the compound doubled to 85 million pounds between 1960 and 1970. In 1971 with the identification of the problem, sales plummeted to 35 million pounds, and the company undertook the voluntary and most responsible action to dispose of spent fluid. Temperatures of 2000°F are needed to destroy the substance, yet Monsanto agreed to perform the service for its customers. In spite of this, many industrial users continue to dispose of the liquid improperly--as a dust control agent in parking lots or simply as a waste in landfills. Leaching from such sources continues to contaminate aquatic systems, resulting in a continuing rise in PCB levels in both birds and fish.

PCBs are but one example of chemical pollutants that find their way into the environment. Once this happens, we have to restrict and then prohibit the discharge of the harmful contaminant.

Effluent Guidelines: U.S. EPA

The effluent guidelines for each industry group listed in Table 1 have been prepared by the EPA and promulgated for compliance by 1977 and 1983 water pollution control goals. The magnitude of the effort undertaken is suggested by the number and variety of industries classified:

Table 1. Status of effluent guidelines: May 1976 (Source: U.S. Environmental Protection Agency)

Industry Groups	Number of Sub-Categories	Date Proposed[a]	Date Promulgated[a]
Group 1, Phase 1			
Fiberglass	1	8/22/73[b]	1/22/74
Beet sugar	1	8/22/73	1/31/74
Feedlots	2	7/ 7/73	2/14/74
Glass	6	9/ 7/73	2/14/74
Cement	3	9/ 7/73	2/20/74
Phosphate	3	10/ 7/73	2/20/74
Rubber	4	10/11/73	2/21/74
Ferroalloy	3	10/18/73	2/22/74
Asbestos	7	10/ 5/73	2/26/74
Meat	4	10/30/73	2/28/74
Poultry	5	4/24/74	
Inorganics	22	10/11/73	3/12/74
Cane sugar	2	10/29/73	3/20/74
Grain mills	6	10/11/73	3/20/74
Fruits and vegetables	5	11/30/73	3/21/74
Electroplating	1	12/ 7/73	3/28/74
Plastics and synthetics	13	11/ 9/73	4/ 4/74
Nonferrous	3	12/ 4/73	4/ 8/74
Fertilizers	5	12/26/73	4/ 8/74
Leather tanning	6	4/ 8/73	4/ 9/74
Soap and detergent	19	12/14/73	4/12/74
Timber products	8	12/20/73	4/18/74
Organic chemicals	3	12/ 7/73	4/25/74
Petroleum refining	5	1/15/74	5/ 9/74
Builders paper	1	12/17/73	5/ 9/74
Dairy	11	1/14/74	5/28/74
Pulp and paper	5	2/ 6/74	5/29/74
Seafood	14	1/ 3/74	6/26/74
Iron and steel	12	2/19/74	6/28/74
Textiles	7	2/ 5/74	7/ 5/74
Steam electric	4	3/ 4/74	10/ 8/74
Group 1, Phase II			
Glass	6	8/21/74	1/16/75
Rubber	7	8/23/74	1/10/75
Meat	6	8/28/74	1/ 3/75
Timber	7	8/26/74	1/16/75

Table 1.   (Continued)

Industry Groups	Number of Sub-Categories	Date Proposed[a]	Date Promulgated[a]
Asbestos	4	8/29/74	1/ 9/75
Grain mills	4	8/17/74	1/ 3/75
Plastics and synthetics	11	9/20/74	1/23/75
Fertilizer	2	10/ 7/74	1/14/75
Phosphates	3	1/27/75[b]	
Ferroalloys	5	2/24/75[b]	
Inorganics	41	5/22/75[b]	
Seafoods	19	1/30/75[b]	12/ 1/75
Cane sugar	5	2/27/75[b]	
Nonferrous	5	2/27/75[b]	
Electroplating	3	4/24/75[b]	
Organics	4	1/ 5/76[b]	
Fruits and vegetables	51	10/21/75[b]	4/16/76
Pulp and paper	10	2/19/76[b]	
Iron and steel	23	3/29/76[b]	
Foundries			
Carbon and alloy			
Group 2			
Furniture	4	11/14/74	6/ 2/75
Asphalt paving	4	1/10/75	7/24/75
Paint and ink	4	2/26/75[b]	7/28/75
Auto and other laundries			
Fish hatcheries	3		
Transportation	7		
Converted paper			
Petroleum and gas extraction	4	9/15/75	
Steam supply	2		
Coal mining	4	10/17/75	
Water supply	15		
Mineral mining	17	10/16/75	
Explosives	4	3/ 9/76	
Miscellaneous chemicals			
Carbon black	4	5/18/76	
Adhesives and sealants			
Gum and wood chemicals	6	5/18/76	
Hospitals		5/ 6/76	
Photographic processing			
Pharmaceuticals			
Pesticides			
Machinery and mechanical products			
Ore mining and dressing	7	11/ 1/75	
Food and beverages			
Clay and gypsum			
Concrete products			

---

[a]Published in Federal Register.
[b]Interim final guidelines.

The best summary of the complex situation represented in the chart appears in the following except from the Council on Environmental Quality 1976 Report:

EPA issues effluent limitation guidelines for each industry, defining the pollution loads allowable under the 1977 standards of "best practicable technology" and the 1983 standard of "best available technology, economically achievable." Table 1 summarizes EPA's progress in issuing these guidelines.

Guidelines issued to the pulp and paper and iron and steel industries between June 1975 and April 1976 are exceptionally important, both economically and environmentally. The pulp and paper industry uses more process water than any other U.S. industry and is one of the industries most significantly affected by the legislation (see the Economics section of this chapter for further discussion of these impacts). The iron and steel industry has posed some of the nation's most serious water pollution problems, especially where several plants are grouped together, as in the Mahoning River Basin in Ohio. In an unusual action in March 1976, EPA issued special effluent guidelines for eight steel plants in the Mahoning Valley. These plants have been allowed substantially lower abatement requirements than those applied to steel mills in the rest of the nation. According to EPA, enforcement of national regulations for these older facilities of U.S. Steel, Republic Steel, and Youngstown Sheet and Tube would cause "severe economic and employment disruptions."

In another unusual action in April 1976, EPA withdrew effluent guidelines for organic chemicals, excluding butadiene, as a direct result of legal challenge by the industry.

EPA continues to work on the remaining industrial categories, but much of the agency's effort has been focused on these very important and difficult industries.

EPA must also issue other major guidelines pertaining to "new sources," discharges proposed by industry after enactment of Public Law 92-500, and to pretreatment of industrial wastes that are to be discharged into municipal waste treatment systems. The "new source performance standards" are frequently equivalent to the 1983 limitations for existing industries. The development of pretreatment standards for existing industries continues. Pretreatment guidelines issued through May 1976 are given in Table 2.

The guidelines are translated into individual abatement requirements through the National Pollution Discharge Elimination System (NPDES) by requiring permits for every point source discharger. As indicated in Table 3, the number of permits issued for industrial sources continues to increase, with 90 percent of major dischargers and 67 percent of all industrial dischargers receiving

Table 2. Status of pretreatment regulations (Source: U.S. Environmental Protection Agency)

Industry	Number of subcategories	Pretreatment regulations			
		Number for existing sources		Number for new sources	
		Proposed	Promulgated	Proposed	Promulgated
Dairy	12	12	12	12	12
Grain mills	10	10	6	10	10
Fruits and vegetables	8	8	8	8	8
Seafood	33	33	33	33	14
Sugar	8	8	3	8	1
Textile	7	7	0	7	7
Cement	3	3	3	3	3
Feedlots	2	2	2	2	2
Electroplating	5	5	0	5	0
Organic chemicals	7	7	3	7	3
Inorganic chemicals	49	49	0	49	22
Plastics and synthetics	20	20	0	20	20
Soap and detergent	19	19	15	19	19
Fertilizer manufacturing	7	7	0	7	7
Petroleum refining	5	5	0	5	5
Iron and steel manufacturing	12	12	0	12	12
Nonferrous metal	8	8	0	8	3
Phosphate manufacturing	6	6	0	6	3
Steam electric power	4	4	0	3	3
Ferroalloy	7	7	0	4	3
Leather	6	6	0	6	6
Glass	14	14	4	14	13
Asbestos	11	11	7	11	11
Rubber	11	11	0	11	11
Timber	13	13	0	13	13
Pulp and paper	5	5	5	5	5
Builder paper and board	1	1	1	1	1
Meat products	15	15	4	15	10
Paint formulating	1	1	0	1	1
Ink formulating	1	1	0	1	1

permits as of March 31, 1976. The rate at which additional permits are issued will probably decrease as more time and effort are required to reach agreement with the remaining major industrial sources.

There have been unexpected delays in implementing the complicated administrative requirements of the 1972 amendments. Effluent guidelines have not been issued for all industries, but many firms have received permits and will meet the 1977 deadlines; others will not practicably be able to do so.

Beyond these administrative delays, there is some evidence that the system is not achieving the tight pollution controls required by the legislation. Three steps are necessary to satisfy the law's requirements. First, EPA prepares effluent guidelines to meet the mandated abatement standards (i.e., best practicable technology and best available technology). Second, each polluter receives a permit requiring him to satisfy the effluent guidelines. Third, the discharger reduces his effluents in accordance with the schedule and requirements stated in the permit. Delays occur when guidelines are not prepared according to schedule, when special technological problems exist in writing the permit, or when technology or resources impede effluent reduction by the discharger.

Several consultants to the National Commission on Water Quality (NCWQ) concluded that effluent guidelines prepared by EPA cannot meet the requirements of the legislation because they are based on inadequate technology. The consultants feel that more stringent (and therefore more expensive) abatement requirements are necessary. EPA does not agree with these conclusions, and there have been no court decisions requiring EPA to strengthen its guidelines.

Table 3. Status of permits issued under the NPDES: January 1976
(Source: U.S. Environmental Protection Agency)

Types of Dischargers	Total identified dischargers	Permits issued as of June 1975	Permits issued as of January 1976
Industrial (and other non-municipal)	41,454	21,639	26,958
Major	4,655	2,797	4,213
Minor	36,799	18,842	22,745
Municipal	20,664	16,664	16,845
Major	4,604	2,714	4,375
Minor	16,060	13,950	12,470
Federal facilities		1,988	2,062
Major			226
Minor			1,836
Total		40,291	45,865

There is general agreement that the permitting program can be accelerated by having more states assume the permitting authority. As indicated in Table 4, four states were given this authority from July 1, 1975, through July 6, 1976. However, the prospects are dim for the states to assume these responsibilities in the near future. An EPA report released in December 1975 concludes that progress toward decentralization by formal program delegations "has reached a point of diminishing returns," because few states have the staff capability to assume large-scale delegation. The report also notes that insufficient funding for state agencies is the single most important obstacle to a more effective division of labor between EPA and the states.

Table 4. States assuming NPDES responsibilities (Source: U.S. Environmental Protection Agency)

State	Date assumed	State	Date assumed
California	May 14, 1973	Minnesota	June 30, 1974
Oregon	Sept. 26, 1973	Maryland	Sept. 5, 1974
Connecticut	Sept. 26, 1973	Missouri	Oct. 30, 1974
Michigan	Oct. 17, 1973	Hawaii	Nov. 28, 1974
Washington	Nov. 14, 1973	Indiana	Jan. 1, 1975
Wisconsin	Feb. 4, 1973	Colorado	March 27, 1975
Ohio	March 11, 1974	Wyoming	Jan. 30. 1975
Vermont	March 11, 1974	Virginia	March 31, 1975
Delaware	April 1, 1974	S. Carolina	June 10, 1975
Mississippi	May 1, 1974	N. Dakota	June 13, 1975
Montana	June 10, 1974	Nevada	Sept. 19, 1975
Nebraska	June 12, 1974	N. Carolina	Oct. 19, 1975
Georgia	June 28, 1974	New York	Oct. 28, 1975
Kansas	June 28, 1974		

Regardless of the efficacy of this plan, presently we still face the serious problem of surface waters that contain wastes. These waters go on into the world's biosphere. As they make their way slowly to the ocean, they are used, partially treated, and then reintroduced to the watercourse with other contaminants from non-point and point sources. Eventually, the waters reach the coast where the tides mix them with the sea. This mixing zone, the estuary, is the most biotically productive nursery ground in the world. As we will see in a later chapter, the impact of waste-filled freshwater on that environment is a problem of quite another order of magnitude!

CHAPTER SUMMARY

1. As water flows from a mountain as a stream, certain groups of plant and animal life selectively reside in communities along its course as a consequence of stream gradient; dissolved oxygen, temperature, pH, nutrient levels of the water; the filtrable and non-filtrable solids present; and other variables.

2. By discharging wastes into a stream, man influences the balance of the plant and animal communities, helping bacteria, algae, and other organisms to harm or kill certain life forms.

3. The "carrying capacity" of the stream determines whether the stream locally can "recover," and the degree of that recovery directly affects the plant and animal life downstream.

4. Certain indicators of water quality include BOD levels, pH, diversity index, abnormal levels of natural organics and the presence of synthetic organics.

5. Because all influences in the river at any given point affect the quality of life downstream, the accrued pollutants through many watersheds ultimately flow to the freshwater/saltwater interface of the estuaries. There, great damage is wrought or great benefits are reaped due to the inflowing freshwater quality.

SOURCES

Atmospheric Contribution to the Chemistry of Lake Water. Eds. D.H. Matheson and F.C. Elder. Supplement to Vol. 2, 1976.

Bennett, G.W. Management of Lakes and Ponds. New York: Van Nostrand Reinhold Co., 1970.

Biological Aspects of Thermal Pollution. Eds. P.A. Krenkel and F.L. Parker. Nashville, Tennessee: Vanderbilt University Press, 1969.

Biological Methods for Assessment of Water Quality. Eds. J. Cairns, Jr. and K.L. Dickinson. Philadelphia: American Society for Testing Materials, 1973.

Bozman, F.H. and G.E. Likens. "Acid Rain: A Serious Regional Environmental Problem." Science, 184 (June 1974).

Clark, J.R. "Thermal Pollution and Aquatic Life." In Man and the Biosphere, Eds. P.R. Ehrich and J.P. Holdren. New York: W.H. Freeman & Co., 1971.

Cleaning Our Environment: The Chemical Basis for Action. Sub-Committee on Environmental Improvement. Washington, D.C.: The American Chemical Society, 1969.

Cole, G.A. Limnology. St. Louis, Missouri: The C.V. Mosby Co., 1975.

Council on Environmental Quality. Environmental Quality-75: The Sixth Annual Report of the Council on Environmental Quality. Washington, D.C.: GPO, 1975.

Eckenfelder, W.W. Water Quality Engineering for Practicing Engineers. New York: Barnes and Noble, Inc., 1970.

Ecological Toxicology Research: Effects of Heavy Metal and Organohalogen Compounds. Eds. A.D. McIntyre and C.F. Mills. New York: Plenum Press, 1974.

Ehrlich, P.R. and A.H. Ehrlich. Population, Resources, Environment: Issues in Human Ecology. San Francisco: W.H. Freeman and Co., 1972.

Hammer, M.J. Water and Waste-Water Technology. New York: John Wiley & Sons, Inc., 1975.

Handbook of Water Resources and Pollution Control. Eds. H.W. Gehm and J. I. Bregman. New York: Van Nostrand Reinhold Co., 1976.

Managing Water Quality: Economics, Technology, Institutions, Ed. A.V. Kneese. Baltimore, Maryland: Johns Hopkins Press, 1968.

McKee, J.E. and H.W. Wolf. Water Quality Criteria. Resources Agency of California, State Water Quality Control Board, Publication 3-4.

National Commission on Water Quality. Staff Draft Report. November, 1975.

Odum. E.P. Fundamentals of Ecology. Philadelphia: W. B. Saunders Co., 1971.

Palmer, C.M. Algae in Water Supplies. Public Health Service, U.S. Department of Health, Education, and Welfare, No. 657. Washington, D.C.: U.S. Government Printing Office, 1962.

The Practice of Water Pollution Biology. U.S. Department of the Interior, FWPCA. Washington, D.C.: U.S. GPO, 1969.

Rudd, R.L. Pesticides and the Living Landscape. Madison, Wisconsin: University of Wisconsin Press, 1964.

Self-Monitoring Procedures: Basic Parameters for Municipal Effluents. U.S. EPA. Washington, D.C.: U.S. GPO, 1974.

Steen, E. Dictionary of Biology. New York: Barnes and Noble, 1971.

Study Group on Mercury Hazards. "Hazards of Mercury." Environmental Research, 1, No. 1 (March 1975).

U.S. Environmental Protection Agency. Environmental Impact of Highway Deicing. Washington, D.C.: GPO, 1971.

_____. "Scientists Drilling in Floor of Atlantic for Fresh Water." Environment News. Boston, Mass.: U.S. EPA, New England Regional Office, October 1976.

_____. "Region V Enforcement Views on the Toxic Act Implementation." Environment Midwest (February 1977).

SUGGESTED READING

Boughey, A.S. Fundamental Ecology. Scranton: International Textbook Co., 1971.

Commoner, Barry. The Closing Circle. New York: Alfred A. Knopf, 1972.

Ehrenfeld, D. Conserving Life on Earth. New York: Oxford University Press, 1970.

Ehrlich, P.R. and A.H. Ehrlich. Population, Resources, Environment: Issues in Human Ecology. San Francisco: W. H. Freeman and Co., 1972.

Garlauskas, A.B. "Conceptual Framework of Environmental Management." Journal of Environmental Management, No. 3 (1975).

Garrels, R.M. et al. Chemical Cycles in the Global Environment. Los Altos: William Kaufmann, Inc., 1975.

Handler, P. Biology and the Future of Man. New York: Oxford University Press, 1970.

Leopold, Aldo. A Sand County Almanac. New York: Oxford University Press, 1970.

Wagner, R. H. Environment and Man. New York: W. W. Norton and Co., 1971.

_____. The Biosphere. San Francisco: W. H. Freeman and Co., 1970.

CHAPTER NINE

WATER USE AND TREATMENT

CONTAMINATION OF PUBLIC DRINKING WATER

The water in the park has been contaminated with sewage. Persons who have consumed water here may develop gastro-enteritis with nausea, vomiting, diarrhea, and cramps. This is a self-limited disease which should get better by itself.

July 11, 1975   Richard Sims
                       Superintendent
                       Crater Lake National Park

The clean, blue waters of Crater Lake in Oregon's Cascade Mountains draw visitors from all over the world, but carelessness, greed, and stupidity led to the gross pollution of the water these visitors drank in 1975. Thousands of persons drank spring water that was con-taminated by raw sewage from Crater Lake Lodge, a privately operated facility within the park. Lodge operators then attempted to keep information of the situation from park officials and the public.

The following quotes from the Eugene, Oregon Register Guard were later supported by a Congressional investiga-tion:

"More than 100 employees were sick on June 30th. But, Richard Sims, park superintendent, said he had been told of no more than 10 ill-nesses on any given day.

Lodge employees ill with diarrhea and nausea were handling food."

Dr. Mark Rosenburg of the Communicable Disease Center in Atlanta ordered the park closed after the illness became widespread. He said samples taken in May 1975 showed contamination and that even the new system being proposed for the park would not meet state standards.

Crater Lake Lodge operator, Ralph Peyton, concluded the closure had cost him hundreds of thousands of dollars in sales and that ". . . it's all thanks to you newspapers who (sic) publicize bad news."

All forms of life need ample quantities of safe water. The predictions are that in the future there will be inadequate amounts of it. By the year 2020, the United States will require 1200 billion gallons of water per day, but the estimated total usable surface water supply from rainfall will be only 700 billion gallons per day. The condition of those surface waters is barely acceptable in many public water supply systems and poor in others. Clearly, to have sufficient amounts of clean water, we will have to reuse much of it many times over. This means that after each use we must purify it to the acceptable level directed by public health standards.

Recent Findings of the Public Health Service

The present status of the country's water supplies is alarming. In 1970 the Public Health Service examined 969 representative public water supply systems in nine geographic areas. They concluded that (1) "many systems are delivering water of marginal quality on the average; (2) many are delivering poor quality in one or more areas of their water distribution system; and (3) the deficiencies identified with most water systems justifies (sic) real concern over the ability of most systems to deliver adequate quantities of safe water in the future." The major findings were these:

Status of Water

- An insufficient number of bacteriological samples were analyzed for 85 percent of the water systems --and 69 percent of the systems did not even analyze half of the numbers required by the PHS Drinking Water Standards.

- 36 percent of 2,600 individual tap water samples contained one or more bacteriological or chemical constituents exceeding the limits in the Public Health Service Drinking Water Standards.

  . . . 9 percent of these samples contained bacterial contamination at the consumer's tap evidencing potentially dangerous quality.
  . . . 30 percent of these samples exceeded at least one of the chemical limits indicating waters of inferior quality.
  . . . 11 percent of the samples drawn from 94 systems using surface waters as a source of supply exceeded the recommended organic chemical limit of 200 parts per billion.

Status of Physical Facilities

- 56 percent of the systems evidenced physical deficiencies including poorly protected groundwater sources, inadequate disinfection capacity, inadequate clarification capacity, and/or inadequate system pressure.

- In the eight metropolitan areas studied, the arrangements for providing water service were archaic and inefficient. While a majority of the population was served by one or a few large systems, each metropolitan area also contained small inefficient systems.

Operator's Qualifications

- 77 percent of the plant operators were inadequately trained in fundamental water microbiology; and 46 percent were deficient in chemistry relating to their plant operation.

Status of Community Programs

- The vast majority of systems were unprotected by cross-connection control programs, plumbing inspection programs on new construction, or continuing surveillance programs.

Status of State Inspection and Technical Assistance Programs

- 79 percent of the systems were not inspected by State or County authorities in 1968, the last full calendar year prior to the study. In 50 percent of the cases, plant officials did not remember when, if ever, a state or local health department had last surveyed the supply.

If we consider the problems here in relation to the hydrologic cycle, we can focus on three areas of concern: (1) the quality of the water entering the public drinking water supply system; (2) the adequacy of treatment it receives before and during transmission to consumers; and (3) the quality of treatment given the wastewater before it returns to the surface water to become some other community's drinking water supply. Earlier we considered the first problem area. Now we'll examine the adequacy of raw water for drinking and the efficacy of treatment in recycling that water.

The Safe Drinking Water Act, 1974

Most surface and groundwater require treatment before they can be drunk. Surface waters contain non-point source sediments, microbiological organisms, organic chemicals, and occasionally radioactive fallout. Subsurface waters increasingly contain sewerage pipe leakage, subsurface injected waste fluids, intruding ocean water, and contaminated surface seepage, especially from urban stormwater runoff and disposal on land of sludge from treatment. The variety of contaminants which will have to be removed before the water is suitable for drinking originates from the watershed's character and prior use made of the water.

According to an EPA report "Salt Water Intrusion in the United States" published in July 1977, 50% of the national population and 95% of the rural population obtain water from subsurface supplies. Some states depend on ground (subsurface) water for over 85% of public water supplies. Nationwide, the general population, industry, commerce obtain about 20% from beneath the surface. As we have mentioned before, much of the underground water is contaminated with dissolved solids. While U.S. Public Health Service fixed the public drinking water limit at 500 ppm, about 2/3rds of the underground water contains at least 1,000 ppm dissolved solids, and beneath these aquifers are saltier waters of 10,000 ppm. These and ocean waters are potential intruders of fresh water supplies.

Forty-three states indicate salt water intrusion problems. The most severly intruded of them are coastal metropolitan areas. There are, however, 22 states with inland salinity problems from a number of manmade and natural sources. Most intrusion problems are created by excessive demands on subsurface reservoirs, surface water impoundments, landfills, underground water storage, mining, septic tanks, leaks, and spills. These contamination routes are then complicated by natural or manmade avenues for contaminated water movement, such as faults, improper oil exploration, canal construction, and channel dredging, thus interrelating and confusing identification and remedy.

The burden which greater need for underground water places upon society is considerable. First, the salt water must be treated; second, the salt removed must be isolated to inhibit its return to the open aquatic system; third more energy is required to remove, treat, and distribute purified salt water; fourth, to prevent increased concentrations of salts, the underground supply must not be removed more rapidly than it is replenished; and fifth, contingency plans must be made for depletion of underground reservoirs entirely. Before even step one can commence, the water must first be analyzed for appropriate treatment.

Public Law 93-523, the Safe Drinking Water Act of 1974, proposes that selected chemicals or organisms within those categories be tested and then reduced if excessive. Let's examine the Drinking Water Quality Regulations and Proposals as of May 1, 1976. The Drinking Water Act specifies the parameters (criteria) and maximum contaminant levels for the types of water systems (community and non-community), monitoring requirements (numbers of samples per month related to population), as well as the monitoring report procedure. There are certain worrisome omissions in the proposed list of contaminants: viruses, carcinogens, antibiotics, and hormones. Especially critical are those contaminants which are in practically undetectable amounts and for which methods of analyzing and procedures for treating and monitoring have yet to be determined.

The Act requires the water treatment staff not only to ascertain the contaminants present in drinking water but also to indicate their concentration and the type of treatment to use. Many contaminants might cause odors and tastes, color, pH, and other characteristics not falling within the parameters of the Safe Drinking Water Act; treatment procedures will have to remedy these characteristics as well.

Our ability to detect and measure the presence of certain exotic pollutants far exceeds the technology available to remove them. This is added impetus to local officials to prevent contamination in the first place. In water management, the old saw about "better safe than sorry" has new significance.

The general range of treatments available are as follows. We'll examine several types first and consider briefly the purpose of each.

Ten Processes for Treating Drinking Water

1.   Aeration. When air is bubbled through water or water is sprayed into the air, the concentrated gases in solution diffuse to the atmosphere where they become less concentrated. As a result, hydrogen sulfide (rotten-egg odor), carbon dioxide, and volatile organics (unattractive odors and tastes) will leave the water. Volatile organics are lightweight molecules, like those of ether or isopropyl alcohol, that evaporate readily upon aeration. Other chemicals, such as inorganics, may become oxides and settle to the bottom of the tank as solid particulates. The pH of the water probably will not be at extremes when carbon dioxide and other gases escape from solution into the atmosphere.

2.   Coagulation and Sedimentation. A coagulant, such as an inert synthetic polymer, causes the bulk of the pollutants to clot together into a dense mass that settles to the bottom. This process can remove (suspended) organic and inorganic materials from the water.

3.   Lime-soda Softening. High calcium lime, $CaCo_3$, and slaked lime, $Ca(OH)_2$, react with the salts of bicarbonate, sulfate, chlorides, and nitrates. If not removed from water supplies, they cause hardness and scaling in hot water systems, and they inhibit soaping. These salts would probably be higher in concentration in groundwater than surface water.

4.   Zeolite Softening. Zeolite is a naturally occurring ion exchange material. It is made of silicate mineral structured in a giant network resembling a sponge. It is negatively charged throughout, so it can be pre-loaded with soluble positive ions like sodium ($Na+$). Placed in water containing calcium and magnesium ions ($Ca++$, $Mg++$), the zeolite mineral with sodium ions presents an exchange opportunity: the calcium and magnesium ions for the

sodium ions. Because of the different attractions and relative solubility of the calcium and magnesium ions compared to the sodium ion, zeolite can take up the unwanted ions, leaving sodium in solution. Later, the zeolite can be removed, backwashed, filled with sodium, and used again.

Other ion exchange softeners have been developed from hydrocarbons. They can either be predominantly negative or predominantly positive, depending upon which ions are to be removed from the contaminated water.

5 & 6. <u>Slow and Rapid Sand Filtration</u>. The water to be treated flows either slowly (.1 gallons per minute per square foot) or rapidly (2-3 gallons per minute) over sand filters. The former procedure yields 1-3 mg. of suspended solids per liter of water, while the latter yields 2-5 mg. of suspended solids/l.

7. <u>Disinfection</u>. This technique applies a chemical agent, usually chlorine (or sometimes ozone), to kill waterborne bacteria. Chlorine, it is suspected, reacts with hydrocarbons to form possible carcinogens, whereas ozone does not. Though both eventually escape as gas, chlorine remains in solution longer than ozone and thereby provides longer-lasting protection. Disinfection may also reduce taste and odor, depending upon the kind of waste treated and the type of disinfectant used.

8. <u>Activated carbon</u>. Animal and wood charcoals have very large surface-areas-to-weight ratios. Activated carbon, familiar in household aquarium filters, decolorizes, clarifies, and filters the water. In addition, phenols (from coal tars) and cyanides (from gas works, coke ovens, and metal plating) are removed by carbon columns. Like the ion exchange columns, activitated charcoal can be regenerated by heating, so it is predicted that its use will become more widespread.

9. <u>Special Chemical Treatment</u>. Toxic materials, organics, and metals may require a special environment, such as a high or low pH range, to favor a physical or chemical reaction which will remove the unwanted material from solution or suspension.

10. <u>Desalinization</u>. Various properties of water and solutions permit separation of water from salts. In addition to lime-soda softening, water may be boiled rapidly (flash distillation) and condensed, leaving the salts as solids. Ion exchangers remove low salt concentrations. Molecular filters separate colloidal particles from solution and dissolve molecules on the basis of size. When a fluid passes through the selectively permeable matter most large molecules above a certain size are retained. Other methods are possible, though costs and other considerations influence the choice.

INORGANIC
CHEMICALS

Treatment:	Iron & Manganese	Metals	Chloride	Calcium Carbonate	Organic Chemicals	Toxic Inorganics and Organics	pH	Turbidity	Micro-Biological Bacteria	Color	Odor and Taste
1. Aeration	x	-	-	-	x	-	x	-	-	-	x
2. Coagulation-Sedimentation	x	x	-	x	x	x	x	x	-	x	x
3. Lime-Soda Softening	x	x	-	x	x	x	x	x	-	x	x
4. Zeolite Softening	x	x	-	x	x	x	x	x	-	x	x
5. Slow Sand Filtration	x	x	-	x	x	x	-	x	-	x	x
6. Rapid Sand Filtration	x	x	-	x	x	x	-	-	x	x	x
7. Disinfection	-	-	-	-	x	-	-	-	x	x	x
8. Activated Carbon	-	-	-	-	-	x	-	-	-	x	x
9. Special Chemical Treatment	x	x	-	x	x	x	-	x	-	x	x
10. Desalinization	-	-	x	-	x	-	-	-	-	-	-

Figure 35: *Common water treatment processes for water quality parameters.*

Distribution of Drinking Water

Pumping and distribution facilities in the United States are generally inadequate. Not only must such a system function for years, but also it must not permit deterioration of the water once it passes initial quality control checks. In some cases, the engineering problems for a system can be staggering. For example, water pressure to the user must be great enough to reach the topmost elevation in the line, but it must not be so great as to damage appliances. In tall buildings, booster pumps on every few floors force water up to the next higher ones. The volume of deliverable clean water relates to pressure because peak hours of use during the day or emergency demands may reduce the pressure and/or decrease the volume substantially. Therefore, storage areas for water may have to be placed along the distribution line to supplement the water supply. At each point where plumbing connections are made there is opportunity for grease, oil, metals, and possibly harmful organisms to enter the system. Consequently, the system must be carefully monitored to prevent possible contamination.

We see, then, that a system for distributing public drinking water must deliver safe water that is aesthetically appealing and adequate in pressure and amount. And lastly, the cost of the system to the public must be affordable.

Collection of Water for Treatment

Once water is used in homes, hospitals, factories, and garages, or other facilities, the water will contain various wastes that pollute the natural environment if released untreated. The sewerage system itself may be a source of contamination because of materials used (asbestos-cement piping) or because of illegal connections or deteriorating conduits. Moreover, some older collection systems are designed so that stormwater from surface runoff empties into the sanitary sewer line. In this situation, the total waste fluctuates in volume and contaminants. Separate sewer systems are now required in most areas, and the construction of combined sewers which carry both stormwater and sewage is strongly discouraged. If the sudden increased volume created by the stormwaters is more than a treatment plant can process, a portion of the sewage may be shunted past the treatment plant directly into the receiving waters--untreated. Urban runoff is an immense non-point pollution source and is a focus of growing national concern.

Urban Runoff

There is no best method for the control and treatment of urban stormwater. However, management programs certainly must include controls for source, collection, storage, and treatment. These programs must allow for conditions of climate, existing sewerage, topography, potentially available public treatment works, and the receiving waters.

Source control aims at avoiding stormwater runoff in the first place. Since rainfall or snowmelt is the primary water source, we must see to it that private and public drainage areas make maximum use of soil absorption. For example, we might direct more runoff than we do now from rooftops, parking lots, and driveways to grass or to sand or gravel drainage areas so that a substantial amount of water would soak into the soil. In most cases, street sweeping is an effective means of reducing the amount of suspended and dissolved solids that enter stormwaters. However, the sources of street debris, the amount of sediment contributed by non-street areas, the weather, and the season greatly vary the effectiveness of street sweeping.

Some pollutants may be prevented from entering stormwater readily, while others are not amenable to controls. Two pollutants are noteworthy problems--dog feces and salt. Animal feces in most heavily populated urban areas and on beach-front recreation areas are a troublesome aesthetic problem and a primary source of nutrient stormwater loading as well. Dog feces, salt, and other urban runoff contaminants may be shunted into roadside ditches, trenched drains, unsealed lagoons, and other open lands where they could penetrate subsurface waters. Any subsurface water contamination can be harmful: about 30% of all urban drinking water comes from underground. Each new contaminating source requires more energy for more treatment; therefore, higher delivery costs result.

Street salting is another source of stormwater pollutants. Major highways in Connecticut and Massachusetts may take up to 44,000 lbs. of salt per mile of road every winter. Some of these highways are routed within the urban stormwater collection area. In these areas, the use of sand followed by street sweeping might be an alternative to salting icy roads.

During collection, water can be delayed en route to the plant and temporarily stored. Inflatable bladders placed in the sewer line can slow or retain a large quantity of stormwater, but to be effective the sewer lines must be free of obstructing sediment and rocks. Additional off-line storage of water can be done by redirecting stormwater flow to special tanks, bags, or abandoned treatment plants. Later, such water is returned through the sewerage system for treatment.

New construction standards attempt to prevent clean water from entering the sewer, to end infiltration due to faults in construction and materials (e.g., groundwater seepage), and to stop inflow from illegal connections (e.g., domestic roof gutters). Clearly, designs for such systems must consider daily wastewater flow patterns within the collection area, as well as topography, weather, soil conditions, underground networks of pipe or wire laid by utilities, property values, projected growth of the community, and the likelihood of having adequate means for wastewater discharge.

As we can readily see, the environmental impact of urban stormwater discharged to the waterways can be great. The amount of BOD from combined sewers has been shown to have approximately half that of a sanitary sewer and it has about three times the sediment load. To comply with PL 92-500 waste-water discharge limitations, municipalities will have to give a higher priority to stormwater management than they have to date.

For a comprehensive investigation into EPA projects dealing with the problem of stormwater runoff we refer you to John A. Lager and William G. Smith's Urban Stormwater Management and Technology, An Assessment, U.S. EPA No. 67012-74-040, Washington, D.C.: U.S. Government Printing Office, December 1974; Nationwide Evaluation of Combined Sewer Overflows and Urban Stormwater Discharges, Volume I, Executive Summary. Cincinnati, Ohio: Municipal Environmental Research Laboratory, Office of Research and Development, U.S. EPA, September 1977; and Evaluation of Fluidic Combined Sewer Regulators under Municipal Service Conditions. Cincinnati, Ohio: Munici-pal Environmental Research Laboratory, Office of Research and Development, U.S. EPA, August 1977.

Wastewater

Now, let's return to our subject of collection systems to consider one major engineering concern--hydrogen sulfide gas (H_2S). This gas is highly flammable, poisonous, and carries the foul odor we associate with rotten eggs. Unlike oxygen with a normal range of 3-10 ppm in water, H_2S is very soluble in water, dissolving as much as 4000 mg/l. H_2S is a pH-dependent chemical. At a pH of 9, about 90% of the gas will dissolve; at 7, about 50%; and at a very acid pH 5, only 1% is left, meaning that 99% of the gas escapes into the atmosphere. If the sewer has inadequate venting to allow the gas to dissipate, then it can be trapped in a pocket. In such concentrations H_2S kills if it is breathed and it explodes if it is ignited. Reports of sewer line explosions are not uncommon. Workers wear gas masks to protect against H_2S poisoning when investigating any unknown situation in the sewer system.

The H_2S is produced by natural processes of decomposition by the anaero-bic (without oxygen) bacterial digestion of domestic sewage and tannery, paper mill, textile, and chemical plant wastes. As little as .05 ppm can be tasted in drinking water; therefore, tap water at this or greater levels would be unsuitable for baking, brewing, and confectionary and beverage manufacturing. High concentrations of hydrogen sulfide are deleterious to certain industrial processes, photographic developer compounding, and boiler operations. Furthermore, hydrogen sulfide at certain levels is toxic to most plant and animal life, although some of those associated with sewage flourish in it. A few data indicate the range of some of those levels:

Concentration of H$_2$S	Maximum Time of Exposure	Animal
0.86	24 hrs.	trout
1.0	-	mayfly larvae
3.3	24 hrs.	carp
4.3	24 hrs.	goldfish
750.0	-	blood worm larvae

Overall, the most formidable problem in building sewerage systems is to prevent leakage into groundwaters. Sewers must be sealed and routinely checked for breaks. Preventative maintenance is especially important when the sewer line is near to or in the water table or underlying porous rock stratum. The costs for energy loss, treatment facilities, and health restoration must be weighed against those measures necessary to ensure a totally enclosed sewage transportation system.

Water Treatment

According to PL 92-500, all publicly owned treatment works must meet secondary treatment standards by July 1, 1977. Even higher standards or higher levels of treatment may be required to meet state water quality standards. Primary treatment merely screens and settles solids present in sewage. There is minimal biological treatment. A chemical flocculent may be added to induce settling and the effluent may be chlorinated to kill bacteria. Chlorine or ozone is sometimes added as the final step in sewage treatment when it is necessary to kill additional levels of bacteria. Public Law 92-500 requires that communities also employ a secondary treatment process which removes up to 85 percent of the biochemical oxygen demand (BOD) and all the suspended or filtrable solids. Secondary treatment standards are now 30 mg/l BOD And 30 mg/l suspended solids for a monthly average water flow, 45 mg/l for a seven day flow and a maximum of 60 mg/l on a daily basis.

Many treatment plants must remove phosphorous because those receiving streams are tributaries to lakes already heavy with concentrations of natural and man-made pollutants (such waters are "eutrophic"). Other treatment plants must reduce ammonia because even low levels are toxic to fish life. The Ely, Minnesota, advanced wastewater treatment plant is capable of removing phosphorous nutrients from the final effluent. The tertiary facility was added to the city's existing secondary treatment plant; it "polishes" the water by removing organic phosphorous by activated carbon action. Figure 35 shows the Ely wastewater flow schematic. Communities interested in studying the economics, energy requirements, and environmental benefits of an advanced wastewater facility are directed to EPA's publication, Environmental Impacts of Advanced Wastewater Treatment at Ely, Minnesota, one of the Ecological Research Series, published in August 1976.

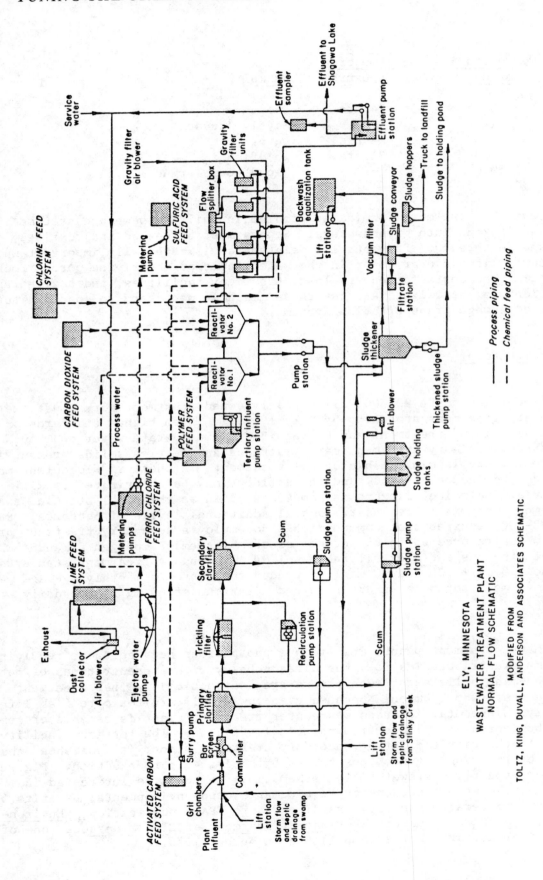

ELY, MINNESOTA
WASTEWATER TREATMENT PLANT
NORMAL FLOW SCHEMATIC

MODIFIED FROM
TOLTZ, KING, DUVALL, ANDERSON AND ASSOCIATES SCHEMATIC

Process piping
Chemical feed piping

Figure 36: *Ely, Minnesota wastewater treatment plant normal flow schematic modified from Toltz, King, Duvall, Anderson and Associates Schematic.*

Secondary treatment aims chiefly at reducing the sticks, greases and oils, plastic bags and containers, leaves, paper, and various sediments as well as biochemical oxygen-demanding agents--like digested and undigested food wastes containing fats, carbohydrates, and proteins. Secondary treatment doesn't remove phosphorous, nitrogen, metals, and some organics; therefore, advanced wastewater treatment processes must be continued, as the diagram of the Ely, Minnesota system shows. However, chemicals such as slaked lime can be added to the primary, secondary, or specialty units for phosphorous removal. Phosphate levels can be held down to 1 ppm when the calcium in slaked lime ($Ca{+}{+}$) reacts with the phosphate compound, $PO_4^{\equiv}$ and forms a fairly insoluble compound, $Ca_3(PO_4)_2$, which settles out of the solution with the phosphorous. Phosphorous must be removed in publicly owned treatment plants in Ohio that process over 1,000 gallons of waste per day and discharge into Lake Erie or its tributaries. Other waste products, such as ammonia and heavy metals, may be removed by means used to treat drinking water and by special procedures too detailed for us to consider here.

Treatment Plant Construction

Federal funds are available under PL 92-500 for 75% of the cost of preliminary planning, design plans and specifications, and the actual construction of wastewater treatment facilities. Proposed plants must use the best practicable waste treatment technology, and the treatment technique selected must be shown to be cost-effective. Best practicable technology is determined by evaluating alternative waste treatment processes. Alternatives that must be considered include (1) treatment and discharge into navigable waters, (2) land application and utilization, and (3) reuse of treated wastewater. Cost effectiveness means it achieves the needed degree of pollution control at the least cost in money, in environmental impacts, and in other non-monetary costs. (See bibliography, How to Obtain Federal Grants to Build Municiapl Wastewater Treatment Works.)

As an example of cost-effectiveness, it is most likely that a regional treatment plant is cost-effective in urban areas, while least likely to be so in rural ones. In cities large regional plants can provide better treatment of more water through computerized operations, in-plant frugality, and minimal but expert staffing. However, in sparsely populated regions, the guiding wastewater treatment principle resides in the profundity of that simple statement, "Mother Nature knows best." Here a large plant is not needed, and a small plant is comparatively less cost-effective. Further, new study costs show the plant in many areas simply cannot be afforded.

This principle is not applied when housing development locations and densities exceed the soil's capacity to assimilate septic tank and leach field wastes. It is also not applied when, instead of using suitable soils and dispersal, a sewer line is put in. Both cause problems: too many septic tanks may putrefy the surroundings, while availability of sewerage systems may encourage further development. Neither may be suitable for the community.

Appropriate land use balances the natural capabilities of air, land, and water.

Discharging Wastewater and Disposing of Sludge

The Water Pollution Control Act differs from earlier wastewater management legislation in that it concentrates on effluent standards rather than on the assimilative tolerances of the receiving waters. The Act requires that treated water be returned to the waterway when the discharge meets either the secondary effluent standard or that standard plus any specified conditions, such as the removal of phosphorous. If, however, the discharge goes to land surfaces instead of to a water treatment facility, then the discharge site must provide for storage during winter months when the water or soils may be frozen. For such discharge we should consider carefully the principles of surface runoff, absorption by soil, and general contamination of groundwater recharge areas; otherwise, pollution along some other pathway in the hydrologic cycle might occur. Specifically, we must consider soil types, drainage patterns, soil depth, depth to groundwater, groundwater movement, distance from wastewater to disposal site, proximity to well fields, as well as individual state regulations governing discharge of wastewater. (See bibliography, two reports: Evaluation of Land Application Systems and Costs of Wastewater Treatment.)

A more complicated problem for us, however, is the disposal of materials removed from the water during treatment. Collectively the materials are called sludge. Sludge continuously accumulates during the stages of treatment. It is deliberately concentrated and thickened by treatment until virtually de-watered. At this point, sludge may be subjected to aerobic (with oxygen) or anaerobic (without oxygen) bacterial digestion. Both types of digestion produce methane gas. Many plants use the methane for their in-plant fuel requirements instead of purchasing gas from a utility company. In this bacterial digestion and subsequent releasing of volatile gases, the total sludge volume reduces. The volume may also be diminished by exposure to air at high pressure and temperature--the wet air oxidation process. The sludge can also be incinerated to diminish its bulk further, or instead it might be applied to farmland as a soil conditioner. Some reports indicate that sludges produced from industrial wastewaters contain heavy metals which may leach into the soil and to the groundwaters--to appear once more as pollutants.

In short, sludge-handling is not a simple task. Sludge can be so thick and abundant that it must be transported by conveyor and truck or train. The odors are noxious and the methane gas produced is toxic and explosive. Air pollution laws impose rigid, high-cost control systems, making transportation and controlled land disposal a common problem.

The extent to which we treat the water really depends upon its next use. We presumed that all treated water would be returned to the receiving waters where it would continue down the watershed. However, the effluent might go elsewhere. For example, refineries in California use the effluent of the Central Costa Sanitary District as cooling water for public buildings. Such water must be chlorinated and low in solids and organics; otherwise, bacteria may flourish in the cooling tanks, gradually building residues of such mass that cooling towers have collapsed under the unexpected weight. Alternative use of treated water allows modifications in the treatment process, but strenuous efforts must be made to close the alternative-use loop so that partially treated water is returned for final treatment before discharge into the ambient receiving waters.

Treating Wastewater for Drinking Water Use

Given the reusability of treated water and the double demands in the future for more and safer water, we might be most practical to return the treated wastewater to the drinking water distribution system. There might then be one treatment center. Entering water would be treated to drinking quality, distributed, used, collected, treated, and then pumped right back into the drinking water distribution system.

Of all the biospheric systems considered, however, the best use-and-treatment system is that which incorporates the natural processes occurring in air, soils, and water. An understanding of those processes and an application of that knowledge to increase the use of natural processes is not a "regression"; it would be the least costly, most promising, and refreshing step forward that could be imagined. The U.S. EPA's renewed effort to employ natural processes is discussed further in Chapter 14.

CHAPTER SUMMARY

1. Our supply of healthful useable water for plant and animal consumption and industrial processing is diminishing, but not our overall global water supply. To ensure adequate supplies of water for these and other purposes, a range of treatments are available, the individual one determined by the prior and intended use of the water.

2. Ten types of treatment are used to make water suitable for drinking: 1) aeration; 2) coagulation and sedimentation; 3) lime-soda softening; 4) zeolite softening; 5 & 6) slow and rapid sand filtration; 7) disinfection; 8) activated carbon; 9) special chemical treatment; 10) desalinization.

3. Once treated, potable water must be sanitarily distributed to users at proper pressure, at peak times, and without pollution enroute. Pumping and distribution facilities in the U.S. are generally inadequate.

4. Collecting water for treatment poses problems because of numerous inadequate or outdated sewerage systems--e.g., combined storm and sanitary sewer lines; under-capacity of treatment plants to treat a short-term, high volume load of water which, therefore, must be shunted untreated into

receiving waters.

5. Urban runoff is a critical non-point pollution source that Pl 92-500 demands planners to contend with if they are to handle adequately storm water pollution.

6. Wastewater collection entails numerous problems for planners and commissioners to address--the danger of explosion or poisoning from H_2S; leakage from lines into groundwaters; meeting PL 92-500, July 1, 1977 standards for secondary treatment; constructing cost-effective treatment plants; disposing of sludge. One challenge for technologists is to develop adequate, cost-effective means for treating wastewater to be "reused" as drinking water.

SOURCES

Costs of Wastewater Treatment by Land Application. Washington, D.C.: Office of Water Program Operations, U.S. EPA, June 1976.

Evaluation of Land Application Systems. Washington, D.C.: Office of Water rogram Operations, U.S. EPA, March 1975.

How to Obtain Federal Grants to Build Wastewater Treatment Works. Denver, Colorado: General Services Administration, U.S. EPA, May 1976.

"Interim Primary Drinking Water Standards, U.S. EPA. Federal Register, 40, No. 1 (March 14, 1975).

Kibby, Harold and Donald J. Hernandez. Environmental Impacts of Advanced Wastewater Treatment at Ely, Minnesota. Corvallis, Oregon: U.S. EPA. Corvalis Environmental Research Laboratory, Office of Research and Development, August 1976.

McKee, Jack E. and Harold W. Wolf. Water Quality Criteria. State Water Quality Control Board, No. 3-A. Sacramento, Calif.: The Resources Agency of California, 1963.

Public Law 92-500, Federal Water Pollution Control Act Amendments of 1972. Washington, D.C.: GPO, 1972.

Public Law 93-523, Safe Drinking Water Act of 1974. Washington, D.C.: GPO, 1974.

Recommended Standards for Water Works. Great Lakes-Upper Mississippi River Board of State Sanitary Engineers, 1968.

Recommended Standards for Sewage Works. Great Lakes-Upper Mississippi Board of State Sanitary Engineers, 1971.

Reid, Frank. "Drinking Water Quality Regulations: Measuring, Monitoring and Managing (attached chart, "Drinking Water Quality Regulations and Proposals: Status as of May 1, 1976). Water and Sewage Works, June 1976.

U.S. Department of Health, Education, and Welfare. Community Water
    Supply, Significance of National Findings. Washington, D.C.: GPO,
    July 1970.

U.S. Environmental Protection Agency. Alternative Waste Management
    Techniques for Best Practicable Waste Treatment. Washington, D.C.:
    GPO, October 1975.

_____. Urban Stormwater Management and Assessment. Washington, D.C.:
    GPO, 1974.

Wastewater Quality and Treatment. American Water Works Association.
    New York: McGraw-Hill Book Co., 1976.

Water Treatment Plant Design. American Water Works Association. New
    York: McGraw-Hill Book Co., 1969.

CHAPTER TEN

COASTAL ZONES

A PERSPECTIVE

The clear waters of Sebago Lake flow into the Presumpscot River and flow downstream to mix with the tides. The estuary had been a resource rich in fish, waterfowl, and shellfish and served the early settlers well.

In 1842, a paper mill was built on the river and log drivers brought timber for processing. By 1880 this mill was the largest in the world. For over 100 years its untreated wastes poured into the river and the estuary was no longer an asset to the community.

A 1963 study estimated that there were over 7.3 million pounds of sludge in the estuary smothering most of the mudflat habitat of shellfish. Waste wood fibers decomposed, generating noxious hydrogen sulfide gas and consuming most of the available oxygen.

The paper plant was not the only contributor to the plight of facilities in the watershed until 1971. A rendering plant discharged 2,300 gallons of water a day from its hide processing operations. The estuary has been closed to shellfish harvesting since 1946 because the high bacteria count makes the fish unsafe for human consumption. Citizens complained about the foul smell of hydrogen sulfide and the damage it caused to the paint on their houses. Rafts of sludge rose from the bottom and, mixed with unsightly masses of foam, floated back and forth in the tidal flow. The estuary was decidedly not an asset to the community.

During the 1960's the situation began to change for the better. Early efforts were patchwork and insufficient. Lime pellets were spread from a helicopter to ease the hydrogen sulfide problem, but they were ineffective and created still more problems. Then the company installed a primary clarifier, followed in 1976 by secondary activated sludge treatment. A native eelgrass was planted throughout the estuary to clarify the water, stabilize sediments, and provide

a habitat for aquatic organisms. The recovery has
been dramatic. There are no rafts of sludge, no
odor of hydrogen sulfide, and the water appears much
clearer. Striped bass in the 25 lb. range are being
caught in the estuary for the first time in memory.

Much still needs to be done, but company, community,
council of governments, and state are working together to restore the estuary.

> Bradbury D. Blake, "A Profile of Estuarine
> Pollution and Recovery." Allagash Environ-
> mental Institute, University of Maine at
> Portland-Gorham, 1975.

Tidal Movements

The coastal zones, where continents touch oceans and fresh water meets
salt, have been there since the earth cooled and the waters fell. When this
natural interface became so contaminated that it required pollution controls,
Congress wrote and passed the Coastal Zone Management Act in 1972. Thirty
states were asked to define their concept of "coastal zone" for planning purposes. There is little agreement among the states in their definitions--
"within 2 miles of the coast," Delaware; "the coastal strip between mountains and sea, generally about five miles wide," California; "200 feet inland from high tide," Washington. For the purposes of this manual, therefore, we will use the natural definition: the shoreline intertidal zone
where freshwater meets saltwater.

The shorelines shift constantly with wind and wave action. Glacial
formation and melt waters have caused the Atlantic Coast shoreline to shift
by hundreds of miles. The shoreline was at the continental shelf when the
glaciers advanced, but it was far inland when they receded. At one time,
all of Florida and a sizable part of the present coastline up to Maine were
under water.

Daily shifts in the shorelines occur with each tide. Tides, the result
of gravitational pull of the Sun and Moon, vary with the change in angles
among Earth, Sun, and Moon. Tidal periodicity is threefold: the 24-hour
tidal fluctuation is a result of Earth's rotations. The 28-day tidal
fluctuation is a result of the Moon's orbiting, and the twice-a-year neap
and spring tides result from the Sun and Moon aligning. The gravitational
force pattern which moves the ocean's waters is always changing from the two
extreme conditions shown in Figure 37--a straight line to a right angle
alignment of Earth, Sun, and Moon.

The gravitational attraction between any two masses is directly proportional to the mass of the body but inversely proportional to the cube
of the distance: $F = \dfrac{M}{d^3}$. Therefore, while the Sun is 26 million times

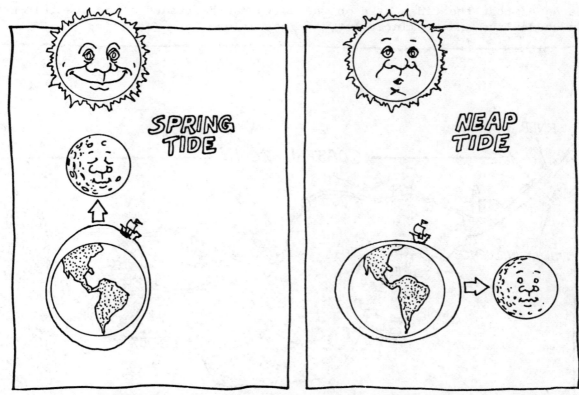

Figure 37: *Solar and lunar forces in conjunction cause spring tides, and in opposition cause neap tides. The moon exerts 2.15 times the attractive force of the Sun.*

greater in mass than the Moon, it is 389 times farther from the Earth. Both exert a force on the Earth (and the Earth on them), but the Moon's "F" is 2.15 times greater than the Sun's. Hence, we have big tides from the Moon and slight tides from the Sun. Both solar and lunar forces add to or cancel each other's pull, at the former position distorting the waters like a football; in the latter, returning them more nearly to the shape of a soccerball. Simply stated, both masses pull at the waters, which then rock and wave over the ocean floors, but the Moon has the more influence.

Declination, Earth's tilt to the Sun and its position to the Moon, places the points of the football in different planes at different times. Again, the tides may be higher or lower, depending upon the geographic location and the celestial relationships. The wind and high and low pressure cells can also dramatically affect the wave action of the waters, especially the high (sometimes of hurricane force) velocities of low pressure cells that lift the tides and drive their waters far inland.

The tides vary in height, approximately 3 feet at Cape May, New Jersey; 4 feet on Long Island; 7 feet on Stamford, Connecticut; 50 feet at the Bay of Funday. They rise against the river mouths and compress the freshwaters into continuous mounds with incredible force, thrusting back on the waters behind them that are moving toward the ocean. The impact of these waters striking each other may result in only the smallest ripple of waves far upstream. On the Delaware River, the tidal effects reach 100 miles upstream near the Trenton-Morrisville Bridge. Newark Bay and the Hackensack River, the East and Hudson Rivers, and the Connecticut and Rhode Island Rivers have long inland tidal waters. Though far-reaching, the most dramatic differences that the tides make on the Earth can be traced along the thin margin where land and sea intersect, the estuaries.

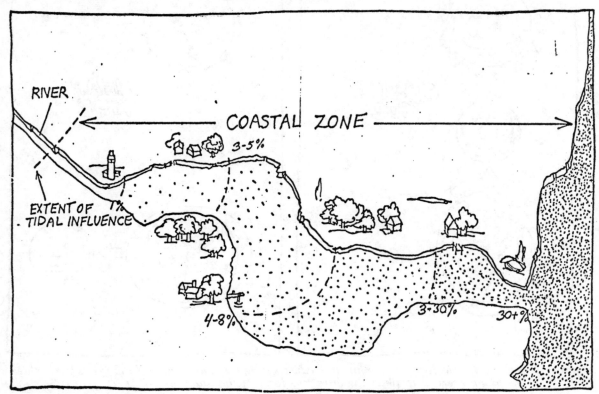

Figure 38: *The percent of tidal influence in the Coastal Zone decreased landward. The approximate, proportional effect correlated with distance is suggested in this diagram.*

Through these estuarine waters, the downward-flowing rivers meet the seas. The tides exchange enormous volumes of water across a very narrow threshold. Great currents of changing salinity, depth, and motion beget myriad physical, chemical, and biological habitats. Each compounded set of conditions creates a potential home safe from predators, rich with food, regularly cleansed of wastes . . . everything from a special ecological niche. The estuaries are Mother Nature's proving grounds, full of an incredible variety of life that is fair game for any competitor.

Salinity

Are estuaries so different from other water zones? How have the non-point pollutants, the untreated urban runoff, the heated water affected the estuaries? There are numerous standard instruments applied to measure conditions in the estuaries. There are gradients in: suspended and dissolved solids, light penetration, volume of water movement, densities of water, diversity and number of plants and animals (plankton, free-floating and benthic, bottom-dwelling), the nutrients, the productivity, and dozens of other parameters.

Foremost, estuaries range in salt concentrations from fresh to brackish to sea waters. Generally, the quantitative range for salt content is this:

Fresh water (rivers, lakes, streams)   500 ppm*

Brackish waters (upper estuary)   500-8,000 ppm

Brackish waters (lower estuary)   8,000-33,000 ppm

Open ocean   33,000-37,000 ppm

At any <u>single</u> geographic point, however, the salinity resolutely changes with the tide, the stratification between the surface freshwater and subsurface saline waters, and the temperature--as the density of the dots in Figure 39 suggests:

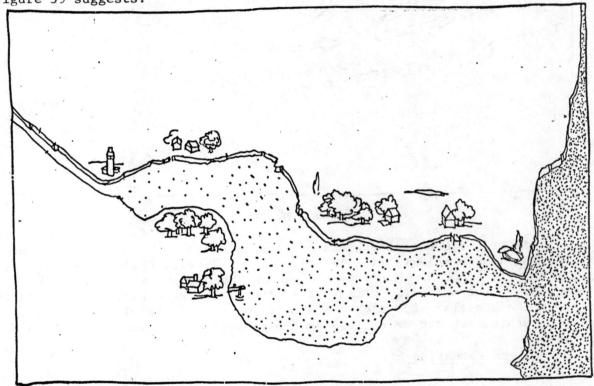

Figure 39: *Salinity gradient.*

Estuarine waters also stratify by salinity level. When rivers or streams flow into the relatively shallow estuary (10-20 feet deep), the less dense, fresh waters flow seaward at the surface, while the denser, more saline waters flow upstream along the bottom. This tends to stratify the circulation pattern of the water and to minimize vertical mixing of the two water masses. During the warm months, flows from rivers and streams are generally warmer than ocean flows, so layering patterns are more pronounced (warm water masses are lighter than cool water masses). Wintery conditions, storms, and heavy stream runoff break up those patterns mixing the waters (see Figure 40).

---

* "Parts per million" (ppm) is useful to compare with concentrations mentioned earlier in this manual. However, marine and coastal oceanographers, and marine biologists, refer to salinity in parts per thousand (ppt or %): e.g., 8,000 ppm (as above) would be 8 ppt.

Figure 40: *River/estuary.*

Salinity influences the kinds of organisms that will inhabit the estuarine niches. Some animals like jellyfish are drifters, while others are free-swimming, like tomcod. Others move about on the bottom, such as fiddler crabs; some stay in the mud, like clams; or in tunnels, like worms; or attached to rocks, like mussels. But each has a need for certain levels of salinity, and therefore each can be extinguished by abrupt alterations in salt concentration.

Nutrients and Estuarine Life

More than any other large-scale zone, estuaries are rich in nutrients --in fact, they carry more nutrients than any other land or water form of substantial size. Estuaries receive nutrients, especially nitrogen and phosphorous, and suspended solids from land runoff. The nutrients become circulated by salinity and tidal patterns and then entrapped by marshlands, submerged plant forms, and sedimentary deposits. The larger, coarse-grained suspended solids first are scattered near the faster running main channel of the inflowing river: the finer silts and organics later settle in quieter eddies nearby. As flows and circulation currents subside, mud and sand settle bottomward, forming organically rich layered flats and bars. At times of high tides and wind action, the bits are rescattered, reformed, or carried out into the ocean currents. The heavier stones, pebbles, and shells are left behind.

Farther from the mainstream, aquatic vegetation emerges. Cattails and Spartina root and spread, thereby stabilizing the shoal. These plants retain other circulating sediments, increase in numbers, and gradually build extensive wetlands. Moist, nurturing, stable, warm and vegetated marshes become a nursery and feeding ground for thousands of clams, oysters, crabs, menhaden, flounder, shadrockfish, bluefish, ducks, geese, and muskrats. Here on the shorelines of the world is nature at its most bountiful.

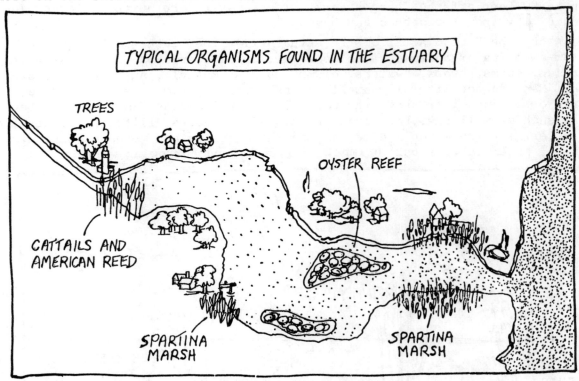

Figure 41: *Typical organisms of estuary.*

Weather conditions periodically alter the normal flow patterns and re-distribute the estuaries' sediments. Particulate resuspension reduces light penetration, and photosynthesis is minimal. However, in the estuaries the waters are shallow and frequently choppy from flow turbulence, wind action, and tidal exchange, and therefore are easily reoxygenated. The dissolved oxygen seldom drops below 6 ppm, unless waters are polluted. Further, there is usually a high concentration of phytoplankton in the surface waters, and the light does not have to penetrate deeply to cause them to photosynthesize and generate oxygen. It is possible, however, that under conditions lethal to benthic organisms, large, stagnant areas result. In 1965 Hurricane Agnes caused just such a condition by heavy sedimentation followed by turbidity and anoxia in the waters of the Chesapeake Bay. Shellfishing has still not returned to normal in the Bay's upper areas.

More obvious to us than salinity or nutrient levels are the estuaries' unusual physiographies. Like watersheds, they differ because of their geo-logic history, glacial actions, drainage patters, and freshwater loads, as well as the weather and latitude and longitude. Major estuaries are those of the Chesapeake Bay, the Delaware Bay, the Passaic River, the Hudson River and New York Harbor, the Thames River, the Connecticut River, Narragansett Bay, Buzzards Bay, Boston Harbor, Passamaquoddy Bay, Casco Bay, and Penob-scot Bay. Cape Cod Bay and Long Island Sound tend to have more saline oceanic currents than the others. Thus, while estuarine conditions are found along shoreline areas and at the mouths of smaller bays and harbors, the waters of larger bays and sounds are mainly characterized as marine.

Marine waters which cover the continental shelf (a coastal plain formerly exposed during the last glacial period, extending from shoreline to a point seaward 600 feet deep) have sediments from the estuarine waters as deep as 90 feet off the Georges Bank. These waters are quite different in productivity from the open ocean beyond.

Along the bottom areas of the estuary live the benthos (the aquatic bottom-dwelling organisms), such as algae, sponges, rocky corals, barnacles, hydroids, worms, crabs, oysters, clams, snails, mussels, anemones, and starfish. Many do not literally dwell on the bottom, but may be fastened to riprap or pilings left above the water level at low tide. Most of the benthos, such as mollusks, horseshoe crabs, and barnacles, filter nutrients from the water. At the water's edge, and in the cattails and reeds live the larval fish, shellfish, crabs, shrimps, jellyfish, and burrowing worms.

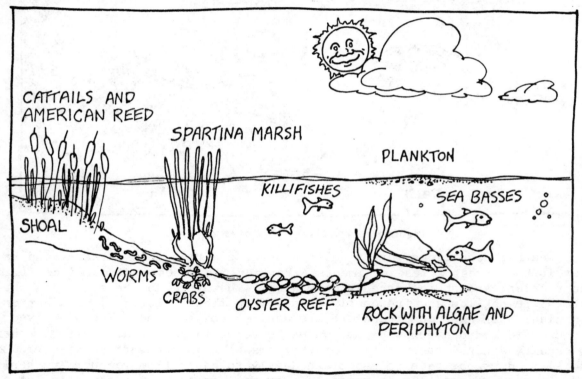

Figure 42: *Spartina, cattails, etc.*

At times, anadromous fishes, such as sea-running smelts, trout, and salmon, migrate through to spawn in the shallow, sandy freshwater upriver. The water's surface is roiled by schools of menhaden as they leap to escape a predator from beneath. Waiting patiently, blue heron, seagulls, osprey, and eagles stalk and then plunge at this prey. Raccoon, otters, ducks, geese. . .and the human hunters and fishers all know the estuarine waters to be a cornucopia.

Drifting through the upper layers of water, the phytoplankton (plant plankton that live unattached in the water) begin the journey to the sea. They travel with the zooplankton (animal plankton) eggs and larval forms

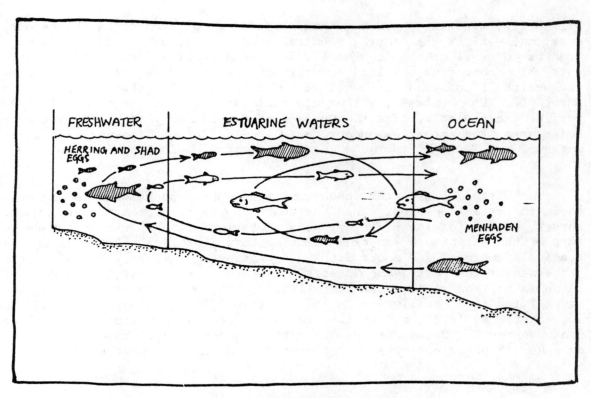

FRESHWATER   ESTUARINE WATERS   OCEAN

HERRING AND SHAD EGGS

MENHADEN EGGS

Figure 43: *Fresh, estuarine, and ocean fish.*

and juvenile stages of all the bottom dwellers and free swimmers just described. A fine-meshed plankton net dragged through the water concentrates these drifting forms. A 10X or 20X dissecting scope reveals a teeming mass of nearly translucent forms. The tiny green and brown ones with chlorophyll, the phytoplankton, are ingredients in "plankton soup" for the zooplankton. The plankton, in turn, are food for the filter-feeding bottom organisms, and even tiny swimming fish which strain nutrients from the filmy waters.

Estuarine Productivity

Of all the major land and water zones in the world, the estuaries are the most prolific. The diversity of biotic niches is so vast that a great number of individuals of many different species have virtually unlimited opportunities to feed, survive, and reproduce. Land-washed freshwater pours nutrients, though sometimes toxins as well, continuously into a shallow, warm, constantly mixed basin with an infinity of hiding places. The three to four million years of life on Earth have seen hundreds of thousands of successful mutations and adaptations survive and flourish in the estuaries. If we compare the tons of plant materials in a marsh in the Mississippi and one in Narragansett Bay with those of a wheat field in the Midwest, we see that both marshes exceed the yield of the wheat field (Fig. 44).

Yet this world of the estuary is as vulnerable to pollution as other land and water areas, and even more so than most because it receives the combined effects of so many kinds of contamination. Erosion from croplands contains an unnatural load of insecticides, herbicides, and pesticides.

Oil spills, dredgings, and heat and chemical discharges along the estuary drastically alter the natural conditions of it. About 80% of the O_2 we breathe comes from oceanic phytoplankton, and to live they must have nutrients which come from the land and through the estuaries. Since we harvest the wealth of the coastal zones, we are concerned that they not contain mercury, DDT, PCBs, viruses, pathogenic bacteria, or some new chemical of undetermined accumulative effect. Our health depends on that of the estuaries, and that of the estuaries on our control of pollutants flowing into those waters.

The striped bass offers one example of what happens when we neglect these interrelationships. The Chesapeake Bay is the primary spawning and nursery ground for the migratory striped bass that inhabit the inshore waters of the Atlantic Ocean from Maine to North Carolina. Bass support extensive commercial and sport fishing operations. In 1970, 783,000 sports fishermen of the north and mid-Atlantic states spent about $100,000,000 to catch 14 million striped bass totalling 73,000,000 pounds in weight. Commercial landings totalled an additional 11,000,000 pounds worth $2,500,000 at market. But PCBs, oil spills, bacterial counts, and floods have recently contaminated the Chesapeake Bay breeding grounds. There has been no hard evidence of pollutant effects yet, but we can surely expect some.

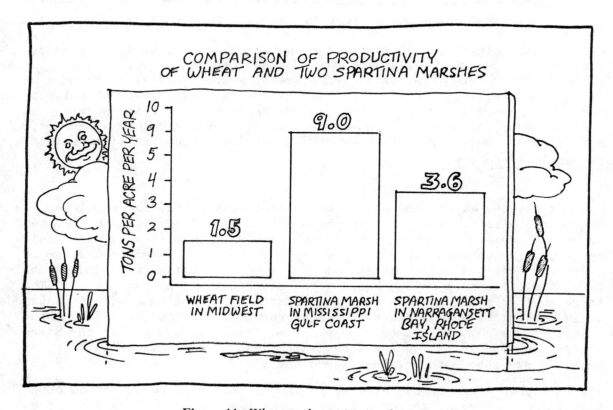

Figure 44: *Wheat and spartina productivity.*

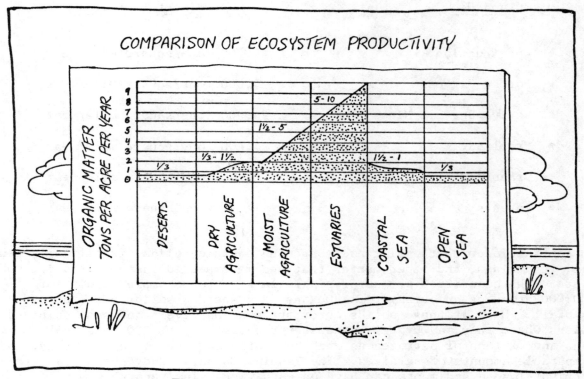

Figure 45: *Comparison of ecosystem productivity.*

Together with the Atlantic coast, the estuaries support two-thirds of the commercially valuable fishing areas of the United States. But researchers John and Mildred Teal estimated that from 1922-1954 the productive shallow coastal water and marsh in the U. S. dropped from 7.4 million acres to 5.3 million acres--a loss of more than 25% in 32 years. When harbors, marinas, oil storage areas, shipyards, and coastal cities are built upon filled wetlands, not only are those lands lost for food production, but also they carry pollution that accompanies the operation and maintenance of such facilities and uses. In addition to the normal silts and sediments from agriculture, there are even greater amounts from in-stream and shoreline construction, commercial lumbering, mining, and farming.

Estuarine Pollution--Inorganics and Organics

If we look at the following chart, we begin to see the powerful effects of shoreland sedimentation on estuaries. This list compares the sediment produced annually from one square mile of watershed by six land-uses, though the first two are temporary or intermittent uses:

Land Use	Sediment Produced
● Construction	48,000 tons/square mile/year
● Forest Harvest	24,000 tons/square mile/year
● Active Surface Mines	24,000 tons/square mile/year
● Cropland	4,800 tons/square mile/year
● Grassland	240 tons/square mile/year
● Forests	24 tons/square mile/year

In combination with the silt are suspended organic solids, fertilizers, sewage, renderings, and other matter that become embedded in the estuarine mud flats. The quantities are surprisingly large. For example, a city of 100,000 produces an average of 280 tons of suspended solids per hour of rainfall. Most of these solids enter streams and rivers and some combined sewers where they may bypass wastewater treatment. The 280 tons include .4 tons and .2 tons of nitrogenous and phosphatic compounds, respectively, and comparable amounts of sulfites. The Yaquina Estuary Study shows what effect nutrient-loaded sediments can have on estuaries. The report summarized that:

1. The amount of sulfide released to the overlying waters of benthic tidal flats may contribute to the total atmosphere a volume of sulfur that may be as great as all of the sulfur produced during fossil fuel combustion;

2. furthermore, these interstitial waters may carry, under certain conditions, such a high concentration of sulfide that it is toxic to many tidal organisms;

3. and sulfides react with dissolved oxygen, removing oxygen from the overlying waters, creating a hazard to plants and animals.

The sequence of biochemical events which led to these findings illustrates the interrelatedness of land-use and environmental health:

● Inorganics, such as clays, silts, and soils from non-point sources and organics, such as bacteria, plant matter, and sewage enter the estuary.

● Estuarine tidal action, currents, and salinity stratifications distribute the fine particles from slower water onto tidal flats, bars, and shoals.

- The naturally active bacteria metabolize the nutrients. The usual chemical action of respiration requires that the energy-depleted carbon be released as carbon dioxide and the hydrogen as water. In this last reaction, free oxygen has to be available:

$$4H_3O^+ + O_2 \rightarrow 6H_2O \text{ or } 4H^+ + 2O^= \rightarrow 2H_2O$$

- Under high sedimentation and therefore high turbidity, there is low photosynthesis and therefore low dissolved oxygen levels. The hydrogen ion, consequently, may not be able to find oxygen.

- If it can't, the hydrogen will then seek sulfur if it is available. In this case it is because of the high nutrient deposition. Sulfides are usually found in organic sediments, but may also be found in the inorganic ones. The reaction is akin to that of oxygen with hydrogen:

$$4H^+ + 2S^= \rightarrow 2H_2S$$

- Hydrogen sulfide, which is very soluble in water, exists in any of the following forms, depending on the pH of the water:

$$(1\% \text{ soluble}) \; H_2S \leftrightarrow HS^- \leftrightarrow HS^- + S^= \; (90\% \text{ soluble})$$
$$\qquad\qquad (pH \; 5) \quad (pH \; 7) \qquad (pH \; 9)$$

- At the normal seawater pH of 6.5-7.0, the predominant sulfide is HS^-. This reacts with iron to form ferrous sulfide, FeS, which gives the dark layering to sand bars. Normally, the iron present will be enough to continue to keep taking the HS^-, keeping it from participating in some other reaction. But when iron compounds are trapped behind dams upstream, an excess of sulfides is in the estuary.

- With an excess of HS^- ions, the photosynthesizing bacterium, <u>Thiobacillus</u>, uses the ions, converts them into $S^=$ which, within minutes, can be catalyzed by the metals in neighboring deposits (nickel, manganese, calcium, magnesium, etc.) to combine with any remaining dissolved oxygen, thereby further depleting available oxygen for biota—to sulfites, thiosulfates, sulfate, or free sulfur. That creates an even worse situation.

- Not only is the oxygen level now reduced, but also these last complex ions can combine further with oxygen to make sulfur dioxide, SO_2—one of the atmosphere's most severe pollutants.

- The hydrogen sulfide species, H_2S, is toxic to fish, crustaceans, polychaetes, and other benthic macroinvertebrates.

(Earlier statements indicated that concentrations of
.86 ppm killed trout. Studies also show that at the
pH of 7.6-8.0, hydrogen sulfide as low as .075 ppm is
harmful to walleye and suckers, and particularly to
eggs and fry. These reactions harm freshwater fish, too.)

● Even more dangers accrue. At the lower end of the pH
scale, the hydrogen sulfide is no longer soluble and escapes as a gas into the air, adding another of the atmospheric pollutants to global circulation. As we know, hydrogen sulfide is toxic to breathe and is explosive upon
ignition.

This series of reactions and cycles is just one of many hundreds of biochemical and energy interrelationships that begins in the watershed and is carried to the estuaries. Another type is related to temperature elevation in
the estuarine waters--i.e., thermal pollution.

Let's examine an actual case of thermal pollution in a southern U. S.
coastal area. The Florida Power and Light Company operates two fossil fuel
plants at Turkey Point, Florida. During the study period 1968-1970, each
produced 432,000 killowatt-hours and utilized 630 cubic feet/second of cooling water removed from the bay north of Turkey Point. Water temperature rises 6-7° C when passing through the plant. There is a drop of 1-2° C when
the water passes from the plant to the mouth of the Grand Canal. Water entering the bay, therefore, is usually elevated 5° C above the ambient water
temperatures. The principal findings in this case were these:

1. Average temperature elevations above 4° C caused almost
barren conditions where few animals and almost no macroalgae
or sea grasses occurred. The area at Turkey Point which was
elevated above 4° C with two fossil fuel units and 1230 cfs
flow was approximately 75 acres.

2. Average temperature elevations between 3 and 4° C above
ambient summer water temperatures caused serious depletion in
the biota; and this damage was not compensated for by increased
production due to warming in winter. At Turkey Point the area
between 3 and 4° C was approximately 100 acres.

3. Average temperature elevation between 2 and 3° C caused damage to the biota in summer; but this was reversed by the increased
production in winter. At Turkey Point the area between 2 and 3° C
was approximately 125 acres.

4. A total area of about 300 acres showed a decline in abundance
of animals which was statistically measurable for at least part
of the year. In approximately 125 acres the increased winter
catches compensated for the low summer catches and in approximately 250 acres winter recovery indicated that there would be

relatively rapid recolonization if the discharge were stopped.
The inner barren zone of about 50 acres would recover slowly
if at all due to the death of the rhizomes of the Thalassia
and changes in the sediment.

5. Areas with fluctuating temperature were not as severly damaged as those areas constantly exposed to elevated temperatures.

6. Most animals were caught in areas where red algae Laurencia
or Digenia were abundant; less were taken in Thalassia and least
where little or no algae or seagrasses occurred.

7. With the increased temperature and increased flow expected
with the nuclear generators, damage to the area will escalate
unless alternate methods of cooling are implemented.

Assuming, for example's sake, that the nature and extent of thermal pollution is worth considering and that the results are sufficiently validated
to test that assumption elsewhere, let's move the problem of discharging
great amounts of heated water into a northeastern coastal area. If the heated water could be prevented from entering the estuary, one problem could be
solved, but what else could be done with such heated water? Again, we have
an actual instance to consider, but in this case the findings come from experimentation on the northwest coast. In the late 1960s, a water project
conducted on the Mackenzie River in Oregon experimentally used thermal waters
for agriculture. The findings in the Springfield Project were impressive:

- Increased yield and quality of crops through control of
  soil temperature and moisture content.

- Prevention of frost damage through heat dissipation from
  warm water application during frost conditions.

- Prevention of sunburn on soft fruits through control of
  humidity and atmospheric temperature.

- Lengthening of growing season for row crops and the possibility of double cropping.

- Introduction of new crops.

- Prevention of cold water shock.

- Fuller fruits and nutmeats through humidity control.

- The effect of thermal water irrigation on soil reduced leaching and runoff of herbicides, fertilizers, and pesticides.

In this project thermally heated water was used for frost control, irrigation,
and undersoil heating for a period of 5 years on 70 acres of orchard for

frost control and on 100 acres for row-crop planting. Thermal water from the Weyerhauser Company's Springfield mill was pumped 2 miles to the test site, seven adjoining farms. The project anticipated the installation of a thermonuclear generating plant and concomitant thermal water disposal problems. The major conclusions are these:

1. Water, after being used for irrigating the farms in the Springfield Project, has been returned unheated to the Mackenzie River; no detrimental effects were observed, and the enormously expensive cooling procedures which totally waste heat were not required.

2. No fruit buds in thermal-water-protected orchards were damaged by a severe spring freeze. A full crop of peaches was produced in the project orchards. Unprotected orchards in the surrounding countryside produced no crop to a very light crop of peaches.

3. Less warm water than cold was required for irrigation; less damage to trees, lower water costs, and reduced nutrient leaching from the soil accompanied the use of warm water.

4. Undersoil heating of greenhouse-covered soils increased yields of asparagus by 44-95%; market readiness of rhododendron nursery stock advanced by one year; Japanese cucumber growth was markedly increased and could produce an estimated $100,000 per acre crop.

5. The warm water was used to cool plants during hot summer periods above 85° F (near the temperature at which plant growth decreases and injury may occur). The plants were not harmed by the process and were kept under the plant-injury temperature.

6. There were no increases in fungi, molds, or bacterial infestations in any of the crops.

7. The multi-use thermal water system would be approximately one-third the cost of other systems combined to provide irrigation and frost protection.

Results from the Springfield Project suggest that it is possible to convert a thermal water discharge problem into an environmental benefit at a cost-effective return. If there were a "Turkey Point Problem" in New England, there could be a "Springfield Project Solution" there as well. The implications of these two separate studies are pertinent not only for power producers and agriculture, but also for industry and public recreation, pyrolitic waste disposal and steam heat customers, and other producer/consumer energy couples. The major goal in extrapolating such findings to solve an analogous New England case is to protect the estuary.

A summary from an actual Presumpscot River rehabilitation story follows here as a concluding perspective on the significance of the estuary to a community and on the practicalities of solving land-use conflicts in such an area.

In the Presumpscot River estuary in Maine, papermill wastes and untreated sludges resulted in "the building of sludge depositions in the estuary which smothered the mudflat habitat of shellfish and worms. The decomposition of wood fibers caused large amounts of noxious hydrogen sulfide gas to be generated, causing an extremely serious problem." Associated problems included low dissolved oxygen, high coliforms in shellfish, and the elimination of pollution-intolerant organisms. Subsequently, there were losses of local food resources, reduction in shellfishing employment, lowering of land tax appraisals, and the closing of recreational beaches. After 100 years of pollution and attempts to halt it, this opinion was reached:

> The estuary and lower river will never be as productive as they were in the days of Chief Skittergusset. The area surrounding the Presumpscot will probably continue to develop; that is the basis of our economic system and seems to be an underlying factor that shapes our society. How the resources of the Presumpscot are used will reflect the attitudes of society towards the natural resource ethic and the growth ethic. If the growth ethic prevails, only a segment of society will benefit, and the area's value will be realized largely in monetary terms and short run benefits. The natural ecosystem, just recovering from more than a hundred years of destruction by pollution, will be injured by uses incompatible with the ecosystem and crowded out by too much development. If a natural resource ethic is incorporated, the restored estuarine ecosystem would be regarded as an integral part of the regional community. . . providing benefits for all people of all generations.

CHAPTER SUMMARY

1. The coastal areas contain the most productive habitats in the world. U. S. estuarine and wetlands areas are diminished and polluted, however, and in response the Congress has enacted the Coastal Zone Management Act, involving 35 states.

2. Estuaries are intertidal zones where fresh and saltwaters mix. Physically they stratify by salinity, temperature, and topography. Chemically, they differ in elements, concentrations, and nutrients. Ecologically, they have ideal conditions for accommodating the diversity of species.

3. Point and non-point sources inexorably provide cropland soil, mine tailings, manufacturing wastes, landfill leachates, urban stormwater, municipal sewage--ad infinitum--into this ideal ecological system.

4. The estuaries are accumulating land-use debts. Sulfide depositions and nuclear plant hot-water discharges are two types of pollutants which have a record of usury. Alternatives to the discharge of pollutants into the nation's surface waters are possible and reasonable.

5. Thermal wastewater, for example, increased yield and quality of fruit and vegetable crops in the Mackenzie River, Oregon, experimental "Springfield Project."

SOURCES

Bella, David A. Tidal Flats in Estuarine Water Quality Analysis. Corvallis, Oregon: U. S. EPA, June 1975.

Berry, James W. and Herman H. Miller, Jr. A Demonstration of Thermal Water Utilization in Agriculture. Washington, D. C.: GPO, April 1974.

Boone, Joseph G. and Benjamin M. Florence. The Status of the Striped Bass and Maryland's Role in the Fortunes of This Valuable Fish. Annapolis, Maryland: Chesapeake Bay Foundation, June 1976.

Lippson, Alice Jane. The Chesapeake Bay in Maryland. Baltimore, Maryland: Johns Hopkins Press, 1973.

Roessler, Martin A. and Durbin C. Tabb. Studies of Effects of Thermal Pollution in Biscayne Bay, Florida. Washington, D. C.: GPO, August 1974.

Sherwood, Arthur W. Understanding the Chesapeake: A Layman's Guide. Cambridge, Maryland: Tidewater Publishers, 1973.

SUGGESTED READING

Clark, John. Coastal Ecosystems: Ecological Considerations for Management of the Coastal Zone. Washington, D. C.: The Conservation Foundation and the National Oceanic and Atmospheric Administration, 1974.

Darnell, Rezneat M., et. al. Impacts of Construction in Wetlands of the United States. Springfield, Virginia: National Technical Information Service, 1976.

Emery, K. O. "The Continental Shelves," in The Ocean. Ed. Philip Morrison. San Francisco: W. H. Freeman and Co., 1969.

Engel, Leonard, et. al. The Sea. New York: Time, Inc., 1961.

Marx, Wesley. The Frail Ocean. New York: Ballantine Books, 1976.

Myers, Phyllis. Zoning Hawaii. Washington, D. C.: The Conservation Foundation, 1976.

Steward, R. W. "The Atmosphere and the Ocean," in The Ocean. Ed. Philip Morrison. San Francisco: W. H. Freeman and Co., 1969.

Wend, Edward. "The Physical Resources of the Ocean," in The Ocean. Ed. Philip Morrison. San Francisco: W. H. Freeman and Co., 1969.

Zim, Herbert S. and Lester Ingle. Seashores: A Guide to the Animals and Plants along the Beaches. New York: Golden Press, 1965.

CHAPTER ELEVEN

THE ENVIRONMENT AND HUMAN HEALTH

A PERSPECTIVE

The most terrible outbreak of cholera in this Kingdom
is probably what took place . . . a few weeks ago. Within two hundred and fifty yards of the spot where Cambridge
Street joins Broad Street, there were upwards of five hundred fatal attacks of cholera in ten days. . . . The greater number of cases terminated in a few hours.

I requested permission to take a list of the deaths . . .
which was kindly granted. . . . I found that nearly all
deaths had taken place within a short distance of the pump
(at Broad Street). There were only ten deaths in houses decidedly nearer to another street pump. In five of these
cases, the families of the deceased persons informed me that
they had always sent to the pump on Broad Street as they pre-
ferred the water to that of the pump which was nearer. In
three other cases, the deceased were children who went to
school near the pump on Broad Street.

I had an interview with the Board of Guardians of the St.
James' Parish on the evening of Thursday, 7th September,
1849 and represented the above circumstances to them. In
consequence of what I said, the handle of the pump was removed the following day.

> Excerpted from a report by John Snow
> of London, England, in George Berg's
> Water Pollution

Asiatic cholera is a severe infection of the intestinal tract produced
by the Vibrio comma bacterium. The cholera vibrio is a short, comma-shaped
bacterium, flagellated at both ends, which grows rapidly in the small intestine
and breaks down the cell walls. This process begun, the tissues can no longer retain body fluids and, in severe infections, the loss of fluids can cause
death. The vibrio bacterium is passed with feces into the water and, if the
infected wastewater leaks into the drinking water supply, the kind of situation described by Mr. Snow in the chapter's perspective follows quickly. The
immediate solution to the environmental problem of September 7th, 1849 was
sublime.

The biosphere contains many different types of health hazards. Some are
natural, like the vibrio bacterium, some manmade, like PCBs, others are com-

plex mixtures, such as photochemical oxidants. The types which relate most closely to the air, soil, and water principles which we have discussed from various perspectives up to this chapter are those agents which cause short-term or long-term toxic changes in human health and which are essentially ubiquitous in the biosphere.

These agents are chemicals whose atoms bond together by means discussed earlier and in forms that may differ from normally functioning biochemicals by a mere twist of one atom on one side of a molecule or another, or by the substitution of a group of atoms for another group. Most of the hazardous chemicals closely resemble the normal life chemicals; thereby, the attackers are well disguised. Such poisons (toxins), each having a special tactic, can work swiftly, creating a condition that is acute. Others are slow and persistent, creating one that is chronic. Regardless of the degree of effect they have, they usually invade alone, but can collectively as well. They are always obstinate until they meet their match.

Chemical Toxins

Let's consider how man specifically contracts toxic diseases and what the toxins can actually do to the highly complex human system. Any category of chemical, natural or synthetic, is a toxin if it induces one or more adverse biological effects. Short-term acute or long-term chronic effects may appear in a human of any age--a fetus, a newborn, a toddler, a child, an adolescent, or an adult. The consequences of such toxic attacks may range from mild illness to death. Acute toxic effects are normally easy to recognize and to link to particular chemicals. Therefore, manmade toxins causing acute health problems usually can be prevented from contaminating humans by pre-release screenings in laboratory tests. Chronic toxins, however, are not so analyzable, and often go undetected. Such toxins can have very broad, long-term effects, inducing cancer (carcinogenicity), birth defects (teratogenicity), or gene damage (mutagenicity). Sweepingly, chronic toxicity may also impair the general function of a person's system of immunity and it may be associated with psychobehavioral disorders. To complicate matters, these chemicals can also interact to produce an effect that neither one causes alone--an action we describe as "synergistic." Such chemicals include food additives, pesticides, or drugs, and the time and site of interaction are usually unknown. Even more worrisome than these known toxins and their symptoms are the anticipated introduction of new toxic chemicals of which we have little or no knowledge and over which we have little or no control.

Acute Toxicity

The most obvious way in which people are affected adversely by chemicals, excluding microorganisms, is acute poisoning. Officially, about 5,000 deaths per year in the U. S. are attributable to this cause,[1,2] * and there is reason

---

* Sources are indicated in notes at the end of the chapter rather than in the text, because of frequent citation of research data.

to believe that this is a conservative figure. The numbers of non-fatal poisonings and other toxic reactions from chemical products used by consumers in the home each year are listed in Figure 46. The majority of these poisonings occur in children under the age of five. Prevention of such accidental poisoning requires safe packaging and the use of less hazardous ingredients whenever possible.

POISONINGS AND OTHER TOXIC REACTIONS FROM CHEMICAL CONSUMER
PRODUCTS PER YEAR (see ref. 2)

Product	Number injured
Laundering, cleaning, and polishing products	
Poisoning from soaps, detergents, cleaners	40,000
Poisoning from bleaches	35,000
Poisoning from disinfectants, deodorizers	20,000
Poisonings from furniture polish	20,000
Poisonings from lye corrosives	15,000
Other poisonings from laundering, cleaning, & polishing products	20,000
Other injuries from laundering, cleaning, & polishing products	100,000
	250,000
Pesticides	
Poisoning from insecticides	35,000
Poisoning from rodenticides	20,000
Other poisoning from pesticides	20,000
	75,000
Cosmetics*	
Injuries from perfume & toilet water	20,000
Injuries from lotions & creams	10,000
Other injuries from cosmetics	30,000
	60,000
Miscellaneous	
Poisonings from airplane glue	25,000
Poisonings from lighter fluid	15,000
Poisonings from kerosene	15,000
Poisonings from turpentine	25,000
Poisonings from other flammable liquids	10,000
	90,000
Total all products	475,000

* Injuries from cosmetics are chiefly skin eruptions, loss of hair, severe allergic reactions, etc., sufficiently serious to restrict activity for 1 day or require medical attention.

Figure 46

Acute toxic effects can result from dermal and respiratory tract exposure to chemical toxins one contacts at work, but no adequate studies support estimates of either the number or the severity of such cases.

A more subtle kind of poisoning is found in the indirect acute and chronic effects of community air pollutants-- chiefly sulfur dioxide and particulates--on the incidence of common respiratory diseases. Although we know that these diseases are primarily infectious ones, increases of acute respiratory illnesses in children and adults have been associated clearly with high pollutant levels, taking into consideration the effects of weather and other variables.[3]   A recent study of some families in New York and Chicago indicates that in several of the adult groups respiratory illness increased by more than 30 percent with heightened levels of air pollution.

Chronic Toxicity

Chronic toxicity is any adverse health effect which develops over time from a chemical or physical pollutant. The most frequent are occurrences of the pollutant itself (or its metabolized form) being incompletely excreted. Repeated exposure builds up concentrations of it in sensitive organs. Heavy metals such as lead and mercury typify these toxins. Because of the slow accumulation over months of exposure and the gradual onset of non-specific symptoms (gastric distress, irritability), lead and mercury poisoning are seldom recognized. Generally, they damage severely the nervous system and the kidneys. In addition, mental retardation and childhood hyperactivity are well-recognized effects of lead poisoning in children.

Many kinds of dust present in the work environment cause long-term debilitating lung diseases called pneumoconioses.[5] About 125,000 coal miners suffer from a particular variety called "black lung," a disease causing 3,000 to 4,000 deaths each year.[6] Similar conditions are asbestosis from asbestos and asbestos-like fibers, byssinosis from cotton, bagassosis from sugar cane, and silicosis from various silica-laden dusts. Overall, about 9,000 people die yearly from these occupational dust-related diseases.

The widely prevalent lung diseases--bronchitis, emphysema, and asthma-- are aggravated by occupational and communal air pollutants. Many pollutants interact with certain weather conditions to intensify the severity of such illnesses. Figure 47 shows that the daily percentage of asthma attacks increases with greater SO_2 concentrations when the ambient temperature is at 50° F and higher, but the attack rate remains constant, regardless of SO_2 concentration, at temperatures between 0° and 30° F. Temperature is independent of the relationship between weather conditions such as inversions and air pollutant concentrations. Such findings suggest that land-use planners should consider programs for pollution control that are guided by the interrelationships of pollutants, air temperature, and the general health of the community's residents.

Routes of Human Exposure

We've touched on three major routes of human exposure to chemicals: skin/

mucous membrane contact, ingestion, and inhalation. For drugs, there is a fourth route: the "parenteral," such as intravenous or intramuscular injection. The effects of chemicals may be restricted to the initial site of exposure, such as the skin or lungs, or may become generalized in later absorption.

RELATIONSHIP BETWEEN ASTHMA AND POLLUTION

Shown is the asthma attack rate versus daily sulfur dioxide concentration within three temperature ranges. (see ref. 17)

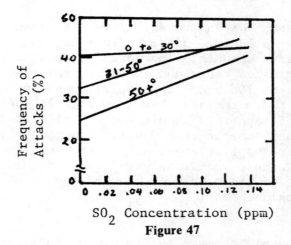

SO$_2$ Concentration (ppm)

Figure 47

Depending on the chemical, exposure may occur through more than one of these routes. For example, with household aerosol-propelled insecticides, exposures are by direct skin contact, by eating contaminated food, and most importantly, by inhalation. There are several routes of exposure for hair sprays, deodorants, and other aerosol products. Children living in dilapidated inner-city housing often risk serious lead poisoning both by eating peeled lead-based paint and by inhaling lead particulates from automobile exhaust which seeps into the building.[7]

Asbestos is another multiple-entry toxin. Asbestos and asbestos-like mineral fibers--which may be human carcinogens*--may be inhaled, swallowed in drinking water, or ingested. Mentioned earlier, the Silver Bay, Minnesota iron ore tailings release into Lake Superior tons of waste which contains asbestos. Asbestos and similar fibers found in many urban water supplies possibly originate from asbestos-cement water conduits.[8]

We can see that toxins come from many sources and invade man at every moment and in all parts of the body--all this as he goes about his everyday activities.

---

*Ed. note: There is much controversy about whether ingested asbestos is carcinogenic. We encourage the reader to remember that research is actively proceeding in the many areas of public health that we are discussing.

Categories of Toxic Chemicals

The spectrum of chemicals naturally present in the biosphere is broad enough, but now thousands of synthetic chemicals are in the biosphere. They are commercially produced at the rate of about 500 new ones yearly. A survey of the basic natural and synthetic toxic chemicals we know about indicates the nature of the problem of toxic and hazardous substances.

Simple Organics

Some of the simplest, most universal materials--arsenic, barium, cadmium, chromium, lead, mercury, selenium, silver, fluoride, and nitrates--can be harmful, particularly in large amounts. Inorganic arsenic is normally present in soil in the parts per million range and in seawater in parts per billion. The drinking water standard is .05 ppm. Some animals concentrate arsenic by accumulating it from all of the materials they ingest. Although there is no study showing the incidence of cancer in people whose diet contains prawns, these shellfish contain as much arsenic as 170 ppm.[9] Contamination by quantities of arsenic in freshwater supplies apparently increases frequency of cancer: of 40,000 southwestern Taiwanese who drank water from arsenic contaminated artesian wells, 20 percent of those over 60 year of age--i.e., those with the longest exposure--had skin cancer.[10]

Other studies of people exposed to arsenic by inhaling and/or ingesting arsenical insecticides and by inhaling inorganic arsenic from copper smelting operations do indicate correlation between arsenic intake and skin and lung tumors. Nitrates and nitrites, simple inorganic ions widely distributed in nature, pose recognized public health hazards. Nitrates in drinking water can

INCIDENCE OF SKIN CANCER

Age-specific prevalence rate (percent) as a function of arsenic concentration (ppm) in well water. (see ref. 10)

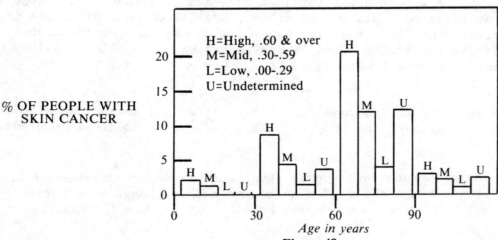

Figure 48

come from fertilizer runoff; they can be converted--more readily by babies--
to nitrites which can block the oxygen-carrying capacity of blood. (Babies
have less stomach acidity than adults, a characteristic making them more tolerable to certain bacteria which reduce nitrate compounds to nitrites.) The
nitrite then diffuses through intestinal walls into the blood stream. There
it reacts with hemoglobin and causes a condition called "methemoglobinemia,"
in which hemoglobin cannot carry oxygen. The symptom is a bluish appearance--
hence "blue babies," those newborns afflicted by low oxygen levels.

Substantial amounts of nitrate can be found in some vegetables such as
spinach. Nitrate levels in vegetation increase with the use of phenoxy herbicides such as 2,4-D. Nitrates and nitrites are deliberately added to cured
ham, bacon, and sausage to preserve the red color during storage and cooking.
Some other uses of nitrite in foods ostensibly help to prevent botulism, but
the usefulness of nitrite for all of these purposes is questionable because
instruction on safe use is inadequately documented. The unnecessary introduction of nitrate/nitrite additives in foods, particularly for "cosmetic purposes," has aroused special concern because nitrite tends to combine with secondary and tertiary amines, other chemicals naturally present in various foods,
to form nitrosamines--a class of substances with high carcinogenic, teratogenic, and mutagenic potential.[11,12] Recent experiments suggest that substantial
nitrosamine formation may be catalyzed by bacteria in the intestine and by
acid in the stomach. Even more recent evidence indicates that oxides of nitrogen, such as those present in air pollutants, can combine with nitrosate
amines to form airborne nitrosamines, creating yet another source of contamination for air and water supplies.[13]

Natural Organics

Clearly, "natural" is not necessarily synonymous with "harmless." Naturally occurring toxic organic chemicals--in the amounts and locations where they
have occurred for millennia--have coexisted on Earth with surviving species of
plants and animals without totally exterminating all members of any current individual life form. The following are examples of some familiar natural foodstuffs containing toxic organic chemicals:

- Peach pits, bitter almonds, lima beans, and cassava contain particular sugars (cyanogenic glycosides) which can
  be hydrolyzed to release hydrogen cyanide enzymes liberated upon crushing. Despite cooking and other procedures
  to remove most of the cyanide, peripheral neuropathy from
  long-term cyanide poisoning is a major problem among poor
  people in Nigeria, for whom cassava is a dietary staple.

- A number of foods contain substances that destroy or make
  unavailable certain vitamins. Raw soybeans have an enzyme
  (lipoxidase) that destroys carotene. Raw egg white contains a protein (avidin) which binds diotin (vitamin H) so
  strongly as to make it unavailable for use.

- Some fungi, particularly the <u>Aspergillus</u> genus, produce potent toxins. Aflatoxin, produced by <u>Aspergillus flavus</u> mainly on groundnuts, is one of the most powerful carcinogenic materials known. Another famous composite of fungal toxins is produced in rye infected with <u>Claviceps purpurea</u>. Humans who eat contaminated rye may suffer hallucinations and convulsions or gangrenous destruction of limb tissue, known in previous centuries as Saint Anthony's fire. However, most antibiotics are fungal toxins whose major reactions are to bacteria rather than animals.

- A number of plants contain substances that affect the central nervous system: the stimulants in coffee (caffeine) and tobacco (nicotine); and the mind-altering substances in poppies (morphine), peyote cactus (mescaline), and Mexican mushroom (psilocybin).

<u>Synthetic Organics</u>

Figure 49 below shows six general classes of organic chemicals of which man synthesizes several billion pounds per year. All classes, cyclic intermediates, plastics, rubber, surface-active agents, and others (except pesticides) increased in 1970 over production in 1967. All classes reported increased hundreds-fold since 1964.[6,14] These materials have been degraded into other forms or they persist in original form--somewhere in the world.

SYNTHETIC ORGANIC CHEMICALS

1970 production and percent increase in production from 1967 and from 1949. (see ref. 8, 10)

Class of chemical	1970 production (billions of lbs)	Increase 1967-1970	Increase 1949-1970
Cyclic intermediates	28.3	38%	N/A
Plastics, resin material, & plasticizers	20.6	36%	1,130%
Synthetic rubber & rubber processing	4.7	16%	350%
Surface-active agents	3.9	12%	810%
Pesticides	1.0	-2%	710%
Others	79.7	33%	550%
Total or weighed average	138.2	32%	N/A

Figure 49

The portion of these chemicals that are harmful to man is simply unknown. In fact, no general screening exists for determining their possible harmful effects on chemical production workers, distributors, or applicators, not to mention the general public. The disturbing aspect is the latency period between the introduction of the chemical and the appearance of symptoms. Therefore, we face the double dilemma of neither knowing which of these are toxic nor knowing how long each one's latency period lasts before adverse effects appear. Consider the case of polyvinyl chloride, PVC.

Polyvinyl chloride plastics were first introduced on a large scale in the 1950s. Production grew about 15 percent per year until 1970, when it reached four billion pounds (included in the category of "Others" in Figure 49. Recently several cases of a previously rare form of liver cancer, angiosarcoma, have been detected among the workers engaged in polymerizing vinyl chloride. A few years ago this same chemical was shown to produce cancer in laboratory animals. In all cases, the latency period for these workers has been more than 12 years. Average latency time for all tumors that may result from exposure to a given carcinogen can be as many as 30 to 40 years. Billions of pounds of polyvinyl chloride compounds have been and are now being produced for many uses, including propellants for aerosols.

The agricultural chemicals--fertilizers, pesticides, fungicides, and herbicides--are thought to be likely toxic organics, although their effects in most cases are unknown for reasons given above. Some, like DDT, have been identified as harmful and are in control programs. In 1973, 95 percent of all DDT in humans was ingested from dairy and meat products. Since then, the federal ban on DDT has reduced its residues in those two food groups and, as expected, residues in humans. Findings by the National Human Monitoring Program call for restrictions--if not a complete ban--on DDT. In 1967 it found DDT in 99+ percent of all the human tissue samples taken; in 1973, 100 percent. However, the residue level in 1970 was 7.87 ppm and in 1973 down to 5.89 ppm. DDT residues in young children are declining more consistently than in older persons, an indication of the recent decline in intake. The parent DDT is found in decreasing proportion to one of its metabolites, DDE. DDE found in human tissues today indicates DDT that entered the tissue years ago.[8]

Aldrin, a boll weevil control, breaks down into Dieldrin. Both are chlorinated hydrocarbons that degrade slowly to biologically inactive products. Widespread contamination from Aldrin appeared in the 1960s. Used in 1955 to kill sand flies in St. Lucie County, Florida, it killed instead 1,000,000 fish of 30 different species and halted reproduction for weeks in those fish that survived. Later it was demonstrated to accumulate in fish, then in fish-eating predators such as eagles, which were debilitated by the high concentrations of the toxin. Aldrin/Dieldrin impaired the eagles' ability to produce adequately thick egg shells. Once Aldrin/Dieldrin was proven to be carcinogenic to laboratory animals, it was presumed to be carcinogenic to humans as well.[8]

Upon learning of these specific cause-effect relationships, authorities of the EPA banned the use of these chemicals in 1971. Application dropped from 21,000,000 pounds in 1966 to 10,000,000 in 1974 and to 273,000 pounds in 1975 (mostly for termite control). However, Aldrin/Dieldrin still persists in undiminished concentrations in the midwestern United States because of heavy use in the 1960s. Other reports confirm their persistence in air and water, though in 1975 relatively low amounts found in songbirds confirm the general decline in use of these chemicals nationwide.

In humans, the trend is a constant level of Aldrin/Dieldrin in 99 percent of human tissues in all age groups for 1970-1973. The intake levels are dropping somewhat. Diminished residue levels show now in potatoes, cereals, and grains to which the pesticide had been applied previously, while levels are constant in dairy products, meat, fish, and poultry--all of which are second-order consumers of the contaminated cereals and grains. With information campaigns on the harmful effects of DDT and Aldrin/Dieldrin and regulations limiting their sale and use, we can project reductions of both in the biosphere.[8]

PCBs, as mentioned in Chapter 8, are also long-lasting toxic chemicals. Recognized for their toxicity to lower-order organisms in the food web, they too are being removed from the biosphere. While acute toxicity in humans is low, since 1966 a fascinating record of food web accumulations has been developing that bodes ill for man. PCBs are accumulated by organisms that feed on others; the increased accumulation concentrates along the food chain. In the United States it is estimated that over 40 percent of the population has one part per million absorbed in adipose (fat) tissue.[15] In 1968, a severe form of skin disease was diagnosed in Japanese families that consumed rice oil contaminated with Kanechlor 400 (a PCB with 48 percent chlorine content). The "Yusho syndrome" is characterized by swelling of the upper eyelids, visual impairment, acne-like blemishes, and heightened pigmentation of the skin. Patients also exhibit neurological disorders and hearing impairments. When PCBs were diffused through the placental membranes of pregnant mothers, babies were smaller than average and had similar symptoms. Most patients recovered slowly because the PCBs apparently are retained for a very long time.

As in the case of Aldrin/Dieldrin, once PCBs' effects were known, efforts began to remove them from the market. The actions show results: in 1971, PCBs were present in levels as high as .36 ppm in 5 percent of 360 composite foods-- meat, fish, poultry, or grain products; in 1972, 12 percent of the foods analyzed contained PCBs, but average levels in meat, fish, and poultry had declined, the highest level detected having dropped to .15 ppm. In 1973 and 1974, residues in food fell both in the range of food and the level of PCBs in each food tested. The last analysis showed PCBs in 4 percent of the foods, at a level of about .05 ppm. Dietary intake dropped from an estimated .1 ppm. per kilogram of body weight in 1971, to .02 in 1973, and .001 in 1974. While residues in foodstuffs generally have declined, PCBs still appear in the system.[8,15] Producers of PCBs have voluntarily cut production by half, but the use persists because of the expense of destroying this synthetic organic. Further restrictions on the application of PCBs may be necessary before environmental levels as a whole stabilize and decline. By these examples, however, we can see some of the impacts which organic chemicals have upon the biosphere and its individual life forms.

Microorganisms

There are many other sources of illness for humans. Viruses cause

Poliomyelitis, chicken pox, and the swine flu. Rickettsia cause typhus and Rocky Mountain spotted fevers, while bacteria infect man with scarlet fever, pneumonia, tuberculosis, diphtheria, bubonic plague, cholera, strep throat, and gangrene. Single-cell organisms and multi-celled animals cause dysentery; malaria; pinworm, tapeworm, and hookworm infections; and hundreds of other debilitating diseases. The history of successes and failures in recognizing and controlling the source of such microorganisms and their entry into the human system is a long and troublesome one that continues.

There are 76 viruses known to be pathogenic to man. Those found in our swimming and drinking waters include adenoviruses, Coxsackie viruses, ECHO viruses, viruses of infectious hepatitis, polioviruses, and reoviruses. Of the viral illnesses, only infectious hepatitis is known to be waterborne; polio is suspected to be. Because some viruses are known carcinogens in certain animals, they are suspected carcinogens in man.

Bacterial waterborne diseases include intestinal illnesses, such as dysentery, typhoid fever, paratyphoid fevers, cholera, and gastroenteritis, as well as the less common tuberculosis, anthrax, brucellosis, tularemia, leptospirosis, and others. To survive in water, these bacteria and other microorganisms must cope successfully with the full range of environmental conditions that include variations in levels of oxygen, pH, temperature, sunlight, nutrients, sediments, and chemicals. They also must elude their natural predators. Consequently, the probability seems small that the right number and type of viruses, bacteria, and other microorganisms should be present at the right time and the right place to cause serious infections, yet they can be, and the infections may be widespread. An outbreak of typhoid fever involved 437 people at Zermatt, Switzerland in 1963; an epidemic of gastroenteritis caused by Salmonella typhimurium sickened 18,000 people in Riverside, California in 1965.[16] More recently, another intestinal infection, carried by Shigella Flexneri and Shigella heidelberg, incapacitated 2,500 people in Madera City, California in 1965.

Impacts on Cancer

In 1900 microorganisms caused 31% of all deaths in the U.S. Pneumonia, influenza, tuberculosis, and gastritis were the number one killers then. With immunization and antibiotics, controls of such diseases were possible and fewer people died. In 1900, heart disease and cancer held the 4th and 8th positions and were responsible for 12 percent of the deaths. In 1978 they are now 1st and 2nd, and cause 50 percent of the deaths.[8,17,18,19] Microorganisms seem controllable with rapid-response immunization and bactericidal programs. However, genetic mutations threaten always to produce a virulent strain, like that thought to cause the enigmatic "Legionnaire's Disease." "Legionnaires' Disease," thought to be a bacterial infection, killed 27 people who attended a convention in Philadelphia in 1976. In 1977 more cases were diagnosed across the country.

The annual death rate from heart disease rose from 137.4/100,000 population in 1900 to 362 in 1970. Deaths from cancer climbed from 64/100,000 to 162.8. Cancer killed 358,000 U. S. citizens in 1974; about 1,000,000 are now under treatment for it. About one third of the cancers are of the skin; the rest seriously or fatally attack other areas of the body.[8] Generally, cancer is the unchecked growth of certain cells. Specifically, its other names relate to the body area attacked:

- In connective tissue: <u>sarcoma</u>

- In internal and external lining (lung, breast, skin): <u>carcinoma</u>

- In the circulatory systems: <u>leukemias</u> or <u>lymphomas</u>.

It is estimated that 60-90 percent of all cancer is related to environmental factors, including cigarette smoking, occupational exposures, natural agents such as solar and cosmic radiation, natural asbestos, and aflatoxins. Probably 90 percent of all causes of cancer are directly attributable to environmental chemicals.[8,20-23]

The majority of known environmental carcinogens are at the workplace. Above normal frequencies occur in workers having contact with known or suspected carcinogens such as asbestos, arsenic, benzopyrene, bis-chlorolethyl-ether, benzidine, coal tar, carbon black, and vinyl chloride. Benzidine, for example, was related to bladder tumors in 1965; 17 of 76 (21%) coal tar dye plant workers exceeded the national frequency of .0132% for bladder cancer. Because of the long latency period for tumors, many more workers are expected to have bladder tumors during the 1980s. Similar correlations between workplace and carcinogens are made for people who are smokers and whose employment brings them into contact with asbestos and/or vinyl chloride. Other job-related cancers include lung cancer in uranium miners of Colorado; skin cancer in cutting and shale oil workers; nasal-sinus cancer in wood workers; lung cancer and pleural mesotheliomas in insulation handlers; and cancer of the pancreas in organic chemists.[8]

Surprisingly, only very weak regulations protect workers whose jobs expose them to specific pollutants.[24] There is no general requirement for safety testing and standard-setting for industrial chemicals before workers handle them. Of the tens of thousands of toxic substances found on the job, fewer than 500 have official standards for exposure to them. Even these few standards could prevent only the most obvious and immediate toxic effects. Little or no margin of safety is allowed between the minimal levels of known toxic pollutants and permissable levels. Figure 50 shows the greater pollutant level allowed workers than allowed the general population.

Let's examine more closely the various causes of lung cancer, returning briefly to asbestos workers as a case in point. Those who are non-smokers contract lung cancer at normal rates, but a cigarette smoker who works with asbestos has eight times the risk of dying of lung cancer as similar smokers of the same age who do not work with asbestos, and 92 times the risk of laborers who neither work with asbestos nor smoke.[8]

ENVIRONMENTAL VERSUS OCCUPATIONAL STANDARDS
(see ref. 25)

Pollutant	Environmental Standard *	Occupational Standard **
Sulfur dioxide (ppm)	Annual arithmetic mean=.03	5
Carbon monoxide	Maximum 24 hr once/yr=.14	
	Maximum 3 hr once/yr=.50	
	Maximum 8 hr once/yr=9	50
Nitrogen dioxide (ppm)	Maximum 1 hr once/yr=35	
	Annual arithmetic mean=.5	5
Particulates (milligrams/cubic meter)	Annual geometric mean=.075	res- 5 pirable fraction
Lead (in micrograms/cubic meter)	Maximum 24 hr once/yr=.26	total 15 dust
	30-day mean=1.5	200

* Environmental Protection Agency standards for community air pollution exposure (except for lead standard--from California Air Resources Board)
** Occupational Safety and Health Administration (OSHA) Standards, levels based on 8 hours per day of exposure

Figure 50

The best documented and most significant data on cancer from environmental chemicals are those on tobaccos. It has been suspected for several decades that heavy tobacco smoking is directly and causally related to chronic lung disease, especially cancer. Over 29 studies published from 1939 to 1964 generally substantiate the causative role smoking plays, one of the most important demonstrating clearly that cases of lung cancer increased with cigarette smoking.[26,27]

Mortality rates from lung cancer in men and women have increased alarmingly over the last few decades in the United States and have now reached epidemic proportions. Many studies cite evidence on how urban air pollution contributes to lung cancer, and they identify numerous classes of chemical carcinogens in polluted urban air. Such research has shown an excess of lung cancer deaths in smokers living in polluted urban areas, compared with those living in non-polluted rural areas.[29] Similar strong, regional variations in the incidence of a wide range of other organ cancers are now well recognized.[30-37]

Another environmental factor links oral cancer and dietary habits. Oral cancer accounts for 35 percent of all Asiatic cancers, and is clearly related to the chewing of Betel nuts and tobacco leaves. The high incidence of liver cancer among the Bantu and natives of Guam may well be due to dietary contam-

ination by aflatoxin,[38] the powerful cancer-causing fungus mentioned earlier,
and to eating Cycad plants.[39-41] Widespread gastric cancer in Japan, Iceland,
and Chile is probably connected to the predominant fish diet: secondary amines
natural in fish and the added nitrite preservative may react to form nitrosamines. Coincidentally, numerous cases of cancer of the esophagus in Zambia,
the Calvados area of France, and other geographic areas may be related to nitrosamines in alcoholic drinks. Nitrosamines in experimental animals have
caused cancer of the esophagus.[36,37,42-44]

Usually, the more potent the carcinogenic agent, the sooner it is identified as a cause of cancer. Very low levels of aflatoxins and nitrosamines can
produce cancer in experimental animals, but even these low levels have been
found in certain foods. Weaker carcinogens such as atmospheric pollutants,
certain pesticides, and food additives may escape detection by biological
tests. Undetected and with prolonged latency periods, they may cause more
harm in the long run than the most powerful carcinogens.

Impacts on Birth Defects

Three major categories of human teratogens (agents that produce birth defects) have so far been identified: viral infections; x-irradiation; and chemicals, such as mercurials, thalidomide, and diethylstilbestrol.[45]

Thalidomide, for example, is a drug that was widely marketed in Europe
in the late 1950s and early 1960s for use by pregnant women with "morning sick-
ness." An alert medical practitioner associated the drug with a recent incidence of malformed limbs of a peculiar type in thousands of newborns. Thalidomide was detected as a human teratogen only because of the dramatic and unusual nature of the birth defect it produced: paired defects, or bilateral ampu-
tations of limbs. If it had been responsible for a similar incidence of unseen
effects, such as congenital heart defects, it probably still would be in use as
a "safe drug."

Impacts on Mutations

A mutation is defined as any inheritable change in the genetic material.
This may be a chemical transformation of an individual gene (gene or point
mutation) that causes it to have an altered function. Alternatively, the
change may involve a microscopically visible rearrangement, or gain, or loss
of parts of a chromosome (chromosome aberration). In studying an individual
defect in a human, it isn't always possible to tell whether the defect is due
to point mutation or chromosome aberration.

The first clue that environmental pollutants may influence the genetic
constitution of future populations appeared some four decades ago with the discovery that ionizing radiation induces mutations. The subsequent development
of atomic energy has heightened the potential for such changes in genes and

therefore heightened our concern for finding safeguards to help to minimize radiation exposure. Once radiation-induced mutagenesis was discovered, there were reasons to suspect that some chemicals would cause similar effects, but proof was delayed until World War II when mustard gas was shown to induce mutations in fruit flies. Many and varied types of chemicals have subsequently proved to be mutagenic. The likelihood that some highly mutagenic ones may come into wide use, or indeed already are in wide use, now seriously concerns us.[46-49]

Mutations may occur in any somatic (body) or gene (ovum or sperm) cell. Often the particular cell involved dies, resulting in only brief and local damage. However, if the cell's genetic role changes while the cell's capacity to divide is unharmed, the mutation can be transmitted to descendant cells. These effects may result in cancer in the body cells of the adult or the embryo, or in birth defects in body cells of the embryo. Mutations in germ cells are more serious than birth defects because they can be transmitted to future generations. Since some genetic control manages every part of the body and every body process, gene alterations to germ cells potentially hold changes for all conceivable types of future structure and process. Approximately one-fourth of spontaneous human abortions show some chromosome aberrations. We have no way of knowing at present how many of the remaining three-fourths are by gene mutations or by undetectable chromosome aberrations. If the embryo survives until birth, varieties of physical abnormalities may appear. Many inherited diseases are caused by mutations, and many more diseases will prove to be genetically linked. While individually rare, collectively such mutations comprise serious problems in the area of public health.

The great majority of genetic mutations are of the mildly harmful or at best neutral variety, as established experimentally and as deduced from the principle of natural selection.[47] Natural selection has previously eliminated those individuals whose mutant genes caused abnormalities that were fatal. As a result, a near balance exists between the introduction of new mutant genes into the population and elimination of old mutant genes by natural selection. With present high standards of living and health care in the United States, many individuals carrying mutations that in the past would have caused death or reduced fertility now survive and propagate. The equilibrium is thus out of balance, and new mutants are being added to the population faster than they are being eliminated by natural selection. Now that many infectious diseases have been eliminated or are under control, it is likely that future medical problems increasingly will prove genetic in origin--such as resistant staphylococcus, syphilis spirochetes, certain insects, and other highly publicized dangers to our health.

Conclusion

Any hope of linking particular chemical exposures with current health effects calls for public education about the ingredients of chemical products. Information about the product composition now is regarded generally as trade information. Such secrecy prevents medical investigations, deprives specialists on toxic effects of useful data for their investigations in animal studies, and prevents the public from choosing materials selectively, as well as from calling for a given product to be withdrawn from the market if the ingredients are considered especially dangerous. In addition to full access to information, the consumer's and the general public's interest should be adequately represented at all formal and informal stages of the decision-making and agency-industry discussions that precede the marketing of a new product. Decisions made by the regulatory agencies solely under the lobbying influence of pertinent industries have a discouraging history. As far as the public's interests are concerned, the system of checks and balances is largely absent from current regulatory practice. Apart from legal action after exposure to a hazardous or dangerous product, a consumer has virtually no power to influence regulations of drugs and other products.

Generally, the contrasting of benefits and risks has led to many short-term benefits for industry and few benefits and many risks for the consumer. Although clearly detrimental to the consumer, such present "review" practices are often detrimental to an industry, for it may suffer major economic setbacks when hazardous products in which it has invested--e. g., Kepone--are banned from the market. Such problems encourage those minimal constraints on industry that are characteristic of decision-making by regulatory agencies. Responsibility for stronger constraints must be shared with the regulatory agencies by the legislature, the scientific community, and the consumers and citizens. Until this happens consumers have inadequate ways to protect their own rights and interests--and their environment.

CHAPTER SUMMARY

1. Environmental health risks are natural, like the cholera bacterium; man-made, like PCBs; or complex mixtures of both, such as the high incidence of cancer in those who smoke, handle asbestos, or both.

2. Most environmental risks are (1) acute short-term and linked to identifiable agents, and chronic long-term and often not readily associated with specific causes. Acute agents include consumer products such as laundry and cleansing agents, pesticides, cosmetics, and inappropriately handled volatiles. In addition, simple elements--lead, arsenic, mercury, fluoride, nitrates, and others--can be harmful in excessive amounts, specific routes of exposure, and over time of exposure.

3. Chronic agents take time to show symptoms, such as coal dust which causes black lung disease; asbestos, asbestosis; cotton, byssinosis; sugar cane, bagassosis; and other occupationally related diseases.

4. Acute and chronic agents invade the body through skin/mucous membrane contact, ingestion, inhalation, or intravenous/intramuscular injection. Health records are beginning to reveal the types of agents, routes of entry, sources of contact, and symptoms of illness. It is difficult to draw hard conclusions about any one-to-one relationship between cause and effect because humans are mobile, change jobs, and the potential toxic agents are virtually everywhere.

5. The federal legislation controlling use of certain known toxins, such as Aldrin/Dieldrin, PCBs, DDT, and others has led to a marked reduction in these accumulating toxins in plants, secondary consumers (cattle, sheep, poultry, fish), and tertiary consumers (humans).

6. Viruses and bacteria are naturally occurring organisms which cause disease. Some have become resistant to controls, while others may be mutants that will always be threats, such as the bacterium thought to cause "Legionnaires' Disease."

7. The major toxins are carcinogenic (causing cancer), teratogenic (causing birth defects), or mutagenic (causing genetic mutation).

8. The majority of known environmental carcinogens are at the workplace. For example, non-smokers contract lung cancer at normal rates, but a cigarette smoker who works with asbestos has eight times the risk of dying of lung cancer as similar smokers of the same age who do not work with asbestos, and 92 times the risk of laborers who neither work with asbestos nor smoke.

9. Agents that cause birth defects are viral infections, x-rays, and chemicals such as those associated with mercury, thalidomide, and diethylstilbestrol.

10. Agents that cause mutations in somatic (body) cells or gene (ovum or sperm) cells are radioactivity, chemicals such as mustard gas, and others which are suspected. It is likely in the future that certain environmental factors will relate to mutant forms of bacteria (such as recently publicized, drug-resistant venereal disease types), the perennial cold virus, hospitals' nemesis, staphylococcus, and those bacteria carried by certain insects.

11. The future exposure to environmental toxins depends upon the consumers' role in the decision-making and in the agency-industry discussions that precede the marketing of a new product. Consumer knowledge is the critical factor.

SOURCES

[1]*Final Report*, National Commission on Production Safety (Washington, D. C.: GPO, 1970).

[2]*Accident Facts* (Chicago: National Safety Council, 1972).

[3]I. T. T. Higgins and B. G. Ferris, Jr. "Epidemiology of Sulphur Oxides and Particulates," *Proceedings of the Conference on Health Effects of Air Pollutants* (Washington, D. C.: National Academy of Sciences, National Research Council, 1973).

[4]J. G. French, et. al., "The Effect of Sulfur Dioxide and Suspended Sulfates on Acute Respiratory Disease," Arch. Environ. Health 27 (1973).

[5]I. L. Selikoff, "Occupational Lung Diseases," Environmental Factors in Respiratory Disease (New York: Academic Press, Inc., 1972).

[6]Panel on Chemicals and Health, President's Advisory Committee, Chemicals and Health (Washington, D. C.: Science and Technology Policy Committee, National Science Foundation, 1973).

[7]"Control of Lead Additives in Gasoline--Fuel Regulations," Federal Register, 38:33734 (6 December 1973). See also Federal Register, 28 (November 1973) for EPA's position on the health implications of air-borne lead.

[8]Council on Environmental Quality, The Sixth Annual Report of the Council on Environmental Quality (Washington, D. C.: GPO, 1974).

[9]C. Hueper, Occupational and Environmental Concerns of the Respiratory System (New York: Springer-Verlag New York, Inc., 1966).

[10]W. P. Tseng, et al., "Prevalence of Skin Cancer in an Endemic Area of Chronic Arsenicism in Taiwan," J. Natl. Cancer Institute, 40-453 (1968).

[11]W. Lijinsky and S. S. Epstein, "Nitrosamines as Environmental Carcinogens," Nature, 225:21 (1970).

[12]P. N. Magee, "Toxicity of Nitrosamines: Their Possible Human Health Hazards," Food Cosmet. Toxicol., 9:207 (1971).

[13]D. H. Fine, et. al., "N-Nitroso dimethyline in Air," Bull. Environ. Contam. Toxicol., 15:739 (1976).

[14]U. S. Tarrif Commission, Synthetic Organic Chemicals--United States Production and Sales, 1970 (Washington, D. C.: GPO, 1973).

[15]Karim A. Ahmed, "PCB's in the Environment," Environment, 18, No. 2 (March 1976).

[16]B. J. Dutka, "Coliforms Are an Inadequate Index of Water Quality," Journal of Environmental Health, 36, No. 1 (1973).

[17]American Cancer Society, Cancer Facts and Figures (New York: American Cancer Society, 1973).

[18]U. S. Department of Health, Education, and Welfare, The Strategic Plan (Washington, D. C.: GPO, 1973).

[19]S. S. Epstein, "Environmental Determinants of Human Cancer," Cancer Research, 34:2425 (1974).

[20]World Health Organization Expert Committee, World Health Organization Technical Report, No. 276 (1964).

[21]J. Higginson, "Present Trends in Cancer Epidemiology," Proceedings of the 8th Canadian Cancer Research Conference (1969).

[22]E. Boyland, "The Correlation of Experimental Carcinogenesis and Cancer in Man," in Experimental Tumor Research, ed. Hornberger and Karger (1964).

[23]S. S. Epstein, "The Political and Economic Basis of Cancer," Technology Review, 78:1 (1976).

[24]"Occupational Carcinogenesis," Ann. New York Acad. Sci., 271 (1976).

[25]Barry Commoner, "Workplace Burden," Environment, 19:15 (1973).

[26]U. S. Department of Health, Education, and Welfare Report of the Committee to the Surgeon General (Washington, D. C.: GPO, 1964).

[27]E. C. Hammond and D. Horn, "Smoking and Death Rates, J. A. M. A., 166:1159, 1294 (1950).

[28]J. Clemmesen, "Bronchial Carcinoma--A Pandemic," Can. Med. Bull., 1:37 (1954).

[29]National Academy of Sciences, Particulate Polycyclic Organic Matter (Washington, D. C.: National Academy of Sciences, 1972).

[30]W. C. Hueper, "Environmental Carcinogenesis in Man and Animals," Ann. N. Y. Acad. Sci., 108:963 (1963).

[31]A. G. Oettle, "Cancer in Africa, Especially in Regions South of the Sahara," J. Natl. Cancer Inst., 33:383 (1964).

[32]H. F. Kraybill and M. B. Shimkin, "Carcinogenesis Related to Foods: Contamination by Processing and Fungal Metabolites," Adv. Cancer Res., 8:191 (1964).

[33]R. W. Miller, "Environmental Agents in Cancer," Yale J. Biol. Med., 37:487 (1965).

[34]D. Schmal, "Exogenic Factors in Human Carcinogenesis and Methods for Their Detection," Neoplasma, 15:273 (1968).

[35]Higginson.

[36]J. Kmet and E. Mahboubl, "Esophageal Cancer in the Caspian Littoral of Iran: Initial Studies," Science, 175:846 (1972).

[37]Lijinsky and Epstein.

[38]Aflatoxin--Scientific Background, Control, and Implications, ed. Goldblatt (New York: L. A. Academic Press, 1969).

[39]G. L. LaQuer, et. al., "Carcinogenic Properties of Nuts from Cycas Circinalis Indigenous to Guam," J. Nat. Cancer Inst., 3:319 (1963).

[40]P. Keen and P. Martin, <u>Trop</u>. <u>Geogr</u>. <u>Med</u>., 23:44 (1971).

[41]<u>Liver Cancer</u>, IARC--WHO Scientific Publications No. 1 (Lyons, France: World Health Organization, 1971).

[42]N. D. McGlashan, et al. "Carcinogenic Properties of Nuts from Cycas and Oesophageal Cancer," <u>Lancet</u>, 2:1017 (1968).

[43]N. D. McGlashan, "Oesophaegeal Cancer and Alcoholic Spirits in Central Africa," <u>Gut</u>, 10:643 (1969).

[44]"Assessment of Scientific Information on Nitrosamines," Report of an ad hoc Study Group of the EPA, 1976.

[45]S. S. Epstein, <u>Environment and Teratogenesis in Pathology of Development</u> (Baltimore: Williams and Wilkins Co., 1973).

[46]S. S. Epstein and M. S. Legator, <u>The Mutagenicity of Pesticides: Concepts and Evaluation</u> (Cambridge, Mass: MIT Press, 1971).

[47]<u>Report of the Advisory Panel on Mutagenicity</u>, Department of Health, Education, and Welfare, Report of the Secretary's Commission on Pesticides and Their Relationship to Environmental Health (Washington, D. C.: GPO, 1969), p. 565.

[48]J. F. Crow, "Chemical Risk to Future Generations," <u>Scientist and Citizen</u>, 10:113 (1968).

[49]L. Lederberg, in Epstein and Legator's <u>The Mutagenicity of Pesticides: Concepts and Evaluation</u>, p. x.

CHAPTER TWELVE

ENERGY, CONSERVATION, AND RESOURCE ALTERNATIVES

A <u>PERSPECTIVE</u>

A thought. Is energy too big--too complex and powerful?
Granted we need tremendous amounts of energy. And a large
demand means technologically-intensive energy sources. But
with big energy sources, we get big problems. Huge systems
are designed to be safe--except when they're not.

The massive gas system almost collapsed without gas [in
the winter of 1977]. Sure, who knew that there wouldn't
be enough gas at a certain price. But too many people
depended on it, especially industrial and residential consumers who previously had some alternatives. What about
poor gas users who froze to death in coal country because
they tied themselves into the giant gas machine which just
had to grow bigger?

Then there are huge power grids which have all sorts of fail-
safe devices which "always" work--except when something goes
wrong. Remember the big power failure in the Northeast not
too many years ago, (and again in the summer of 1977)? And
we have the big "nukes" with redundant safety systems--
superbly engineered, with lots of radioactive waste to dispose of, all which will be done "safely"--except when it's
not. Not to say that large coal plants won't be big potential polluters, notwithstanding all the possible safeguards.
At least it's easier to control pollution of one large coal
burning plant than many small ones.

Now we have supertankers and super ports. Admittedly, the
tanker issue is now muddled by a plague of seemingly endless accidents largely due to a mixture of incompetent
leadership, poor navigation, inadequate and untrained
personnel, abysmal maintenance, lack of adherence to rules
and standards, old fatigued ships and careless control and
supervision topped by some seemingly callous owners who
don't seem to care. Statistically, they are safer. Fewer
tankers mean fewer accidents, and multi-compartment construction helps. But what if it fails? There will be a
lot of oil out there.

We can't conclude that it is necessary to do away with all
these huge power sources. But we can say that in some in-
stances, small energy sources may not be a bad idea. Point

is, there's a lot to say for small generating systems.
Home solar set-ups, local wind-based systems, residential,
commercial and industrial total energy systems based on
local generators, alternate coal and cellulose (wood)
firing boilers, regional geothermal and tidal energy come
to mind as well as local storage devices for good load management. There's also a lot to say for regional self-suf-
ficiency where possible. Wood farming in Maine; coal fired
heating systems in West Virginia and Ohio; geothermal plants
in California; gas in Texas; offshore oil in the Northeast
all make a lot of sense--when, of course, they make sense.

There's nothing wrong with bigness in energy, but progress
doesn't always necessarily mean bigness either.

Louis Naturman, Energy, Spring 1977

Energy and the Environment

All citizens, especially those with land-use planning responsibilities,
need to understand the relationship between "energy" and the natural systems
in our environment. Here is the problem in overview.

We dig coal from the ground with machines that take energy to manufacture and to assemble them. In turn, these are run by people who need energy
for transportation to work sites to run those machines. We then pump or
truck or railroad the extracted coal to a power plant where the coal burns,
makes steam, and the steam then drives a turbine. As the coal burns, heat
and particulates enter the atmosphere. Air pollution equipment to control
emissions requires energy to build and to operate it. But with electrical
energy we also have waste. The electricity generated from the turbine then
goes to a manufacturing plant to drive machinery. There is less power at
the site of need due to energy loss in conductor resistance and friction.
Consequently, there is less power to machine and assemble a lathe, or a car,
or a stove, or a toy, and then to package, ship, sell, and use it. At some
point we also discard it. A city truck powered with diesel fuel and directed by people picks up the item and carries it to a landfill where it is
covered. And there, very slowly, it disintegrates.

From this, some observations about energy and natural systems should be
clear:

- We have limited materials on Earth which can be taken apart for
  their energy.
- Both in extracting energy sources from the Earth and in converting them to other forms we lose energy into space and we generate hazardous pollutants.
- Costs of energy will rise dramatically forever: as supplies go
  down, demands will escalate. We will have to pay for a safer,
  healthier environment.

Clearly, citizens can help to conserve energy, slow the depletion of critical reserves, upgrade environmental health, and make energy costs affordable by (1) slowing the rate at which energy-rich materials are extracted from the Earth; (2) reducing the total amount of material converted; (3) lowering the amount of air- and water-borne pollutants released into the atmosphere; and (4) minimizing energy-wasteful modes of living.

Energy Defined

Some people equate "energy" to oil or electricity; others, to motion and work; some, to enthusiasm and still others to money. By reviewing a few basics we should be able to respond better to such varied associations:

- Energy is the ability to do work or to produce change.
- Potential energy is the capacity to do work that a body possesses because of its position or condition. For example, water behind a dam has potential energy because of its height above sea level and the pull of gravity.
- Kinetic energy is energy a body possesses because it is in motion.
- The kinetic energy of a body with mass "m" moving at a velocity "v" is one half the product of the mass of the body and the square of the velocity: i.e., $1/2 \ mv^2$. (See Figure 51.)
- "Work" is the transfer of energy through a force acting upon and displacing a given body--e.g., lifting a weight.
- The energy expended, equal to the work performed, is the product of the force, "f," and the distance, "d": i.e., f x d = work.
- Power is the amount of energy expended.
- It is common to convert energy from one form to another; however, the "Law of Conservation of Energy" says that energy neither can be created nor destroyed.
- The theory of relativity says of mass and energy that one can be converted into the other; thus, the "Law of Conservation of Energy" includes both.

Forms of Energy

In addition to movement, we are interested in other energy forms:

- Chemical energy (a form of potential energy because of the position of the atoms and the condition of their charges) to digest foods, to ignite fires, and to generate heat and light.
- Heat energy used for warmth, steam power, and electricity.
- Electrical energy stored in batteries containing chemicals or transmitted through wires.
- Electromagnetic-wave energy for radio, television, radar, lasers, sonar.
- Solar energy to grow food, to illuminate, to warm.
- Water energy to drive turbines for electricity.

All forms of potential energy have the capacity to do work and become

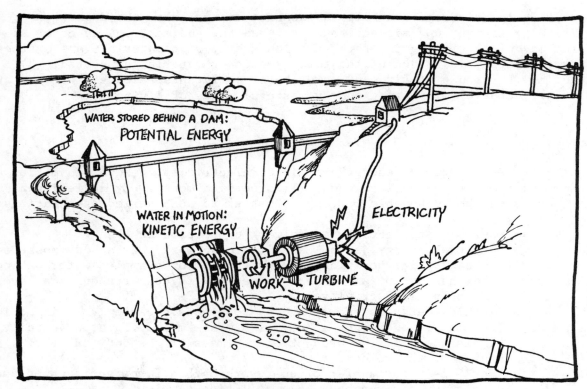

Figure 51: *Potential and kinetic energy.*

kinetic in doing work. Therefore, when we use the word "energy" here we are talking about forms of energy--either those that are in reserve or those in transformation that are doing some type of work. The ongoing source of energy is the Sun. Except for the heat generated within the Earth and the energy of the gravitational force of the Sun and Moon, the principal future source of energy is still the Sun. Its photons strike the Earth, lighting the sky, heating the land and waters, and stimulating plant photosynthesis. The consequences of converting sunlight into available energy is schematically represented in Figure 52. It shows how energy becomes work.

The types of work are myriad. Through discoveries and inventions and constructions, we collect and redirect solar energy to our human purposes. From left to right, in Figure 52, the Sun heats the Earth's atmosphere and land/water surfaces. Water evaporates, air circulates, rivers flow, lightning sparks, the tides rise and fall. Plant chlorophyll absorbs photons and retains or transmits the energy to other chemicals. The Earth transitionally presses these chemicals--in the form of decayed plants and animals-- into peat, coal, petroleum, shale oil, and natural gas. All of these types can translate motion or heat into yet other kinds of energy: electricity, light, sound, magnetism, and food. These kinds of energy can perform specific types of work, as suggested by the products and services that we consumers purchase.

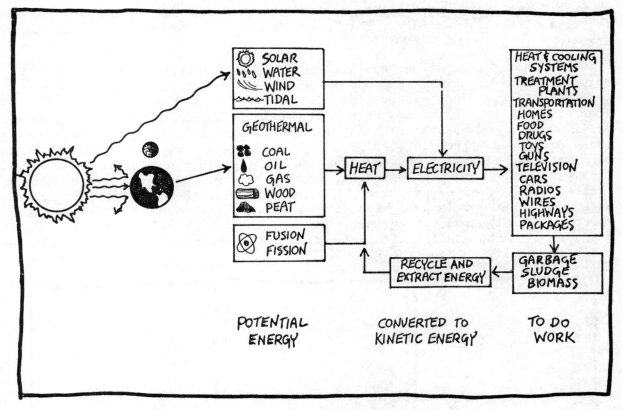

Figure 52: *Solar energy.*

The general consumer categories and the percentages of U.S. energy demand and supply in 1970 are summarized in Energy and Power as follows:

- Transportation: 24.6%
- Industrial: 37.2%
- Residential and Commercial: 22.4%
- Conversion and transmission loss: 15.8%

From Order to Randomness

To convert matter into energy, it must readily be manageable. Its potential must be high. It must be transferrable safely and at low cost to the place where the energy will be put to work. And, the procedure for converting matter into useful work must be simple. A general statement about the familiar types of matter that we have discussed is that the most manageable are ones that are highly ordered, concentrated, or pure in chemical structure and physical position. Wood, coal, gas, and uranium all have these characteristics. In ordered form, they are good fuels. But, when the conversion process begins to change the matter into another energy form, then the original structure and position change into disordered form. Progressively, the component atoms and molecules are less and less easily used to produce more energy. The matter is less and less able therefore to perform work. Thus, we can understand that "Energy runs downhill." Just as in Chapter 1 we saw we were "stuck mit" universal laws, so another states that as energy is used it takes a less useful form. That disposition of energy is called "entropy."

Our knowledge that our energy inevitably is "running down" must guide our selections of which atoms and molecules we want to transform into what. Let's consider a down-to-earth specific example: we tap rubber trees, dig out iron ore, refine copper, and then boil, smelt, extrude, stretch, wrap, bend, drill, press, and assemble--an automobile. Energy goes into every one of those processes. The finished product, a car, is a very highly ordered set of molecules. It takes a tremendous amount of energy just to make the parts, to say nothing of making the ships, trucks, trains, conveyors, doors, chutes, crates, and hoists needed to get them into place in the first place. Yet as soon as that car is assembled, it begins to go "random": the exhaust roils about in the atmosphere; the worn tire goes into the backyard; the spark plugs land in the local sanitary landfill; the fenders rust. The car eventually is totally random (see Figure 53).

Figure 53: *Car going random = increase in entropy.*

The transition of the car from a highly ordered to a highly disordered state exemplifies only one item going random in a comparatively short time. All of the Universe is going random: the planetary system, the Sun, and all of the energy concentrated on the Earth. It is nature. But, the frightening phenomenon on Earth is that we humans are rushing Earth's randomness. We collect bits and pieces of energy as fast as we can, fashioning them into buildings, cars, bridges, computers, telephones, airplanes, and myriad other forms. These highly ordered structures go random. The going random is synonymous with generating pollution.

The randomness of the car--the particulates, the tire, the plug, the rust--is pollution. The more cars we make, the more pollution we have. By the Law of Conservation of Energy, everything must go somewhere: the air pollutants, the garbage, the old ships, the polyethylene bags all go somewhere--down the rivers, into oceans, septic tanks, landfills, or just "out the window." In fact, we might say that the higher our gross national product, the greater is randomness and pollution! Now, we have to spend more energy than ever before just moving, sifting, filtering, screening, separating, precipitating, and picking up all the pieces. In fact, 4-6% of the nation's energy use between 1975 and 1983, according to the National Research Council, will be expended on just such activities. Herein lie responsibilities and opportunities for land-use planners.

Prudent land-use master plans will contain land-use regulations and development densities aimed at the lowest possible energy demands and, therefore, the least possible pollution. To prepare such a plan, the authors will need to research the energy requirements of various facilities and the potential and alternative energy sources available for installing, operating, and maintaining them.

Domestic Energy Resources of the United States

The relationship between U.S. energy demands and U.S. energy supplies calls for us to plan effectively to preserve our resources. Energy resources are measured in Quads.* A Quad is an enormously large quantity of energy useful in comparing the work capacities of various energy forms. Figure 54 shows that between 1975 and 2000 energy demand in the U.S. will increase from 80 to 160 Quads, the total being about 2,900 Quads, and shows anticipated sources of that energy. What it does not show is what happens after the year 2000.

Of the 2,900 Quads projected for consumption, about 500 could be saved by conservation efforts, estimates the Department of Energy. That still leaves 2,400 Quads to find. The Figure shows that by the year 2000 the principal type of energy will be fossil fuel--coal, gas, and petroleum. Yet even with advanced technology, all of the remaining reserves of gas and petroleum in the U.S. only can yield some 2,130 Quads. Estimates for other sources are projected in Figure 55.

---

*A Quad is 10^{15} British thermal units (1,000,000,000,000,000 Btus). A Btu is the amount of energy needed to elevate the temperature of a pound of water by one degree Fahrenheit. A "calorie" is the amount of energy needed to elevate the temperature of a milliliter of water one degree Centigrade.

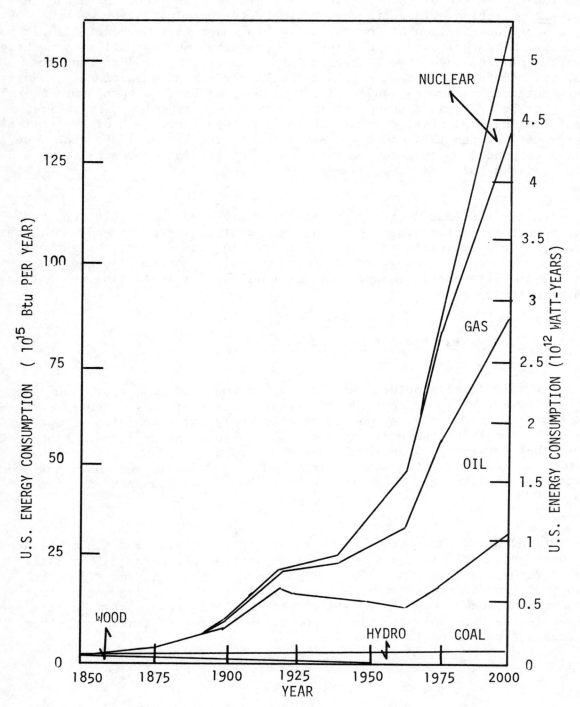

U.S. energy consumption between 1850 and 1970 with a projection to 2000. Oil, gas, and nuclear fuel use are expected to expand through the turn of the century with total fuel consumption doubling from present use rates. Energy consumption data are from U. S. Bureau of Mines.

Figure 54

DOMESTIC ENERGY RESOURCES OF THE UNTED STATES
(in Quads, and available at only twice present costs)

	Natural Gas	Petroleum	Oil Shale	Coal	Geothermal	Solar	Fission	Fusion
With known technology	600-1,050	800-1,100	1,200	4,800 7,000	.066	.154	1,800	-0-
Theoretical advanced technologcal potential	-0-	-0-	4,600	-0-	-0-	28,000	128,000	∞*

Figure 55

*In excess of 3,000,000,000 Quads

Natural Gas and Petroleum

The U.S. will increase its use of oil between 1970 and 1990 from 20,000,000 to 31,000,000 barrels per day. Only 7,500,000 will be domestic oil, and its price will increase until equal to that of foreign oil--by the mid-1980s.

Natural gas is found in association with petroleum. It volatilizes from the liquid petroleum, rises, and becomes trapped by an impervious rock stratum. Past discoveries of oil in the United States relate to natural gas in the ratio of one barrel of oil to 6,500 cubic feet of gas. According to Energy and Power, from the projected ultimate total amount of oil, 165 billion barrels (136 billion already discovered), it follows there will be about 1,075 trillion cubic feet of natural gas. Projecting, the peak of natural gas production will be reached between 1975 and 1980, although the discoveries in Alaska (30 billion barrels, a 10 year supply in the U.S.) means the Alaskan oil and gas will retard the rate of decline in available U.S. reserves.

As natural gas supplies dwindle, gas companies are building plants to convert petroleum by-products (propane, butane, and naptha) into "synthetic natural gas," which costs about twice as much as natural gas. If demands are high, petroleum (and therefore synthetic natural gas) will run out around 2025; if in low demand, around 2070 (estimates Energy, spring 1977). In either situation, the prices will advance about 10% per year, based on projected reserves and costs to extract them. No one knows actual figures, but trends are clear.

Some attendant environmental problems with continued dwindling petroleum and natural gas supplies are (1) spills from ocean transport vessels; (2) consumption of great quantities of chemicals for enhanced (tertiary) oil recovery--i.e., reconstituting a well and reclaiming more oil; and (3) pollution from coal burning to supplant waning oil and gas supplies. A brief comment about the first two problems suggests the nature of these concerns.

First, about 16,000,000 metric tons of petroleum run into the oceans annually. About 15% is from tanker accidents, 80% from cargo tank cleaning and ballasting operations, and 4% is from cleaning tanker bilges and fueling the ships themselves. Spillage increased from 67,000 tons in 1974, to 188,000 tons in 1975, to over 200,000 tons in 1976. The great fear is that with ever larger tankers there will be ever more tons of spill. The tankers are large: 572 of them over 175,000 tons in September 1975. Accidents which occured from August 1974 through December 1976 are chronicled below:

Date	Tanker	Petroleum spills in Metric Tons	Location	Cause
8/9/74	Metula	53,600	Strait of Magellan	Grounding
10/22/74	Universe Leader	2,600	Bantry Bay	Valve open
1/6/75	Showa Maru	4,500	Strait of Malacca	Grounding
1/10/75	Afran Zodiac	391	Bantry Bay	Tug accident
1/29/75	Jakob Maersk	85,000	Porto de Leixos	Grounding, explosion
1/31/75	Corinthos	143	Marcus Hook	Explosion
8/15/75	Globtik Sun	2-3,000	Gulf of Mexico	Collision
11/13/75	Olympic Alliance	2-3,000	Dover Strait	Collision
5/12/76	Urquiola	30,000	La Coruna	Grounding, explosion
12/15/76	Argo Merchant	25,000	Nantucket Shoals	Grounding
12/24/76	Oswego Peace	7	Groton, Conn.	
12/27/76	Olympic Games	443	Marcus Hook	Grounding
12/30/76	Grand Zenith	27,000	Off Nova Scotia	Sinking

Figure 56

Second, there is a heavy cost for oil recovery. It is tempting to think of improved oil recovery procedures as a way to augment shrinking petroleum reserves. There are 28×10^6 bbls of recoverable oil which we could extract with existing technologies, but the cost is too great. When the price per barrel reaches $15.00, recovery becomes economical. Of the chemical flooding, carbon dioxide miscible, and thermal recovery methods, only the last method is economical. Chemical flooding requires 24 pounds of surfactant, alcohol, and polymer to recover 1 barrel of oil--very high cost recovery. Other more expensive techniques may be possible, such as deep hydraulic fracturing of oil and gas-bearing shales. Valid results from present testing of these principal recovery methods will not be available until 1985.

Shale Oil

A substantial amount of oil can be extracted from tar sands and oil shales. The largest tar-sand deposits are in northern Alberta. They hold some 300 billion barrels. The world supply of shale oil is estimated at 3,100 billion barrels, but of the world total, only 190 billion barrels are considered recoverable. The rest is far too costly to extract. The main cost variables are the amount of oil in the deposits and the large quantity of water needed for processing. There is little shale oil recovery in process now--only prototypical work. It is thought that substantial capital investment will not be made until oil sells at $20.00 a barrel. The selling price may trigger a major hazard--a water shortage, since the extraction of shale oil consumes such massive quantities of water. Figure 57 (from Energy, spring 1977) cites the following figures for comparing water consumption for oil shale conversion and other energy conversion processes:

Typical Water Use for Power
And Energy Conversion Processes

Power (1,000-MW unit at 85% load factor)	Water consumption (acre-feet/year)		
	Dry-tower cooling	Wet-tower cooling	Cooling pond
Fossil-fired plant	500-5,000	15,000	9,000
Nuclear plant (PWR, BWR)[1]	--	25,000	--
Nuclear plant (HTGR)[1]	--	15,000	--
Oil shale conversion			
1 million bbl/day	--	155,000	
50,000 bbl/day	--	80,000	
Coal gasification 250 million cubic feet per day[2]	6,000	10,000	
Coal liquefaction 100,000 bbl/day	10,000	25,000	

[1]PWR--Pressurized Water Reactor; BWR--Boiler Water Reactor; and HTGR--High Temperature Gas Reactor.
[2]Includes water for a source of hydrogen and for process steam.

Figure 57

Coal

Coal is the world's most abundant and available energy resource--about 7.6 trillion metric tons are now available to us. Presently worldwide some 3 billion tons per year are mined. At this rate, the first 10% has already been removed, the middle 80% of the total supply will be mined during the 300-year period from 2000 to 2300, leaving the last 10% to be mined after that period. The U.S. holds about 20% of the world's coal supply. In the U. S., coal comprises over 90% of the nation's recoverable energy reserves. Oil and gas are easier to extract, less costly to transport, and more efficient and clean to burn. Coal combustion produces carbon dioxide which disperses into the ambient air. The concentration of this gas in the past 100 years has increased in the atmosphere from 290 ppm to 320 ppm, and may reach some 375-400 ppm by the year 2000. Theoretically, atmospheric CO_2 absorbs solar rays reflected from the Earth, thereby retaining heat close to the Earth's surface. At the present rate of coal use for energy, we conceivably could raise the temperature of the Earth by 1° C by 2000. Other effects of coal burning include particulates and sulfur dioxide gas, removable by various combustion and pollution control devices. Yet air pollution control often means <u>more</u> coal must be burned to fuel the manufacture of the control devices and to maintain their operation.

We may remove sulfur from the coal before or during combustion or we may "scrub" sulfur oxides from the flue gas before it is emitted. However, the most promising pollution abatement technique appears to be the fluidized bed-boiler in which pulverized coal is burned with limestone (CaO, calcium oxide) in a combustion chamber to which large volumes of air are added to make the matter behave as a fluid. The calcium oxide combines with the sulfur to form a solid, calcium sulfate, $CaSO_4$. Other combustion products, such as fly ash and soot particles, can be removed from flue gas by electrostatic precipitators of the type described in an earlier chapter.

We can also clean the coal <u>and</u> deliver it economically by converting it to a gas or liquid fuel. The technology for coal gasification goes back to the last century when "water gas" was manufactured at municipal gas works and used for street lighting. The challenge today is to make gasification economical and clean. Low Btu synthetic natural gas is possible to produce, but it is not thought today to be economical to do so. High Btu gas, however, is not in sight at current gas prices.

Geothermal Energy

Geothermal heat is theoretically an enormous source of energy, but the amount of it available economically is not great. The heat conducted from the Earth's interior through hot springs and volcanoes is about .3 of a Quad. We need 80-160 Quads per year between now and the year 2000. The prospects for geothermal energy are reviewed below by the National Academy of Sciences in <u>Energy for Rural Development</u>:

Geothermal energy, the natural heat contained within the Earth, is generally too deeply buried to be of use. However, in areas of the world that have experienced recent volcanic activity, geothermal resources may exist that can be exploited economically. These are usually found in regions of hot springs or areas where the deep hot rock is known to be fractured or to have pore spaces that permit water or steam to be circulated to carry heat to the surface.

Geothermal energy is distributed widely over the world, but localized geographically; it is a resource that can be used only near natural occurrences. When it is present, however, it provides a source of energy for electricity generation, space heat, drying, and refrigeration that is competitive with other technologies.

Technology for exploiting geothermal sources is in use in many countries. Geothermal turbine systems appear to have lifetimes of about 30 years or more. The lifetime of wells appears to be at least 10-15 years--longer in the case of hot-water wells used in conjunction with space heating systems.

The United States, Mexico, Japan, and New Zealand, run geothermal powered hot-water and steam systems with a reliability of 80-95%, but not without environmental problems. Geothermal hot-water and steam wells contain high concentrations of toxic, odorous hydrogen sulfide, dissolved salts, and other air and water pollutants. Therefore, such a heat source can be used only in a closed system which returns the cooled water to the subterranean reservoir. If the water is not pumped back into the ground, lands may slump for lack of support. Careful observations are being made for slumps and potential earthquakes, particularly in Japan. To date no serious subsidence or slippage has been reported.

Solar Energy

The Sun contributes about 99.98% of the Earth's total energy; the remainder is geothermal and tidal. The category of "solar energy" includes wood fuel, farm waste, photosynthesis fuel, hydropower, wind power, direct conversion, and space heating. These are considered "renewable" energy sources, as opposed to nuclear, fossil, and geothermal energy which are "non-renewable" sources. The Department of Energy estimates that these solar or renewable energy sources could produce possibly 25% of the U.S. energy requirements by the year 2020. Most of the solar energy generated would be for practical applications in rural areas: domestic and commercial water heating; heating and cooling of buildings; drying of agricultural and animal products; and salt production by evaporation of seawater and inland brines.

We already have solar-warmed air for space heating as well as water for domestic bathing, laundering, and general heating. In certain parts of the country, solar-heated homes compete economically with fossil-fuel heated ones, especially as the latter fuels dwindle. Currently solar heating is about 25% less expensive than heat by resistive electricity and slightly more expensive on the average than gas and oil heat. Solar heating will be more affordable as the technology is refined, and as the fossil fuel supplies diminish and therefore rise in price. Solar energy is both economical and environmentally advantageous. Let's examine a number of solar energy sources, some of which bear on planning decisions about land-use densities and development.

Let's consider the solar energy sources listed above in relation to their potential for providing future energy.

1. Wood-fuel in 1850 yielded 90% of U. S. energy. By 1910, the figure dropped to 10%, coal the major replacement of wood. Later wood-fuel became almost insignificant, and natural gas and petroleum replaced coal. Now there is a temporary upsurge in coal use as it replaces a greater share of the nation's total needs, as gas and petroleum fall off and nuclear power slowly increases as a source. Wood probably never again will fill much of the national energy need. Wood availability depends on tree growth: there is neither land nor time to grow enough wood to compete with fossil or nuclear fuels.

2. Farm Waste we include in the category of "biomass," a collective term for waste from organic matter, which is potentially convertible to energy. A Department of Energy report suggests that by the year 2000 we could have energy equivalent to 1,500,000 barrels of oil per day by burning biomass. The U.S. EPA has been supporting experimental conversion of biomass into methane, especially from the household and animal wastes produced in the rural western United States. Economic conversion of biomass into transmissable energy means collecting large quantities of raw materials, as in metropolitan areas and in regional collection systems. There are a few state-wide programs for biomass conversion. As other fuel sources diminish, biomass becomes more economical as an energy source, but currently the technology is low and the capital requirements are high. Therefore, it is unclear how economic a source of energy biomass may be in the future.

3. Photosynthesis-fuel is energy stored in chlorphyll-bearing plants; most of it is consumed by herbivores. The energy loss here is great: of the organic material synthesized by a plant, about 80-90% of it is stored. But, when an animal consumes the plant, he has spent energy in seeking it, and spends even more in eating, metabolizing, and then defecating the plant. The available energy is about 10% of that originally in the plant. Estimates in Energy and Power indicate that for humans the penalty for "bulk-handling" food is even greater! Of some 10,000 Kilocalories of food produced per capita per day in America, about 15% is wasted in handling and processing. Of the remaining 8,500 Kilocalories, some 6,300 fuel the animals that produce about 900 Kilocalories of meat, while 2,200 Kilocalories go into the human diet as plant materials. Therefore, the final food supply of meat and plants per person is about 3,100 Kilocalories daily, making field-to-table efficiency about 31%--comparable to an electrical power station.

4. Hydropower provides about 4% of the total U.S. Energy. The United States has already developed a large portion of the potential resource. Among the

major projects are those in the Tennessee Valley, the St. Lawrence River, the Niagara Frontier, the Colorado River (Hoover and Glen Canyon Dams), and the Columbia River system. Hydro-electricity is almost entirely non-polluting. (Building the reservoirs, however, does produce pollution.) There will be other major water power developments in the United States, especially when water supplies are needed for energy extraction, as in shale oil conversion. For example, contracts for federal reservoirs have been pending on 55,000 acre-feet (1 acre of water, 1 foot deep) in the Colorado River Basin for oil shale prototype development projects. Even when oil prices rise to $20/barrel, hydroelectric power will not produce a substantially higher percentage of energy than it does now. According to Pauline and Weishaus in Ecology, that and the following are some reasons why more dams will not be constructed:

- Hydroelectric power developed to its fullest would fill only a scant portion of our energy needs.
- Water availability for hydroelectric plants can be cut by dry spells.
- Water sources are fixed and therefore water power is not so readily transmissable as other energy sources.

5. Wind power has long been used to pump water and to grind grain. However, the great size of high energy production windmills and electrical generating stations pose difficult engineering problems that make them unlikely sources of energy in the future. Small--scale windmills, supplemented with some mechanical (water reservoir) or electrical (battery) storage system, would suit single-family and farm needs. Due to intermittent wind conditions the problem of storage is the major constraint on planning extensive wind-power generators in the future.

6. Direct conversion of solar light into energy is accomplished by generating electricity from materials which release electrons from their surfaces in a photovoltaic cell. Such cells, however, are a long way from providing competitive energy. Direct conversion of light to usable power is an ideal environmental goal--no moving mechanical parts, no air, water, or thermal pollution, and no consumption of fossil fuels; unfortunately, conversion costs are staggeringly high. In 1970, for example, capital costs per kilowatt capacity at a fossil fuel station were about $500; the same capacity from a photovoltaic station would cost $2,000,000. But, the cost has since dropped dramatically, as the summary chart at the end of this section demonstrates. (By 1980 costs should be 1/50th of the price in the chart.) A few small photovoltaic cell units of about 10% efficiency are available in Japan, England, France, and the United States.

7. Space heating by direct solar radiation is common in many parts of the world. Highly economical small-scale heat collectors can be made for private use. A flat collector plate, with baffles for moving air or with pipes for carrying H_2O, is painted black to absorb sunlight. Then a glass plate that admits most of the Sun's rays covers the pipes. The energy is absorbed by the blackened collector sheet and pipes and then slowly pumped either to storage containers or to the area to be heated. Combined conventional and solar heating devices have proven to be quite practical. In addition to household use, agricultural use of solar heating includes drying crops either by exposing harvested material to the heat or by passing

solar-heated air through and over the materials. The technology and materials are simple, making such systems highly reliable and cost-effective.

In summary, solar-generated energy is generally practical at present for needs satisfied by wood-fuel, farm waste, photosynthesis-fuel, hydropower, wind-power, and indirect radiation. However, solar-generated energy is impractical for producing electricity. To be so, the technological problems must be solved and the costs made competitive with other electricity-generating sources. Some cost comparisons for several types of energy plants are as follows (figures based on those appearing in Energy for Rural Development and Physical Science):

Type of Plant	Cost Per Kilowatt
Fossil Fuel	$ 500
Geothermal	150-500
Hydroelectric (small)	1,000
Wind-for electrical	3,000-6,000
Wind-for water pumping	5,000-10,000
Photovoltaic	100,000-150,000
Nuclear	750

Fission

Fission is the splitting of nuclei of heavy elements such as uranium. Most U.S. reactors use U_{235} because it splits more easily than other forms. But, U_{235} will be in short supply by the end of the century. Another isotope of uranium form, U_{238}, is also fissionable and in greater supply. By "breeding," uranium 238 absorbs neutrons in a "breeder reactor" and transforms into fissionable plutonium 239, or thorium 232 becomes fissionable uranium 233. Natural uranium, in which uranium 235 is rare, contains a large amount of uranium 238, so that a starter supply is ample and, therefore, more fissionable material is produced than the original amount. The breeder reactor, in effect, generates a superfluity of fissionable wastes. One great fear is that material in its waste form will eventually leak into underground water supplies, the atmosphere, or the oceans. Exposed nuclear wastes can be lethal for thousands of years, as some of the half-lives (when the radioactivity reaches half of its original strength) of radioisotopes indicate: strontium 90, 29 years; cesium 137, 30 years; plutonium 238, 86 years; plutonium 239, 24,400 years; plutonium 240, 6,600 years; and americium 241, 433 years. Another great fear about developing such nuclear energy is that the surfeit of fissionable materials will require a waste management and control system that is "theft-proof." Otherwise, the world can be subject to a blackmail threat of unknown magnitude. Indeed, a recent issue of Rolling Stone magazine reported the diversion of a nuclear cargo from Germany to Israel. Presumably other such diversions can occur. For safe use of nuclear energy we must have compliance to laws governing their use and sale, as well as compliance to guidelines for safe, secure storage of the wastes. Storage is immensely simplified if waste volume is small.

To handle wastes from fission the Department of Energy has set 1985 for establishing a pilot repository for high-level radioactive wastes. In the meantime, the Nuclear Regulatory Commission is testing a waste solidification process in which an erosion-resistant glass is sprayed around the waste. The wastes will later be placed in the repository (probably stable geological formations as deep as 2,000 feet). By the late 1980s there will be an accumulation of more than 25,000 metric tons of radioactive uranium from spent fuel, so the needs for safe containment are clear.

As a result of the operational hazards and unresolved issues about government liability for accidents, since May of 1976, 53 of the 68 new power plants granted permits were forced to delay construction. On July 21, 1976, the U.S. Court of Appeals of the District of Columbia ordered the Nuclear Regulatory Commission not to issue any more permits or licenses for nuclear power plants until it could better document its contention that any disposal of wastes would not harm the environment. NRC then won a stay of mandate and has since issued provisional licenses. While utilities are still spending millions of dollars expanding waste storage facilities, nuclear fuel processing plants, which reprocess and recycle the uranium, are not operating. Another major environmental problem of nuclear energy conversion facilities is thermal pollution. Reactor heat must be removed to prevent an explosion, and water is the most practical coolant. Most nuclear plants dissipate their waste heat by discharging coolant waters into a moving river, a large pond (1,000-2,000 acres per 1,000 megawatt plant), or into the air with wet (evaporative) or dry (closed cycle) cooling towers. Costs determine which method is used. All have environmental impacts, probably the dry cooling tower the least, although it costs the most.

Fusion

Nuclear fusion--the reaction which combines hydrogen isotopes, deuterium, and tritium--does not produce the same dangerous wastes that fission does. However, the heat generated by fusion reaction is so great that no known substance can contain it. Without containment, the heat cannot be concentrated to generate steam for turboelectric power. Present research is aimed at developing means to hold fusion plasma in enormously strong magnetic fields, but operational units are thought to be 25 to 50 years away.

Other research utilizing lasers to fuse deuterium and tritium pellets has proven to be quite promising that a major technological breakthrough seems likely. There is some hope that fusion technology will allow us to supplant fission--with all of its problems--by fusion, which is a safe, virtually inexhaustible source of electrical energy.

Figure 58 illustrates the difference between fission and fusion reactions, the former being a splitting apart and the latter being a combining.

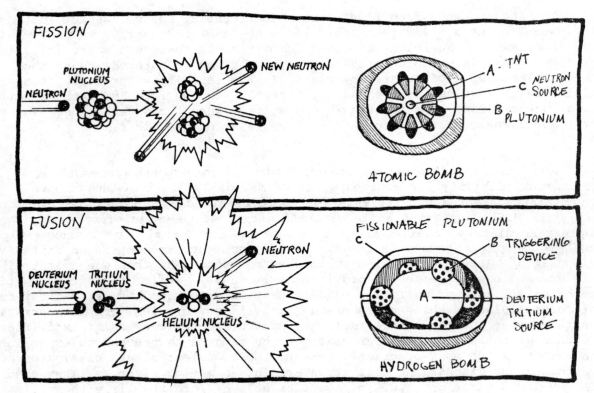

Figure 58: *Fission and fusion.*

Wind, Tide, Hydropower, and Other Sources

It is evident by now that the best means to deliver energy through existing transportation and power transmission grids is by use of fossil fuels and nuclear energy. Wind, tides, hydropower, and other solar and non-solar sources are in general (1) technically undeveloped; (2) very capital intensive for expansion beyond present production levels; (3) and/or they are contrary to the vested business, commercial, and political interests of private and world institutions.

Wind, for example, is inconstant over time and geography. The large mechanical or electrical units would be extremely difficult engineering feats. Like direct solar heating and electrical units, wind-powered energy plants must have some storage medium (elevated water, storage batteries, etc.) to even the flow of electricity during shifts in weather conditions. A number of ingenious proposals for using both sources of energy are under test, and they promise utility at least to rural communities.

Tidal power is obtained from the filling and emptying of any bay or estuary that can be closed by a dam. The only full-scale tidal-electrical plant so far built is on the Rance estuary on the Channel Island coast of France. Its capacity will eventually be 320 megawatts. The world's total expected tidal power, however, is only 2% of the total hydrologic power; hydrologic power provides only about 10% of the total world need.

Additional hydrologic power is some time off, with most of the potential in undeveloped Africa, South America, and Southeast Asia where economic barriers prevent construction of hydroelectric facilities. In the U. S.

there is not much undammed water except that which will become economically feasible when oil shale and other fossil fuel projects requiring water for processing become economical.

Other sources of primary energy have been discussed. There are advantages and disadvantages to each. Some are affordable or accessible enough to allow communities to experiment with them, perhaps to profit by the outcome. In the meantime, there is much that communities can do to abate the demand for energy-consuming land-use developments, and thereby stretch out the present energy supply.

Energy and Environmental Protection: Implications for Planners

It follows from this consideration of energy sources that new, speculative resources are an investment for the future, not a means to remedy problems today. It is clear that the quality of life worldwide depends on present and future use of technically and economically available energy from all sources. As the transition takes place, there are hundreds of ways local governments can restrict energy demands, use available resources, and practice responsible environmental management. The basic principals are to:

A. Reduce the amount of wastes, and therefore waste handling and treatment.
B. Use natural systems whenever technically, economically, and environmentally appropriate.
C. Apply energy husbandry, especially through careful assessment of alternative land-use.
D. Recognize that there is no single answer; rather, keep options open and use all practical resources.

An Ounce of Prevention

Source reduction of wastes that enter the hydrologic cycle or those that end up in landfills is also energy reduction. Fewer waste products mean less energy needed to (1) make new replacement products; (2) transport that product to and from the point of consumption; and (3) reclaim it from discharge into the open biosphere. Domestic disposals and phosphorous detergents offer familiar examples of waste problems which call for source reduction.

Garbage disposals produce waste. They take electricity and flush-water to disperse waste from a concentrated to a diluted solution. Efficient treatment of disposal wastes must restore them to a concentrated solution again. Finally, these wastes add nutrients to the open biosphere in such volume that they add to general water pollution abatement costs.

Like disposals, phosphorous-laden detergents introduce biological nutrients that feed massive algal blooms. These blooms in turn pollute potential surface and, later, ground waters that might otherwise require little pretreatment before use as drinking and industrial water supplies. The findings on use of detergents vs. soaps are these:

- A complete ban on all detergents would be best environmentally.
- The next best solution is to launder with a combination of soap and washing soda, hydrated sodium carbonate, also called sal soda, $Na_2CO_3(H_2O)_{10}$.
- Low phosphate or non-phosphate detergents are the third choice.
- At the least, less detergent--whether non-phosphate or phosphate-- than recommended by manufacturers is often very effective for cleaning needs.

In addition, studies point out that bleaches and antiseptics do not sterilize more than soap alone, and the value of "whiteness" from brightner additives is exactly that, a <u>value</u>, and not a preference based on the actual <u>healthfulness</u> of whiter clothes, for they are not more hygienic.

To make the point explicit, to coarse-filter 30 MGD (million gallons per day) of wastewater requires <u>4,400</u> kilowatt hours per year. But, if phosphorous also has to be removed the same amount of water requires <u>27,400</u> kilowatt hours per year--roughly six times the cost. It <u>pays</u> not to pollute!

Industrial wastes, too, require less cost to treat when the concentrates are handled before they become diluted by entering the receiving waters. Contrary to the idea that the "solution to pollution is dilution," it takes <u>less</u> energy to treat <u>concentrated</u> wastewater, since costs escalate in proportion to the volume of water handled. Any time water has to be moved anywhere it costs energy.

<u>Biomass Conversion and Heat Exchange</u>

As a matter of course, master plans for an area should include energy conservation by use of natural systems and exploiting yet untapped energy sources. In wastewater treatment we have examples of both Biomass Conversion and Heat Exchange.

A. Biomass energy recovery and recycling systems use the fuel potential of the organic solids, such as domestic disposal wastes, to create a useable form of energy. Three major biomass energy conversion processes are:

- <u>Anaerobic digesters</u>--bacteria metabolize organic wastes, respiring methane, CH_4, and carbon dioxide, CO_2. The methane is used to fuel plant operations.
- <u>Incinerators</u>--the heat of combustion of organics produces steam which can be used to heat buildings or to drive small electric generators to do other work.
- <u>Pyrolysis</u>--an experimental heat and chemical method of forming gas and oil for in-plant combustion.

B.   Heat exchange between warm incoming wastewater and the plant's circulating water space-heating system can also conserve energy. In Cleveland,
Ohio a treatment plant handling 220,000 gallons of heated wastewater per
day uses ten heat exchangers to warm eight buildings during winter. The
direct fuel oil savings is about 124,000 gallons, for a dollar savings of
about $50,000. Another way to take advantage of the natural systems and to
save water treatment costs is to install a dual water supply. Not widely
practiced and expensive to initiate, such systems nonetheless are energy
conservative for some communities. In a dual system, the water quality meets
two standards. The drinking, cooking, washing water--about 15% of the normal
total supply--would have to meet the high quality standards of the Safe
Drinking Water Act. The remaining 85% would be piped separately for cleaning,
flushing toilets, watering lawns, and industrial processing. In England and
Wales some 40 communities have separate domestic (potable) and industrial
(non-potable) water supply systems. Two U.S. cities, St. Petersburg,
Florida and Colorado Springs, Colorado, have second systems for distributing
treated municipal wastewater for irrigation and lawn watering. Dual systems
offer greater energy savings when the wastewater to be treated before drinking
purposes is heavily polluted and requires energy expensive treatment.

C.   Husbandry of Energy Resources--When clean water has entered the
home, run through the disposal, and become sewage, we must pay to clean it up
again. The cost increase is proportional to the degree of dispersal, or
randomness. Therefore, the line of attack is to retard dispersal. One way
is to keep sewage out of the public treatment system. EPA's policy on the
funding of sewage collection systems aims at cost-effective wastewater
handling with greater pollution control benefits. Funding of sewage collection systems requires that:

1.   The collector systems be proven necessary, cost-effective, and
     eligible under "substantial human habitation" definition (average
     population densities of 1.7 persons per acre, one household for
     every two acres or more, on October 18, 1972), with two-thirds of
     the sewage flow-through originating from the habitation.
2.   New sewers must dispose of wastes from present systems from homes
     of the existing population; and the present system must be shown
     to be (a) a public health hazard; (b) or a ground- or surface-water
     contaminant, or (c) in violation of a point source discharge re-
     quirement of PL 92-500.
3.   The proposal for sewer funding must demonstrate, where population
     densities are less than 10 persons per acre, that alternatives
     are clearly less cost-effective than new facilities. The alterna-
     tives to be evaluated include the following (from "Funding of Sewage
     Collection Systems Projects," EPA memorandum):

     - measures to improve operation and maintenance of existing septic
       tanks, including more frequent inspections, timely pumpouts, and
       prohibition of garbage grinders
     - new septic tanks
     - holding tanks and "honey wagons"
     - various means of upgrading septic tanks, including mounds, al-
       ternate leaching fields and pressure sewers
     - other sytems to serve individual households or a cluster or house-
       holds. Such systems include, for example, wastewater separation,

water conservation and recycle systems where feasible.

The means for improving operation and maintenance of existing septic tanks is based upon the use of the natural system of anaerobic digestion, as mentioned above. Digestion is followed by filtration through soils in a leach field. Commercial and industrial wastes often can be processed through small-scale package treatment plants.

All of these systems—septic tanks, package treatment plants, waste-water treatment facilities—produce sludge. Sludge is now a "solid waste" problem. In its concentrated state, the waste actually becomes a potentially marketable energy resource, a subject explored in the next section.

Where none of the measures in paragraph 3 above are appropriate, the waste enters the public treatment system. Here, too, there are means for applying energy conservation actions. The major treatment plant cost categories for potable and non-potable wastewater treatment facilities are:

- Electricity—electric pumps to move water or sewage are the major electricity consumers; sludge incineration may also require the installation of electrically powered air pollution control equipment.
- Gas—natural gas may be used to dry sludge; once dried, however, it may then be incinerated, sometimes with another fuel added. Natural gas may also have to be purchased for heating the physical plant.
- Chemicals—the manufacture and transportation of chemicals, some derivatives of petroleum and natural gas, represent high energy consumption indirectly.

Finally, care can be given to the type of wastewater treatment process. Some consume more energy than others. A complete cost-effectiveness analysis must be made before the figures below relate to a particular community. (Additional data appears in EPA's "Energy Conservation in Municipal Wastewater Treatment," Office of Water Program Operations, March 1977).

Process	Capacity (MGD)	Energy Requirement Thousand KWH/Yr
Trickling filters with course filtration (Southern US)	30	4,401
Activated sludge w/o incineration (Southern US)	30	8,915

Activated sludge w/nitrification and chemical clarification (Northern US)	30	14,549
Activated sludge – higher than secondary (Northern US)	30	27,400
Independent physical/ chemical – secondary treatment (Northern US)	30	7,063
Independent physical/ chemical – higher than secondary treatment (Northern US)	30	17,435
Ponds	30	8,182
Land treatment by infiltration/percolation	30	8,132

Figure 59

A number of practices in new and updated plants can minimize energy needs, particularly electrical ones. The following suggest some directions that designers can specify in building or modifying existing structures:

- Use the motion of incoming wastewater to mix in treatment chemicals rather than use power-driven stirring devices.
- Minimize water lift requirements to reduce pumping demands. For example, a 40-foot lift in a 100 MGD plant requires 10,000,000 kilowatt hours/year of electricity, or about $300,000.
- Choose equipment on an annual cost basis, not on initial capital cost. For example, pumps can be bid at a guaranteed kilowatt hour per thousand gallons, and this figure used to calculate annual cost.
- Install variable speed controls or else closely match pumping equipment to average need. Throttled pumps do not operate at an efficient level.
- Use elevated storage to meet peak demand without pumping.
- Peak water demand (usually for lawn watering) coincides with peak electricity demands.
- Charge a premium for water delivered during peak periods; the higher charges tend to decrease demand.

Solid Waste

Solid waste, like polluted water, also costs energy to treat or to dispose of safely. However, solid waste increasingly is being used as an energy resource. Such resource recovery is cost-effective in communities where disposal costs are over approximately $10.00 per ton. Overall economic feasibility must be proven, however, if municipal solid waste recovery is to become widespread.

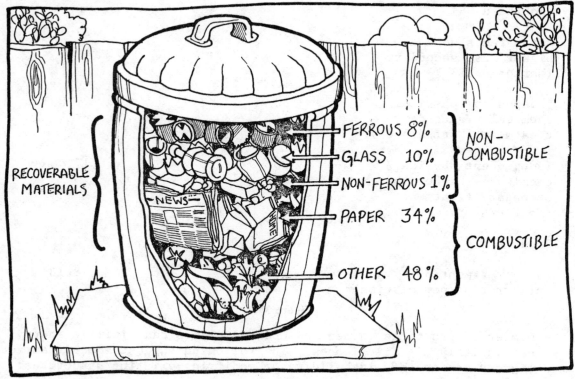

Figure 60: *Solid waste.*

The resource potential of solid wastes, reported in the U. S. EPA's August 1977 Environment Midwest, is shown on Figure 60. At the present rate, by 1990 we will accumulate over 200 million tons of solid waste per year. The metropolitan areas generate 70% of the nation's waste. In that waste are the following annual resource equivalents:

- 8 million tons of steel (enough for 5 million standard-size cars).
- 700,000 tons of aluminum (15% of annual national consumption).
- 9.5 million tons of glass (46 million bottles).
- The energy equivalent of 180 million barrels of oil.

Three general approaches can retrieve these national resources. In increasing order of energy demands, these are:

- Waste reduction laws
- Source separation
- Mixed waste recovery.

Waste Reduction Laws

These laws are intended to encourage recyclable containers and to end manufacture of products for quick disposal, e.g., packaging restrictions and beverage container deposits. Energy costs decline for the local communities which have less solid waste for collection and disposal. From the perspec- . tive of "environomics" it is sound to plan for lesser amounts of energy to transform, for that means less energy needed to recover those materials we no longer can use in present form.

Under the Resources Conservation and Recovery Act (RCRA), administered by EPA, states will designate Regional planning areas to develop solid waste management plans. At this stage, local governments will share with states the decision-making about which agency will conduct the planning and then carry out the plans. One of the options surely will be source separation, as well as mixed waste recovery.

Source separation at the point of generation, the home, has been tried in a number of communities. For example, under EPA sponsorship, the 23,000 people of Marblehead, Massachusetts have been separating paper, glass, and cans from other wastes in their homes. The city reduced its refuse total by 30% and earned $15-25 per ton on the recycled materials. The economics for mixed waste recovery is also favorable.

Mixed Waste Recovery

The value of individual efforts for energy savings becomes apparent when another resource recovery approach--mixed waste recovery--is considered. Instead of sorting and organizing at home, source separation occurs at a central facility. Such recovery offers overall net energy production, especially in large metropolitan areas where environmentally sound landfills become more and more costly. Even at capital costs of $5,000-50,000 per ton of daily capacity, mixed waste recovery represents the best alternative in many cities. The basic requirements for efficiency are a market for the recovered materials and a dependable supply of wastes. The latter is not as simple as it sounds, for there are annual variations in the amount and composition of municipal wastes as well as day-to-day differences, particularly between weekends and weekdays.

The basic recovery processes are shredding, magnetic separation of ferrous metals, and air separation. All require energy, but not as much as to process virgin materials into new products. In addition to materials, the solid waste also furnishes energy. The three types are:

- Incineration: direct combustion of the refuse in a boiler to produce steam.
- Solid Refuse Derived Fuel (RDF): separation and size reduction of the combustible fraction.
- Pyrolysis: partial combustion of wastes in an oxygen-deficient atmosphere that produces as a gaseous or liquid fuel.

There are many systems being marketed using these principles or variations of them. In nearly a dozen cities in the U.S., resource recovery systems process between 200-3,000 tons of wastes per day. Yet, of the daily volume of 145 million tons of municipal wastes trucked to U.S. landfills daily, only 6% is recovered. However, as fossil fuels costs rise, Refuse Derived Fuels are sure to become competitive with other sources for any large community.

Diversity of Natural Systems Promotes Energy Conservation

Whether we are solving problems of solid waste, water pollution, air contamination, or energy conservation, our efforts must involve the maintenance of diverse natural ecological systems.

In watersheds where soils are healthy, a diverse population of bacteria, worms, and insects mix inorganic chemicals with decomposing organic litter, furnishing nutrients for plants and animals, simultaneously limiting water runoff, and recharging underground aquifers. As a result, wastes are assimilated, energy stored, and the environment improved.

Furthermore, diverse natural ecological systems work. They work because they were refined over the years. They are very reliable. In fact, man-made systems, such as sewage treatment plants do not work as reliably because man oversimplifies the system, compared to nature. Ecologists, contrasting natural with man-made systems, may disagree as to whether there is a point beyond which additional diversity has no effect, but they are unanimous in agreeing that systems without substantial diversity are quite unstable.

The lesson from nature is that the greatest efficiency in energy use comes with diverse, interconnected energy conversion networks. This means that land-use plans which strive to increase the alternatives for energy conversion will achieve the greatest energy efficiency. This generalization applies to solid waste disposal, wastewater treatment, farming, transportation, recreation, space heating, or any of the other activities of man. There is no way to avoid the laws that govern physical, chemical, and biological interactions: they state that to stay alive we must convert matter into energy. There we have no choice. However, we can and must choose which matter to convert, at what rate, and to what work we will put that energy and ourselves.

CHAPTER SUMMARY

1. Population growth in the future is inevitable and, therefore, so is an increase in energy consumption. Energy resources will consequently rise in cost, making energy conservation of benefit to everyone.

2. Energy is the capacity to perform work. Work is the result of moving a mass through a distance. Potential energy is the capacity for future work, exemplified in water held behind a dam. Kinetic energy, if harnessed, performs work, as it does upon leaving a reservoir and being directed toward an electric turbine.

3. All energy forms are redirected in their total capacity at each stage of conversion from potential to kinetic or from one form to another. The inevitable direction of all energy reserves is degradation. All matter proceeds from order to disorder, or entropy, the amount of entropy ever increasing since much energy is dissipated into unusable forms.

4. All of the known energy forces are three: gravitational, electrical, or nuclear. A review of current energy resources, their potential future contribution to the nation's needs, and an observation about their environmental impact indicates that fossil fuels and nuclear energy will be the nation's energy sources from now through the years 2020-2070.

5. Fusion is not yet technically feasible, but if developed in time, it could become the primary source of all the world's energy needs. It is ample in quantity, inexpensive, and environmentally clean.

6. Other than fossil and nuclear fuels, other sources of energy are either too costly (such as the photovoltaic cells), too dispersed (hydropower), or unreliable (wind power), to contribute more than a small portion of the total energy requirement.

7. Local governments can help conserve energy. Examples in wastewater treatment and solid waste disposal indicate that both water and solid waste should be treated as close to the source of generation as possible and in their most concentrated forms. Natural assimilative capacities of air, water, and soil can handle limited wastes cost-effectively. A number of thermodynamic conversions, such as biomass utilization and heat exchange, can save energy in such facilities as wastewater treatment plants.

8. Solid waste refuse can be segregated at home or at a central facility for recycling materials and for extracting refuse derived fuel. The cost disadvantage will decrease as fossil and nuclear fuel costs increase.

9. The greatest cost advantage possible comes with natural systems treatment of wastes. To function cost-effectively, however, natural systems must be healthy. A measure of that health is a diversity of inorganic and organic matter and living organisms. Preservation of diversity in natural and man-made systems is therefore a high priority.

SOURCES

"Cities Mine Solid Waste Piles in Search for Wasted Profits." Engineering News Record, September 15, 1977, pp. 20-24.

Council on Environmental Quality. Environmental Quality--1976: The Seventh Annual Report of the Council on Environmental Quality. Washington, D.C.: GPO, 1976.

Dales, J.H. Pollution, Property & Prices. Toronto, Canada: University of Toronto Press, 1972.

Fowler, J.M. and K.E. Mervine. Energy and the Environment: An Annotated Bibliography. College Park, Maryland: University of Maryland, Department of Physics and Astronomy, May 1974.

Gannon, Robert. "The Untapped Underground Sea of Pure Water." Popular
    Science, 204 (April 1974), 92-94, 150-51.

"Horizontal Integration: A Reality for Alternative Energy Sources." Energy,
    II, No. 2 (Spring 1977).

How to Obtain Federal Grants to Build Municipal Wastewater Treatment Works.
    Denver, Colorado: Office of Water Program Operations, U.S. EPA, May 1976.

"Is it Time for Deepwater Ports? Do Big Tanker Mean Big Ports?" Energy, II,
    No. 2 (Spring 1977).

National Academy of Sciences. Energy for Rural Development: Renewable Re-
    sources and Alternative Technologies for Developing Countries. Washington,
    D.C.: National Academy of Sciences, 1976.

National Research Council. Implications of Environmental Regulations for
    Energy Production and Consumption. Washington, D.C., June 1977.

"Nuclear Wastes: End Product or Just the End?" Energy, II, No. 2 (Spring 1977).

Pauline, Lawrence J. and Howard Weishaus. Ecology: Man's Relationship to His
    Environment. New York: Oxford Book Co., 1971.

Rhett, John T. "Less Costly Treatment Systems." Mimeographed, August 18, 1976.

Richards, Theodore J. "Off-peak Water Pumping", Water and Sewage Works.
    August 1977, pp. 74-78.

Starr, Chauncey et. al. Energy and Power. San Francisco: W.F. Freeman and
    Co., 1971.

"Tertiary Oil and Gas Recovery: Now It's Becoming More Economical." Energy,
    II, No. 2 (Spring 1977).

Turk, Jonathan and Amos Turk. Physical Science with Environmental and Other
    Approaches. Philadelphia: W.B. Saunders Co., 1977.

"Waste to Watts." Environment Midwest. Washington, D.C.: GPO, August 1977.

"Western Water for Energy Development: Enough Water in the Right Place?"
    Energy, II, No. 2 (Spring 1977).

U.S. Environmental Protection Agency. Energy Conservation in Municipal
    Wastewater Treatment. Washington, D.C.: GPO, March 1977.

Whittaker, Robert H. Communities and Ecosystems. New York: Macmillan Co.,
    1970.

Wilson, Mitchell et. al. Energy. New York: Time Inc., 1963.

CHAPTER THIRTEEN

POLLUTION ABATEMENT POLICIES AND STANDARDS

A PERSPECTIVE

Pollution and waste accumulation have plagued us ever
since man started living in permanent settlements, and
a multitude of solutions have been developed throughout
the centuries reflecting contemporary attitudes toward
sanitation and ideas with respect to a decent environment. Man has always been careful to remove wastes
from his own private dwelling, but he usually has dumped
them immediately outside. This inherent public irrespon-
sibility is a curious, albeit apparently basic, human
characteristic which was in evidence in the ancient
advanced civilizations and is still with us today.
The organized community must therefore protect itself
against the negligence of its own members through regulations, public works programs, and enforcement of
quality levels as defined by itself.

Medieval society tended to ignore the problem almost
entirely, often with dire consequences. Some American
Indian tribes simply moved their camp when the conditions
became intolerable even according to their standards.
During the early Industrial Revolution city fathers
paid some lip service to the need for waste control, but
did little since their interests were centered elsewhere.

The medical profession was the first to discover the real
effects of pollution on human health and well-being during the last century or so, a period that has been characterized by rapid advances in medical science. Sanitary
engineers and public health experts have done much in
more recent decades in the development of methods and
techniques toward waste control. The time has come to
apply this knowledge not as the basis for stop-gap and
emergency measures in crisis situations but in a systematic and preventative way for all urban settlements,
regions, and, indeed, the environment as a whole. If
information or experience is still lacking in certain
areas, it must be identified and the gap filled through
research and experimentation. A positive and constructive
approach is required through (1) the definition of problems;
(2) decisions as to what should be done or what levels of
quality to be achieved; (3) the development of the appropriate technological methods; and, (4) the application of

such solutions within a given or modified political and
administrative framework.

Sigurd Grave, <u>Urban Planning Aspects
of Water Pollution
Control</u>, New York, N.Y.
Columbia University
Press, 1969.

President James Carter submitted to Congress a comprehensive environmental message on Monday, May 23. The message includes more than a dozen new legislative initiatives
or commitments to submit future legislation, five executive
orders, and a wide variety of policy statements and direc-
tives to federal agencies. It expressed the President's
commitment to the goals of environmental protection.

In the introduction to the Message the President stressed
that environmental issues are broad in scope, encompassing
the work-place and the urban environment, as well as conventional concerns about pollution, wilderness and wildlife.

He also stated his belief that environmental protection is
"consistent with a sound economy" and has created--and will
continue to create--many more jobs than it costs. The
President praised the Congress for the major environmental
legislation enacted over the past seven years and he pledged
the Executive Branch to sensitive administration and energetic enforcement of these laws, many of which have yet to
be fully implemented.

He observed that environmental protection is no longer
just a legislative job, and promised that it would receive
"firm and unsparing support" from the Executive Branch.

The Message covers a number of major themes: controlling
pollution and protecting the public health; energy and
the environment; the urban environment; protecting natural resources; preserving our national heritage, the
global environment; and making environmental laws work
more effectively.

<u>Environment Midwest</u>, U.S. EPA,
Region V, Chicago, Illinois, June 1977

One primary goal of this manual is to help local officials and others
concerned with environmental quality to become more familiar with environmental systems. In addition, we also want to affirm the part they must
play in enlisting the political system to help solve environmental problems.

How Political Systems Solve Problems of Natural Systems

Technicians use precise scientific data to make recommendations on specific technical functions. Professionally, they are not public servants who represent the electorate or who oversee their well-being. But local elected and appointed officials are public servants. Their job is to secure, with state and federal counterparts, restoration and maintenance of the electorate's political trust. To do so they must make decisions that benefit that electorate. By extension, then, these public servants are guardians of the biosphere's health.

This chapter is an informal discussion about the legal standards that govern pollution abatement. Just as the natural history of watersheds may be useful in planning to control sedimentation, so we believe that a political history of pollution control legislation may be useful in planning to control land use and development. First, we need to face squarely one reality about environmental problems: there is no single formula for resource management. Yet, it is reasonable to hypothesize that for every national, regional, or local situation, there is some way to balance the need to develop resources with the need to preserve them. The balance point is sought by setting performance standards to meet certain goals. Ideally, standards include consideration of the needs of all parties concerned and they assess the full consequences of implementation.

From Pollution Policy to Pollution Standard

Policy evolves into standards. The steps by which it does so are these:

1. Setting goals: e.g., to eliminate the discharge of all pollutants into the nation's streams by 1985.

2. Identifying water uses to be protected: e. g., uses include recreation, potable supply, and a healthful environment for aquatic biota; these waters must meet certain standards of water quality.

3. Identifying the criteria deemed necessary to support defined uses: e.g., the presence of fecal coliforms in freshwater may indicate the contamination of that water by pathogenic organisms.

4. Declaring quality standards on maximum pollution levels for ambient air and water: e.g., the maximum contaminant level of lead in drinking water is .05 milligrams/liter.

5. Stating effluent and emission standards to restrict the sources of pollution: e. g., no person shall discharge into the atmosphere from any refuse burning equipment emissions of

any air contamination which is darker in shade or density
than that designated as No. 1 on the Ringelmann chart (an
opacity measure);

6. Specifying enforcement procedures: e.g., the owner of any vessel
from which there is discharged any hazardous substance shall
be liable per discharge based on toxicity, degradability, and
dispersal and shall be fined an amount not to exceed $50,000.

Setting Goals

An example of goals is quoted below from the Federal Water Pollution
Control Act Amendment of October 18, 1972:

DECLARATION OF GOALS AND POLICY

Sec. 101. (2) The objective of this Act is to restore and
maintain the chemical, physical, and biological integrity
of the Nation's waters. In order to achieve this objective
it is hereby declared that, consistent with the provisions
of this Act—

(1) it is the national goal that the discharge of
pollutants into the navigable waters be eliminated
by 1985;
(2) it is the national goal that wherever attainable,
an interim goal of water quality which provides for
the protection and propagation of fish, shellfish, and
wildlife and provides for recreation in and on the water
be achieved by July 1, 1983;
(3) it is the national policy that the discharge of
toxic pollutants in toxic amounts be prohibited;
(4) it is the national policy that Federal financial
assistance be provided to construct publicly owned
waste treatment works;
(5) it is the national policy that areawide waste treatment management planning processes be developed and
implemented to assure adequate control of sources of
pollutants in each State; and
(6) it is the national policy that a major research and
demonstration effort be made to develop technology necessary to eliminate the discharge of pollutants into the
navigable waters, waters of the contiguous zone, and
the oceans.

Goals may sometimes seem too general, even though such classifications help
determine where the community's greatest needs lie. Sometimes insufficient
or conflicting technical data about pollution levels cause additional confusion. For example, to propose maximum contaminant levels for the Drinking Water Act, the U.S. EPA suggested that water be monitored routinely for

asbestos fibers. Yet, when the standards were printed (<u>Federal Register</u>, December 24, 1974), EPA dropped the recommendation because there were not enough supporting data to prove an epidemiological relationship between the presence of asbestos in water and health effects. Furthermore, the means for routinely monitoring the quantity of asbestos in water is expensive, cumbersome, and experimental. The EPA has allocated approximately $16,000,000 for 1977 to investigate the relationship between ingested asbestos and human health. In time, then, it may become possible to establish pollution standards which are indeed compatible with the pollution control goals.

Step two, identifying the water uses to be protected, is illustrated for the goal in Sec. 101 (a) (2), above. The National Technical Advisory Committee acting upon that goal to upgrade water quality by 1983, established the following use categories:

<u>Class A</u> - Suitable for public water supply with treatment by disinfection only. Suitable for all other water uses (recreation, etc.), uniformly excellent quality.

<u>Class B</u> - Suitable for bathing and other primary contact recreation. Acceptable for public water supply with appropriate treatment (may require more than just disinfection). Suitable for agricultural and certain industrial processes and cooling uses. Suitable as excellent fish and wildlife habitat. Excellent aesthetic value but not necessarily uniformly excellent quality.

<u>Class C</u> - Suitable for fish and wildlife habitat, boating, fishing and certain industrial process and cooling uses. Not suitable for primary contact recreation (swimming). Under some conditions acceptable for public water supply but only after appropriate regimen of pretreatment. Good aesthetic value.

<u>Class D</u> - Suitable for navigation, certain industrial process and cooling use and migration of certain species of fish. Not suitable for water supply under any conditions. Not suitable for swimming, boating, or fishing. Acceptable aesthetic value only.

In Step 3, identifying criteria, information is first obtained from research. These data set the parameters within which to preserve the use that has been selected for protection. For example, the criteria for water quality which will maintain game fish might include the pH, chlorine concentration, PCBs level, and the dissolved oxygen content. Dissolved oxygen, in this case, is an indicator criterion of quality. If there were high nutrient loadings, bacteria would thrive in proportional numbers and in doing so would consume the oxygen. If the level dropped sufficiently, then fish would die. This minimum survival value needs to be established. The dissolved oxygen criterion might state that a dissolved oxygen level of

TABLE I—LIST OF APPROVED TEST PROCEDURES

Parameter and units	Method	Standard methods	ASTM	EPA methods
General analytical methods:				
1. Alkalinity as CaCO₃ mg CaCO₃/liter.	Titration: electrometric, manual or automated method—methyl orange.	p. 370	p. 143	p. 6.
2. B.O.D. five day mg/liter.	Modified winkler or probe method.	p. 489		p. 8.
3. Chemical oxygen demand (C.O.D.) mg/liter.	Dichromate reflux.	p. 495	p. 210	p. 17.
4. Total solids mg/liter.	Gravimetric 103-105° C.	p. 535		p. 280.
5. Total dissolved (filterable) solids mg/liter.	Glass fiber filtration 180° C.			p. 278.
6. Total suspended (nonfilterable) solids mg/liter.	Glass fiber filtration 103-105° C.	p. 537		p. 278.
7. Total volatile solids mg/liter.	Gravimetric 550° C.	p. 535		p. 282.
8. Ammonia (as N) mg/liter.	Distillation—nesslerization or titration automated phenolate.			p. 134. p. 141. p. 149.
9. Kjeldahl nitrogen (as N) mg/liter.	Digestion + distillation—nesslerization or titration automated digestion phenolate.	p. 469		p. 149. p. 167.
10. Nitrate (as N) mg/liter.	Cadmium reduction; brucine sulfate; automated cadmium or hydrazine reduction.	p. 458 p. 461	p. 124	p. 170. p. 175. p. 188. p. 106.
11. Total phosphorus (as P) mg/liter.	Persulfate digestion and single reagent (ascorbic acid), or manual digestion, and automated single reagent or stannous chloride.	p. 526 p. 532	p. 42	p. 246. p. 248. p. 255.
12. Acidity mg CaCO₃/liter.	Electrometric end point or phenolphthalein end point.		p. 148	
13. Total organic carbon (TOC) mg/liter.	Combustion—infrared method.	p. 257	p. 702	p. 221.
14. Hardness—total mg CaCO₃/liter.	EDTA titration; automated colorimetric atomic absorption.	p. 179	p. 170	p. 76. p. 78. p. 185.
15. Nitrite (as N) mg/liter.	Manual or automated colorimetric diazotization.			
Analytical methods for trace metals:				
16. Aluminum—total mg/liter.	Atomic absorption.	p. 210		p. 98.
17. Antimony—total mg/liter.	Atomic absorption.	p. 210 p. 425		
18. Arsenic—total mg/liter.	Digestion plus silver diethyldithiocarbamate; atomic absorption.	p. 62 p. 210		p. 13.
19. Barium—total mg/liter.	Atomic absorption.	p. 67		
20. Beryllium—total mg/liter.	Aluminon; atomic absorption.	p. 210		
21. Boron—total mg/liter.	Curcumin.	p. 69		
22. Cadmium—total mg/liter.	Atomic absorption; colorimetric.	p. 210 p. 422	p. 692	p. 101.
23. Calcium—total mg/liter.	EDTA titration; atomic absorption.	p. 84	p. 692	p. 102.
24. Chromium VI mg/liter.	Extraction and atomic absorption; colorimetric.	p. 420	p. 692	p. 94.
25. Chromium—total mg/liter.	Atomic absorption; colorimetric.	p. 210 p. 426		p. 104.
26. Cobalt—total mg/liter.	Atomic absorption.	p. 210	p. 103	
27. Copper—total mg/liter.	Atomic absorption; colorimetric.	p. 210	p. 692	p. 106.
28. Iron—total mg/liter.	...do.	p. 210 p. 410	p. 692	p. 108.
29. Lead—total mg/liter.	...do.	p. 210 p. 433	p. 163	p. 110.
30. Magnesium—total mg/liter.	Atomic absorption; Gravimetric.	p. 210 p. 435	p. 692	p. 112.
31. Manganese—total mg/liter.	Atomic absorption.	p. 210 p. 416	p. 692	
32. Mercury—total mg/liter.	Flameless atomic absorption.	p. 201	p. 692	p. 114.
33. Molybdenum—total mg/liter.	Atomic absorption.	p. 210		
34. Nickel—total mg/liter.	Atomic absorption; colorimetric.	p. 443	p. 602	
35. Potassium—total mg/liter.	Atomic absorption; colorimetric; flame photometric.	p. 283	p. 326	
36. Selenium—total mg/liter.	Atomic absorption.	p. 283		
37. Silver—total mg/liter.	Atomic absorption.	p. 210		p. 116.
38. Sodium—total mg/liter.	Flame photometric; atomic absorption.	p. 317	p. 326	p. 116.
39. Thallium—total mg/liter.	Atomic absorption.			
40. Tin—total mg/liter.	...do.			
41. Titanium—total mg/liter.	...do.	p. 157		
42. Vanadium—total mg/liter.	Atomic Absorption; Colorimetric.	p. 210	p. 692	p. 120.
43. Zinc—total mg/liter.	Atomic Absorption; Colorimetric.	p. 444		
Analytical methods for nutrients, anions, and organics:				
44. Organic nitrogen (as N) mg/liter.	Kjeldahl nitrogen minus ammonia nitrogen.	p. 468		p. 140.
45. Ortho-phosphate (as P) mg/liter.	Direct single reagent; automated single reagent or stannous chloride.	p. 532	p. 42	p. 225. p. 246. p. 249.
46. Sulfate (as SO₄) mg/liter.	Gravimetric; turbidimetric; automated colorimetric—barium chloranilate.	p. 331 p. 334	p. 81 p. 82	p. 286. p. 288.
47. Sulfide (as S) mg/liter.	Titrimetric—iodine.	p. 551		p. 294.
48. Sulfite (as SO₃) mg/liter.	Titrimetric; iodide-iodate.	p. 337	p. 261	
49. Bromide mg/liter.	...do.	p. 46	p. 216	p. 29.
50. Chloride mg/liter.	Silver nitrate; mercuric nitrate; automated colorimetric-ferricyanide.	p. 96 p. 307	p. 22 p. 21	p. 81. p. 41.
51. Cyanide—total mg/liter.	Distillation—silver nitrate titration or pyridine pyrazolone colorimetric.	p. 397	p. 556	
52. Fluoride mg/liter.	Distillation—SPADNS.	p. 171 p. 174	p. 101	p. 64.
53. Chlorine—total residual mg/liter.	Colorimetric; amperometric titration.	p. 363	p. 229	
54. Oil and grease mg/liter.	Liquid-Liquid extraction with trichlorotrifluoroethane.	p. 254		
55. Phenols mg/liter.	Colorimetric; 4 AAP.	p. 502	p. 443	p. 232.
56. Surfactants mg/liter.	Methylene blue colorimetric.	p. 339	p. 619	p. 131.
57. Algicides mg/liter.	Gas chromatography.			
58. Benzidine mg/liter.	Diazotisation—colorimetric.			
59. Chlorinated organic compounds (except pesticides) mg/liter.	Gas chromatography.			
60. Pesticides mg/liter.	Gas chromatography.			
Analytical methods for physical and biological parameters:				
61. Color platinum-cobalt units or dominant wave-length, hue, luminance, purity.	Colorimetric; spectrophotometric.	p. 160 p. 202		p. 36.
62. Specific conductance mho/cm at 25° C.	Wheatstone bridge.	p. 323	p. 169	p. 284.
63. Turbidity Jackson units.	Turbidimeter.	p. 350	p. 467	p. 308.
64. Fecal streptococcci bacteria number/100 ml.	MPN; membrane filter; plate count.	p. 689 p. 690		
65. Coliform bacteria (fecal) number/100 ml.	MPN; Membrane filter.	p. 691 p. 689		
66. Coliform bacteria (total) number/100 ml.	...do.	p. 684 p. 679		
Radiological parameters:				
67. Alpha—total pCi/liter.	Proportional counter; scintillation counter.	p. 598	p. 609	
68. Alpha—counting error pCi/liter.	...do.	p. 598	p. 612	
69. Beta—total pCi/liter.	Proportional counter.	p. 598	p. 478	
70. Beta—counting error pCi/liter.	...do.	p. 598	p. 478	
71. Radium—total pCi/liter.	Proportional counter; scintillation counter.	p. 611 p. 617	p. 674	

Figure 61

5 ppm is the minimum that average game fish can tolerate. To be specific, the criteria for the example use identified in Step 2, above, are derived from the Water Pollution Control Act's 71 test procedures for five categories of water quality criteria (see Figure 61).

Criteria are not standards, but once identified, criteria are sometimes seized by public officials as if they were. Such use is often misapplied; for example, smog control particulate criteria in Los Angeles might not be criteria in Boston. Clearly, we have to use appropriate criteria if we are to develop a solid pollution control plan.

In Step 4, quality standards are set based upon the criteria. Quality standards are the maximum levels of pollutants considered tolerable. The criteria and the state of the threatened species or resource help to establish these quality standards. Assuming that the dissolved oxygen criterion for game fish is 5 ppm, the local Conservation Commission, on the basis that sport fishing is a major economic contributor to that community, says that fish must be guarded with substantial safety margins. They might then request the standard to be 7 ppm dissolved oxygen.

Originally, air quality standards were set by local officials who could either use federal criteria for their standards or adopt standards of neighboring communities. Predictably, they found themselves pressured by both federal and community groups to adopt their criteria. As a result, delays, unreliable data, and confusion in setting air and water quality standards confounded everyone. The Clean Air Act in 1970 returned authority for pollution control to Washington. When the U.S. EPA was established in the same year, it became responsible for drawing up the quality standards for various types of industries. The same principle applied to the successor acts, the Water Pollution Control Amendments of 1972 and the Safe Drinking Water Act of 1974.

Like criteria, standards can be represented by numbers, such as a total of 4 coliform bacteria per 100 milliliters of water, 1 Turbidity Unit monthly average, and 380 mg of total suspended solids per 100 milliliters. If possible, the test for meeting the standards should be easy and inexpensive to conduct; furthermore, it must produce reliable data. Test procedures for comparing water samples against the standards are contained in Standard Methods for the Examination of Water and Wastewater, a work started in 1897. Air standards are not so well defined, but the EPA has an urgent program well underway to develop test procedures.

In the fifth step, effluent and emissions standards are stated to prevent or to limit future discharges into air and water sources. Effluent and emissions standards are the cutting edge of pollution abatement, for they clearly indicate the limits of allowable pollution for the various physical, chemical, or biological parameters defined in the federal and state standards. The federal effluent and emission standards in the three Acts mentioned above specify which pollutants will be considered criteria and monitored, what maximum levels of each will be allowed, and what exceptions will be permitted under certain conditions. The EPA has also specified the test procedures to be used for monitoring the enforcement of such standards. When effluent limitations and best management of non-point sources do not adequately protect water quality, further controls are necessary.

However, some of the test procedures seem to be "Catch 22's." The acceptance of a relatively inexpensive, reliable test method can encourage officials to use the criterion the test measures whether the federal standard applies or not. Therefore, it may be difficult either 1) upon identification of a more appropriate criterion to establish a standard, or 2) upon discovery of an easier, less expensive, more reliable test, to ask that the test become the "standard method."

Federal Environmental Laws

In response to public interests and needs, the following major pieces of federal legislation were written and approved. Each is a composite of the six steps to convert a pollution abatement policy into enforceable standards. A summary of the basic intent for each follows the title of each law:

National Environmental Policy Act

Requires that all federal agencies utilize a systematic, interdisciplinary approach in project planning and decision making.

Requires a detailed Environmental Impact Statement for any major federal action significantly affecting the quality of the human environment.

Federal Water Pollution Control Act

Requires that all point source discharges into any water source of body receive a permit from the U.S. EPA or designated state agency; minimum treatment requirements for any such discharges are established (NPDES Permit).

Requires that any discharge of dredged or fill material into water courses or bodies or adjacent wetlands receive a permit from the U.S. Corps of Engineers (Section 404 Permit).

Establishes planning requirements for basins (Section 303), area-wide water quality management (Section 208) and municipal treatment facilities (Section 301).

Clean Air Act

Requires National Ambient Air Quality Standards; requires that states develop implementation plans to protect or attain these standards; prevents deterioration of existing air quality.

Establishes standards of performance for new stationary sources of air pollution.

Establishes national emissions standards for hazardous air pollutants.

Controls the level of emissions from mobile sources.

Noise Control Act

Establishes standards of noise emissions for various devices.

Coastal Zone Management Act

Establishes, through planning grants to states, programs for the management of coastal areas, including regulation of areas of geographic concern for review of land-uses.

Requires that federal activities within the coastal zone be consistent with approved state management plans.

Provides special assistance to states experiencing development related to off-shore oil development.

Endangered Species Act

Regulates the possession of threatened or endangered species.

Prevents any federal activities that would adversely affect the continued existence of a threatened or endangered species either directly or through habitat destruction.

Resource Conservation and Recovery Act

Regulates the disposal of hazardous wastes for the protection of the environment and public health.

Establishes planning programs for state and local governments.

Toxic Substances Control Act

Requires special certification of any newly introduced substance which may be toxic.

Federal Insecticide, Fungicide, and Rodenticide Act

Provides for the registration by U.S. EPA of pesticides and pesticide manufacturing facilities.

Restricts use of registered pesticides to certified applicators.

Safe Drinking Water Act

Establishes National Drinking Water Regulations specifying maximum allowable contaminant levels.

Requires strict state or U.S. EPA enforcement and monitoring of local water supplies for national standards compliance.

Marine Protection Research and Sanctuaries Act

Prohibits dumping of any material into the ocean without a permit from the Corps of Engineers (dredged material) or U.S. EPA (other material).

The sixth and last step in pollution abatement is to enforce the standards. The means to do so must be clear and the test for compliance must be thorough.

The Safe Drinking Water Act

Let's consider in more detail Public Law 93-523, the Safe Drinking Water Act, passed on December 16, 1974. It required the Administrator of the U.S. Environmental Protection Agency to promulgate a set of primary, health-related drinking water regulations for all public drinking water suppliers. Prior to this legislation, only an estimated 9,000 water supplies in the U.S. were being monitored with any frequency, compared to the estimated 42,000 water supplies the EPA believed should be monitored to protect the health of the American public. Charged with the above task, the EPA quickly drew up standards which were published in the Federal Register of December 24, 1975 under the title, "Interim Primary Drinking Water Standards."

The philosophy of enforcing these standards is similar in many respects to that followed in the Clean Air and Water Pollution legislation described earlier. Through rule-making the EPA defines what the minimum quality standards for the water should be (stated in terms of Maximum Contaminant Levels or MCLs), defines the types of public and private water supplies that must be tested (categorized by "community" and "non-community" systems) and even defines the testing frequency for each MCL. Instead of a "permits program" as in the Federal Water Pollution Control Act Amendment of 1972, the EPA instituted a "certification program." The certification program works as follows: The EPA, through its Water Supply Program, sends its technical personnel to inspect and to evaluate individual state laboratories to see that laboratory staff understand the purpose and technical requirements of the law and are capable of carrying out the certification program within the state. Once certified by the EPA, the state laboratory sends out its team of "evaluators" to inspect each of the regional and municipal laboratories under its jurisdiction. Laboratories not meeting minimum requirements for equipment, personnel, and experience are denied certification until they correct these deficiencies. The EPA makes available up to 75 percent funding for upgrading water supply laboratories.

This new law requires record-keeping (five years for bacteriological data and ten years for chemical data), as well as sending immediately to the state laboratory any results from water tests that show that an MCL has been exceeded. The state laboratory then initiates corrective measures, deciding whether it is necessary to alert the public about the contamination. If it is an emergency, we might hear this announcement on the radio or television: "Boil water before drinking." Such a message comes in response to the Safe Drinking Water Act of 1974.

During the years such legislation was being passed, the responsibility for pollution abatement shifted from the federal government to the states, back to the federal government, and now once more back to the states and local governments. The present arrangement, however, operates like a partnership of federal, state, and local governments. The decision-making power that conservation commissions have could be greater than most people believe.

The Water Pollution Control Act

To understand the line of authority from the acts to the local commissions, however, we should examine this partnership among three levels of government. The Water Pollution Control Act, especially, contains provisions to encourage and assist public participation in enforcing the Act's standards. One provision, Section 208, sets up an "Areawide Waste Treatment Management Plan" which involves several local governments in planning and implementing solutions to their common water quality management problems. It established a management structure to carry out the actions specified in the plan and provided grants to cover planning costs.

Areawide planning addresses point source pollution (a "discernible, confined and discrete conveyance," such as municipal and industrial waste discharges that require permits) and non-point source pollution (general and diffuse sources, such as farmland erosion, stormwater runoff, mine seepages, construction siltation, salt water intrusion, etc., not specifically isolable for permitting). Most importantly, areawide planning provides a structure to coordinate the wastewater program with air quality and the management of water supplies and the handling of solid wastes—as well as other related environmental matters.

Under this section, state governors designate "208 Planning Areas." While there are several ways to choose Areas, once the governor designates an Area, he must assign an agency to direct planning there. The planning agency includes elected officials or their representatives from the local governments. The agency designs a plan, while operating agencies or commissions carry out the plan. Planning responsibilities include determining locations for treatment plants, control of non-point sources, land-use development, air quality improvement, methods for solid waste disposal, and similar duties. It is at this level that Conservation/Environmental Commissions become involved.

The Emergence of Conservation/Environmental Commissions

Growing from New England's town meeting tradition, environmental commissioners are part of a duly constituted division of local government, part of the system that makes and/or controls decisions which affect our environment. Ipswich, Massachusetts, threatened by beach and tidal marsh development, articulated a need for laws through which a municipality could conserve its natural resources. In 1957, Massachusetts adopted the first state legislation establishing commissions. By 1968, conservation commissions were enacted in Connecticut, Maine, New Jersey, New Hampshire, New York, and Rhode Island. New Jersey renamed the commissions "environmental commissions" in 1972, and included a revised set of interests they should address:

> An environmental commission shall have power to study and make recommendations concerning open space preservation, water resources management, air pollution control, solid waste management, noise control, soil and landscape protection, environmental appearance, marine resources, and protection of flora and fauna.

With missions as clear as this, we have the necessary means to control the use of resources in the interests of conserving them. The realities, however, of state and local ordinances and the customs of the social institutions will no doubt modify every commissions' modus operandi, but the record of success for commissions seeking a balance among the three interests holds much promise. In addition, commissions generally work closely with other local departments such as Planning Boards, Boards of Health, and Boards of Appeal to get as much representation of public interests as possible. Such a network of cooperation can't help but remind us of that interconnectedness of the natural world and its splendid efficiency when all its interests are in balance.

The legal authority of such commissions extends in many cases to the power to approve or deny any new construction, land use application, or facilities plan. Commissions can bring suit in the name of the community against any person or corporation alleged to be in violation of effluent limits, emissions limits, or other permit conditions. In fact, if a commission sees fit, it can, by working with the state authorities, set effluent limits that are stricter than those required by the federal government. In no case, however, can the commission act to relax the federal effluent limits. This type of power gives conservation commissions a power over the quality of community life that has not existed before, and therein lies the utility of the new governmental federation.

Local, state, and federal governments now have a system for working cooperatively to solve many problems of pollution. The wisdom of creating plans to direct our energies at controlling pollution grew from the knowledge that we ourselves decide the limits of our resources of air, water, soil, and energy.

CHAPTER SUMMARY

1. Pollution policy becomes practical law by going through 6 steps: setting goals; identifying uses to be protected; identifying criteria deemed necessary to support definite uses; declaring quality standards; stating effluent and emissions standards; and specifying the enforcement procedures.

2. For example, by 1983, the Water Pollution Control Act stipulates, the nation's inland waters must be upgraded to Class B. The classes are: A=suitable for public water supply with treatment by disinfection only; B=suitable for bathing and other primary contact recreation; C=suitable for fish and wildlife habitat . . . and certain industrial process and cooling requirements; D=suitable for navigation, certain industrial process, and cooling use and migration of certain species of fish.

3. Pollution control "criteria" differ from "standards." Criteria are the physical or chemical parameters which need to be controlled, say the dissolved oxygen level for game fish. Biological tests might conclude that dissolved oxygen criteria is 5 ppm; below that fish die. Standards might be set above that--perhaps at a level of 7 ppm--to ensure that no fish will die.

4. A most important step is the prevention of further pollution. This is accomplished by setting wastewater effluent and air emissions standards for specific uses and geographical areas.

5. In another example, the Safe Drinking Water Act passed in 1974 requires the U. S. EPA to set primary health-related drinking water regulations for all public drinking water suppliers. Qualifying as a supplier of potable water requires "certification" under which state laboratories send out evaluators to local and regional laboratories. Data banks, public service announcements under conditions of alert, and other requirements give workability to the law.

6. Section 208 of the Water Pollution Control Act sets up Areawide Waste Treatment Management Regions to coordinate plans within that region for all water quality management decisions. Conservation and environmental commissions participate in the implementation.

7. Conservation commissions began in Massachusetts in 1957 and are forerunners of the 208 Planning Areas. These commissions can approve or deny new construction, land-use applications, facilities plans, sewage effluent-limit violators, and permit violators. They cannot, however, relax federal standards.

SOURCES

Citizens' Advisory Committee on Environmental Quality. Community Action for Environmental Quality. Washington, D.C.: GPO.

Guidelines for Reporting Daily Air Quality. Washington, D. C.: GPO.

Citizens' Guide to Action for Clean Waters. Arlington, Vir., Izaak Walton League.

Citizens' Guide to Clean Air: A Manual for Citizen Action. Washington, D.C.: The Conservation Foundation.

Community Air Quality Guides. American Industrial Hygiene Association, 1968.

"EPA's Water Program's Guidelines Establishing Test Procedures for Analysis of Pollutants." Federal Register, 38, Vol. 199, (16 October 1973).

Geldreich, Edwin E. Evaluating Water Bacteriological Laboratories. Washington, D.C.: GPO, 1975.

Ramsey, William and Claude Anderson. Managing the Environment. Basic Book Publishers, 1972.

Ridgeway, James. The Politic of Ecology. E.F. Dutton & Co., 1970.

Sloan, Irving I. Environment and the Law. Dobbs Ferry, New York: Oceana Publications, 1971.

Stern, Arthur. Air Pollution. New York: Academic Press, 1968.

U.S. Department of the Interior, Federal Water Pollution Control Administration. Report of the Committee on Water Quality. Washington, D.C.: GPO, 1968.

U.S. Environmental Protection Agency, Proceedings for the First Microbiology Seminar on Standardization of Methods. Washington, D.C.: GPO, 1973.

U.S. Public Health Service. Standard Methods for the Examination of Water and Wastewater. Washington, D. C.: GPO, 1976.

CHAPTER FOURTEEN

NATURAL SYSTEMS AND LAND-USE PLANNING

A PERSPECTIVE

We take a handful of sand from the endless landscape of awareness around us and call that handful of sand the world.

Once we have the handful of sand, the world of which we are conscious, a process of discrimination goes to work on it. . . . We divide the sand into parts. This and that. Here and there. Black and white. Now and then. The discrimination is the division of the conscious universe into parts.

The handful of sand looks uniform at first, but the longer we look at it the more diverse we find it to be. Each grain of sand is different. No two are alike. Some are similar in one way, some are similar in another way, and we can form the sand into separate piles on the basis of this similarity and dissimilarity. Shades of color in different piles--sizes in different piles--grain shapes into different piles--subtypes of grain shapes in different piles--grades of opacity in different piles--and so on, and on, and on. You'd think the process of subdivision and classification would come to an end somewhere, but it doesn't. It just goes on and on.

One type of understanding is concerned with the piles and the basis for sorting and interrelating them. . . . Another type of understanding is directed toward the handful of sand before the sorting begins. Both are valid ways of looking at the world although irreconcilable with each other.

What has become an urgent necessity is a way of looking at the world that does violence to neither of these two kinds of understanding and unites them into one. Such an understanding will not reject sand-sorting or contemplation of unsorted sand for its own sake. Such an understanding will instead seek to direct attention to the endless landscape from which the sand is taken.

> Robert M. Pirsig, Zen and the Art of Motorcycle Maintenance

> All ethics so far evolved rest upon a single premise:
> that the individual is a member of a community of inter-
> dependent parts. His instincts prompt him to compete
> for his place in the community, but his ethics prompt
> him also to cooperate (perhaps in order that there may
> be a place to compete for).
>
> The land ethic simply enlarges the boundaries of the
> community to include soils, water, plants, and animals,
> or collectively: the land.
>
> Aldo Leopold, <u>A</u> <u>Sand</u> <u>County</u> <u>Almanac</u>

<u>Jobs</u>, <u>Health</u>, <u>and</u> <u>Environmental</u> <u>Quality</u>

Increasingly the people of the United States are equating their concerns for economic stability and well being with environmental quality.
No <u>one</u> person would dare such a statement, unless he were very wealthy and
very healthy. But collectively <u>we</u> are saying that <u>we</u> are becoming as
worried about our exposure to cancer-producing chemicals as we are about
the salary we receive for livelihood from an industry that produces them.
The collective expression is most pointedly and powerfully represented in
the National Environmental Policy Act of 1969. The Act directly addresses
these three related concerns, economics, welfare, and the environment.

> The Congress, recognizing the profound impact of man's
> activity . . . on the natural environment, particularly
> population growth, high-density urbanization, industrial
> expansion, resource exploitation . . . and recognizing . . .
> the critical importance of restoring and maintaining en-
> vironmental quality to the overall welfare and development
> of man, declares that it is the continuing policy of the
> Federal government, in cooperation with states <u>and local</u>
> <u>governments</u>*, to use all practical means and measures, to
> foster . . . the general welfare, to create and maintain
> conditions under which man and nature can exist in produc-
> tive harmony, and fulfill the social, economic and other
> requirements of future generations of Americans."
>
> National Environmental Policy Act

NEPA raises citizens' <u>accountability</u> for balancing economic development, social welfare, and environmental quality. It is a thesis of
this book that indeed progress in all three areas is desirable and achieve-
able. Furthermore, the three areas are so intrinsically related that
neglect of any one can only lead to deterioration in the others.

---

*Emphasis is ours.

Barring disaster, the population of the United States will increase to 250,000,000 by the year 2,000 and be in excess of 400,000,000 by the year 2070. Because of the present great proportion of child-bearing young people in the population, this growth in total numbers will occur even if the birth-rate holds at fewer than 2.1 births per mother (the number required for population replacement). Although 70% of the population now lives in the metropolitan areas, there will be an increase in population everywhere. Growth is inevitable and must be faced.

To put it directly, "Local government decision-makers must ascertain what difference in impact among alternative development patterns do, in fact, exist and must effectively plan and control land use so as to minimize cost burdens and adverse environmental effects." This statement and the figures preceding it are from introductory comments in a recent study, The Costs of Sprawl, prepared for the Council on Environmental Quality (in association with the Department of Housing and Urban Development and the Environmental Protection Agency) by the Real Estate Research Corporation.

This and other studies (many referred to in Sources and Suggested Readings) show the general nature in social, economic, and environmental impact, as well as the extent in discomfort, dollars, pollutants, and energy savings, of change accomplished by informed and willful exercising of a plan. There is, in the face of inevitable growth especially, a case for planning.

The Benefits of Planning

The Costs of Sprawl compares six community prototypes differing in housing and density to six different degrees of community-wide planning. The findings are highly instructive to people who live in the east and west coast megalopolis region because the data collected was primarily about the urban fringes. However, it is also applicable to land development practices and opportunities everywhere.

The following direct quotes indicate many of the conclusions that are of special use to readers of this manual on environmental systems:

1. Planned development of all densities is less costly to create and operate than sprawl in terms of environmental costs, economic costs, personal costs, and energy consumption.

   The environmental advantages of planned development include:

   Twenty to thirty percent less air pollution resulting from reduced automobile travel.

   Conservation of open space.

Preservation of significant wildlife.

Improved site design to minimize noise impacts.

Careful land use design . . . to minimize the amount of soil disturbed and paved over (thus lowering slightly the volume of storm water run-off, sedimentation, and water pollution). . . .

2. Economic and environmental costs (as well as resource consumption) are likely to be significantly less at higher densities to house and service a given population. . . . Some personal costs, however, may increase with increasing density. . . .

Increased density reduces total environmental costs but increases the concentration of pollution. . . . especially air pollution and sediment

Energy and water consumption may be reduced by approximately 40 percent in high density developments. . . from reduced auto transportation, heating and cooling, and lawn watering

3. Thus, while planning results in cost savings, density is a much more influential cost determinant. Clearly, the greatest cost advantages occur when higher density planning developments are contrasted with low density sprawl. . . .

4. When alternative residential developments are considered for a given site. . .development costs increase with density, but not as rapidly as the increase in number of dwelling units which can be accommodated. . . .

For a given site size, air pollution is more concentrated as density increases.

Total energy consumption (excluding transportation) increases approximately 120 percent when the density of a given site increases from two to ten dwelling units . . . per acre (an increase of 500 percent). Residential water use will also increase, but again not as rapidly as the number of dwelling units.

Many personal costs, particularly those associated with privacy and personal ownership, will increase with increasing densities.

5. Variation in certain basic study assumptions leads to the following conclusions:

a. Doubling or tripling the population assumed in the base analysis would allow the community to support additional services, regional parks, community health clinics, and public transportation. Diseconomies of scale would be experienced with regard to solid waste collection; some operating economies are likely to be realized for schools, police, fire, libraries, government administration. Significant economies (both capital and operating) would be found for solid waste disposal and sewage water treatment.

b. The effect of extreme site conditions (poor soil, very flat or steep slopes, absence of ground and surface water sources, high water table, dense or sparse ground cover, extreme climate) will be to either greatly increase development costs or prohibit development altogether.

6. Given a constant amount of floor space (200,000 square feet), shopping center commercial areas will be 20 percent . . . less costly to build and service with roads and utilities than a strip commercial area. . . . Savings are largely due to lower land prices per acre in shopping centers than are found for commercial strips. . . . Environmentally, the strip compares poorly with the shopping center because:

a. The strip is less appealing visually.

b. It takes longer to build (due to incremental construction) thus causing greater sedimentation.

c. The strip configuration encourages stops on shopping trips, thus increasing auto emissions.

Understanding the Role of Government

It is maintainted in the position paper, "A Five Year Water Quality Management Strategy," that the federal government will look increasingly to state and local governments to assist them in implementing national programs. Local governments, therefore, will need to understand the posture and essential strategies of the federal government so that there is a more coordinated and effective effort toward environmental quality control systems throughout the country. The position of the Environmental Protection Agency toward water quality management illustrates well how federal, state, and local governments link in political partnership to solve environmental problems through a focus on natural systems.

EPA exercises its water quality management program, as we have discussed in an earlier chapter, through PL 92-500, the Federal Water Pollution Control Act. Section 208 of the Act sets up Areawide Planning Regions within each state. Another Section, 201, provides for the award of federal money to construct water treatment facilities. The Act called for the areawide planning first, and then the construction of facilities. However, that priority was shifted during the last Administration, probably in consideration of increasing unemployment statistics. Indeed, during 1975 while approximately 10,000 persons were displaced from employment by environmental control restrictions, another 50,000 were employed to construct environmental control facilities. But, now there is evidence, as EPA officials have learned, that:

- many of the wastewater treatment facilities funded or planned for funding are too expensive for the local population. Four examples are in Walton, New York; Dunkirk, Ohio; Greenville, Maine; and Humboldt County, California.

- wastewater treatment plants produce sludge which becomes a solid waste disposal problem.

- incineration of sludge and other solid wastes becomes an air pollution problem.

EPA has developed a five year strategy to:

(1) improve program performance (i.e., focus on result-oriented 208 efforts; avoid secondary air quality and sludge impacts of construction grants; and achieve adequate planning before advanced waste treatment construction).

(2) impact previously under-emphasized environmental problems (e.g., non-point sources, pretreatment, water and nutrient conservation, urban runoff, pits/ponds and lagoons).

The strategy concentrates on facility planning and urban runoff control in selected urban areas, and nationally significant state-identified non-point source priorities. One of the objectives includes pilot urban runoff demonstrations to restrict runoff and thereby to avoid advanced wastewater treatment. Construction of preventive controls is estimated to be one-tenth as costly as that for advanced treatment facilities. Another objective is to test sludge disposal alternatives, such as land application of wastewater. During these implementations, the federal government with the state will exercise greater control over setting of priorities and oversight of local activities.

Public participation will be emphasized throughout. First, the state-wide 208 program establishes priorities, directions, and coordination throughout the state; 208 agencies have the principal responsibility for all water quality management decisions within their areas--involving the public in planning also is a major part of their responsibility.

Currently EPA is reminding its regional administrators to encourage the search for alternatives to provide cost-effective wastewater treatment facilities. A recent review of approved facility plans showed that decision-makers do not always consider prudent alternatives: new or renovated septic tanks, holding tanks, and package treatment systems often are more cost-effective than collection, interceptor, and treatment networks. EPA policy requires that facility plans contain analysis of alternatives involving maintenance and/or new construction of treatment systems for single family homes and small clusters of homes wherever these are feasible in the planning area. Septic tanks, holding tanks, and package plant treatment systems serving small clusters of homes are eligible for funding if they meet certain criteria (PL 92-500, Section 502, CFR 35.920-1 and 35-925-5 [b]; 40 CFR 30.810; FMC 74-7). Systems serving individual homes are not eligible for federal funding; only a group of individual family systems are eligible. These trends—toward broader emphasis on local planning and greater concern for alternatives to advanced wastewater construction—are consistent with the goals of local planning organizations.

Everyone is a potential land-use decision-maker and every land owner can assert influence. The most influential potential planners include planning board members, county executives or commissioners, city managers, and conservation and environmental commissioners. Other major groups with an interest in planning and zoning decisions include: mortgage bankers; land developers; home builders; zoning attorneys; realtors and real estate associations; general business groups, such as the local chambers of commerce or boards of trade; environmental organizations; and local government officials and political leaders. All of these peoples' decisions and actions influence the environment. As we tried to point out in Chapter 1, there is no discontinuity between one action and another, even though there may be a great stretch of distance. In short, all of these people need to consider planning of land-use.

The Elements of Land-Use Planning

The essential elements of responsible land management are a natural resources inventory,* a master plan, and regulations. A schematic might represent the three elements triangularly or linearly as continuously recycling or as an endlessly repeating sequence. Whatever the graphic mode, it is evident that a large amount of valid information helps to form a wide-reaching, solid plan to employ appropriate and fair regulations to control the inevitable population growth and resulting land development.

Resource Data

Information for a master plan can be obtained by land capability analysis: it evaluates the land's and therefore the system's inherent capacity to withstand development. Some land barely covers a rock outcropping, so it cannot retain groundwater or assimilate wastewater. Consequently, it cannot withstand diffuse residential development without regional water and sewage systems. The example may sound absurd, but the practice is common.

---

*Natural resources inventories are the data base used for land capability analysis.

Land Capability Analysis

A land capability analysis assesses the natural and socioeconomic variables such as those exemplified on Figure 62. Federal, state, and local agencies often store many years of data on a region. Local residents, college and university faculty, conservation and preservation groups, outdoor education centers, libraries, and many other professional associations and citizen groups have invaluable records for such an analysis. The U.S. Geoglogical Survey (USGS) prints inexpensive topographic soil survey maps, state Departments of Natural Resources; Fish and Game, Wildlife; Environmental Quality or Protection, and others have banks of data on land capabilities.

Historical socioeconomic land uses can be plotted on analytical maps. Revised USGS maps, for example, overprint new developments in purple. The U.S. Department of Agriculture's Agricultural Stabilization and Conservation Service, which maintains an office in each county, can provide information on the availability of 10-year interval aerial photographs from the Soil Conservation Service. USGS also administers the Earth Resources Observation Systems Program (EROS) at Sioux Falls, South Dakota (phone 605/594-6511, extension 511) and can furnish aerial photography and imagery from airplane and spacecraft with coverage repeated every 18 days for any area in the U.S. Such maps give information on elevation, slope, woodlands, cultivated land, airshed patterns, water surfaces, water temperatures, urban surfaces, and other related matter. Data obtained from these and other sources are imposed over topographic maps with transparent overlays or imprinted over them with codes via computer printout. Values are assigned the overlaid or imprinted material by color or number, so that a visual composite picture emerges that expresses natural land use potentials. These printouts indicate that the land may be more or less suitable for certain types of designated use.

Additionally, the pictures may show potential problems and opportunities. The projections might highlight eroded zones that could add to sedimentation by increased surface runoff, ultimately exacerbating potential floodplain damage. Periodic comparisons might illustrate the change over a period of time in the amount of land lost to agriculture and recreation; the amounts of air and water pollutants; the vagaries of wind and precipitation; the effects of fertilizers and insecticides; the actions of other counties and states. In short, these pictures (or snapshots, as we treated them in Chapter 1) may help put together what is important for all planners to see-- the big picture.

Land Suitability Analysis

The composite representation from computer code or transparent overlays indicates current as well as projected land uses. Therefore, land suitability analysis--the next step after land capability analysis--can be done. Typical factors coded or overlaid include:

SUGGESTED VARIABLES FOR LAND CAPABILITY ANALYSIS

Variable	Suggested Data Source
• Topography (elevation & slope & distinctive features)	US Geological Survey topographic maps
• Soils (locations & characteristics of soil types; drainage, permeability, shrink-swell limits)	US Soil Conservation Service; state soil surveys; county soil and water conservation districts
• Geology (bedrock depth & type; mineral resources; engineering properties; rockiness)	US Geological Survey; state geological survey
• Vegetation (land cover types; forest types; habitats; rare or endangered species of wildlife)	US Forest Service; state forestry departments; aerial photos from state highway or natural resources agencies or local agencies
• Wildlife & Fish (rearing and spawning areas; nesting sites; rare & endangered species)	US Forest Service; state forestry departments; aerial photos from state highway or natural resources agencies or local agencies
• Surface Water (quantity; location; watersheds; hydrology float potential; recharge areas)	US Geological Survey; state natural resources agency
• Groundwater (quantity; location; hydrology; water table)	US Geological Survey; state geological surveys and natural resources agencies
• Water Quality (pH; coliforms; phosphates; benthic organisms; hardness; flow rates; sedimentation)	US Geological Survey; state environmental protection agencies; local water pollution control agencies
• Meteorology (airsheds)	US Weather Bureau
• Air Quality	
• Land Use	State environmental protection agencies; local
• Sewer Service Areas	air quality control agencies
• Water Service Areas	Regional, areawide, and local
• Political Boundaries	planning and/or development
• Population Characteristics	agencies
• Zoning	

Figure 62

Even if precise data or unsophisticated representation of human use of land cannot be made, to begin to collect data is vital. With it, planning can begin. Let's examine a case history that illustrates such land capability and land suitability analysis.

At the site of "Woodlands," 25 miles north of Houston, Texas, a full land capability analysis was performed. Initially the study aimed at satisfying environmental requirements, but developed into an important money-saving tool in site designing. The Woodlands site, almost entirely forested, is on the flat Texas Coastal Plain where a high percentage of the soils are poorly drained. As a result, the site's streams are characterized by a very low base flow and high peaks. Nearly one-third of the site is within the 100-year floodplain of one major creek passing through the area.

Conventional methods for preparing such a site would involve a dense system of drainage tiles, significant deforestation and a concomitant loss of much groundwater recharge--major considerations in a critical area. In contrast, use of natural drainageways would preserve environmental values as well as cost only 25% of the typical approach.

Land capability analysis data for the study was collected for soils, vegetation, topography, and hydrology. Planners used this information to develop a land-use plan which required maximizing recharge, protection of permeable soils, maintenance of water tables, diminution of runoff, retardation of erosion and siltation, increase in base flow of streams, and the protection of vegetation and wildlife habitats.

The soils information was especially critical. Soils were grouped by percentage according to permeability and other characteristics. As a result of the analysis, arterial and collector roads were built on ridge lines away from drainage areas. Intensive development was located in areas of impermeable soils. Minor residential streets were laid out perpendicular to the slopes comprised of excessively permeable soils. The streets in effect served as berms that retarded flow of runoff and increased infiltration of water to the soil. Developers chose permeable pavement for activity areas located over permeable soils.

We see, then, that such capability and suitability analysis can lead not only to environmentally sound decisions on land-use, but also can help developers--private and public--to plan with realistic cost figures for the projects.

The <u>Master</u> <u>Plan</u>

Planning is the conscious selection of policies for land use. Only after planning can guidance tools for growth be employed effectively. In the U.S., 75% of the cities under 30,000 in population have no trained staffs; consequently, they must rely on consultants or community participation for plan designs. The planning process, however, is a political one that ultimately must be responsive to the desires of the community. Therefore, public officials in planning positions need to have ongoing dialogue with their constituents.

The comprehensive study of natural and manmade features in hand, planners draw up a master plan or comprehensive document. This guides their preparation of (1) zoning and subdivision policies and then (2) ordinance implementation tools, such as easements, permit programs, critical areas designation, performance studies, and others. Historically, the master plan had no legal status; only the zoning ordinance did. Now, since the Oregon Supreme Court decision in April 1975, states such as Oregon, Florida, New Jersey, and California require that plans and regulations be consistent, thus making comprehensive master plans much more important for all states in which developments are being proposed.

A comprehensive master plan is ultimately a map of the planned region with an overprint of the land-use policies. If the plan is for a totally undeveloped region, it ideally could draw upon information obtained from a land capability analysis, in which case data would be included from the natural resources inventory. If the plan is for an area already highly developed, then the existing facility itself establishes the plan. The U.S. highway system in some areas <u>is</u> the master plan because either the needs of the area are so contingent upon it or because the physical structures themselves rule out certain alternative land uses. On the average, however, master plans have both general information from broad analyses and specific information from focused studies.

Some of the latter information which would bear upon the environmental elements of the master plan are products of the site plan review. These reviews would address proposed projects or existing resources and would include environmental impact statements, cost/benefit analyses, and energy impact analyses. These three information-gathering devices are discussed later.

Regulations

There are two very important legal guidelines to observe while developing regulations to implement the master plan. In summary:

- The Fifth Amendment to the U.S. Constitution prohibits that private property be taken for public use without just compensation.

- Exclusionary practices that discriminate against groups in society are prohibited.

All land-use planning activities, regulations, and tools should observe carefully these guidelines, with citizens and officials seeking counsel at every step in the land use planning process.

The first point, often referred to as the "Taking Issue," has a long history dating to English customs and abuses which the Bill of Rights sought to redress. Court decisions have subsequently distinguished the limits of land use regulations to prevent them from becoming license to confiscate. In fact, in some situations governments must reimburse land owners who have lost property value as a result of zoning and other land use restrictions. An excellent review of the issue and accepted legal approaches appears in the CEQ study, The Taking Issue, cited at chapter's end.

The second point is more difficult to grasp and is less well defined by the courts. Controversy still exists in state and federal courts as to whether to permit controls which have the effect of excluding housing of a given type or price range--even if the goals are to protect the environment. This controversy is addressed in How Will America Grow?, by the Citizens Advisory Committee on Environmental Quality:

> In March 1975 the New Jersey Supreme Court, in its consideration of a contested Mount Laural Township zoning ordinance, ruled unanimously that localities may not adopt zoning ordinances that exclude low-income persons or families. The Court answered that each community in the State must share the housing needs of the surrounding region.

With these two legal guidelines foremost in their plans, local officials and concerned citizens may now employ a number of legal devices to control the appropriate and responsible use of community lands. One or more of these approaches may be applied to the control area at a given time. Specific variations of each may become precedents at the local level; therefore, information about such changes must be available.

The Site Plan Review

The site plan review (e.g., environmental impact statements, cost/benefit analyses, and energy impact analyses) will arm planners with backup arguments for employing particular master plan compliance regulations.

Environmental Impact Statements

Environmental impact statements are required under the 1969 National Environmental Policy Act for all significant federal projects. The statements are to identify the environmental consequences of the proposed land-use change and to help to bring out information needed to make a well-considered decision regarding such a change. Information reported in the statement can force a change in the proposed work or even prohibit it altogether. The change or moratorium usually occurs after public disclosure of the information.

The terms "for all significant federal projects" is revealing if we examine precisely what it means. Each federal agency can judge if its project is "significant." If it is, it may then proceed with an EIS. But, municipalities generally require such statements. In these cases, EIS information-gathering methods are used by the planning boards to guide their subsequent plans and actions. EISs are not, then, equal in meaning when applied to federal agencies and to municipal ones.

Cost/Benefit Analyses

Of similar but more limited scope, the cost/benefit analyses focus upon concerns of special public interest. Typically, they compare the cost of a single project with the anticipated benefits. To illustrate, the project might be a proposed manufacturing operation. The costs to the community might involve the expansion of schools, extension of sewer lines, addition of police staff, a new fire truck, and similar expenditures. The benefits are revenues to the treasury from added property taxes, sales taxes, and sewer and water charges. A mathematical proportion of cost to benefit quantifies one project at one time for comparison to other projects at past or future dates, thereby giving the master plan designers special insight about the need for and cost benefit of that project.

Energy Impact Analyses

Energy impact analyses are not formal programs, like the Environmental Impact Statements. Rather, they are generic studies intended to help planners to hold down costs and to utilize the natural environment. Often the least polluting technology is also the highest energy consumer. Comparing energy resources, future availability, and alternatives improves the master plan.

Selecting the Tools

With site analysis data in hand, the regulations are selected to make the master plan work. Some of the more familiar regulatory tools to be discussed include:

- Zoning
    (functional criteria vs.
    performance criteria)
- Floodplain zoning
- Planned Unit Development
- Subdivision Regulation
- Phased Development
- Transfer of Development Rights

- Critical Areas
- Easements
- Permit Programs
    (stream encroachment)
- Preferential Tax Assessment
- Capital budgeting
- Pre-emptive purchase

Zoning and Subdivision

Zoning is not a policy but rather the legal instrument that puts in place the policies established by the master plan. The major ordinances are zoning and subdivision. Zones are divisions of land restricted to certain uses by the landowner. The usual classifications are residential, commercial, industrial, and agricultural. There often are sub-classifications. A tract of land zoned "residential" would be the "highest" or most restricted zone; it could not be used for commerce or industry. The least restricted would be an industrial zone, allowing all of the classifications higher than industry to use the zone for development, excluding residential uses. Zoning ordinances may also limit building heights, amount of useable space, set-backs, and other aspects of construction.

Subdivision regulations usually detail controls within the zone. These regulations set standards for project parameters, such as street improvement, houselot layout, procedures for designating private land for public use, and other project requirements. Such ordinances may also influence the way land is used by requiring the developer to meet certain land-use functions and by specifying the performance criteria applied to those functions. A function criterion is a desirable feature or service provided by a parcel of land and its attendant development:

- to provide open space

- to prevent soil erosion

- to prevent degradation of water quality

A performance criterion is a statement of the minimum acceptable measure of the desired function:

- 35% of the parcel to be open space

- 10% maximum increase in soil erosion

- 0% maximum percentage of increase in runoff rate

A functional approach to zoning involves (1) identification of the functions which the community wishes its land to provide; and (2) establishment of the performance criteria for each function. There are often both economic and environmental advantages to carefully drawn up function and performance criteria.

A zoning law or ordinance is not static. The law was probably proposed by a planning commission and enacted by the legislature, usually the city council or county board of commissioners. Changes can be made politically by amending or technically by obtaining "variances" or "special exceptions." These actions may be taken by an appointed Planning Commission or a Board of Zoning Appeals.

Floodplain Zoning

"Floodways" are the stream bed and banks over which the stream normally floods. Serious danger threatens people and property in "floodways." "Floodplains" are the land areas which are flooded normally on an average of every 100 years. Hazardous damage threatens people and property in floodplains.

To control damages on floodways and floodplains, a master plan includes a designation of certain lands for certain uses as "hazardous zoned." "Hazardous zone" designation thereby regulates the uses of land that might result in substantial environmental damage and danger to human life. A comprehensive Floodplain Management plan could include the outright acquisition of floodplain lands to halt development. It could impose restrictions within the floodplain, or require special building codes for flood-proofing of structures already in the plain of probable inundation. This type of regulation can also prohibit the damming of streams, channelization, or construction of levees. If the land in question is publicly owned, it may be designated to serve as a greenbelt for recreation and open space. Recreation and open space usually (1) minimize flooding and (2) provide aesthetic essentials.

To illustrate this application of "hazardous zone" designation to land use planning, let's examine an actual instance. The Planning Advisory Committee of Dakota County, Minnesota, in 1973 developed an environmentally sound "Shoreland Zoning Ordinance" intended to control development in areas around particular lakes and streams within its borders. It controls "Floodplains Soils Districts," defined by specifying the six alluvial soil types. mapped by the U.S. Conservation Service. Special limitations are placed on the use of these soil areas. Their planning document included the following:

(1) Permitted Uses--e.g., agriculture, golf courses, unpaved parking areas, residential lawns and play areas, and utility lines to

the extent that they do not require structures to fill which would restrict the flow capacity of any drainageway.

(2) Prohibited Uses--e.g., septic tank absorption fields, buildings and structures, filling or grading of soils and, in general, any use retarding the soil's capacity to store and absorb floodwater.

(3) Conditional Uses--e.g., roadways, bridges, or utility structures that do not significantly impede floodwaters, on the condition that a permit is issued after a finding that flood-proofing standards will be met and no increased flooding will result.

These restrictions are carefully supported with the technical definitions and standards. Their overall effects are to (1) prevent flood-vulnerable uses at the site; (2) avoid uses which increase upstream or downstream flood damage; and (3) protect water quality by preventing on-site sewage disposal in areas which may be flooded.

Planned Unit Development

This is a single residential development in which density regulations apply to the project as a whole rather than to each individual lot. Thus, instead of requiring 5 houses to be placed each on 1-acre lots, a PUD could allow a five-family dwelling to be located on one lot with four empty lots surrounding it. The average on both situations is 1 house per acre. The desired goal, however, is to apply the concept to a much larger project than this one example. A single development could unify residential, commercial, institutional, and recreational functions into a single neighborhood or community. The ordinance sets minimum requirements for types of structures, relative ratios of land-uses, engineering specifications, conformity to land suitability, and relates to the needs of the expected occupants.

The zoning board reviews the Planned Unit Development on an individual basis to insure that specifications are appropriate and meet all other zoning requirements. An example of how a PUD evolved in Woodlands, Texas, appears earlier in this chapter in the section on land capability analysis.

Phased Development Ordinances

As the words imply, these ordinances set a rate of development for the area. The provisions might indicate not only the timing of future growth, but also the location and type of growth allowed. For example, under the master plan, development might not be allowed until the area were served with sewerage, drainage, parks, roads, utilities, and other selected prerequisites.

Transfer of Development Rights

This process functions to average out the environmental needs of the whole community and the economic motives of the individual members. It provides a way for the community to acquire land for uses that benefit the most, while compensating or not denying those who would stand to gain or lose if a total redistribution of property were actually made. While the individuals retain land ownership, use of those lands is transferred to the public. To put it another way, "Development Rights" are legal tender equal to the dollars which an owner would have gained if he sold his farmland valued at $200 per acre to a developer for $2,000 per acre. On each acre sold, he would gain $1,800. With 10 acres, he would have a total gain of $18,000. But, if the master plan determines that for the public's benefit the land remain agricultural, then the law can give the farmer $18,000 in "Development Rights." The farmer gains $18,000, retains his land, and holds it as farmland in perpetuity.

Now, by prohibiting development on ten acres within the community, there will have to be permitted more people concentrated in some other ten acres of the community. The public owns $18,000 worth of Development Rights. It can reallocate the share granted to the farmland to some other suitable part of the community. In another section, for example, a resident owns land which is suitable for development, but his land is already developed at the community's permissable average. If he wishes to develop that land to a higher density, then he can acquire "Development Rights" from the public. It will cost him $18,000 to buy the rights to increase the number of residents allowable on his land if he owned an additional ten acres. Transferable Development Rights break the linkage between (1) a particular parcel of land and (2) its development potential by permitting the transfer of that potential (its "development right") to another parcel where that development will not be objectionable. The mechanism is a sublime way to redistribute the community's wealth.

Critical Areas

Critical areas are geographic features or uses of material of state concern. Designation requires:

- definition of the type of area to be regulated and the beneficial functions to be preserved

- an inventory and map of the area

- a regulatory system to preserve the area

The areas to be protected have environmental protection as the primary aim. Natural areas, for example, might include wilderness strips, nature preserves, aquifer recharge land, floodplains, steep slopes, scenic rivers, geologic wonders, historic sites, farmlands, and wetlands. But, critical areas could also include lands which serve important public needs, such as sites for sewage disposal, waste treatment, power plants, schools, and recreation. In addition to federal and state designations of critical areas, local governments may also make the designation. Some of the 35 states eligible for federal funds under the Coastal Zones Management Act of 1972 are delineating their own coastal zones as critical areas. Then, they identify for further special concern locations within the zones. Other states may require local governments to carry out a "Critical Areas" program themselves or they may allow a state agency to administer the program.

Easements

An easement is the partial purchase of land. It is an acquired right of use, interest, or privilege just short of ownership. Easements cost less than outright purchases but accomplish the same end. The most familiar form is the utility easement in which a landowner agrees to the presence of an under- or over-ground utility line for a negotiated fee. The owner still holds title to the land, using it as he wishes as long as he does not damage the line.

An environmental easement compels the landowner to forego any alteration or use that may lessen the land's environmental value. A public agency might buy or accept as a donation an easement along a "scenic river." The easement would give the agency the right to forbid the landowner from destroying the woodlands along the river banks. In such a case, the easement cost may be little or nothing.

An agricultural easement, on the other hand, might be quite costly. The easement reserves for agricultural purposes land which otherwise would be very valuable if sold for housing developments. In this case, the easement costs could be very high. The following case from Suffolk County, New York, illustrates how the easement works to preserve farmland. The example appeared in the Sixth Annual Report of the Council on Environmental Quality, 1975: Suffolk County is located on the northeastern end of Long Island. To the west are commuter communities and industrial areas which have spread out from New York City over the past few decades. In contrast, much of the county remains in agricultural use, its soils of glacial origin supporting particularly productive potatoe farms. The county government has undertaken an ambitious $60 million program to purchase development rights to 13,000 acres of farmland. A bond issue will finance the easements: its aim is to preserve permanently 20% of the remaining open farmland in the county.

Farmers were asked to offer to the county options to buy the development rights to all or parts of their land. The county also sought to inform the farmers about the benefits which they themselves would receive--primarily the option of remaining in farming in the face of increasing pressures for land. The response was enthusiastic--381 landowners offered 17,800 acres of development rights for a total of $117 million. This gave county planners the opportunity to choose the best candidate sections for preservation and to piece together large contiguous areas.

Permit Programs

When land use jeopardizes the public interest, local officials may have to impose land use restrictions through a permit program. An application for a permit requires a description of the proposed action, its purpose, and a detailed analysis of the environmental impact. The analysis might consider changes in stream flow, ground water recharge, fish and wildlife survival, stream encroachment, or permanent results of air or water pollution. Almost all permit applications require a public hearing where citizens can review and respond to the land use proposed by the permit seeker.

One of the most successful permit programs involves the regulation of wetlands. Many states, as well as the federal government through the U.S. Army Corps of Engineers and the U.S. Environmental Protection Agency stipulate permits for wetlands development. Connecticut's wetlands permit program is a good example. The Connecticut Inland Wetlands and Waterways Act requires towns and cities in the state to institute a permit program for the regulation of the use of wetlands in their jurisdictions or to allow the state to do so.

The Act recognizes that these inland areas have "ecological, scenic, historic, and recreational values and benefits" and provides for a careful review and potential veto of any wetlands development proposal. "Wetlands" are defined by the Act as land, including submerged land, having any of the soil types designated by the U.S. Soil Conservation Service as poorly drained, very poorly drained, alluvial, and floodplain.

Once an area's wetlands have been mapped, the following uses of it require a permit: any activity that involves operating within or using a wetland that includes removal or deposition of material; obstructions or constructions; alteration or pollution of wetlands. If the activity is judged to be a threat to the area, the applicant must provide detailed data on the wetland that address the possible effects of the proposed action. In reviewing the permit application, the local agency considers: the environmental impact; alternative actions; long-term environmental productivity; irreversible resource losses; public health, safety, and the influence of the nearby lands; and, finally, the suitability of the activity to the area. Regulated activities in violation of the Act can result in a fine of up to $1,000 per day. Collected fines are used to restore the wetlands to their original conditions.

Another permit program is "stream encroachment." Although designed to protect stream banks, stream encroachment regulations can inhibit one of the nation's most severe pollution problems--erosion. Erosion, as we learned earlier, comes from non-point sources (non-point now constitutes 60% of all pollution in the U.S.). At least 50% of all of our country's pollution is plain sediment, "dirt," a mixture of rocks and nutrients. The nutrients, of course, include artificial fertilizers, agricultural insecticides, as well as animal and vegetable matter. Croplands are the greatest contributors of sediment. Urban runoff is another. Not least among the other urban contaminant sources are leaking urban sewerage systems. Leaking rural septic tank systems contribute their share of contaminants to the land. These latter add materially especially in nutrient sediment load. However, cropland runoff remains the chief source of sediment.

Croplands are large, open areas where topsoil is regularly exposed to erosion. There are a number of preventive practices we discussed earlier which can be employed to minimize erosion. Nonetheless, millions of tons of cropland sediments are washed to the sea. The origins of such pollution are so diffuse that successful abatement calls for recognition that the integrity of stream banks is a focus for land use controls. If developments encroach upon those banks, they typically (1) create substantial erosion because of the actual construction, and (2) remove the ground cover as a barrier between non-point sources of sediment and the stream's flowing waters. In addition to reducing topsoil loss, preservation of stream banks also helps to restrict the surface runoff of rainwater. By lowering total sediments and extreme stream flow together, we can substantially reduce potential flood damage. The costs are less in the prevention than in the treatment.

The general strategies which can be used to control such non-point pollution are these:

(1)   Erosion and Sediment Control Plans

Any development, if over a specified minimum of acres of soil to be disturbed or cubic yards removed, requires a plan to control erosion and sedimentation. The plan must be approved by a local agency, usually a county soil and water conservation district. The plan may include timing of the disturbance with respect to season and weather, the placement of sediment catch basins, revegetation of disturbed soil, and temporary mulch covering.

(2)   Setbacks

This regulation declares that strips of land alongside streams will be undisturbed to some fixed boundary line set back from the stream bed. Setbacks prevent disruption of the streambank itself and maintain covered land to filter sediment and reduce water flow into the stream itself.

(3) Watercourse Protection

A permit can be required to alter or to develop a stream and/or its banks. The procedure is very much like that described above for wetlands. Often stream protection regulations are, in fact, drawn up in conjunction with wetlands regulations.

Preferential Tax Assessment

Many state tax laws require that land be taxed at its potential market value, rather than at its actual value. This non-preferential policy imposes an economic hardship on an owner who wants to conserve the environmental value of his land. A farmer might pay taxes of $40/acre for wood-lots or farmland, but suddenly with population expansion he must pay $120 per acre because the land could become a shopping center site. The difference in taxes might be equal to, or be more than, the farmer's cash crop.

Preferential assessment provisions allow the taxing authority to recognize a different tax rate for different land-uses. Under this plan, the farmer might then be able to pay the lower rate and hold his land in wood-lots and tilled property. In addition, it is possible to induce the farmer to maintain the property in those declared conditions by imposing the threat of a retroactive clause which declares that he could be charged the higher tax rate all the way back to the date of the first decision if he decided at a later date to sell the land to the shopping center developer. This device has had limited success in long-term land use control because normally the increase in the value of the land for shopping centers far exceeds the minor penalty of the retroactive tax. Or, the farmer may sell his land to another person who may opt immediately not to preserve but to sell. In short, the device is not binding on successive owners.

Capital Budgeting

Coupled with the phased development ordinances, capital budgeting—also known as capital improvements or investment planning—integrates the development schedule with the development funding. The concept is that growth occurs where public money is allocated. The federal government in part controls public money, usually in the form of matching grants. But, states often can exert even greater control by choosing which committees receive the money for which projects. The states, for example, establish the priority list for grants authorized by the Federal Water Pollution Control Act for sewage treatment facilities. They also heavily influence allocations of federal money for transportation, water resources, and education. Consequently, communities high on the state eligibility lists receive federal funding, build new facilities, and stimulate growth and change.

Therefore, unless planning for capital investment is coordinated with land-use strategy, growth may occur around the new facilities, regardless of the community's land-use plans and intentions. On a national scale, the most glaring example of such undirected growth is that of the Interstate Highway System. From its first links in the early 1950s until 1970, the major planning criterion for these highways was efficient movement of people and goods. The result was a skeleton of interchanges at high speed inter- and intra-community corridors that have changed the very nature of most urban and many rural and natural areas. Accompanying residential, commercial, and industrial land-use has been determined not by land capability analysis, but by time zones, via interstates, from major centers of employment and business. Since the beginning of the 1970s the environmental planning required for such highway construction has helped to arrest the unguided spread of the system. However, the task of solving the problems already cast in concrete and asphalt will continue for years.

To make a capital budgeting plan work, developers must be encouraged to build where the facilities are planned to be installed. For example, Maryland requires that building permits and subdividion plans be consistent with the master plan's assignments for water and sewage facilities. The Office of State Planning in Massachusetts is attempting to discourage investment in infrastructures (sewers, waterlines, roads, schools, etc.) and housing development in suburban and urban areas in order to encourage the restoration and stabilization of older central areas. These are exceptions, however, because the application of capital budgeting to land-use control is a relatively novel practice.

Pre-emptive Purchase

The last of these familiar regulatory tools is pre-emptive purchase. This is simply a straightforward way to look at block development. A local government can purchase a few keystone parcels and thereby preserve a large area. Geographically, large areas of wetlands are often readily controlled through small areas strategically purchased. Purchase and lease-back/sell-back arrangements can accomplish the same ends. Under these regulations, public lands purchased from individual owners can be leased or sold back to them or to others with restrictions on use written into the contract. In the pre-emptive purchase the original acquisition costs may have required substantial sums of money, but in the lease-back/ sell-back arrangements, there are opportunities to recover some of the investment. Variations of the pre-emptive purchase have several names, but are aimed at the same goal: to hold and to preserve large areas of land for environmental protection and, by extension, for the public good.

Project Review

The federal and state governments require--before funds are awarded for development--a rigorous public review. The purpose is to assure that the project reflects the best needs of the public. As a result of public review, local officials and citizens help make land-use decisions. Through participation in the review process, they learn how variations of land-use controls can help to enforce the local master plan.

The principal federal reviews are the Environmental Impact Statement (EIS) and A-95. As discussed earlier, the National Environmental Protection Act requires an EIS for every "major federal action significantly affecting the quality of the human environment." The scope of the regulation includes (1) federal construction programs, such as sewerage, highway, and dam building; (2) administrative actions, such as orders for power plants to convert from oil to coal burning; and (3) federal leases and permits. The review is required even when private proposals seek federal permission or cooperation.

The Environmental Impact Statement

An EIS is not so much a scientific research report as it is a document for full public disclosure. It must contain adequate technical analyses of ecological and socio-economic relationships and their potential environmental impacts. However, these technical analyses often are unable to quantify expected impacts or even to assign probabilities of occurrence. Even if the EIS document could quantify impacts, planners must recognize that the "significance" of environmental impact is a subjective value judgement which must be made on the basis of public opinion and desires.

The reviews are usually coordinated by regional agencies known variously as Regional Planning Commissions, Areawide Coordination Agencies, Councils of Government, and Metropolitan Commissions. These agencies generally have full-time personnel familiar with local programs, planning laws, environmental assessments, and federal requirements. But the agency staff need assistance from other sources. One source is the information and recommendations produced by local policy boards. Conversely, the agency can furnish policy boards and local governments with technical plans and environmental determinations which the local governments could not normally afford.

States also have project reviews. These are normally similar to the federal programs. State reviews can include private actions which may have such impact as to warrant state examination. Some of these reviews pertain to a specific activity, such as power plant siting, "critical areas," developments of regional impact, or other identifiable high import development. A-95 has a similar objective.

The A-95 Review

The Intergovernmental Cooperation Act is implemented in part by the Office of Management and Budget. OMB's Circular A-95 designates some 400 "areawide clearing houses" to review proposals seeking federal monies. Some federal programs may require an EIS as well as an A-95 review. The latter is required for health planning, law enforcement assistance, open space acquisition, and education programs, none of which involve construction. The effect of the two review procedures is to increase the probability that programs will be consonant with environmentally sound alternatives. The land capability analysis, discussed early in this chapter, is one of the principal bases on which a sound plan is established; a review provides the opportunity to test the quality of the analysis and the soundness of the plan.

Benefits of the A-95 Review process can be environmental improvement as well as financial savings. Examples such as these are common:

- A 150-bed hospital in Albuquerque, New Mexico, did not have adequate access to the metropolitan highway system or sufficient parking. After the review, a different site with access and parking was selected.

- Near Mobile, Alabama, an 8-mile highway plan obligated the government to purchase 20 homes in the right-of-way. A recommendation at the review revealed a new routing at a savings of $200,000 in relocation costs.

- In Marcey, New York, the review agency received two proposals—one for a federally funded sewer project, the other toward a new state college. The applicants met, coordinated extension of the sewer to the college, and saved substantial funds.

The state justifies its review on the assumption that the proposal has environmental or socio-economic significance that crosses local political boundaries. Political divisions are not identical to natural divisions, such as watersheds or airsheds. Therefore, actions modifying natural systems can readily involve numbers of political jurisdictions. The state sets up a means to assure protection of interest outside of the project's jurisdiction.

Local involvement in state proceedings resembles that for federal ones. Again, preparation and involvement determine the quality of the information applied in the decision-making actions.

Knowledge and Concern

This discussion of land-use planning tools should give citizens and public officials a general sense of the approaches available. Each tool has a complex technical and legal component that must be carefully and thoroughly designed for local needs. Individuals interested in learning more about these and other land-use tools will find a suggested reading list at the end of this chapter. Of additional help are the periodicals and reports of various professional "umbrella" organizations. These include, among many:

- American Society of Planning Officials

- American Institute of Planners

- National Association of Counties

- Urban Land Institute

- Council of State Governments

- Soil Conservation Society of America

Technical and legal sophistication can only do so much for environmental protection. Local officials, foremost, must have a concern for the health and well being of the human environment; then they must increase their own awareness of the intricate natural relationships among water, air, land, and human activities--as we have emphasized starting with Chapter 1. With such knowledge they can generate the public support necessary to investigate and implement land planning programs. Their actions are a measure of their belief in a "land ethic" that can guide us in keeping all of us and the environment safe and productive.

CHAPTER SUMMARY

1. The people, through congressional legislation and land-use ordinances, are up-grading "environmental quality" to parity with economic and social welfare.

2. Growth in population is inevitable; citizens therefore must consider what that means in environmental quality, economics, and social welfare.

3. The Costs of Sprawl compares 6 housing types at 6 stages of planning, demonstrating higher benefits with careful planning.

4. The federal government will increasingly look to local governments for assistance in implementing land-use management, so local officials need to know the federal position.

5. The essential elements of responsible land management are 1) a land capability analysis, 2) a master plan, and 3) implementing regulations.

6. For 1), a land capability analysis evaluates land, air, water, and socio-economic conditions in the planning region, and then maps the information. Land suitability analysis overlays present or anticipated uses to produce a readout synthesizing land and use limitations.

7. A Master Plan is the conscious selection of <u>policies</u> for land-use. It has no legal status <u>per se</u>, but since the Oregon Supreme Court decision in April 1975, Master Plans and their regulations necessarily must be consistent. Planners develop regulations, but foremost they must 1) uphold the 5th amendment which prohibits taking property without just compensation, and 2) not undertake exclusionary programs that discriminate against certain groups. The regulations are selected to enforce the Master Plan's policies. The Site Plan Review, including Environmental Impact Statements, Cost/ Benefit Analyses, and Energy Impact Analyses, are the information guides for selection of the correct tools.

8. A dozen types of regulations are reviewed to illustrate the range of controls that land-use planners employ.

9. Public hearings involve citizens so that they can contribute to the development of the Master Plan and appropriate land-use regulations. Knowledge <u>and</u> concern are requisites to effective planning.

SOURCES

Bosselman, Fred, and David Callies. <u>The Quiet Revolution in Land Use Control</u>. Washington, D.C.: Council on Environmental Quality, GPO, 1971.

Bosselman, Fred, David Callies, and John Banta. <u>The Taking Issue</u>. Washington, D.C.: Council on Environmental Quality, 1973.

Citizens' Advisory Committee on Environmental Qualty. <u>How Will America Grow</u>? Washington, D.C.: GPO, 1976.

Council on Environmental Quality. <u>Environmental Quality, 1975: The Sixth Annual Report of the Council on Environmental Quality</u>. Washington, D.C.: GPO, 1975.

_____. <u>Environmental Quality 1976: The Seventh Annual Report of the Council on Environmental Quality</u>. Washington, D. C.: GPO, 1976.

<u>Five Year Water Quality Management Plan</u>. Mimeographed, 1977.

Leopold, Aldo. <u>A Sand County Almanac</u>. New York: Ballantine Books, 1970.

McHarg, Ian and Jonathan Sutton. "Ecological Plumbing for the Texas Coastal Plain: The Woodlands New Town Experiment." <u>Landscape Architecture</u>, 65 (January 1975), 78-79.

Nash, Roderick, ed. <u>The American Environment: Readings in the History of Conservation</u>. Reading, Mass.: Addison-Wesley Publishing Co., 1968.

Soil Conservation Society of America. <u>National Land Use Policy: Objectives, Components, Implementation</u>. Ankeny, Iowa: 1973.

Real Estate Research Corporation. The Costs of Sprawl: Environmental and Economic Costs of Alternative Residential Development Patterns at the Urban Fringe. Washington, D.C.: GPO, 1974.

Reilly, William K. The Use of Land: A Citizens' Policy Guide to Urban Growth: A Task Force Report Sponsored by the Rockefeller Brothers Fund. New York: Thomas Y. Crowell Co., 1973.

Rhett, John T. "Less Costly Treatment Systems." Washington, D. C.: US EPA. Mimeographed, August 18, 1976.

U.S. Bureau of Outdoor Recreation. Protection of Nature's Estate. Ed. E.M. Stover. Washington, D.C.: GPO, 1975.

Soil Conservation Society of America. Planning and Zoning for Better Resource Use. Ankeny, Iowa, 1971.

SUGGESTED READING

American Society of Planning Officials. Subdividing Rural America. Washington, D.C.: Council on Environmental Quality, GPO, 1976.

Council of State Governments. The Land Use Puzzle. Lexington, Ky.: n.p., 1974.

Cranston, M., B. Garth, R. Plattman, and J. Varon. A Handbook for Controlling Local Growth. Stanford, Calif.: Stanford University, 1973.

Curtis, V. (ed.). Land Use and the Environment: An Anthology of Readings. U.S. Environmental Protection Agency, Environmental Studies Div., Washington, D.C., 1973.

Ford Foundation. The Art of Managing the Environment. New York: N.Y., 1974.

Kaiser, E.J., et. al. Promoting Environmental Quality through Urban Planning and Controls. Washington, D.C.: U.S. EPA, 1974.

McAllister, D.M. (ed.). Environment: A New Focus for Land Use Planning. Washington, D.C.: National Science Foundation, 1973.

McHarg, Ian L. Design with Nature. Garden City, N. J.: Natural History Press, 1969.

Shoman, Joseph J. Open Land for Urban America: Acquisition, Safekeeping. and Use. Baltimore, Maryland: Johns Hopkins Press, 1972.

Soil Conservation Society of America. National Land Use Policy: Objectives, Components, Implementation. Ankeny, Iowa, 1973.

Soil Conservation Society of America. Planning and Zoning for Better Resource Use. Ankeny, Iowa, 1971.

National Land Use Policy: Objectives, Components, Implemention. Ankeny, Iowa, 1973.

Strong, Ann, and J.C. Keene. Environmental Protection through Public and Private Development Controls. Washington. D.C.: U.S. EPA. 1973.

U.S. Department of Agriculture. Land Use Planning Assistance Available through the U.S. Department of Agriculture, Washington, D.C.: GPO, 1974.

Urban Systems Research and Engineering. Interceptor Sewers and Suburban Sprawl. Washington, D.C.: CEQ, 1974.

The Growth Shapers: The Land Use Impacts of Infrastructure Investments. Washington, D.C.: CEQ, 1976.

Washington Environmental Research Center. Final Conference Report for the National Conference on Managing the Environment. U.S. Environmental Protection Agency, Office of Research and Development. Washington, D.C., 1973.

Whyte, William. The Last Landscape. Garden City, N. J.: Doubleday and Co., 1968.

CONTRIBUTORS

ROBERT S. ANDERSEN received a B.S. in biology from Cleveland State University. He has been employed by the City of Cleveland, Division of Air Pollution Control as an Air Pollution Engineer, and is President of Envisage Environmental, Inc., a private firm involved with analysis of noise, ambient air monitoring, and energy efficiency.

CANDACE M. ASHMUN received her B.S. in physics from Smith College. She has served on the New Jersey Natural Resource Council and is Vice President of the Upper Raritan Watershed Association. A recipient of awards from the United States EPA, she currently serves the New Jersey DRP as a task force member in the division of Water Resources, Solid Waste, and Passaic Basin Flood Control. Candy Ashmun is the Executive Director of the Association of New Jersey Environmental Commissions.

THOMAS J. DUNN, 1973 M.S., Yale School of Forestry and Environmental Studies, concentrated his graduate work in ecological systems analysis and environmental planning. His experience includes management planning for forest lands, urban waterfront areas, and ocean beaches. He has worked as a Resource Planner, an Environmental Planner, and presently serves as a Planning Engineer with the Planning and Systems Development Division, Cleveland Regional Sewer District, Cleveland, Ohio. Mr. Dunn's distinctions include Phi Beta Kappa membership and a B.A. degree summa cum laude, also from Yale, and a graduate fellowship from the National Science Foundation. He is a member of the National Association of Environmental Professionals.

SAMUEL S. EPSTEIN, M.D., received his medical training at the University of London and served as Chief of the Laboratory of Environmental Pathology and Carcinogenics at the Children's Cancer Research Foundation in Boston. He has served on the staff of the School of Medicine of both Harvard and Case-Western Reserve Universities. He has testified on numerous occasions on the effects of food additives and pesticides on humans. In addition, he was the first to document the dangers of NTA as a phosphate substitute in detergents. He is the author of two books and over 150 articles on environmental medicine. Dr. Epstein is presently a professor at the School of Public Health, University of Illinois.

AL B. GARLAUSKAS is the Chief of Water Quality Control Laboratories of the Cleveland Division of Water as well as Assistant Professor in Environmental Studies at Cleveland State Univesity. He holds Bachelor and Master of Science degrees from Case-Western Reserve and Kent State Universities, respectively, and is presently a doctoral candidate. Mr. Garlauskas received a U.S. EPA Environmental Quality Award in 1975 for "outstanding contributions to environmental quality work."

EDWARD J. P. HAUSER received his M. A. in biological sciences and a Ph. D. in education from Kent State University. He is a professor at Lakeland Community College in Mentor, Ohio; past Chairman of the Ohio College Biology Teachers Association; Corporate Board Member of the Holden Arboretum; and a Board Member of the Ohio Chapter of The Nature Conservancy.

LANCE J. MEZGA was graduated from Kent State University with a B. S. in geology and an M.S. in hydrology, and serves as a consultant in these areas at Dalton-Dalton-Little-Newport. Experienced in a number of projects relating to land-use, Mr. Mezga has a special interest in groundwater quality as it is affected by land-use, and has published several papers in this area.

GARY J. NEID received an M.S. in meteorology from Wright State University, and has worked with the City of Cleveland, Division of Air Pollution in his specialty. The Air Quality Forecasting Method that he developed has been adopted in several urban areas. Mr. Neid is an Assistant Professor of Environmental Science at Cleveland State and Vice President of Envisage Environmental, Inc.

ROBERT G. ROLAN, Project Manager and Senior Ecologist at Dalton-Dalton-Little-Newport, received his Ph.D. in zoology and physiology at the University of Nebraska. He has served as Head of the Division of Environmental Sciences and Associate Director of the Institute of Urban Studies at Cleveland State University, and has been the Manager and Principal Investigator of a number of projects relating to Lake Erie. Dr. Rolan is the author of numerous articles and a book on field investigation practices in general ecology.

PAT SMITH is Chairman of the Air Conservation Committee of the Northern Ohio Lung Association. She is also Chairman of the Ohio EPA Citizen Council and Board Member of the Ohio Environmental Council. A graduate of Baldwin-Wallace College, she has received awards from the Ohio Department of Natural Resources, the City of Cleveland, and the U.S. EPA. Mrs. Smith was recently named Chairman of the Occupational Health Mission Group of the American Lung Association.

STEPHEN J. SEBESTA is the Sanitary Engineer for Cuyahoga County, Ohio. He is a Ph.D. candidate in Environmental Engineering at Wayne State University, from which he received an M.A. in Occupational and Environmental Health. Mr. Sebesta has served with both the U. S. Public Health Service and Dow Chemical Company in Advanced Wastewater Treatment Technology. He serves as an Adjunct Assistant Professor at Cleveland State University.

BERNARD I. SOHN is Manager of Environmental Technologies for Millipore Corporation, Bedford, Massachusetts. He has a Bachelor's degree in biochemistry and a Master's degree in business administration. Mr. Sohn holds several patents in membrane technology, and has authored a number of publications in journals of the National Association of Biology Teachers and National Science Teachers Association. He has collaborated in writing textbooks currently used in secondary environmental education, and serves as Commissioner of the Conservation Commission of Brookline, Massachusetts.

CHARLES R. THOMAS received his B.S. and M.S. in biology from Bowling Green State University. He is employed at Dalton-Dalton-Little-Newport as a marine biologist. Mr. Thomas has worked on large water resource projects in the Gulf Coast and Great Lakes states, and has recently completed a study of the impacts of a major railroad improvement project on the wetland and coastal marshes from Massachusetts to Maryland.

GEORGE L. VERCELLI received his M. S. in Sanitary Engineering from New York University and a B. S. degree in civil engineering from Newark College of Engineering. He is head of Environmental Engineering at Dalton-Dalton-Little-Newport, where he has been responsible for numerous projects relating to municipal and industrial wastewater treatment.

APPENDIX A

SOME USEFUL MATHEMATICAL CONVERSIONS

The <u>Metric System</u>

In the Metric System a

>
meter measures length
liter measures capacity
gram measures weight

The following prefixes can be used to show parts or multiples:

*micro-	= 1/1,000,000	mega-	= 1,000,000
milli-	= 1/1,000	kilo-	= 1,000
centi-	= 1/100	hecto-	= 100
deci-	= 1/10	deca-	= 10

The following measures should be of use to you:

<u>Length</u>

10 millimeters (mm) = 1 centimeter (cm)
10 centimeters = 1 decimeter (dm)
10 decimeters = 1 meter (m)
1000 meters = 1 kilometer (Km)

<u>Length Squared</u>

100 square millimeters = 1 square centimeter
100 square centimeters = 1 square decimeter
100 square decimeters = 1 square meter

<u>Length Cubed</u>

1000 cubic mm = 1 cubic cm
1000 cubic cm - 1 cubic dm
1000 cubic dm = 1 cubic m

---

*"Micrometer," abbreviated "u," is used to measure tiny particles. There are some 25,000 micrometers in an inch. "Micron" is sometimes used instead of "micrometer," but they both refer to the same measure.

Capacity (Liquid and Dry Substances)

```
10 milliliters (ml) = 1 centiliter (cl)
10 centiliters = 1 deciliter (dl)
10 deciliters = 1 liter (l)
100 liters = 1 hectoliter (Hl)
10 milligrams (mg) = 1 centigram (cg)
10 centigrams = 1 decigram (dg)
10 decigrams = 1 gram (g)
10 grams = 1 decigram (Dg)
10 decagrams = 1 hectogram (Hg)
10 hectograms = 1 kilogram (Kg)
1000 kilograms = 1 (metric ton (T)
```

English System

In the English System of measurement a

> foot measures length
> quart measures capacity
> ounce measures weight

Here are English equivalents to the preceding metric information:

Length

```
1 mile = 1760 yards = 5280 feet
1 yard = 3 feet = 36 inches; 1 foot = 12 inches
1 rod = 5.5 yards = 16.5 feet
1 micro-inch = one millionth inch or .000001
```

Length Squared

```
1 square mile = 640 acres
1 acre = 4840 square yards = 43,560 square feet
1 square rod = 30.25 square yeards
1 square yard = 9 square feet
1 square foot = 144 square inches
```
An acre is equal to a square, the side of which is 208.7 feet.

Length Cubed

```
1 cubic yard = 27 cubic feet
1 cubic foot = 1728 inches
```

Capacity (Liquid)

```
1 U.S. gallon =.1337 cubic feet = 231 cubic inches = 4 quarts = 8 pints
1 quart = 2 pints = 8 gills
1 British Imperial gallon = 1.2009 U.S. gallons = 277.42 cubic inches
```

1 cubic foot = 7.48 U.S. gallons

Capacity (Dry)

1 bushel (U.S.) = 1.2445 cubic feet = 2150.42 cubic inches
1 bushel = 4 pecks = 32 quarts = 64 pints
1 peck = 8 quarts = 16 pints
1 British Imperial bushel = 8 Imperial gallons = 1.2837 cubic feet =
    2218.19 cubic inches

Weight (Avoirdupois, Commercial)

1 gross or long ton = 2240 pounds
1 net or short ton = 2000 pounds
1 pound = 16 ounces = 7000 grains

Pressure

1 pound per square inch = 144 pounds per square foot = .068 atmosphere =
    2.042 inches of mercury at 62°
1 atmosphere = 30 inches of mercury at 62°F = 14.7 pounds per square inch
1 foot of water at 62°F = 62.355 pounds per square foot = .433 pounds per
    square inch
1 inch of mercury at 62°F = 1.132 feet of water = 13.58 inches of water =
.491 pounds per square inch

The C.G.S. System

The C.G.S. System of measurement, or centimeter-gram-second system, uses
measures of distance, mass, and time to arrive at the following units:

> velocity = 1 centimeter in one second
> acceleration due to gravity = 981 centimeters in
>   one second
> force = 1 dyne = 1/981 gram
> work = 1 erg* = 1 dyne-centimeter
> power = 1 watt = 10,000,000 ergs/second

Equivalencies

Since we must work commonly today with both the Metric and the English
Ssytems, the following equivalencies will be of use:

---

*The erg is such a small unit that "joule" is often substituted. One
joule equals 10,000,000 ergs.

Equivalencies of Length

1 mile = 1.609 kilometers
1 yard = .9144 meters
1 foot = .3048 meters
1 inch = 2.54 centimeters
1 inch = 25.4 millimeters
1 kilometer = .6214 miles = 3,281 feet
1 meter = 3.2808 feet = 1.0936 yards
1 centimeter = .3937 inch
1 millimeter = .03937 inch

Equivalencies of Squared Length

1 square mile = 2.5899 square kilometers
1 square yard = .836 square meters
1 square foot = .0929 square meters
1 square inch = 6.452 square centimeters = 645.2 square millimeters
1 square kilometer = .3861 square miles
1 square meter = 10.764 square feet = 1.196 square yards
1 square centimeter = .155 square inches
1 square millimeter = .00155 square inches

Equivalencies of Cubed Length

1 cubic yard = .7645 cubic meters
1 cubic foot = .02832 cubic meters = 28.317 liters
1 cubic inch = 16.38716 cubic centimeters
1 U. S. gallon = 3.785 liters
1 U. S. quart = .946 liters
1 cubic meter = 35.314 cubic feet = 1.308 cubic yards
1 cubic meter = 264.2 U. S. gallons
1 cubic centimeter = .061 cubic inches
1 liter = .0353 cubic feet = 61.023 cubic inches
1 liter = .2642 U. S. gallons

Equivalencies of Weight

1 long ton = 2240 pounds = .9842 metric tons = .89286 short tons
1 short ton = 2000 pounds = 1.120 long tons = 1.1023 metric tons
1 metric ton = 2204.6 pounds = 1000 kilograms = 1.016 long tons = .9072
    short tons
1 pound = .4536 kilograms = 453.6 grams
1 ounce (avoirdupois) = .9115 ounces (troy)
1 kilogram = 2.2046 pounds = 35.274 ounces avoirdupois
1 kilogram per square millimeter = 1422.32 pounds per square inch
1 kilogram per square centimeter = 14.223 pounds per square inch
1 kilogram-meter = 7.233 foot-pounds
1 pound per square inch = .0703 kilograms per square centimeter
1 calorie (kilogram calorie) = 3.968 British thermal units

Multiplication Factors for Conversion

In addition, the following multiplication factors for converting Metric to English and English to Metric may prove helpful:

acres	x	43560	=	square feet
acres	x	4840	=	square yards
acres	x	4047	=	square meters
acres	x	.0016	=	square miles
barrels of oil	x	42	=	gallons of oil
British Thermal Units	x	2.298×10^{-4}	=	kilowatt-hours
BTus/minute	x	.0236	=	horsepower
BTus/minute	x	17.57	=	watts
cubic feet	x	.0283	=	cubic meters
cubic feet	x	7.4805	=	gallons
cubic meters	x	35.31	=	cubic feet
cubic meters	x	1.308	=	cubic yards
cubic meters	x	264.2	=	gallons
cubic meters	x	1000	=	liters
cubic yards	x	.7645	=	cubic meters
cubic yards	x	764.5	=	liters
feet/second	x	.0114	=	miles/minute
feet/minute	x	.0114	=	miles/hour
feet/minute	x	.3048	=	meters/minute
gallons	x	3.785	=	liters
gallons	x	.1337	=	cubic feet
gallons	x	.0038	=	cubic meters
gallons of water	x	8.34	=	pounds of water
horsepower	x	42.44	=	BTu/minute
horsepower	x	.7457	=	kilowatts
kilograms	x	2.205	=	pounds
kilometers	x	.06214	=	miles
kilowatts	x	56.82	=	BTu/minute
kilowatts	x	1.341	=	horsepower
kilowatt hours	x	3410	=	BTus
liters	x	1.507	=	quarts
liters	x	0.2642	=	gallons
liters	x	.0010	=	cubic meters
meter	x	1.084	=	yards
meters/minute	x	3.281	=	feet/minute
meters/minute	x	.06	=	kilometers/hour
meters/minute	x	.0373	=	miles/hour
miles	x	1.609	=	kilometers
miles/hour	x	88	=	feet/minute
miles/hour	x	1.609	=	kilometers/hour
miles/minute	x	88	=	feet/second
square feet	x	2.2957×10	=	acres
square kilometers	x	.3861	=	square miles
square meters	x	1.1960	=	square yards

square miles	x	640	=	square kilometers
square yards	x	.8361	=	square meters
watts	x	.0586	=	BTu/minute
yards	x	.9144	=	meter

APPENDIX B

BASIC, BRIEF CHEMISTRY

All matter is composed of atoms. An atom is the smallest part of a chemical element that can participate in a chemical reaction. There are about 100 different chemical elements, such as hydrogen, oxygen, nitrogen, carbon, iron, copper, sulfur, lead, and uranium. Elements cannot be decomposed chemically into other substances, though some elements decay radioactively and become known by a different element name, and each element has atoms that differ from those of all other elements. Atoms have a wide range of sizes and weights, the lightest being hydrogen, assigned a weight of 1. The heaviest naturally occurring atom is uranium, with a weight of 239.

Atoms are composed of about a dozen different types of particles. The major ones are electrons, protons, and neutrons. Electrons carry a unit negative electrical charge, protons carry a positive electrical charge, and neutrons are electrically neutral. Electrons have a very small mass: 1,837 of them weigh as much as one proton; and a neutron is only slightly heavier than a proton. A proton only weighs 17×10^{-25} grams.

Protons and neutrons are clustered compactly at the atom's center. An ordinary hydrogen atom consists of only one proton, but the nuclei of all other atoms include both protons and neutrons. Electrons are a relatively great distance from the nucleus. The electrons are in levels or orbitals, each of which has a different quantum of energy associated with that level. On the seven shells, the electrons constantly move about the nucleus. The shells often have different shapes, due to the influence of the numbers of electrons about the nucleus.

Atoms have chemical significance because of the activities of their nucleus or their electrons. Some atoms have more neutrons in them than others--these are called isotopes. Some isotopes are unstable and disintegrate slowly into stable atoms of other elements by emission of nuclear particles and radiant energy. The emissions may provide energy which can be captured and converted into other forms, such as heat from uranium decay. Or they may have harmful effects on the atoms of other molecules, perhaps some in living organisms. This radioactivity can cause metabolic disruption, mutations, and abnormal growth and development.

The more characteristic chemical activity of atoms depends not upon the nucleus but upon the numbers of electrons in the outermost energy shell. If it contains all the electrons it can hold, the atoms have no bonding capacity and are chemically inert, never combining with other atoms. Argon, helium, krypton, and neon are examples. If the outershell contains all the electrons it can hold except one, it has a bonding capacity of one, i.e., H^+, Na^+, Cl^-, OH^-; with an electron deficit of two, it has a bonding capacity of two, i.e., Ca^{++}, Fe^{++}, $SO_4^=$, $CO_3^=$. Atoms combine in numbers according to their bonding capacities. Thus, two hydrogens can combine with one oxygen, H_2O, or one calcium with two hydroxyl, $Ca(OH)_2$.

There are two principal types of atomic bonds--electrovalent and covalent bonds. In an electrovalent bond, electrons transfer from one element to another. The electron donor is left with excess proton charges, e.g., H^+, and the recipient has an electron surplus, Cl^-. These charged atoms are ions which are attracted to each other to form NaCl, common table salt. When the cubical salt crystal dissolves in water, the ions separate from one another and move about freely. In covalent bonding, atoms share electrons rather than giving or receiving them. When carbon bonds to oxygen, it shares two of its four outermost electrons with each oxygen, CO_2, or one with each of four hydrogen atoms, CH_4.

The particle formed by the bonding of two or more atoms is a molecule. Two or more different elements form a molecule which is called a compound. A molecule of a compound is like an atom of an element--the smallest, whole identifiable particle. Properties of compounds differ from those of their parts.

Chemical compounds may be classified as either organic or inorganic. Organic compounds contain both carbon and hydrogen; all others are inorganic. It was thought that only living organisms could synthesize organic compounds, and in nature this is essentially true. Organic compounds include the hydrocarbons, petroleum, natural gas, fats, carbohydrates, and proteins which constitute the bulk dry weight of plants and animals. The principal inorganic compounds are water, acids, bases, salts, and several gases such as carbon dioxide and oxygen.

The atomic weight of an element is its weight relative to the common isotope of oxygen, 16. Hydrogen is 1.008, carbon 12.011, uranium 239, etc. A gram atomic weight is its weight in grams; the gram atomic weight of oxygen is 16 grams.

Chemical elements and compounds can react with one another in various ways, producing new substances with different properties. Some reactions take place spontaneously at room temperature, while others may require start-up energy from heat or some other agent which assists the reaction, an agent called a catalyst. Plants and animals employ organic catalysts in almost all biochemical reactions. These are enzymes.

Some molecules are polar. They have a positive charge near one end and a negative charge near the other; H_2O, water, is a good example. In addition to water, acids, bases, and salts, many organic compounds also are polar, such as the sugars and alcohols. Non-polar molecules do not have different charges. Some non-polar substances are hydrocarbons and fats. Generally polar substances are soluble in water, while non-polar substances are soluble in fats and fat solvents. Polar bonds are important in the structure of water and the stability of DNA molecules, as well as in other biologically significant chemicals.

Most chemical reactions take place in some solution. A solution is a mixture of molecules, ions, or atoms of two or more different substances. The dissolving medium is the solvent; the substances are the solute. The relative types of solutes, their concentrations, and the solution temperature are critical to the progression of chemical reactions. The condition of solutions is altered markedly by addition of certain types of atoms and compounds. When these are in excess or deficiency, the solution may be said to be polluted. Under polluted conditions, normal chemical reactions do not take place, creating a situation of natural imbalance. The goal of environmental controls is to maintain normal chemical balance throughout the natural world.

SOURCES

Greulach, Victor A. and J. Edison Adams. Plant̞s: An Introduction to Modern Botany. New York: John Wiley & Sons, Inc., 1967.

The appendix of the Greulach and Adams text contains an excellent introduction/review of chemistry, "Some Basic Chemistry for Botany Students, pages 599-622. We have freely adapted our preceding three-page overview from their text. We encourage you to examine their full text, for it is succinct, thorough, and eminently useful.

APPENDIX C

COMMON ACRONYMS

The following acronyms often are encountered in discussions of environmental standards, law, and related concerns. The list, to be sure, is basic and minimal. Numerous supplements to it are available, such as that included in the Federal Register at the beginning of each new month. It contains acronyms germane to environmental interests and many others.

AQCR	Air Quality Control Region	ESECA	Energy Supply and Environmental Coordination Act
AUM	Animal unit month	ESSA	Environmental Science Services Administration
BAT	Best available technology		
BLM	Bureau of Land Management	FAA	Federal Aviation Administration
BOD	Biochemical oxygen demand	FBC	Fluidized bed combustion
bgd	Billion gallons/day	FDA	Food and Drug Administration
Btu	British thermal unit	FEA	Federal Energy Administration
CEQ	Council on Environmental Quality	FIFRA	Federal Insecticide, Fungicide, and Rodenticide Act
CEQA	California Environmental Quality Act	FPC	Federal Power Commission
CETA	Comprehensive Employment Training Act	FRES	Forest Range Environmental Study
CO	Carbon monoxide	FWPCA	Federal Water Pollution Control Administration
CO_2	Carbon dioxide	FWQA	Federal Water Quality Act
CPI	Consumer Price Index	FY	Fiscal year
CPSC	Consumer Product Safety Commission	GAO	General Accounting Office
dB	Decibel	GEMS	Global Environmental Monitoring System
DDT	Dichlorodiphenytrichloro-ethane	GNP	Gross National Product
DEP	Department of Environmental Protection	HC	Hydrocarbon
		HEW	Department of Health, Education, and Welfare
DES	Diethylstilbesterol		
DO	Dissolved oxygen	HUD	Department of Housing and Urban Development
DOE	Department of Energy		
EDTA	Ethylene diamine triacetic acid	IAEA	International Atomic Energy Agency
EIS	Environmental Impact Statement	IRS	International Referral System
		LNG	Liquified natural gas
EPA	Environmental Protection Agency	MCL	Maximum contaminant level
		N	Nitrogen
ERDA	Energy Research and Development Administration	NAAQS	National Ambient Air Quality Standard
EROS	Earth Resources Observation System	NAPCA	National Air Pollution Control Administration

NAS	National Academy of Sciences	RDF	Solid refuse derived fuel
NASN	National Air Sampling Network	RPA	Forest and Rangeland Renewable Resources Planning Act
NCI	National Cancer Institute		
NCWQ	National Commission on Water Quality	SAROAD	Storage and Retrieval of Air Quality Data
NEPA	National Environmental Policy Act	SCS	Soil Conservation Service
NFIP	National Flood Insurance Program	SO_2	Sulfur dioxide
		SST	Supersonic transport
NIOSH	National Institute for Occupational Safety and Health	SWIRS	Solid Waste Information Retrieval Service
NO_2	Nitrogen dioxide	UN	United Nations
NO_x	Nitrogen oxide	UNEP	United Nations Environment Program
NOAA	National Oceanographic and Atmospheric Administration	UNESCO	United Nations Educational, Scientific, and Cultural Organization
NPDES	National Pollution Discharge Elimination System		
NPS	National Park System	USDA	U.S. Department of Agriculture
NRA	National Recreation Area	USGS	U.S. Geological Survey
NRC	Nuclear Regulatory Commission	WHO	World Health Organization
NRDC	Natural Resources Defense Council	WRC	Water Resources Council
NRI	Natural Resources Inventory		
O_3	Ozone		
OCS	Outer Continental Shelf		
OMB	Office of Management and Budget		
OSHA	Occupational Safety and Health Administration		
OWRR	Office of Water Resources Research		
P	Phosphorous		
PCB	Polychlorinated biphenyl		
PEP	Public Employment Program		
pH	Negative logarithm of the hydrogen ion concentration		
pOH	Negative logarithm of the hydroxyl ion concentration		
ppb	Parts per billion		
ppm	Parts per million		
PSI	Pollution Standards Index		
psi	Pounds/square inch		
PUD	Planned Unit Development		
qBtu	Quadrillion British thermal units		
QUAD	Quadrillion British thermal units		
RD&D	Research, devlopment, and demonstration		

GLOSSARY

Environmental technologies tend to rely on special vocabularies in order to communicate ideas with precision. Unfortunately, these vocabularies tend to exclude the uninitiated and to compartmentalize a subject which, nonetheless, must be understood by those responsible for making the hard decisions which most affect the environment.

This glossary attempts to bring together many of the key words for the concepts and phenomena central to an understanding of the several ecological disciplines. It has been assembled from five excellent glossaries, to which we refer you here for more detailed treatment:

Resource Conservation Glossary
Soil Conservation Society of America
7515 Northeast Ankeny Road
Ankeny, Iowa 50021

Air Pollution Primer
American Lung Association

A Glossary of Ecological Terms for Coastal Engineers
U.S. Army Corps of Engineers--Paper No. 2-74
Coastal Engineering Research Center
Kingman Building
Fort Belvoir, Virginia 22060

Glossary of Commonly Used Biological and Related Terms in Water and Waste Water Control
U.S. Department of Health, Education, and Welfare
Public Health Service
Division of Water Supply and Pollution Control
Cincinnati, Ohio

Illinois Pesticide Applicator Study Guide
Cooperative Extension Service
College of Agriculture
University of Illinois
Champaign-Urbana, Illinois

ABATEMENT. The method of reducing the degree or intensity of pollution, also the use of such a method.

ACTIVATED CARBON. A highly absorbent form of carbon, used to remove odors and toxic substances from gaseous emissions.

ACTIVATED SLUDGE. Sludge that has been aerated and subjected to bacterial action.

ADHESION. Molecular attraction which holds the surfaces of two substances in contact, such as water and rock particles.

ADSORPTION. The adhesion of a substance to the surface of a solid or liquid; often used to extract pollutants by causing them to be attached to such adsorbents as activated carbon or silica gel. Hydrophobic, or water-repulsing adsorbents, are used to extract oil from waterways in oil spills.

AERATION. 1. The process of being supplied or impregnated with air. 2. In waste treatment, the process used to foster biological and chemical purification. 3. In soils, the process by which air in the soils is replenished by air from the atmosphere. In a well-aerated soil, the soil air is similar in composition to the atmosphere above the soil. Poorly aerated soils usually contain a much higher percentage of carbon dioxide and a correspondingly lower percentage of oxygen. The rate of aeration depends largely on the volume and continuity of pores in the soil. The zone of aeration is the zone between the land surface and the water table.

AEROBIC. 1. Having molecular oxygen as a part of the environment. 2. Growing only in the presence of molecular oxygen, as aerobic organisms. 3. Occurring only in the presence of molecular oxygen (said of certain chemical or biochemical processes, such as aerobic decomposition).

AEROSOL. Solid or liquid particles, usually less than 1 micron in diameter, suspended in a gaseous medium.

AIR POLLUTION. The presence of contaminants in the air in concentrations that prevent the normal dispersive ability of the air and that inter-fere directly or indirectly with man's health, safety, comfort, or the full use and enjoyment of his property.

AIR QUALITY CRITERIA. Levels of pollution and lengths of exposure at which adverse effects on health and welfare occur.

AIR QUALITY STANDARDS. The prescribed level of pollutants in the outside air that cannot be exceeded legally during a specified time in a speci-fied geographical area.

ALGAE. (sing., alga): Simple plants, many microscopic, containing chloro-phyll; forming the base of the food chain in aquatic environments. Some species may create a nuisance when environmental conditions are suitable for prolific growth.

ALGAL BLOOM. Proliferation of living algae on the surface of lakes, streams, or ponds; stimulated by phosphate enrichment.

ALKALI. 1. Any substance capable of furnishing to its solution or other substances the hydroxyl ion (OH negative); a substance having marked basic properties in contrast to acid. The important alkali metals are sodium and potassium. 2. The term is applied less scientifically to the soluble salts, especially sulfates and chlorides of sodium, potassium, and magnesium and the carbonates of sodium and potassium, which are present in some soils of arid and semiarid regions in sufficient quantities to be detrimental to ordinary agriculture.

ALKALINE SOIL. A soil that has a pH value greater than 7.0, particularly above 7.3, throughout most or all of the root zone, although the term is commonly applied to only the surface layer or horizon of a soil.

ALKALINITY. The quality or state of being alkaline; the concentration of OH negative ions.

ALLUVIUM. A general term for all detrital material deposited or in transit by streams, including gravel, sand, silt, clay, and all variations and mixtures of these.

AMENSALISM. The interaction of two species resulting in one species being inhibited and the other not affected.

ANADROMOUS. A life cycle in which maturity is attained in the ocean and the adults ascend rivers and streams to spawn in freshwater (e.g., salmon).

ANAEROBIC. 1. The absence of molecular oxygen. 2. Growing in the absence of molecular oxygen (such as anaerobic bacteria). 3. Occurring in the absence of molecular oxygen (as a biochemical process).

ANAEROBIC DIGESTION. Certain bacteria do not need oxygen to respire; they are anaerobic bacteria. As they consume organic wastes, they produce carbon dioxide, CO_2, and methane, CH_4. Methane is one of the components of natural gas and readily burns in domestic appliances, farm drying operations, and waste treatment plant operations.

ANAEROBIC SEDIMENT. A highly organic sediment with no free oxygen present. Usually rich in hydrogen sulfide.

ANION. Negatively charged ion; ion which during electrolysis is attracted to the anode.

AQUATIC PLANTS. Plants growing in or near water with true roots, stems, and leaves; other than algae.

AQUIFER. A geologic formation or structure that transmits water in sufficient quantity to supply the needs for a water development; usually saturated sands, gravel, fractures, and cavernous and vesicular rock. The term water-bearing is sometimes used synonymously with aquifer when a stratum furnishes water for a specific use.

ASH. The incombustible material that remains after a fuel or solid waste has been burned.

ASSIMILATION. The transformation of absorbed nutrients into body substances.

ATMOSPHERE. The layer of air surrounding the earth.

ATMOSPHERIC AREA. As the federal government uses the term, a segment of the continental United States in which climate, meteorology, and topography--all of which influence the capacity of the air to dilute and disperse pollutants--are essentially similar.

ATOM. The smallest portion of an element that can take part in a chemical reaction.

BACTERIA. Single-cell, microscopic organisms that possess rigid cell walls. They may be aerobic, anaerobic, or facultative; they can cause disease; and some are important in the stabilization of solid wastes.

BASIN. 1. In hydrology, the area drained by a river. 2. In irrigation, a level plot of field, surrounded by dikes, which may be flood irrigated.

BENTHOS. The plant and animal life whose habitat is the bottom of a sea, lake, or river.

BIOASSAY. The employment of living organisms to determine the biological effect of some substance, factor, or condition.

BIOCHEMICAL OXIDATION. The process by which bacteria and other microorganisms feed on complex organic materials and decompose them. Self-purification of waterways and activated sludge and trickling filter wastewater treatment processes depend on this principle.

BIOCHEMICAL OXYGEN DEMAND (BOD). The amount of oxygen required by the biological population of a water sample to oxidize the organic matter in that water. It is usually determined over a 5-day period under standardized laboratory conditions and hence may not represent actual field conditions.

BIODEGRADABLE. The significant breakdown by microorganisms of the physical and/or chemical structure of a compound.

BIOLOGICAL CONTROL. Control of pests by means of living organisms such as predators, parasites, and disease-producing organisms.

BIOLOGICAL MAGNIFICATION. The concentration of certain substances up a food chain. A very important mechanism in concentrating pesticides and heavy metals in organisms such as fish.

BIOMASS. A collective term for garbage, forest wastes, manures, agricultural wastes, algae, or anything living or formerly living which contains energy because of its position or condition and is convertible into usable energy forms.

BIOME. A major community of plants and animals associated with a stable environmental life zone or region (e.g., Northern Coniferous Forest or Great Plains).

BIOTA. The flora and fauna of a region.

BIOTIC FACTORS. Factors of a biological nature such as availability of food, competition between species, predator-prey relationship, etc., which besides the purely physical and chemical factors, also affect the distribution and abundance of species.

BLUE-GREEN ALGAE. A group of algae with a blue pigment, in addition to the green chlorophyll. A stench is often associated with the decomposition of dense blooms of blue-green algae in fertile lakes.

BOD. See Biochemical Oxygen Demand.

BRACKISH. Slightly salty; applied to water with a saline content that is intermediate between that of freshwater streams and sea water; neither fresh nor salty.

BRONCHIAL ASTHMA. Abnormal responsiveness of the air passages to certain substances. An attack consists of a widespread narrowing of the bronchioles by muscle spasm, swelling of the mucous membrane, or thickening and increase of mucous secretions, accompanied by wheezing, gasping, and sometimes coughing.

BUFFER STRIPS. Strips of grass or other erosion-resisting vegetation between or below cultivated strips or fields.

BUILDING CODE. Regulations adopted by state or local government which establish minimum standards of construction related to building materials, hazards, and structural collapse.

CALORIE. A measure of energy quantity. A calorie is the amount of energy needed to elevate the temperature of a milliliter (cubic centimeter) of water one degree centigrade. A Calorie is 1,000 calories.

CANOPY. The cover of leaves and branches formed by the tops or crowns of plants as viewed from above the cover.

CAPITAL BUDGETING. Since capital is often designated for certain types of federal projects or invested by special development interests, there may be no means by which the projects or developments conform to the Master Plan. Capital Budgeting coordinates spending with planning. It often ties in with Phased Development Ordinances.

CARBON CYCLE. The sequence of transformations whereby carbon dixoide is fixed as carbon or carbon compounds in living organisms by photosynthesis or chemosynthesis, liberated by respiration and/or death and decomposition of the fixing organism, used by heterotrophic species, and ultimately returned to its original state to be used again.

CARBON DIOXIDE (CO_2). A colorless, odorless, nonpoisonous gas that forms carbonic acid when dissolved in water; produced during combustion and microbial decomposition.

CARCINOGENIC. Tending to produce or incite cancer.

CARRYING CAPACITY. 1. In recreation, the amount of use a recreation area can sustain without deterioration of its quality. 2. In wildlife, the maximum number of animals an area can support during a given period of the year.

CATALYTIC CONVERTER. An air pollution abatement device that removes organic contaminates by oxidizing them into carbon dioxide and water through chemical reaction; can be used to reduce nitrogen oxide emmissions from motor vehicles.

CATION. Positively charged ion; ion which, during electrolysis, is attracted to the cathode. Common soil cations are calcium, magnesium, sodium, potassium, and hydrogen.

CELLULOSE. A complex carbohydrate occurring in wood and all other vegetable material. Wood cellulose fibers are basic components of lumber and wood pulp and many other useful products.

CHEMICAL ENERGY. Chemical energy (a form of potential energy because of the position of the atoms and the condition of their charges) to digest foods, ignite fires, explode, and generate heat and light.

CHEMICAL OXYGEN DEMAND (COD). A measure of the amount of oxygen required to oxidize organic and oxidizable inorganic compounds in water. The COD test, like the BOD test, is used to determine the degree of pollution in an effluent.

CHLORINATED HYDROCARBON INSECTICIDE. A synthetic pesticide that contains hydrogen, carbon, oxygen, and chlorine. Chlorinated hydrocarbon insecticides are persistent insecticides that kill insects mainly by contact action. They are insoluble in water, and are decomposed by alkaline materials and high temperatures. Examples are DDT, aldrin, chlordane, dieldrin, heptachlor, lindane, toxaphene, and methooxychlor.

CHLORINATOR. A device for adding a chlorine-containing gas or liquid to drinking or wastewater.

CHLORINE RESIDUAL. The quantity of chlorine remaining in water or wastewater at the end of a specified contact period. The demand for any given water or waste varies with the amount of chlorine applied, time of contact, and temperature.

CHLOROPHYLL. Green photosynthetic pigment present in many plant and some bacterial cells. There are seven known types of chlorophyll; their presence and abundance vary from one group of photosynthetic organisms to another.

CHRONIC TOXICITY. A polonged exposure to a pesticide that may result in injury or death.

CLARIFIER. In wastewater treatment, a settling tank which mechanically removes settleable solids from wastes.

CLAY (Soils). 1. A mineral soil separate consisting of particles less than 0.002 millimeter in equivalent diameter. 2. A soil textural class. 3. (Engineering) A fine-grained soil that has a high plasticity index in relation to the liquid limits.

CLIMATE. The sum total of all atmospheric or meteorological influences, principally temperature, moisture, wind, pressure, and evaporation, which combine to characterize a region and give it individuality by influencing the nature of its land forms, soils, vegetation, and land use.

CLIMAX. The highest ecological development of a plant community capable of perpetuation under the prevailing climatic and edaphic conditions.

CLUSTER DEVELOPMENT. A variation in subdivision design which permits building lots to be made smaller and grouped on part of a site, thereby leaving the remaining land open for recreational or conservation purposes. Such a plan generally maintains the same overall density as the conventional subdivision design.

COAGULATION. The clumping of particles in order to settle out impurities; often induced by chemicals such as lime or alum.

COAL. Coal, like petroleum, is believed to be a derivative of compressed and chemically altered living matter, primarily plants. It is a black, combustible mineral solid used as a fuel to produce heat, coke, coal gas, water gas, and as a source of chemicals to make many food substances and pharmaceuticals.

COHESION. Holding together; force holding a solid or liquid together, owing to attraction between like molecules; decreases with a rise in temperature.

COLIFORM. A group of bacteria used as an indicator of sanitary quality in water. The total coliform group is an indicator of sanitary significance, because the organisms are normally present in large numbers in the intestinal tracts of humans and other warm-blooded animals.

COLLECTOR. A mechanical device designed to remove suspended particles from gaseous emissions arising from industrial processes. Types include:
Bag-type - A filter in which the filtering medium is a fabric cylindrical bag.
Cyclone - A collector in which an inlet gas stream is made to move vortically; its centrifugal forces tend to drive suspended particles to the wall of the cyclone.
Dust - Any device used to remove dust from exhaust gases.
Fly ash - Equipment used to remove fly ash from combustion gases.

Mechanical – A device in which inertial and gravitational forces separate dry dust from gas.

Multicyclone – A dust collector consisting of a number of cyclone collectors that operate in parallel; the volume and velocity of combustion gas can be regulated by dampers to maintain efficiency over a given load range.

COMMINUTOR. A device that grinds solids, making them easier to treat.

COMMUNITY. 1. An aggregation of organisms within a specified area. 2. People living within the same district, city, etc., under the same laws.

COMPACTION. 1. To unite firmly; the act or process of becoming compact. 2. In geology, the changing of loose sediment into hard firm rock. 3. In soil engineering, the process by which the soil grains are rearranged to decrease void space and bring them into closer contact with one another, thereby increasing the weight of solid material per cubic foot. 4. In solid waste disposal, the reducing of the bulk of solid waste by rolling and tamping.

COMPOSTING. A controlled process of degrading organic matter by microorganisms. Techniques include:

Mechanical – A method in which the compost is continuously and mechanically mixed and aerated.

Ventilated cell – The compost is mixed and aerated by being dropped through a vertical series of ventilated cells.

Windrow – An open-air method in which compostable material is placed in windrows, piles, or ventilated bins or pits and is occasionally turned or mixed. The process may be anaerobic or aerobic.

CONSERVATION. The protection, improvement, and use of natural resources according to principles that will assure their highest economic or social benefits.

CONSERVATION DISTRICT. A public organization created under state enabling law as a special-purpose district to develop and carry out a program of soil, water, and related resource conservation, use, and development within its boundaries; usually a subdivision of state government with a local governing body. Often called a soil conservation district or a soil and water conservation district.

CONSERVATION OF, ENERGY. The Law of Conservation of Energy says that energy can neither be created nor destroyed. The Theory of Relativity says of mass and energy that one can be converted into the other; thus, the Law of Conservation of Energy includes both concepts.

CONSERVATION STANDARDS. Standards for various types of soils and land uses, including criteria, techniques, and methods for the control of erosion and sediment resulting from land disturbing activities.

CONSUMERS (Biology). Heterotrophic organisms, chiefly animals, that ingest other organisms or particle organic matter.

CONTOUR. 1. An imaginary line on the surface of the earth connecting points of the same elevation. 2. A line drawn on a map connecting points of the same elevation.

CONVECTION. The transfer of heat through a liquid or gas by the actual movement of the molecules.

COPROPHAGIC. Animals that eat feces.

COST/BENEFIT ANALYSIS. A comparison between dollar costs and dollar returns. The ratio gives a number comparable over time or type to other projects. It is one of the three analyses required for a site plan review.

COVER. 1. Vegetation or other material providing protection. 2. Fish, a variety of items including undercut banks, trees, roots, and rocks in the water where fish seek necessary protection or security. 3. In forestry, low-growing shrubs, vines, and herbaceous plants under the trees. 4. Ground and soils, any vegetation producing a protecting mat on or just above the soil surface. 5. Stream, generally trees, large shrubs, grasses, and forbs that shade and otherwise protect the stream from erosion, temperature elevation, or sloughing of banks. 6. Vegetation, all plants of all sizes and species found on an area, irrespective of whether they have forage or other value. 7. Wildlife plants of objects used by wild animals for nesting, rearing of young, resting, escape from predators, or protection from adverse environmental conditions.

CRITICAL AREAS. Critical areas are geographic features or uses of material of concern to a state. Designation requires a definition of the type of area to be regulated and the beneficial functions to be preserved; and an inventory and map of the area.

CULTURAL EUTROPHICATION. Acceleration by man of the natural process of enrichment (aging) of bodies of water.

DECIBEL. The unit of measuring the intensity of sound. Zero on the decibel scale is the slightest sound that can be heard by humans--rustling leaves, breathing. The Scale: eardrum ruptures (140 decibels--jet taking off); deafening (100 decibels--thunder, car horn at three feet, loud motorcycle, loud power lawn mower); very loud (80 decibels--portable sander, food blender; continued exposure brings about loss of hearing, impossible to use phone); loud (60 decibels--city playground, average restaurant or living room); faint (20 decibels--courtroom or classroom, private office, a whisper at five feet).

DECOMPOSER. An organism, usually a bacterium or a fungus, that breaks down the bodies or parts of dead plants and animals into simpler compounds.

DECOMPOSITION. The breakdown of organic waste materials by bacteria. Aerobic process refers to one using oxygen breathing bacteria, while anaerobic refers to a process using bacteria which breathe an inorganic oxidant. Total decomposition occurs spontaneously in the open (dumps and landfills) or can be harnessed in waste treatment equipment to work under controlled conditions.

DEMOGRAPHY. The statistical study of human vital statistics and population dynamics.

DEPLETION CURVE (Hydraulics). A graphical representation of water depletion from storage-stream channels, surface soil, and groundwater. A depletion curve can be drawn for base flow, direct runoff, or total flow.

DETERGENT. A detergent, like soap, is made up of long molecules that have, at one end, regions of positive and negative electrical charges that are strongly attracted to water molecules; on the other end is a chemical character that is attracted to grease molecules. This allows soap and detergents to pick up oils and fats from dishes and carry them away in wastewater.

DETRITUS. Matter worn from rocks by mechanical means; generally, alluvial deposits.

DEW POINT. The temperature at which a known quantity of moisture in the atmosphere condenses into rainfall.

DIAMETER BREAST HIGH. The diameter of a tree 4.5 feet above ground level. Abbr. DBH. The additional abbreviations OB- and IB- are used to designate whether the diameter refers to the measurement outside or inside the bark.

DIGESTER. In a wastewater treatment plant, a closed tank that decreases the volume of solids and stabilizes raw sludge by bacterial action.

DISCHARGE (Hydraulics). Rate of flow, specifically fluid flow; a volume of fluid passing a point per unit time, commonly expressed as cubic feet per second, million gallons per day, gallons per minute, or cubic meters per second.

DISSOLVED OXYGEN. The amount of gaseous oxygen (O) dissolved in a liquid-- usually water. Abbr. D.O.

DISSOLVED SOLIDS. The total amount of dissolved material, organic and inorganic, contained in water or wastes. Excessive dissolved solids make water unpalatable for drinking and unsuitable for industrial uses.

DISTILLATION. The removal of impurities from liquids by boiling.

DIURNAL. 1. An event, process, or specific change that occurs every day; usually associated with changes from day to night. 2. Pertaining to those organisms that are active during day time.

DIVERSITY. The variety of species within a given association of organisms. Areas of high diversity are characterized by a great variety of species; usually relatively few individuals represent any one species. Areas with low diversity are characterized by a few species; often relatively large numbers of individuals represent each species.

DRAINAGE, SOIL. Soil drainage refers to the frequency and duration of periods when the soil is free of saturation; for example, in well-drained soils the water is removed readily but not rapidly; in poorly drained soils the root zone is waterlogged for long periods unless artificially drained, and the roots of ordinary crop plants cannot get enough oxygen; in excessively drained soils the water is removed so completely that most crop plants suffer from lack of water. Strictly speaking, excessively drained soils are a result of excessive runoff due to steep slopes or low available waterholding capacity due to small amounts of silt and clay in the soil material.

EASEMENT. A limited right over land owned by someone else. An easement may be for a certain number of years or be perpetual in duration. An affirmative easement gives the owner of the easement the right to use the land for a stated purpose. A negative easement is an agreement with a private property owner to limit the development of his land in specific ways. Examples are utility, environmental, and agricultural easements.

ECOLOGY. The study of interrelationships or organisms to one another and to their environment.

ECOSPHERE. The mantle of earth and troposphere inhabited by living organisms.

ECOSYSTEM. A community, including all the component organisms, together with the environment, forming an interacting system.

EDAPHIC. A term referring to the soil conditions or types as ecological factors.

EDGE EFFECT. The change increase (usually increase) in species diversity and density in the transitional area between communities.

EFFLUENT. 1. Solid, liquid, or gas wastes which enter the environment as a by-product of man-oriented processes. 2. The discharge or outflow of water from ground or sub-surface storage.

ELECTRO-MAGNETIC WAVE ENERGY. Electro-magnetic waves of certain frequencies transmit energy through the atmosphere, water, and space which can be received and converted into audible and visible wave frequencies, e.g., radio, television, radar, sonar, etc.

ELECTROSTATIC PRECIPITATOR. An apparatus that removes particles from a stream of air through an electric field and collects the charged particulates on electrodes.

EMISSION FACTOR. The statistical average of the amount of a specific pollutant emitted from each type of polluting source in relation to a unit quantity of material handled, processed, or burned. E.g., the emission factor of oxides of nitrogen in fuel oil combustion is 119 pounds per 1,000 gallons of fuel oil used. By using the emission factor of a pollutant and specific data regarding quantities of material used by a given source, it is possible to compute emissions for that source--information necessary for an emission inventory.

EMISSION INVENTORY. A list of primary air pollutants emitted into a given community's atmosphere, in amounts (commonly tons) per day, by type of source. The emission inventory is basic to the establishment of emission standards.

EMISSION STANDARD. The maximum amount of pollutant permitted to be discharged from a single polluting source.

EMPHYSEMA. See pulmonary emphysema.

ENERGY. The capacity to do work or to produce change. It may take a number of forms, among them mechanical, chemical, and radiant, and can be transformed from one form to another, but cannot be created or destroyed.

ENERGY IMPACT ANALYSIS. One of the site plan review requirements, the energy impact analysis helpd planners conserve energy in all forms by indicating the energy costs of alternative constructions, locations, transportation routings, and other energy-consuming factors.

ENTROPY. The tendency for concentrated, or ordered, matter to become disordered and to disintegrate. Entropy is the increase in randomness of any energy system.

ENVIRONMENT. The sum total of all the external conditions that may act upon an organism or community to influence its development or existence.

ENVIRONMENTAL IMPACT STATEMENT. One of the three analyses required for a site plan review. Under the 1969 National Environmental Policy Act, environmental impact statements are required for all significant federal projects--although each agency may decide whate is "significant." Now, states are requiring equivalent impact statements for state and private constructions of significance.

EPIDEMIOLOGY. The study of diseases as they affect populations rather than individuals, including the distribution and incidence of a disease; mortality and morbidity rates; and the relationship of climate, age, sex, race, and other factors.

EPILIMNION. In lakes, the layer of water above the thermocline. It is the area where main primary productivity takes place.

EPISODE (Pollution). An air pollution incident in a given area caused by a concentration of atmospheric pollution reacting with meteorological conditions that results in a significant increase in illnesses or deaths.

EQUILIBRIUM. 1. The condition in which a population or community is maintained with only minor fluctuations in composition over an extended period of time. Sometimes called dynamic equilibrium. 2. A dynamic interaction of two opposing chemical or physical processes occurring at equal rates.

EROSION. 1. The wearing away of the land surface by running water, wind, ice, or other geological agents, including such processes as gravitational creep. 2. Detachment and movement of soil or rock fragments by water, wind, ice, or gravity. The following terms are used to describe different types of water erosion:

Accelerated erosion - Erosion much more rapid than normal, natural, or geologic erosion, primarily as a result of the influence of the activities of man or, in some cases, of other animals or natural catastrophies that expose base surfaces, for example, fires.

Geological erosion - The normal or natural erosion caused by geological processes acting over long geologic periods and resulting in the wearing away of mountains, the building up of floodplains, coastal plains, etc. Also called natural erosion.

Gully erosion. The erosion process whereby water accumulates in narrow channels and, over short periods, removes the soil from this narrow area to considerable depths, ranging from 1 to 2 feet to as much as 75 to 100 feet.

Natural erosion. Wearing away of the earth's surface by water, ice, or other natural agents under natural environmental conditions of climate, vegetation, etc., undisturbed by man. Also called geological erosion.

Normal erosion. The gradual erosion of land used by man which does not greatly exceed natural erosion.

Rill erosion. An erosion process in which numerous small channels only several inches deep are formed; occurs mainly on recently cultivated soils. See rill.

Sheet erosion. The removal of a fairly uniform layer of soil from the land surface by runoff water.

Splash erosion. The spattering of small soil particles caused by the impact of raindrops on wet soils. The loosened and spattered particles may or may not be subsequently removed by surface runoff.

EROSIVE. Refers to wind or water having sufficient velocity to cause erosion.

ESTUARY. That portion of a coastal stream influenced by the tide of the body of water into which it flows, for example a bay or mouth of a river, where the tide meets the river current; an area where fresh and marine waters mix.

EUTROPHICATION. The process whereby a body of water becomes highly productive due to the input of large quantities of nutrients. It may have high dissolved oxygen concentrations near the surface during the day and low concentrations during the night. The bottom waters usually have low dissolved oxygen and high organic concentrations at all times of the day.

FACILITY. The building, tanks, collecting pipes, distribution system, and associated electrical, lighting, plumbing, and other construction components of an air or water treatment facility.

FALL OVERTURN. A physical phenomenon that may take place in a body of water during early autumn. The sequence of events leading to fall overturn include: (1) cooling of surface waters, (2) density change in surface waters producing convection currents from top to bottom, (3) circulation of the total water volume by wind action, and (4) vertical temperature equality. The overturn results in a uniformity of the physical and chemical properties of the entire water mass.

FAUNA. The animal life of a region.

FECAL COLIFORM. A group of bacteria normally present in large numbers in the intestinal tracts of humans and other warm-blooded animals.

FECAL STREPTOCOCCUS. A group of bacteria normally present in large numbers in the intestinal tracts of warm-blooded animals other than humans. By assessing the ratio of coliforms to streptococci in a water sample, a rough estimate can be made of the relative contribution of fecal contamination from the two mentioned possible sources.

FISSION. Fission is the splitting of nuclei of heavy elements such as uranium. Uranium$_{235}$ is able to be split easily compared to other forms of uranium. One, U_{238} absorbs neutrons in a nuclear reaction and changes into fissionable plutonium, 239, or thorium, 232. By fission it is possible to create more nuclear fuel than is consumed. Most US reactors use U_{235}, made of the limited quantity of uranium oxide, U_{308}. When the oxide supply ends, products of breeder reactors become unlimited sources of fissionable materials. But, since they produce more than they use, the world's supply of dangerously radioactive wastes would increase dramatically. See also ENERGY, FUSION.

FLOCCULATION. The process by which suspended colloidal or very fine particles are assembled into larger masses or floccules which eventually settle out of suspension.

FLORA. The sum total of the kinds of plants in an area at one time.

FLOODPLAINS. The land areas adjacent to a stream which are flooded with an average frequency of once in one hundred years.

FLUE GAS SCRUBBER. A type of equipment that removes fly ash and other objectionable materials from flue gas by the use of sprays, wet baffles, or other means that require water as the primary separation mechanism, also called flue gas washer.

FLY ASH. Particulate pollutants exhausted into the atmosphere.

FOSSIL FUELS. Fuels derived from the remains of ancient plant and animal life; coal, oil, and natural gas.

FUMES. Particulate or gaseous emissions formed from the chemical reactions of condensation of cooling vapors.

FUNGI. Simple plants that lack a photosynthetic pigment. The individual cells have a nucleus surrounded by a membrane, and they may be linked together in long filaments called hyphae, which may grow together to form a visible body.

FUSION. Fusion combines light nuclei such as deuterium and tritium, rare forms of hydrogen, to produce energy. Deuterium is found in some hydrogen atoms, while tritium comes from lithium. The deuterium-tritium fusion occurs as low temperatures, compared to the deuterium-deuterium fusion. The latter, however, could give us almost unlimited raw materials for the reaction. The technology to do so, though, is still developing. Commercially available energy from fusion is many years away. See also, ENERGY, FISSION.

GAGING STATION. A selected section of a stream channel equipped with a gage, recorder, or other facilities for determining stream discharge.

GEOMORPHOLOGY. That branch of both physiography and geology that deals with the form of the earth, the general configuration of its surface, and the changes that take place in the evolution of land forms.

GEOTHERMAL HEAT. Geothermal heat emanates from the motion of molten rock within the Earth's core. Historically, the energy came from collapsing, compressing gaseous molecules into the extremely dense body of the planet Earth. Also, certain matter formed into elements which are now radioactive and emit energy in the form of atomic particles. Near the surface, this matter is collected for atomic energy production.

GRADIENT. Change of elevation, velocity, pressure, or other characteristics per unit length, slope.

GREENHOUSE EFFECT. The absorption of light wave energy by the Earth's surface and its release as heat into the air. Thus, a passage of light occurs but the heat mass is retained like glass does in a greenhouse.

HABITAT. The environment in which the life needs of a plant or animal organism, population, or community are supplied.

HAZARDOUS WASTE. Waste materials which by their nature are inherently dangerous to handle or dispose of, such as old explosives, radioactive materials, some chemicals, and some biological wastes; usually produced in industrial operations or in institutions.

HEADWATER. 1. The source of a stream. 2. The water upstream from a structure or point on a stream.

HEAVY METALS. Metals present in municipal and industrial wastes that pose long-term environmental hazards; they include boron, cadmium, cobalt, chromium, copper, mercury, nickel, lead, and zinc.

HERBICIDE. A chemical substance used for killing plants, especially weeds.

HETEROGENEOUS WASTE. A body of waste material made up of dissimilar components. (e.g., municipal refuse, which contains metals, glass, paper, plastics, food wastes, yard wastes).

HETEROTROPH. An organism that feeds on organic materials.

HI-VOLUME SAMPLER. A filtering apparatus for measuring and analyzing suspended particular pollutants.

HOLDING POND. A pond or reservoir usually made of earth built to store polluted runoff.

HOLOLOGICAL APPROACH. Analysis of a system (e.g., as to heat budget) where the system is taken as a whole and treated as a "black box" where only input and output are considered.

HOLOPHYTIC. Obtaining food after the manner of a green plant.

HOMEOSTASIS. The tendency of a system to remain at or return to normal, after or during an outside stress.

HOUSING CODE. Regulations adopted by state or local government, applicable to both new and existing housing, establishing minimum standards for sanitary facilities, light and ventilation, screening, minimum size of bedrooms, maximum number of occupants in relation to total floor area, heating facilities, and other requirements considered necessary for decent, safe, and sanitary housing conditions.

HUMIDITY, ABSOLUTE. The actual quantity or mass of water vapor present in a given volume of air, generally expressed in grams per cubic foot or in grams per cubic meter.

HUMIDITY, RELATIVE. The ratio of the actual amount of water vapor present in the portion of the atmosphere under consideration to the quantity that would be there if it were saturated.

HUMUS. That more or less stable fraction of the soil organic matter remaining after the major portion or added plant and animal residues have decomposed, usually amorphous and dark colored.

HYDRAULICS. A branch of science that deals with practical applications (as the transmission of energy or effects of flow) of water or other fluid in motion.

HYDROCARBONS. Compounds containing hydrogen and carbon that are subdivided into alicyclic, aliphatic, and aromatic groups based on their chemical activity and atomic structure.

HYDROELECTRIC ENERGY. The kinetic energy (moving energy) of water falls against turbines which rotate conductive wires between magnetic poles, inducing the flow of electrons through the wires. The flowing electrons are electricity.

HYDROGEN SULFIDE (H_2S).   A poisonous gas with the odor of rotten eggs that is produced from the reduction of sulfates in and the putrefaction of a sulfur-containing organic material.

HYDROLOGIC CYCLE.   The circuit of water movement from the atmosphere to the earth and return to the atmosphere through various stages or processes, as precipitation, interception, runoff, infiltration, percolation, storage, evaporation, and transpiration.

HYDROLOGY.   The science dealing with the properties, distribution, and circulation of water and snow.

HYDROXIDE.   A compound of an element with the radical or ion OH negative, as sodium hydroxide, NaOH.

HYPOLIMNION.   The region of a body of water that extends from the thermocline to the bottom and is essentially removed from major surface influences.

IGNEOUS ROCK.   Rock formed by solidification from a molten or partially molten state; primary rock.

IMPOUNDMENT.   Generally, an artificial collection or storage of water, as a reservoir, pit, dugout, or sump.

INCINERATION.   The controlled process by which solids, liquid, or gaseous combustible wastes are burned and changed into gases.

INDICATOR.   1. In biology, an organism, species, or community that shows the presence of certain environmental conditions. 2. In chemistry, a substance that, by means of a color change, identifies the endpoint of a titration.

INFILTRATION.   The gradual downward flow of water from the surface through soil to ground water and water table reservoirs.

INTERMITTENT STREAM.   A stream or portion of a stream that flows only in direct response to precipitation. It receives little or no water from springs and no long-continued supply from melting snow or other sources. It is dry for a large part of the year, ordinarily more than 3 months.

INVERSION.   The state of the atmosphere in which a layer of cold air is trapped near the Earth's surface by an overlaying layer of warm air; may cause serious air pollution problems.

ION.   An atom or group of atoms which has become electrically charged either by loss or by gain of one or more electrons.

KEMMERER WATER SAMPLER.   An instrument designed to collect a known volume of water from a predetermined depth. The sampler construction essentially consists of a brass cylinder with closable rubber stoppers on each end.

KINETIC ENERGY. Kinetic energy is energy a body possesses because it is in motion. The kinetic energy of a body with mass "m" moving at a velocity "v" is one-half the product of the mass of the body and the square of the velocity: Kinetic Energy = $1/2 \ mv^2$.

LAGOON. 1. In geology, a shallow sound, channel, pond, or lake connected with the sea. 2. In sewage treatment, a reservoir or pond built to contain water and animal wastes until they can be decomposed either by aerobic or anaerobic action.

LAND. The total natural and cultural environment within which production takes place; a broader term than soil. In addition to soil, its attributes include other physical conditions, such as mineral deposits, climate, and water supply; location in relation to centers of commerce, populations, and other land; the size of the individual tracts or holdings; and existing plant cover, works of improvement, and the like.

LAND CAPABILITY. The suitability of land for use without permanent damage. Land capability, as ordinarily used in the United States, is an expression of the effect of physical land conditions, including climate, on the total suitability for use without damage for crops that require regular tillage, for grazing, for woodland, and for wildlife. Land capability involves consideration of (1) the risks of land damage from erosion and other causes and (2) the difficulties in land-use owing to physical land characteristics, including climate.

LAND CAPABILITY ANALYSIS. A report prepared for regional planning which describes the quality and quantity of such factors as topography, soil, geology, vegetation, fish and wildlife, surface water, groundwater, weather, air quality, current land-use, sewer service, water service, political boundaries, population characteristics, and present zoning restrictions.

LAND CAPABILITY CLASS. One of the eight classes of land in the land capability classification of the Soil Conservation Service; distinguished according to the risk of land damage or the difficulty of land-use; they include:
Land suitable for cultivation and other uses.
    <u>Class I</u> - Soils that have few limitations restricting their use.
    <u>Class II</u> - Soils that have some limitations, reducing the choice of plants or requiring moderate conservation practices.
    <u>Class III</u> - Soils that have severe limitations that reduce the choice of plants or require special conservation practices, or both.
    <u>Class IV</u> - Soils that have very severe limitations that restrict the choice of plants, require very careful management, or both.
Land generally not suitable for cultivation (without major treatment).
    <u>Class V</u> - Soils that have little or no erosion hazard, but that have other limitations, impractical to remove, that limit their use largely to pasture, range, woodland, or wildlife food and cover.
    <u>Class VI</u> - Soils that have severe limitations that make them generally unsuited for cultivation and limit their use largely to pasture or range, woodland, or wildlife food and cover.

Class VII - Soils that have very severe limitations that make them unsuited to cultivation and that restricts their use largely to grazing, woodland, or wildlife.

Class VIII - Soils and landforms that preclude their use for commercial plant production and restrict their use to recreation, wildlife, water supply, or aesthetic purposes.

LAND CAPABILITY MAP. A map showing land capability units, subclasses, and classes or a soil survey map colored to show land capability classes.

LAND FORM. A discernible natural landscape, such as a floodplain, stream terrace, plateau, or valley.

LAND SUITABILITY ANALYSIS. A report prepared for planning which describes the quality and quantity of potential projected land-uses, such as housing, industry, commerce, agriculture, energy production and transmission, institutions, transportation, conservation, recreation, open space, cultural and historical sites, floodplain use, and drinking water supplies. Land suitability data is often overlaid onto land capability data to give a composite perspective of what is the appropriate use for the particular region's capability.

LAND-USE PLAN. The key element of a comprehensive plan; describes the recommended location and intensity of development for public and private land uses such as residential, commercial, industrial, recreational, and agricultural.

LARVA. A sexually immature form of any animal unlike its adult form and requiring changes before reaching the basic adult form.

LATITUDE. Angular measurement in degrees north or south of the equator. Lines denoting latitude are also called parallels. (One minute of arc of meridian is one nautical mile.)

LAW OF DIMINISHING RETURNS. When other factors in production do not change, successive increases in the input of one factor will not yield proportionate increases in product; for example, fertilizer can be used so heavily that additional applications will give little or no increase in yield.

LAW OF SUPPLY AND DEMAND. The quantity of a commodity that will be produced or offered for sale (supply) varies directly with the price. The quantity of a commodity that potential buyers are willing to take (demand) varies inversely with the price. The greater the amount of a given product offered for sale on a given market at a given time, the lower the price per unit at which the entire amount can be sold.

LC_{50}. Amount of pesticide in water or air required to kill 50 percent of a test animal population in a 24-hour period. Usually expressed in parts per million (ppm) or micrograms per liter.

LD$_{50}$. Amount of pesticide taken orally or dermally required to kill (lethal dose) 50 percent of a test animal population. Usually expressed in milligrams of pesticide per kilogram of body weight of the test animal.

LEACHATES. Liquids that have percolated through a soil and that contain substances in solution or suspension.

LIME. From the strictly chemical standpoint, refers to only one compound, calcium oxide (CaO); however, the term is commonly used in agriculture to include a great variety of materials that are usually composed of the oxide, hydroxide, or carbonate of calcium or of calcium and magnesium; used to furnish calcium and magnesium as essential elements for the growth of plants and to neutralize soil acidity. The most commonly used forms of agricultural lime are ground limestone (carbonates), hydrated lime (hydroxides), burnt lime (oxides), marl, and oyster shells.

LIMITING FACTOR. A factor whose absence, or excessive concentration, exerts some restraining influence upon a population through incompatibility with species requirements or tolerance.

LIMNOLOGY. The study of freshwater bodies, physically, biologically, and chemically.

LITTER. 1. In forestry, a surface layer of loose organic debris in forests, consisting of freshly fallen or slightly decomposed organic materials. 2. In waste, that highly visible portion of solid waste that is generated by the consumer and is carelessly discarded outside of the regular disposal systems; accounts for about 2 percent of the total solid waste volume.

LONGITUDE. The angle at the pole between the meridian of the place and some standard meridian. For American maps, the standard meridian is the one passing through Greenwich, England.

MACROORGANISMS. These organisms retained on a U.S. standard sieve no. 30 (openings of 0.589 mm); those organisms visible to the unaided eye.

MAP, TOPOGRAPHIC. A representation of the physical features of a portion of the Earth's surface as a plane surface, on which terrain relief is shown by a system of lines, each representing a constant elevation above a datum or reference plane.

MARSH. A periodically wet or continually flooded area where the surface is not deeply submerged; covered dominantly with sedges, cattails, rushes, or other hydrophytic plants. Subclasses include freshwater and saltwater marshes.

MARSH, TIDAL. A low, flat area traversed by interlacing channels and tidal sloughs and periodically inundated by high tides; vegetation usually consists of salt-tolerant plants.

MASTER PLAN. A comprehensive document, optimally based upon land capability and land suitability analyses, including a map which serves the community as a guide to land use. It is used to guide planners in preparing zoning and subdivision ordinances, and in enforcing those ordinances with appropriate tools, such as easements, permit programs, critical areas designation, performance studies, and others.

MEGA-. A prefix meaning 1 million.

MEROLOGICAL APPROACH. As opposed to the "black box" approach, a method which attempts to investigate an ecosystem as individual units making up the whole system.

MESO-. A prefix referring to or of the middle.

METABOLISM. The sum of all chemical processes occurring within an organism; includes both synthesis (anabolism) and breakdown (catabolism) of organic compounds.

METHANE (CH_4). An odorless, colorless, and asphyxiating gas that can explode under certain circumstances; can be produced by solid waste undergoing anaerobic decomposition.

MICRO-. A prefix meaning 1/1,000,000, abbreviated by the Greek letter   .

MICROORGANISMS. Those organisms retained on a U.S. standard sieve no. 100 (openings of 0.149 mm); those minute organisms invisible or only barely visible to the unaided eye.

MILLI-. A prefix meaning 1/1,000.

MORAINE. An accumulation of drift, with an initial topographic expression of its own, built within a glaciated region chiefly by the direct action of glacial ice. Examples are ground, lateral, recessional, and terminal moraines.

MULCH. A natural or artificial layer of plant residue or other materials, such as sand or paper, on the soil surface.

MULTIPLE USE. Harmonious use of land for more than one purpose; i.e., grazing of livestock, wildlife production, recreation, watershed and timber production. Not necessarily the combination of uses that will yield the highest economic return or greatest unit output.

NATIONAL FOREST. A federal reservation, generally forest, range, or wildland, which is administered by the Forest Service, U.S. Department of Agriculture, under a program of multiple use and sustained yield for timber production, range, wildlife, watershed, and outdoor recreation purposes.

NATIONAL MONUMENT. An area owned by the federal government and administered by the National Park Service, U.S. Department of Interior, for the purpose of preserving and making available to the public a resource of archaeological, scientific, or aesthetic interest.

NATIONAL PARK.   An area of unusual scenic or historic interest owned by the federal government and administered by the National Park Service, U.S. Department of the Interior, to conserve the scenery, the flora, and any natural and historical objects within its boundaries for public enjoyment in perpetuity.

NATURAL AREA.   1. A site or area in its natural state, undisturbed by man's activities.   2. An area set aside indefinitely to preserve a representative unit of a major forest, range, or wetland type primarily for the purposes of science, research, or education.

NATURAL GAS.   A light hydrocarbon mixture, mostly methane, CH_4, and ethane, C_2H_6, but also propane, C_3H_8, and butane, C_4H_{10}.   Natural Gas is usually found in association with petroleum, but trapped in impervious rock above the petroleum, and probably derived from it.

NATURAL RESOURCES.   Naturally occurring resources needed by an organism, population, or ecosystem, which, by their increasing availability up to an optimal or sufficient level, allow an increasing rate of energy conversion.

NEKTON.   Those aquatic animals able to swim efficiently, and not mainly at the mercy of currents.

NICHE.   An organism's habitat and functional role in the community.

NITROGEN CYCLE.   The sequence of biochemical changes undergone by nitrogen, wherein it is used by a living organism, liberated upon the death and decomposition of the organism, and converted to its original state of oxidation.

NITROGEN FIXATION.   The conversion of elemental nitrogen (N_2) to organic combinations or to forms readily useable in biological processes.

NOISE POLLUTION.   The persistent intrusion of noise into the environment at a level that may be injurious to human health.

NONPOINT POLLUTION.   Pollution whose sources cannot be pinpointed; can best be controlled by proper soil, water, and land management practices. See pollution, point source.

NUTRIENTS.   1. Elements, or compounds, essential as raw materials for organism growth and development, such as carbon, oxygen, nitrogen, phosphorus, etc.   2. The dissolved solids and gases of the water of an area.

OLIGOTROPHIC LAKES.   Deep lakes that have a low supply of nutrients; thus they support very little organic production.   Dissolved oxygen is present at or near saturation throughout the lake during all seasons of the year.

ONCOGENIC.   A substance that causes tumor formations.

OPEN SPACE. A relatively undeveloped green or wooded area provided usually within an urban development to minimize feelings of congested living.

ORGANIC FERTILIZER. By-product from the processing of animals or vegetable substances that contain sufficient plant nutrients to be of value as fertilizers.

ORGANIC GARDENING. A system of farming or home gardening that utilizes organic wastes and composts to the exclusion of chemical fertilizers.

ORGANIC PHOSPHORUS INSECTICIDE. A synthetic compound derived from phosphoric acid. Organic phosphorus insecticides are primarily contact killers with relatively short-lived effects. They are decomposed by water, pH extremes, high temperature, and microorganisms. Examples are malathion, parathion, diazinon, phorate, TEPP, dimethoate, and fenthion.

ORGANIC SOIL. A soil that contains a high percentage (greater than 20 or 30 percent) of organic matter throughout the solum.

ORGANISM. Any living thing.

OSMOSIS. The tendency of a fluid to pass through a semipermeable membrane, as the wall of a living cell, into a solution of higher concentration, so as to equalize concentrations on both sides of the membrane.

OUTFALL. Point where water flows from a conduit, stream, or drain.

OVERTURN. The period of mixing (turnover), by top to bottom circulation, of previously stratified water masses. This phenomenon may occur in spring and/or fall; the result is a uniformity of physical and chemical properties of the water at all depths.

OXIDANT. The ability of some oxygen-containing compounds to oxidize other compounds. Specific examples include ozone, peroxyacetyl nitrates, and nitrogen dioxide.

OXIDATION. Combination with oxygen; addition of oxygen or other atom or group; removal of hydrogen or other atom or group.

OXYGEN SAG. The temporary decrease in oxygen concentration due to reduced photosynthesis or increased oxygen demand.

OZONE (O_3). A pungent, colorless, toxic gas; one component of photochemical smog.

PARASITE. An organism that lives on or in a host organism during all or part of its existence. Nourishment is obtained at the expense of the host.

PARTICULATES. Finely divided solid or liquid particles in the air or in an emission. Particulates include dust, smoke, fumes, mist, spray, and fog.

PATHOGEN. An organism capable of producing disease.

PEAT. Unconsolidated soil material consisting largely of undecomposed or only slightly decomposed organic matter accumulated under conditions of excessive moisture.

PERCOLATION TEST. A measurement of the percolation of water in soil to determine the suitability of different soils for development including private sewage systems such as septic tanks and drainfields.

PERMIT PROGRAMS. Land may not be used for a different purpose without a permit. The application for permit then requires a description of the proposed action, its purpose, and a detailed analysis of the environmental, and/or energy impact. The Permit Program is used to control wetlands, or discharge of pollutants into navigable waters, or encroachment upon stream banks, for example.

PESTICIDE. Any chemical agent used for control of specific organisms; such as insecticides, herbicides, fungicides, etc.

PETROLEUM. A heavy hydrocarbon mixture ranging from heptane, C_7H_{16}, and decane, $C_{10}H_{22}$, in gasoline to compounds with up to forty carbon atoms. Probably petroleum is formed from the decaying mixture of plants and animals which become modified by chemical reactions promoted through pressure and heat created by overlying rock and soil.

pH. A numerical measure of acidity or hydrogen ion activity. Neutral is pH 7.0. All pH values below 7.0 are acid, and all above 7.0 are alkaline.

PHASED DEVELOPMENT ORDINANCES. These provisions set the timing of future growth as well as the location and type of growth allowed. They often tie in closely with Capital Budgeting.

PHOTOCHEMICAL PROCESS. The chemical changes brought about by the radiant energy of the sun acting upon various polluting substances. The products are known as photochemical smog.

PHOTOCHEMICAL SMOG. A combination of photochemical gases, liquids, and particles in a polluted atmosphere.

PHOTOPERIOD. Refers to the number of hours of light or darkness in the day.

PHOTOSYNTHESIS. The manufacture of carbohydrates from carbon dioxide and water in the presence of chlorophyll using sunlight as an energy source.

PHYTOPLANKTON. Unattached microscopic plants of plankton, subject to movement by wave or current action.

PLANKTON. Those organisms passively drifting or weakly swimming in marine or freshwater.

PLANKTON BLOOM. A sudden rapid increase (usually geometric) to an enormous number of individual plankters under certain conditions.

PLANKTON NET. A cloth net, usually coneshaped, used to collect plankton. Plankters separated from water by means of a net are generally referred to as net plankton and represent only a fraction of the total population.

PLANNED UNIT DEVELOPMENT. A special zone in some zoning ordinances which permits a unit of land under control of a single developer to be used for a variety of uses and densities, subject to review and approval by the local governing body. The location of the zone is usually decided on a case-by-case basis. Density regulations apply to the project as a whole rather than to each individual lot. A single development could unify residential, commercial, institutional, and recreational functions in a single neighborhood. Abbr. PUD.

PLASTICS. Man-made materials containing primarily carbon and hydrogen, with lesser amounts of oxygen, nitrogen, and various organic and inorganic compounds. Plastics, technically referred to as "polymers" are normally solid in their finished state, but at some stage in their manufacture, under sufficient heat and pressure, they will flow sufficiently to be molded into desired shape. Thermoplastics, such as polyethylene, polyvinyl chloride (PVC), polystyrene, and polyropylene, become soft when exposed to heat and pressure and harden when cooled. Thermosetting plastics, such as phenotic and polyester, are set to permanent shapes when heat and pressure are applied to them during forming, and reheating will not soften these materials.

PLAT. A plan or map showing land lines or subdivisions usually with few, if any, other features.

POINT SOURCE (POLLUTION). A stationary source of pollution, such as a smoke stack or discharge pipe.

POLLUTION. The condition caused by the presence in the environment of substances of such character and in such quantities that the quality of the environment is impaired or rendered offensive to life.

POTENTIAL ENERGY. Potential energy is the capacity to do work that a body possesses because of its position or condition. For example, water behind a dam has potential energy because of its height above sea level and because of the force exerted upon it by gravity.

POWER. Power is the amount of energy expended. See also, ENERGY.

ppm (PARTS PER MILLION). One pound in 500 tons; one ounce in 8,000 gallons; one inch in 16 miles.

PRECIPITATION. A general term for all forms of falling moisture, including rain, snow, hail, sleet.

PRECIPITATORS. Devices using mechanical, chemical, or electrical means for collecting particulates.

PRE-EMPTIVE PURCHASE. In order to block development of a large area, ordinances permit the local government to purchase key parcels of smaller ones. The goal is to hold access routes so that development of the larger area is discouraged.

PREFERENTIAL TAX ASSESSMENT. Taxing authorities may assess land differentially by use rather than by location. To illustrate, farmland within an urban area could be taxed at a lower rate than commercial land immediately contiguous.

PRIMARY WASTE TREATMENT. The first stage in wastewater treatment in which substantially all floating or settleable solids are mechanically removed by screening and sedimentation.

PRODUCER (BIOLOGY). An organism that can use radiant energy to synthesize organic substances from inorganic materials.

PULMONARY EMPHYSEMA. An anatomic change in the lungs characterized by a breakdown of the walls of the alveoli, which can become enlarged, lose their resilience, and disintegrate.

PYROLYSIS. The process of chemically decomposing an organic substance by heating it in an oxygen-deficient atmosphere. High heat is usually applied to the material in a closed chamber, evaporating all moisture and breaking down materials into various hydrocarbon gases and carbon-like residue. The gases may be collected with suitable equipment and used or sold. The residue may be further processed into useful materials, such as carbon, sand, and grit, or can be used as landfill.

Quad. A measure of energy quantity, a Quad is 10^{15} British thermal units. A British thermal unit, Btu, is the amount of energy needed to elevate the temperature of a pound of water by one degree Fahrenheit.

RANGE. 1. Rangeland; and many forestlands that support an understory or periodic cover of herbaceous or shrubby plants suitable for grazing without impairing other forest values. 2. In biology, the geographic area occupied by an organism.

REACTION, SOIL. The degree of acidity or alkalinity of a soil, usually expressed as a pH value. Descriptive terms commonly associated with certain ranges in pH are extremely acid, less than 4.5; very strongly acid, 4.5-5.0; strongly acid, 5.1-5.5; medium acid, 5.6-6.0; slightly acid, 6.1-6.5; neutral, 6.6-7.3; mildly alkaline, 7.4-7.8; moderately alkaline, 7.9-8.4; strongly alkaline, 8.5-9.0; and very strongly alkaline, more than 9.0.

REDUCERS. Organisms, usually bacteria or fungi, that break down complex organic material into simpler compounds, also called decomposers.

REFUGE, WILDLIFE. An area designated for the protection of wild animals, within which hunting and fishing is either prohibited or strictly controlled.

RESPIRATION. The complex series of chemical and physical reactions in all living organisms by which the energy and nutrients in foods are made available for use. Oxygen is used and carbon dioxide released during the process.

REVIEWS. Public reviews are ordinarily required by federal and state governmetns to ensure that any project reflects the knowledge and interest of citizens who are influenced by and may contribute to the project. The environmental impact statement and the A-95 are the principal federal review programs.

RINGELMANN CHART. A series of charts, numbered 0 through 5, that equate smoke densities, 0 being clear and 5 completely opaque. They are occasionally used for measuring opacity of smoke from stacks and in setting emission standards.

RIPARIAN RIGHTS. The rights of an owner whose land abuts water. They differ from state to state and often depend on whether the water is a river, lake, or ocean.

RIVER BASIN. A major water resource region. The U.S. has been divided in 20 river basin areas.

RUNOFF (HYDRAULICS). That portion of the precipitation on a drainage area that is discharged from the area in stream channels. Types include surface runoff, groundwater runoff, or seepage.

SAND. 1. A soil particle between 0.05 and 2.0 millimeters in diameter. 2. Any one of five soil separates: very coarse sand, coarse sand, medium sand, fine sand, and very fine sand. 3. A soil textural class.

SANITARY LANDFILL. A site on which solid wastes are disposed of in a manner that protects the environment; wastes are spread in thin layers, compacted to the smallest practical volume, and covered with soil by the end of each working day. Various methods include:
Area - Wastes are spread and compacted on the surface of the ground and cover material is spread and compacted over the top.
Quarry - Wastes are spread and compacted in a depression; cover material is generally obtained elsewhere.
Ramp - A variation of the area and quarry method in that the cover material is obtained by excavating in front of the working face. A variation of this method is known as the progressive slope method.
Trench - A method in which the waste is spread and compacted over the waste to form the basic cell structure.
Wet area - A method used in swampy areas where precautions are taken to avoid water pollution before proceeding with the area landfill technique.

SAPROBIC. Living on dead or decaying organic matter.

SCAVENGER. An animal that eats animal wastes and the dead bodies of animals not killed by itself.

SCENIC EASEMENT. An easement restricting development in order to protect roadside views and natural features.

SCRUBBER. A device that uses a liquid filter to remove gaseous and liquid pollutants from an air stream.

SECCHI DISK. A device used to measure visibility depths in water. The upper surface of a circular metal plate, 20 centimeters in diameter, is divided into four quadrants and so painted that two quadrants directly opposite each other are black and the intervening ones white. When suspended to various depths of water by means of a graduated line, its point of disappearance indicates the limit of visibility.

SECONDARY WASTE TREATMENT. The removal of up to 90 percent of the organic material from sewage by the metabolic action of bacteria.

SEDIMENT. Solid material, both mineral and organic, that is in suspension, is being transported, or has been moved from its site of origin by air, water, gravity, or ice and has come to rest on the earth's surface either above or below sea level.

SEICHE. Periodic oscillations in the water level of a lake or inland sea that occur with temporary local depressions or elevations of the water level.

SEPTIC TANK. An underground tank used for the deposition of domestic wastes. Bacteria in the wastes decompose the organic matter, and the sludge settles to the bottom. The effluent flows through drains into the ground. Sludge is pumped out at regular intervals.

SETTLEABLE SOLIDS. Solids in a liquid that can be removed by stilling the liquid.

SETTLING BASIN. An enlargement in the channel of a stream to permit the settling of debris carried in suspension.

SEWAGE. The total organic waste and wastewater generated by residential and commercial establishments.

SEWAGE SLUDGE. Settled sewage solids combined with varying amounts of water and dissolved materials that is removed from sewage by screening, sedimentation, chemical precipitation, or bacterial digestion.

SHALE OIL. Oil is trapped between layers of shale, an impermeable rock through which liquids and gases cannot penetrate. The amount of petroleum between layers is small; therefore, much rock must be gathered, processed, and discarded to harvest significant quantities of oil. The process requires great quantities of water, thus imposing a secondary use of natural resources with potential for water table reduction and surface water contamination.

SITE PLAN REVIEW. A report of narrower focus than the land capability analysis. The review includes environmental impact statements, cost/benefit analysis, and energy impact analysis. The review helps planners to select precise enforcement tools to govern appropriate and desired land use assignments.

SLOPE. The degree of deviation of a surface from horizontal, measured in a numerical ratio, percent, or degrees. Expressed as a ratio or percentage, the first number is the vertical distance (rise) and the second is the horizontal distance (run), as 2:1 or 200 percent. Expressed in degrees, it is the angle of the slope from the horizontal plane with a 90° slope being vertical (maximum) and 45° being a 1:1 slope.

SLOPE CHARACTERISTICS. Slopes may be characterized as concave (decrease in steepness in lower portion), uniform, or convex (increase in steepness at base). Erosion is strongly affected by shape, ranked in order of increasing erodibility from concave to uniform to convex.

SLUDGE. A semi-fluid mixture of fine solid particles with a liquid.

SMOG. A polluted atmosphere in which products of combustion such as hydrocarbons, soot, sulfur compounds, etc., occur in detrimental concentrations for human beings and other organisms, especially during foggy weather.

SMOKE. Liquid or solid particles under one micron in diameter.

SOIL. 1. The unconsolidated mineral and organic material on the immediate surface of the earth that serves as a natural medium for the growth of land plants. 2. The unconsolidated mineral matter on the surface of the earth that has been subjected to and influenced by genetic and environmental factors of parent material, climate (including moisture and temperature effects), macro- and micro-organisms, and topography, all acting over a period of time and producing a product--soil--that differs from the material from which it is derived in many physical, chemical, biological, and morphological properties and characteristics.

SOIL CONSERVATION COMMITTEE, COMMISSION, OR BOARD. The state agency established by state soil conservation district enabling legislation to assist with the administration of the provisions of the state soil conservation districts law. The official title may vary from the above as new or amended state laws are made.

SOIL MAP. A map showing the distribution of soil types or other soil mapping units in relation to the prominent physical and cultural features of the Earth's surface. The following kinds of soil maps are recognized in the U.S.: detailed, detailed reconnaissance, reconnaissance, generalized, and schematic.

SOLAR ENERGY. Light energy of many frequencies emanates from the Sun. Certain frequencies are captured by the cytochromes, light sensitive chemicals, in plant cells which use light in chemical reactions to do other work. Other solar energy effects are evaporation, major air currents, and melting ice. Manufactured photo-voltaic cells can convert solar frequencies into electricity which then can be consumed or stored in batteries as chemical energy.

SOLID WASTE. Useless, unwanted, or discarded material with insufficient liquid content to be free flowing. Types include:
>   <u>Agricultural</u> - The solid waste that results from the rearing and slaughtering of animals and the processing of animal products and orchard and field crops.
>   <u>Commercial</u> - Solid waste generated by stores, offices, and other activities that do not actually turn out a product.
>   <u>Industrial</u> - Solid waste that results from industrial processes and manufacturing.
>   <u>Institutional</u> - Solid wastes originating from educational, health care, and research facilities.
>   <u>Municipal</u> - Normally, residential and commercial solid waste generated within a community.
>   <u>Pesticide</u> - The residue resulting from the manufacturing, handling, or use of chemicals for killing plant and animal pests.
>   <u>Residential</u> - All solid waste that normally originates in a residential environment. Sometimes called domestic solid waste.

SOLID WASTE MANAGEMENT. The purposeful, systematic control of the generation, storage, collection, transport, separation, processing, recycling, recovery, and disposal of solid wastes.

SPHAEROTILUS. A slime-producing, nonmotile, sheathed, filamentous, attached bacterium usually associated with raw sewerage enrichment.

SPRING OVERTURN. A physical phenomenon that may take place in a body of water during the early spring. The sequence of events leading to spring overturn include: (1) melting of ice cover, (2) warming of surface waters, (3) density changes in surface waters producing convection currents from top to bottom, (4) circulation of the total water volume by wind action, and (5) vertical temperature equality. The overturn results in a uniformity of the physical and chemical properties of the entire water mass.

STACK. An upright pipe that exhausts waste emissions into the atmosphere.

STAND. 1. An aggregation of trees or other growth occupying a specific area and sufficiently uniform in composition (species), age arrangement, and condition to be distinguishable from the forest or other growth on adjoining areas. 2. The number of plants per unit of area other than trees.

STREAM GAGING. The quantitative determination of stream flow using gages, current meters, weirs, or other measuring instruments at selected locations.

STREAM LOAD. Quantity of solid and dissolved material carried by a stream.

STRIPCROPPING. Growing crops in a systematic arrangement of strips or bands which serve as barriers to wind and water erosion.

STRIP MINING. A process in which rock and top soil strata overlying ore or fuel deposits are scraped away by mechanical shovels. Also known as surface mining.

SUBDIVISION. The division or redivision of a lot, tract, or parcel of land into two or more areas either by platting or metes and bounds description.

SUBDIVISION REGULATIONS. An ordinance based on the police power of government to protect the public health, safety, and general welfare. It establishes standards for the subdivision and the development of land, generally including location and width of streets, size and shape of lots, provision of water and sewage disposal facilities, surface water drainage, control of erosion, preservation of floodplains, provision of public land for schools and recreation, and other related items. It does not include land use regulations. It is one of the major methods for implementation of the comprehensive plan.

SUBSISTENCE FARM. A low-income farm where the emphasis is on production for use by the operator and his family.

SUBSOIL. The B horizons of soils with distinct profiles. In soils with weak profile development, the subsoil can be defined as the soil below the plowed soil (or its equivalent of surface soil), in which roots normally grow.

SUBSTRATE. 1. In biology, the base of substance upon which an organism is growing. 2. In chemistry, a substance undergoing oxidation. 3. In hydrology, the bottom material of a waterway.

SUCCESSION. The progressive development of vegetation toward its highest ecological expression, the climax; replacement of one plant community by another.

SULFUR DIOXIDE (SO_2). A heavy pungent, colorless gas formed primarily by combustion of coal, oil, and other sulfur-bearing compounds, but also produced in chemical plants while processing metals and burning trash.

SULFUR OXIDES. Pungent, colorless gases formed primarily by the combustion of fossil fuels; considered major air pollutants; sulfur oxides may damage the respiratory tract as well as vegetation.

SUMMER KILL. Complete or partial kill of a fish population in ponds or lakes during the warm months; variously produced by excessively warm water, by a depletion of dissolved oxygen, and by the release of toxic substances from a decaying algal bloom, or by a combination of these factors.

SURBER STREAM BOTTOM SAMPLER. A compact, lightweight, portable, quantitative bottom sampler especially suitable for sampling organisms from the stone or gravel bottoms of shallow streams possessing a strong current.

SUSPENDED SOLID. Any solid substance present in water in an undissolved state, usually contributing directly to turbidity.

SYNERGISM. Total effect of all interactants when acting together is greater than the sum of interactants acting individually.

SYSTEMIC PESTICIDE. A pesticide that is absorbed by treated plants or animals and translocated via their circulatory systems to most tissues.

TAILINGS. In mining, second grade or waste material derived when raw material is screened or processed.

TAKING ISSUE. A court position on the conflict between land use regulations that benefit the public while they simultaneously deprive a private individual of property without just compensation.

TAXONOMY. 1. The science of classification; laws and principles governing the classifying of objects. 2. Classification, especially of animals and plants, into taxonomic units, such as species, genus, family, and order.

TERTIARY WASTE TREATMENT. Wastewater treatment beyond the secondary or biological stage that includes removal of nutrients such as phosphorus and nitrogen, and a high percentage of suspended solids; also known as advanced waste treatment.

THERMAL POLLUTION. A term describing the act of changing the natural temperatures of bodies of water by dumping warmer water into them.

THERMOCLINE. The transition zone between the warm epilimnion and cold hypolimnion of stratified bodies of water; temperature change equals or exceeds $1^{\circ}C$ for each meter of depth.

TIDAL MARSH. Low, flat marshlands traversed by interlaced channels and tidal sloughs and subject to tidal inundation; normally, the only vegetation present is salt-tolerant bushes and grasses.

TITRATION. The determination of the volume of a solution needed to react with a known volume of sample, usually involving the progressive addition of the solution to the sample until the sample has reacted fully.

TOPOGRAPHY. The relative positions and elevations of the natural or man-made features of an area that describe the configuration of its surface.

TOPSOIL. 1. Earthy material used as top-dressing for house lots, grounds for large buildings, gardens, road cuts, or similar areas. It has favorable characteristics for production of desired kinds of vegetation or can be made favorable. 2. The surface plow layer of a soil; also called surface soil. 3. The original or present dark-colored upper soil that ranges from a mere fraction of an inch to two or three feet thick on different kinds of soil.

TOTAL COLIFORM. The gram negative bacteria that are normal inhabitants of fecal discharges. The total coliform group is recognized in the drinking water standards of public health criteria.

TOTAL HARDNESS. The total dissolved salts in water expressed as total parts of dissolved salts in a million parts of water.

TOXICANT. A substance that through its chemical or physical action, kills, injures, or impairs an organism; any environmental factor which, when altered, produces a harmful biological effect.

TOXICITY. Quality, state, or degree of the harmful effect resulting from alteration of an environment factor.

TRANSECT. A cross section of an area used as a sample for recording, mapping, or studying vegetation and its use.

TRANSFER OF DEVELOPMENT RIGHTS. A "right" is an assigned dollar value to a unit of land. All units within a region have the same dollar value. There are a fixed number of rights in a region. To prohibit development in one area and shift it to another, rights must be bought from the owner of the former and sold to the owner of the latter. Thus, there is equitable distribution of dollars but deliberately unequal use of land.

TRANSPIRATION. The photosynthetic and physiological process by which plants release water into the air in the form of water vapor.

TREATMENT TANK. A water-tight tank designed to retain sewage long enough for satisfactory decomposition of the solids to take place; septic tanks and aerobic sewage treatment tanks.

TRIBUTARY. - Secondary or branch of a stream, drain, or other channel that contributes flow to the primary or main channel.

TROPHIC. Relating to the processes of energy and nutrient transfer from one or more organisms to others in an ecosystem.

TROPHIC LEVEL. The level in a nutritive series of an ecosystem in which a group of organisms in a certain stage in the food chain secures food in the same general manner. The first or lowest trophic level consists of producers (green plants); the second level of herbivores; the third level of secondary carnivores; and the last level of reducers.

TURBIDITY. 1. The cloudy condition caused by suspended solids in a liquid. 2. A measurement of the suspended solids in a liquid. 3. Conditions in the atmosphere that reduce its transparency to radiation.

UNIVERSAL SOIL LOSS EQUATION. An equation used to design water erosion control systems: A = RKLSPC wherein A is average annual soil loss in tons per acre per year; R is the rainfall factor; K is the soil erodibility factor; L is the length of slope; S is the percent slope; P is the conservation practice factor; and C is the cropping and management factor. (T = soil loss tolerance value that has been assigned each soil, expressed in tons per acre per year).

VALENCE. That property of an element that is measured in terms of the number of gram atoms of hydrogen that one gram atom of that element will combine with or displace; for example, the valence of oxygen in water, H_2O, is 2; the valence of hydrogen is one.

VARIANCE. 1. In pollution, permission granted by regulatory agencies to pollute for a limited period of time, usually while corrective measures are being taken. 2. In zoning, permission granted by zoning boards for departure from standards of the zoning ordinance.

WASTE TREATMENT. Any of the physical or chemical processes whereby the qualities of given waste are made more compatible or acceptable to man and his environment.

WASTEWATER. Water that carries wastes from homes, businesses, and industries; a mixture of water and dissolved or suspended solids.

WATER POLLUTION. The addition of harmful or objectionable material to water in concentrations or sufficient quantities to adversely affect its usefulness or quality.

WATER QUALITY CRITERIA. A scientific requirement on which a decision or judgement may be based concerning the suitability of water quality to support a designated use.

WATER QUALITY STANDARDS. Minimum requirements of purity of water for various uses; for example, water for agricultural use in irrigation systems should not exceed specific levels of sodium bicarbonates, pH, total dissolved salts, etc.

WATER RIGHTS. The legal rights to the use of water. They consist of riparian rights and those acquired by appropriation and prescription. Riparian rights are those rights to use and control water by virtue of ownership of the bank or banks. Appropriated rights are those acquired by an individual to the exclusive use of water, based strictly on priority appropriation and application of the water to beneficial use and without limitation of the place of use to riparian land. Prescribed rights are those to which legal title is acquired by long possession and use without protest of other parties.

WATER RIGHTS, CORRELATIVE DOCTRINE. When a source of water does not provide enough for all users, the water is reapportioned proportionately on the basis of prior water rights held by each user.

WATERSHED AREA. All land and water within the confines of a drainage divide or a water problem area consisting in whole or in part of land needing drainage or irrigation.

WATERSHED MANAGEMENT. Use, regulation, and treatment of water and land resources of a watershed to accomplish stated objectives.

WATER TABLE. The upper surface of groundwater or that level below which the soil is saturated with water; locus of points in soil water at which the hydraulic pressure is equal to atmospheric pressure.

WET DIGESTION. A solid waste stabilization process in which mixed solid organic wastes are placed in an open digestion pond to decompose anaerobically.

WET SCRUBBER. An air cleaning device that literally washes out the dust. Exhaust air is forced into a spray chamber, where fine water particles cause the dust to drop from the air stream. The dust-laden water is then treated to remove the solid material and is often recirculated.

WIND EROSION EQUATION. An equation used for the design of wind erosion control systems; $E = f(IKCLV)$ wherein E is the average annual soil loss, expressed in tons per acre per year; I is the soil erodibility; K is the soil ridge roughness; C is the climatic factor; L is the un-sheltered distance across the field along the wind erosion direction; and V is the vegetative cover.

WORK. Work is the transfer of energy through a force "F," acting upon and displacing a given body a given distance, D: Work = F x D. See also, ENERGY.

ZONING. A legal device, an ordinance based on the police power of government to protect the public health, safety, and general welfare. It may regulate the type of use and intensity of development of land and structures to the extent necessary for a public purpose. Requirements may vary among various geographically defined areas called zones. Regulations generally cover such items as height and bulk of buildings, density of dwelling units, off-street parking, control of signs, and use of land for residential, commercial, industrial, or agricultural purposes. A zoning ordinance is one of the major methods for implementation of the comprehensive plan.

ZOOPLANKTON. Unattached microscopic animals of plankton having minimal capability for locomotion.

Index

INDEX

A-95 review, 259-60
Actinomycetes, in soil, 85
Activated carbon, in water treatment, 142-43
Aeration, in water treatment, 143, 143
Air. See also Air pollution
  continental, 43
  inversions, 47-8
  maritime, 43
  masses, 43-5
  polar, 43
  pressure, 45
  tropical, 43
Air inversion, 47-8
Air pollution
  abatement and control, 69
  by aerosols, 64
  by asbestos, 67-8
  by beryllium, 67-8
  by carbon monoxide, 65-6
  by carbon soot, 67
  by fluorides, 67
  forms of pollution, 62
  by heavy metals, 67
  by lead, 67
  major sources of, 62
  by mercury, 67-8
  miscellaneous, 67-9
  by nitrogen dioxide, 65
  particulates, 63
  pesticides, 68
  photochemical oxidants, 67-8
  standards, 64
  by sulfur dioxide, 63
  by tobacco smoke, 68
  urban, 54-7
Air pollution abatement and control, 69-73
  baghouses, 71
  cyclone collectors, 70-1
  electrostatic precipitators, 71-3
  legislation. See individual Acts;
  scrubbers, 72-4
Air Pollution Index, 57
Airsheds, 52-8
  fluorine, 54

  flourocarbons in. 53-4
  inversions and, 55
  ozone layer's affect on, 53-4
  in urban areas, 54-7
Areawide Planning Agencies, 241-2
Asbestos
  in air, 67
  influences on human health, 178-9
  in water, 68
Atomic Energy Act of 1954, 109
Atomic Energy Commission, 69
Atmosphere
  airsheds and, 52
  composition of, 40
  ionosphere of, 40
  jet stream, 40
  ozone in, 53
  stratosphere of, 40
  troposphere of, 40
  winds in, 40-3
Bacteria
  coliforms, 121
  disease-causing, 191
  fecal coliform, 121-2
  as indicator organisms, 121-3
  in soil, 85
  total coliform, 121-2
Barometric pressure, 45
Bioaccumulation, 126
Biochemical oxygen demand (BOD)
  from combined sewers, 145-6
  measurement of, 118
  in relation to dissolved oxygen, 113-20
Biomass conversion, 213-14
  anaerobic digesters, 214
  incinerators, 214
  pyrolysis, 214
Birth defects
  teratogens, 188
  thalidomide, 188
Bishop's Ring, 52
Bureau of Land Management, 103
Cancer, 185-8
  and aflatoxins, 188
  carcinogens, 185-8
  environmental causes of, 185-8

315

Life in a Multi-Cultural Society:
Egypt from Cambyses to Constantine and Beyond

Studies in Ancient Oriental Civilization • Volume 51

ERRATA SHEET

Chapter 7: "A Cult Function for the So-Called Faiyum Mummy Portraits?" by Lorelei H. Corcoran

1) The final two lines (following the word "between") are missing from the second paragraph on page 57:

> the use of a triptych of panel portraits in a domestic context and the veneration of Roman ancestor busts.

2) Footnote # 3, page 57 is missing:

> 3. See also his comments (1982, pp. 24–27) on "other paintings" that he describes as being produced for veneration or commemoration.

Chapter 9: "The *Kbn.wt* Vessels of the Late Period" by John Coleman Darnell

1) The final four lines of page 69 are repeated at the top of page 70.
2) The middle portion of the sentence which straddles pages 70–71 has been deleted, and footnote 12 is missing; the sentence in full, with the footnotes, is:

> The rushed operations of Antigonos occurred in November,[12] Antigonos attempting to take advantage of the height of the Nile and press on to Memphis with his fleet.[13]
>
> 12. According to Seibert 1969, p. 221, Antigonos left Egypt at the end of November.
>
> 13. D. Bonneau (1964, pp. 77-8) misunderstood Antigonos' strategy, and assumed that the inundation prevented the naval operations of Demetrios. These were hampered by Ptolemy and his small vessels. The operations which the officers decline to carry out due to the inundation (Diodorus XX.76, cited by Bonneau, p. 78 note 1) are land operations, proposed as a last hope of invasion after the failure of the primary, naval plan.

Chapter 34: "Implicit Models of Cross-Cultural Interaction: A Question of Noses, Soap, and Prejudice" by Robert K. Ritner

1) Page 287 should be as follows (*Please see the reverse*):

"Cultures in Conflict," yet the question of cultural animosity was ignored by all speakers.[16] Old concepts of cultural synthesis or subjugation are giving way to theories of cultural separation.[17] While this separation should perhaps please everyone, allowing Greek and Egyptian culture to be "vital" independently, I fear that it can be taken too far, and am suspicious of the underlying motives in *overstressing* the absence of interaction, and wonder whether cultural "vitality" is again confused with cultural "purity."

Consider the 1989 discussion by Heinrich von Staden on the question of the influence of Egyptian medicine on the Alexandrian physician Hierophilus.[18] Von Staden admits certain similarities in terms of pulse taking, drugs, and disease theory, but his arguments are often carried by adjectives, not evidence: Egyptian pulse theory is dismissed as "struggling but insistent,"[19] Egyptian disease theory is "not alien" to the Greek (von Staden 1989, p. 5), the Egyptian physician's touch is "aggressive," the Greek's is "restrained" (von Staden 1989, p. 15). Egyptian enema treatments are said to represent "a pathological preoccupation with the anus ... bound to elicit an ethno-psychological study of Pharaonic Egypt sooner or later" (!!!)[20] It should be added that one Egyptian enema specialist is known to have had enough Greek patients to require the services of a well-paid interpreter; here at least there is cross-cultural preoccupation![21] Having accused the Egyptians of neurotic cleanliness,[22] von Staden then faults them as dirty, for not knowing soap (von Staden 1989, p. 15). Soap, as we know it, was invented in 1787 by the French surgeon Nicolas Leblanc, prompted by an earlier offer of a state prize by Louis XVI.[23] Until then, "soap" had been imported from the Arabs, and had consisted of fats *and natron from the Wadi Natrun*. This was the "soap" that had been available to the Greeks — and before them to the Egyptians. Von Staden's arguments show the survival of the old notion of the low class, cultureless Egyptian, whose influence on superior culture is *unthinkable*.

Old feelings of cultural superiority die hard, but what is important is that such prejudices are often the feelings of *scholars*, not those of the people they study. A good case in point is the famous quotation of Polybius on the Alexandrian population as excerpted by Strabo (XXIV. 14). According to Polybius, the mercenary troops are numerous, rough, and uncivilized, the Alexandrians are mongrels, but the native Egyptians are acute and civilized (οχυ και πολιτικον). This favorable characterization of the Egyptians has generally confounded Classicists, whose models of Egyptian culture were determined by contemporary stereotypes of natives as cultureless, rude, second-class citizens.

---

16. "Ptolemaic Egypt: Cultures in Conflict" held December 2–3, 1988 at the Brooklyn Museum. Lecturers instead emphasized cooperation and cross-influence between cultures. A direct question posed by this author regarding the validity of the notion of "cultures in conflict" generated complete disavowal.

17. See A. Samuel 1989, passim; idem 1983, especially pp. 105–17 ; and Bagnall 1988, pp. 21–27.

18. Reviewed by myself 1989, pp. 39–40.

19. Von Staden 1989, p. 10. Egyptian influence here is said to be "not inconceivable."

20. Von Staden 1989, p. 12. This hyperbolic bombast derives from the author's distortion of Egyptian disease theory, which prescribed enemas and emetics for internal complaints in preference to bleeding. A reasoned analysis is found in Steuer 1948 and Steuer and Saunders 1959.

21. Admitted grudgingly in von Staden 1989, p. 26. The author insists that this must be an isolated case in Alexandria since "evidence of this kind is very rare"; in fact, evidence *of any kind* from Alexandria is "very rare" and generalizations about medical interactions are mere speculation. Bagnall 1981, p. 18, attempts to find in this transaction "deeper and darker aspects" of the Greek "exploitative attitude" since it involves mercenary motives. Bagnall is unaware of the theoretical basis of the Egyptian treatment, which is dismissed as "primitive" and "a toy" (in contrast to "Hellenistic science"): "I forbear to offer modern parallels to exotic practices like this becoming fashionable." Smirking remarks aside, the supposed "toy" of suppository and enema treatment remains a basic adjunct to modern medical practice; it is in no sense "exotic." Where, however, is the "Hellenistic science" of bleeding?

22. Von Staden 1989, p. 12: "legendary obsession with personal cleanliness."

23. A good, popular account of the tragi-comic development of modern soap is found in Bodanis 1986, pp. 206–09.

STUDIES IN ANCIENT ORIENTAL CIVILIZATION • No. 51

THE ORIENTAL INSTITUTE OF THE UNIVERSITY OF CHICAGO

THOMAS A. HOLLAND, Editor

Richard M. Schoen, Assistant Editor

LIFE IN A MULTI-CULTURAL SOCIETY: EGYPT FROM CAMBYSES TO CONSTANTINE AND BEYOND

Edited by

JANET H. JOHNSON

THE ORIENTAL INSTITUTE OF THE UNIVERSITY OF CHICAGO

STUDIES IN ANCIENT ORIENTAL CIVILIZATION • No. 51

CHICAGO • ILLINOIS

Library of Congress Catalog Card Number 92-60741

ISBN: 0-918986-84-2

The Oriental Institute, Chicago

© 1992 by The University of Chicago. All rights reserved.

Published 1992. Printed in the United States of America.

Cover Illustration: Facsimile Drawing of the Central Portion of the Rosetta Stone. After Stephen Quirke and Carol Andrews, *The Rosetta Stone, facsimile drawing with Introduction and Translations* (London: The Trustees of the British Museum, 1988).

TABLE OF CONTENTS

LIFE IN A MULTI-CULTURAL SOCIETY: EGYPT FROM CAMBYSES TO CONSTANTINE (AND BEYOND)

in conjunction with the

Fourth International Congress of Demotists

The Oriental Institute, The University of Chicago
September 4–8, 1990

Tuesday, September 4
James Henry Breasted Hall, The Oriental Institute

1:00–1:15 *OPENING REMARKS*
  JANET H. JOHNSON, The Oriental Institute, The University of Chicago
  WELCOME
  WILLIAM M. SUMNER, Director, The Oriental Institute, The University of Chicago

1:15–6:00 *EGYPTIAN SOCIETY FROM CAMBYSES TO CHRISTIANITY*
  Chair: WILLY CLARYSSE, Katholieke Universiteit Leuven

  KARL-THEODOR ZAUZICH, The University of Würzburg*
    Ein Zug nach Nubien unter Amasis

  LISA HEIDORN, The Oriental Institute, The University of Chicago* and § (1991)
    The Persian Claim to Kush in Light of Evidence from Lower Nubia

  H. S. SMITH, University College London*
    Foreigners in the Documents from the Sacred Animal Necropolis at Saqqara,
    an Interim Report

  J. D. RAY, Cambridge University*
    The Jews in Late Period Egypt

BREAK

  JAN QUAEGEBEUR, Katholieke Universiteit Leuven*
    Greco-Egyptian Double Names as a Feature of a Bi-Cultural Society,
    The Case Ψοσνεῦς ὁ καὶ Τριάδελφος

  ROBERT S. BIANCHI, Brooklyn Museum*
    A Group of Seated Male Figures from the Faiyum

  SHARON HERBERT, Kelsey Museum of Archaeology, The University of Michigan
    Excavations at Coptos: Reflections of Ethnicity in the Archaeological Record

  THELMA K. THOMAS, Kelsey Museum of Archaeology, The University of Michigan*
    Greeks or Copts?: Documentary and Other Evidence for Artistic Patronage during the
    Late Roman and Early Byzantine Period at Heracleopolis Magna and Oxyrhynchus

---

* after the name and affiliation of the participant indicates inclusion of the paper in this volume.

§ and a year after the name and affiliation of the participant indicates the publication of the paper elsewhere.
  Please consult the *Bibliography* for the complete reference.

BREAK

MARILINA BETRÒ, The University of Pisa
Aspects of Cultural Interactions in Greco-Roman Egypt: The Medical-Botanic Culture

JOHN DARNELL, The Oriental Institute, The University of Chicago*
Kbn - triremes

DOMINIC MONTSERRAT, University College London§ (1991)
Puberty Rituals in Roman Egypt

ALAN K. BOWMAN, Oxford University
Property, Status, and Ethnicity in Early Roman Egypt

Wednesday, September 5
James Henry Breasted Hall, The Oriental Institute

9:00–12:00   *LITERATURE & LITERACY*
Chair: LUDWIG KOENEN, The University of Michigan

ALESSANDRO ROCCATI, The University of Rome*
Writing Egyptian: Scripts and Speeches at the End of Pharaonic Civilization

DOROTHY THOMPSON, Cambridge University*
Literacy in Ptolemaic Egypt

JAN MERTENS, Katholieke Universiteit Leuven*
Bibliography and Description of Demotic Literary Texts: A Progress Report

W. J. TAIT, University College London*
Demotic Literature and Egyptian Society

BREAK

HEINZ-JOSEF THISSEN, The University of Marburg
*Das demotische Gedicht vom Harfner als Produkt der Begegnung
mit griechischer Literatur*

PETER PICCIONE, The Oriental Institute, The University of Chicago
Did Setne play Senet?

STANLEY BURSTEIN, California State University, Los Angeles*
The Egyptian History of Hecataeus of Abdera

1:30–5:00   *BILINGUAL TEXTS*
Chair: JOHN D. RAY, Cambridge University

RICHARD STEINER, Yeshiva University
Was the Scribe of P. Amherst 63 Bilingual?

BEZALEL PORTEN, Hebrew University*
Aramaic-Demotic Equivalents: Who is the Borrower and Who the Lender?

WILLIAM BRASHEAR, Staatliche Museen, Berlin*
Egyptians and Greeks in an Early Laographia Account (P. Berol. 25161)

ANN ELLIS HANSON, The University of Michigan*
The Agricultural Accounts of Lucius (P. Mich. inv. 880, P. Princ. 3.152)

JAMES MIDGELY, Macquarie University*
P. Macquarie inv. 499: A Bilingual Text from the Macquarie University Collection

BREAK

EMMANUEL TASSIER, Katholieke Universiteit Leuven*
Greek and Demotic School-Exercises

E. VAN'T DACK, Katholieke Universiteit Leuven/Koninklijke Academie van België*
L'armée, microcosme d'un monde multiculturel?

S. HÉRAL, Katholieke Universiteit Leuven/Sorbonne*
  Archives bilingues de nomarques dans les papyrus de Ghôran
LUDWIG KOENEN, The University of Michigan*
  Early Roman Texts from Oxyrhynchus

5:15–7:00   *BYZANTINE EGYPT*
Chair: BEZALEL PORTEN, Hebrew University
  TERRY WILFONG, The Oriental Institute, The University of Chicago§ (1990)
    The Archive of a Family of Moneylenders at Jême
  JAMES KEENAN, Loyola University, Chicago§ (1990)
    Evidence for the Byzantine Army in the Syene Papyri
  J. JOEL FARBER, Franklin & Marshall College§ (1990)
    Legal and Financial Problems of People in the Patermouthis Archive
  G. HUSSON, The University of Rouen§ (1990)
    Les maisons de Syène dans les archives de Patermouthis
  LESLIE MACCOULL, The Society for Coptic Archaeology§ (1990)
    Christianity at Elephantine/Syene/Aswan

Thursday, September 6
James Henry Breasted Hall, The Oriental Institute

8:30–1:15   *CHURCH & STATE*
Chair: ROBERT K. RITNER, The Oriental Institute, The University of Chicago
  WERNER HUSS, The University of Bamberg*
    Gedanken zum Thema "Staat" und "Kirche" im ptolemäischen Ägypten
  JOHN F. OATES, Duke University*
    The Basilikos Grammateus in the Ptolemaic Administration
  LINDA RICKETTS,[†] The University of North Dakota*
    The Administration of Late Ptolemaic Egypt
  SCHAFIK ALLAM, The University of Tübingen*
    Observations on Egyptian Law Courts
  CARY J. MARTIN, University College London*
    Demotic Contracts as Evidence in a Court Case

BREAK

  LANNY BELL, The Oriental Institute, The University of Chicago
    Alexander as an Egyptian God-King
  E. LANCIERS, Katholieke Universiteit Leuven*
    Die ägyptischen Priester des ptolemäischen Königskultes
  HERWIG MAEHLER, University College London*
    Visitors to the Temple of Khnûm on Elephantine: Who Were They?

BREAK

  J. K. WINNICKI, The University of Warsaw
    Pkalasiris—a Libyan or a Syrian God in Roman Egypt?
  ROGER V. MCCLEARY, Kelsey Museum of Archaeology, The University of Michigan*
    Ancestor Cults at Terenouthis in Lower Egypt: A Case for Greco-Roman Oecumenism
  LORELEI CORCORAN, Memphis State University*
    A Cult Function for the So-Called "Faiyum Mummy Portraits"?
  J. VAN HAELST, Centre National de la Recherche Scientifique
    Les débuts du christianisme dans la province égyptienne à la lumière des découvertes papyrologiques

3:00–6:00   *ROUND TABLE/CLOSING REMARKS*
            Chair: RICHARD SALLER, The University of Chicago
                WILLY CLARYSSE, Katholieke Universiteit Leuven*
                    Some Greeks in Demotic Documents
                ROGER BAGNALL, Columbia University§ (forthcoming)
                    Languages, Literacy, and Ethnicity in Late Roman Egypt
                ROBERT K. RITNER, The Oriental Institute, The University of Chicago*
                    Implicit Models of Cross-Cultural Interaction: A Question of Noses, Soap, and Prejudice

BREAK

                EVERYONE, *Round Table*

Friday, September 7
Pick Hall, Room 218

8:30–11:15   *QUESTIONS FROM DEMOTIC TEXTS*
            Chair: A.-H. NUR-EL-DIN, The University of Cairo
                MARK SMITH, Oxford University§ (1991)
                    Did Psammetichus I Die Abroad?
                OLA EL-AGUIZY, The University of Cairo*
                    Is Demotic a New Script?
                SVEN VLEEMING, The University of Leiden*
                    The Tithe of the Scribes (and) Representatives
                EUGENE D. CRUZ-URIBE, Northern Arizona University*
                    The Lake of Moeris: A Reprise

BREAK

                URSULA KAPLONY-HECKEL, The University of Marburg*
                    Thebanische Feldermessung nach enchorischen Dokumente
                RENATE MÜLLER-WOLLERMANN, The University of Tübingen*
                    Demotische Termini zur Landesgliederung Ägyptens
                JOSEPH MANNING, The Oriental Institute, The University of Chicago
                    On the Status Designation "Occupation Title + B3k + Divine Name" in Ptolemaic Demotic Texts

The Oriental Institute, Rooms 212, 216, and 220

11:30–1:00   GEORGE R. HUGHES, JANET H. JOHNSON, ROBERT K. RITNER, & STAFF
            Chicago Demotic Dictionary Project